To Leta Marie Friesen, who shared my life for sixty-two years,
and to those who came from our union.

Contents

PART 3
An Adventure into Bliss

PART 4
Putting on a Military Uniform

PART 5
An Irrational Choice That Changed Our Lives

Contents

PART 6

Developing a Second Career

PART 7

Arizona, Here We Come!

Contents

Appendices

Preface

Three generational moments remain riveted in my memory. Generational moments are when one is keenly aware of the mortality of human existence. One realizes with a sharpened focus that we are connected with each other.

The first such moment for me came when I was leaving home, essentially for the first time, to enroll in a high school academy several hundred miles away. My parents took me to a small village where I was to meet my prearranged ride to the academy.

Still in my early teens, I felt anxious and was unsure of how to say good-bye. I had experienced my father as a rather harsh and demanding person. It hadn't occurred to me that both my parents also felt uncomfortable about this moment. I remember being surprised when my father began to laugh nervously. It was the first time that I became aware of his gentle side as well as his frailty. He didn't know how to say good-bye either.

The second event touched me at the very core of my being. Our only daughter had asked me to walk her down the aisle of the church, then turn around and conduct her wedding ceremony. We met the groom's parents for the first time on the day of the wedding, and she opted to have us spend our time as an extended family the afternoon before the wedding rather than spend our time and energy doing a wedding rehearsal. We spent our time doing things like riding the famous cable cars in San Francisco, sharing lunch in a well-known historic restaurant, et cetera.

When the hour for the ceremony arrived, I remember walking her down the aisle of the church. I was overwhelmed with emotion. At a deep, visceral level, I suddenly became aware how quickly time passes and how rapidly changes occur. She was leaving our home forever to begin her own family.

I had literally performed hundreds of weddings in various settings. In that moment, the emotions that I experienced were so overwhelming that I was on the verge of tears. As I left my position as father of the bride and stood before them as a clergyman, the emotional impact was so powerful that I could barely speak. During the ceremony, I shared with our daughter how she affected her mother and my life.

I also shared our pride in her as she began her developmental journey into adulthood. I pointed out a number of key moments that focused on her sense of adventure, including attending the University of the Andes in Colombia, South America, during a national revolution. I gave her the best wishes of her mother and me as she began this new adventure.

The setting of the third such occasion happened during our sixtieth wedding celebration. Our children and grandchildren (with the exception of one son, his partner, and one granddaughter) had gathered in a cozy corner in a restaurant of the beautiful Westin Hotel in Shanghai, China, for this very special event.

Following dinner, I was attempting to articulate some of the different ways that their mother and grandmother, who was traveling down the lonely road of dementia, had impacted all of our lives. Unexpectedly, I experienced an overwhelming emotion similar to that which I had experienced at our daughter's wedding decades earlier.

As a frequent public speaker, I have rarely been at a loss for words. On this occasion, however, the affirmations that I wanted so much to share were unexpectedly swept away in waves of emotion. Tears flowed, and sobs gobbled up my words. While I clearly knew what I wanted to say, words simply didn't come. This profound encounter shook my equilibrium to the very core of my being. I knew at this moment that everything in our family was changing forever.

In the pages that follow, I also want to identify some of the ways in which a significant shift in my world view occurred while expressing profound appreciation for those who nurtured me in my early developmental years.

An important breakthrough for me occurred when I left home in spite of my parents' fears that I might grow away from their humble, conservative roots. I now certainly understand some of their fears. I was leaving home, essentially penniless, before my seventeenth birthday, to enroll in a small college a thousand miles away, a college that they viewed as being much too liberal. They were afraid that they were forever losing me.

Their anxious and stern admonitions resulted in heavy guilt feelings, but something inside of me told me that I had to go. A week or so before I was to meet two friends from the small academy that I had attended to travel together to a small Michigan church-oriented college, I experienced a magical evening that also affirmed my decision to go against my father's warning. It occurred on the evening of a full moon while working on a neighbor's farm.

After dinner, I had escaped into a nearby field. Sitting against a shock of wheat and facing the full moon, I attempted with considerable anxiety to anticipate what my future might entail and thought about the pros and cons of leaving. The affirmation of that night will forever be etched in the very core of my being. Even today, the period of the full moon is a time of reflection and a deep sense of peace.

When the actual moment of departure came, I can still vividly remember my father's words: "I won't stop you, but I won't give you my blessing." With these words ringing in my ears, I left my home.

This life-changing decision has been affirmed in a number of ways. These changes will be discussed in the following pages. Three experiences profoundly challenged the provincial way in which I had been viewing the world. Serving as an army chaplain immeasurably broadened my horizons. Becoming a "jumping padre" with the 82nd Airborne—in spite of a terrifying fear of heights—was, in many respects, a delayed puberty rite that I hadn't completed in earlier life.

Perhaps the most dramatic move in this shift resulted from my experience with the Trio Indians, who had no awareness that an outside world existed. The Trios, classified by many as primitive, had no written language. They became my teachers in ways that I never anticipated.

Other influential experiences included my work as a psychologist, becoming a member of the Sons of Orpheus male choir, and my longtime involvement in Rotary International.

As I've gotten older, I have often found myself wishing that I knew more about progenitors, particularly my grandparents and their parents. What were their life journeys like? What were their dreams and their goals, and what strategies did they use in attempting to live out these dreams and achieve these goals? How did they celebrate? How did they deal with adversity and disappointment? More succinctly, how has their journey impacted my life?

In the following pages, I have attempted to share some of the "stuff of my life" as well as how the different events in my life have unfolded. I would be pleased if some who are not numbered among my descendants find these pages helpful and perhaps interesting as they assess where their lives have taken them.

I am aware that many people intend to tell their stories, but the years pass and their intentions become a passing dream. I would also be pleased if those not directly related through bloodlines would be inspired to share their stories for those who follow them.

I have a hunch that their progeny will want to know where they have come from and will want to experience the richness of knowing their connections to their families of origin.

In a larger sense, we are all related.

Acknowledgment

Thanks to Dr. Bill Miller for his many hours of editing and proof-reading the manuscript, as well as to Will Files for his expert computer advice and his assistance on final review on a previous edition. Lori Conser has performed her role as managing editor on the current edition in a superb manner.

Reflections at Eventide

Part I

Roots and Early Years

Before the Beginning

In many respects, the early days of my parents' lives are something of a blur to me. When I questioned them about their history and lineage, they didn't seem to know much. I will speculate later about my parents' lack of clarity about where they had come from.

Their parents (both the Friesen and the Wiens side of the family) had either come with their parents from the Ukraine or were born shortly after their arrival in eastern Nebraska. Both families had lived in the Ukraine for nearly one hundred years.

Before going to the Ukraine, the Friesen side of the family came from Friesland, currently the northern province of the Netherlands. (While I have no proof, I suspect that the Wiens side of the family may have come from Vienna, which is known in Austria as Wien.)

I further suspect that, following their being scattered during times of persecution, the Mennonites were identified by the region from which they had come.

My clan of Anabaptist, who objected to a church governed by state or nation, also objected to serving in the military, primarily because they saw the violence of military action in much the same way that they saw violence in general. Military service, in their view, was contradictory to their commitment as followers of Jesus Christ.

This particular group of Anabaptists gathered around the leadership of Menno Simons, a former Roman Catholic priest from Friesland. After a dozen years as a Roman Catholic priest, he made a decision to break with Catholicism and joined the Anabaptists in 1536. This group, who were to become known as Mennonites, were driven out of Friesland by militant members of the Lutheran Church in part because of their refusal to preserve the church by military force if necessary.

A story from this era may be mythical. It is said that a group of Lutherans on horseback were in hot pursuit of Menno Simons. Simons apparently had the faster horse and managed to get ahead of his pursuers when he came upon a stagecoach. He leaped up on the coach with the driver and signaled his horse to go on. When his pursuers caught up with the stagecoach, they asked if anyone had seen Menno Simons. They were obviously unaware that they were speaking to him. He is said to have leaned down from the driver's seat to ask the passengers in the coach section if any of them had seen Menno Simons. Nobody knew who he was. When the pursuers heard the passengers' responses, they galloped off in search of their quarry.

In this time of major dislocation, a number of Mennonites lost their lives. Stanley Voth, the editor of *Henderson Mennonites: From Holland to Henderson*, reports that the "number of martyrs between 1525 and the death of the last Dutch martyr in 1574 is variously estimated at 1500 to 2500. Menno Simons was frequently forced to move his family for their safety."

A friend of Menno's, Tyaard Reniex, of Kimswerd in Friesland, was executed in 1539 for giving Menno refuge. John Thielmann, in his book, *Escape to Freedom*, states that "Mennonites were hung, drowned, or dragged down the streets by horses while tied by the feet."

After a painful period of being refugees, a number of these Mennonites settled in Prussia. Although they prospered, their Lutheran and Catholic neighbors often viewed them with considerable suspicion. The Mennonite emphasis on loving the enemy and their insistence on not serving in the military often created a stressful relationship with their neighbors, who saw the defense of both the fatherland and the church as a primary Christian duty.

In the late 1780s, the Mennonites received offers from the Russian government that would have a significant impact on their future. The Russian empress, Catherine the Great, had recently wrested the land north of the Black Sea from the Turks and was eager to have people of a European background build it into an agricultural resource. This grassy land, barren of trees, was reportedly occupied exclusively by nomad bands of Tartars, Turks, and Armenians.

Steady streams of Mennonite settlers moved to accept this offer as rapidly as they could acquire exit passes. In addition to the economic opportunities, the Russian government allowed them almost unlimited freedom to practice their religious values, establish their own schools, and be in charge of their civil affairs. The next hundred years or so was to be a time of prosperity. In 1870, there were widespread rumors that the privileges they had enjoyed were about to be revoked. While there is no comment in Voth's book about the czar's edict, I heard from some source (I don't remember where) that the Mennonites were given ten years to make the choice to become Russian citizens with all the duties of citizenship, including service in the military, or to leave their lovely farms and get out of Russia.

In the early 1870s, a delegation was sent to scout the United States. Some of the Mennonites had seen this as a hostile land, a home for exiled convicts and roaming tribes of Indians who attacked settlers without notice. They wondered how they could maintain their pacifist position in a land like this. (I also heard that India was seen as a possible site for relocation, although I could find no support for this notion in Voth's book. If this indeed had been a viable option for relocation, our family's history would obviously have been very different had they selected it.)

The delegation from the United States came back with favorable reports, apparently encouraged by Mennonites who had earlier migrated to the New World. During the last two decades of the nineteenth century, Voth reports that approximately eighteen thousand migrated to the United States. It is reported that one hundred thousand Mennonites who stayed in Russia prospered, despite the increasingly restrictive new laws.

Those who remained could not have foreseen the Communist revolution that swept over the country like a hurricane. During this time, the new government took over their farms, and most of these Mennonite residents were never heard from again. Apparently, few traces remain of any remnants of those who stayed behind. (However, I did meet an Alex Redekopp, who told me that his Mennonite father had chosen to stay in Russia. He said that his father, who had married his Ukrainian mother, was essentially a refugee who hid out in different villages after the Mennonites who had remained were dispersed. Alex came to Canada on a relocation program shortly after World War II, without knowing the English language.)

John Thielmann describes his dramatic escape from Ukraine via China just as the revolutionary forces were taking over some thirty-five years after those who chose to come to United States had emigrated. Apparently, he had help from Mennonites who were farmers in Manchuria until he was able to get a visa to the United States. Thielmann states that his family who remained in Russia mysteriously vanished.

If my forefathers had not taken the risk to leave everything and instead had chosen to make the needed compromises to keep their lovely farms in the Ukraine, the history of those of us who followed them would have been dramatically different.

2

My Family of Origin

A number of descriptive word pictures will be given about my father throughout this document. While I do know that he was born in Fairbury, Nebraska, on February 13, 1909, I know very little about his childhood or teenage years or when his family moved to western Nebraska.

Prior to moving to Nebraska, his parents lived for a time in Meade, Kansas, a prominent Mennonite community. A couple of his siblings, who did not survive childhood, are buried in Meade. I had very little contact with my father's sisters during my growing-up years.

On occasion, I would briefly visit the Friesen grandparents' home in Madrid, Nebraska. I don't remember any holiday time with either set of grandparents. My grandmother ran a small creamery while my grandfather served as the village marshal.

My mother, Leona Wiens, was born in Henderson, Nebraska, on February 26, 1906. She had five siblings. I had more contact with this set of uncles and aunts than I did with my father's side of the family.

I don't know when she moved with her family to the Holdrege Ranch, four miles south of Madrid, Nebraska. I do know that my Grandfather Wiens purchased several sections of land of this vast ranch when it foreclosed and sold at auction. I remember wandering as a child through a number of bedrooms and parlors of the primary ranch house. There were large, separate barns for horses and cattle as well as a number of other buildings that held farm machinery.

I was born in a house near the ranch house, which was located near the icehouse. I assume that the ranch manager originally occupied this house.

Like her mother, my mother was tormented by a host of fears. Her strategy of sharing her concern for us was to warn us of the dangers that lurked everywhere. She wore a large apron as part of her daily wardrobe. While issuing these warnings, her brow was deeply furrowed as she was wringing her hands inside that apron.

On one occasion, she warned us with deep concern in her voice not to sneak off and go swimming. She then recited stories of boys who adventurously went swimming in a river without permission. Their bodies were found days later, somewhere downstream. When one is five or six years old, these kinds of stories are both captivating and intimidating.

Interestingly, the small North Platte River, the nearest body of water other than a two-foot-deep horse water tank in our yard, was twenty miles away. We seldom traveled that kind of distance. As I view it now, she attempted to show her care and concern by warning us of the dangers that, in her mind, were lurking everywhere.

Mother had a softer side. She often memorized poems of considerable length and recited them on various occasions. A pious woman, she often sang hymns while doing her chores around the house. Deeply immersed in her religious beliefs, there was also, in my view, an obsessive component to her religious convictions. She lived in fear that she in some weak moment might offend the Almighty and be doomed to "the eternal fires of hell." She was also deeply concerned about the spiritual welfare of her offspring.

My parents established what was known as a family altar. Each morning, they set aside a time to read the bible and other religious materials, which was followed by a lengthy prayer time on bended knees. During these prayers, they would pour out their concerns to

God. The names of each of their children would be recited daily in these prayers. They maintained this practice throughout their lives.

I vividly remember one occasion years later when my younger brother and his family happened to make a visit home at the same time as me and my family. Both our families lived more than a thousand miles in different directions from our childhood farm home. As both families were leaving, my father had us form a family circle in the yard of his home. In his prayers on our behalf, he began to sob and tearfully prayed that this "family circle would not be broken in heaven."

I understood and appreciated the context of his prayer and valued his concern. As we were driving out of the family farmyard, our puzzled teenage daughter wondered why Grandpa was so "shook up." The differences in the traditions and religious orientation in our immediate family were so immense that she couldn't gasp his concern. Perhaps my father intuitively recognized when I initially left home under his protest several decades earlier that such a gap would occur.

In later years, when I would be home for a rare visit, my mother expressed a deep concern that I had become a registered Democrat. As a diehard Republican, she was fiercely loyal to President Richard Nixon. After his forced resignation from the presidency, she expressed deep disappointment that he had been so misunderstood and unfairly driven out of office.

She held strong disdain for President Jimmy Carter, even though he was a deeply religious man. I don't think that she could fathom that a Democrat could be a person of faith. One Saturday evening, I teased her by suggesting that Jimmy had just finished the preparation for the Sunday school class that he was to teach the following day. Her response was to become agitated. She made comment to the effect that he was a religious fraud.

3

Early Childhood Years

The stock market crash resulted in dramatic shockwaves and indescribable stress. Overnight, banks closed. When the banks reopened, the deposits that people thought they had were wiped out. Businesses collapsed. People lost everything they had, including their homes, their livelihoods, and most importantly their hope. Many who have been considered wealthy now were paupers. The nation was in total chaos. The year was 1929.

It was the same year that a young couple, married on June 26, 1928, announced the birth of their firstborn, whom they named Eugene Wesley Friesen. His birth took place on a farm near the small western Nebraskan village of Madrid. The date was Friday, September 13, 1929. My mother, a first-generation immigrant, held a number of superstitious views, including that on Friday the thirteenth, ominous events could occur. I can only speculate how she integrated these deeply internalized fears with the fact that her firstborn arrived on this fateful date.

This national financial crisis was devastating and complicated matters for a newly married couple beginning life together with extremely limited finances. In addition to the financial market crash, a severe drought hit the Midwest states hard, especially Oklahoma, Kansas, and Nebraska. Massive dust storms and plagues of grasshoppers followed in the early thirties.

One of my early memories is of the great dust storms of the early 1930s. As a child of perhaps six or seven years old, I can still visualize these great walls of dust that must have reached several thousands of feet into the sky.

On one particular occasion, my father picked us up from school early as a massive storm was approaching. Shortly after we got to our home, the storm-induced darkness fell upon us. It was if night had suddenly fallen. Without a lighted kerosene lamp, one could not see one's hand in front of one's face. Dust and dirt reached a measurable depth inside our home before the storm passed. (Incidentally, we did not get electricity at our home until I was ten or eleven years old.)

I read somewhere that the top soil blown away during these horrendous storms is said to have circled the earth three times before the atmosphere was cleansed. These storms were complicated by the drought that followed. Swarms of grasshoppers so thick that it was difficult to walk without stepping on them also plagued our part of the Midwest. They devoured every piece of vegetation, including watered gardens, within hours of their arrival.

While I have some memories of the intense drought, I can't imagine how stressful it must have been for those responsible for caring for their families. As a small child, I had some awareness that my parents were facing the crisis of survival. I was aware that my father made trips to the county courthouse for reasons that I then didn't know how to interpret. I only could read on their faces that we were facing some kind of doom. The atmosphere of our home during these stark days was as dark as the clouds of dust had been.

I must have a recessive gene somewhere that prompted me to take risks that left me shaking in my boots (I say more about this when I speak of my ordeal of going through jump school and earning my paratrooper wings). I have no memory of an event that must have occurred somewhere around my third birthday, but it is one that my super cautious mother shared with me. Every farm had a steel-framed windmill with a ladder, which made it possible to climb to the top in the event repairs were needed. The windmill on our farm was about forty feet high. I'm told that I climbed much of the way to the top of the windmill before my mother, who was terrified of heights, spotted me. She calmly talked me down the ladder. I was told that she then put the fear of God into me about heights—a fear that I haven't entirely conquered to this day.

On one occasion when I was in grade school, our family was visiting Will Roger's shrine, which was perched on a mountain cliff near Colorado Springs. I felt faint as I was standing on the veranda; it was built on a cliff overlooking the beautiful vista. I ran back from the outlook toward the security of the wall of the main building.

I have two preschool memories. One evening we were returning from some event in the middle of a very cold winter, probably from some church event or a visit with a neighbor several miles away. We rarely went anywhere. We were in our unheated Ford Model T. My mother, my younger brother, and I were all under a heavy layer of blankets while my father drove the car. My mother's words reassured me that we would be home, where it would be warm, soon.

About five months before my fourth birthday, my brother and I were told that my parents' bedroom was off limits. Since our home was rather small, this was a significant limitation. Several women shuffled in and out of the room. Eventually my brother and I were invited in to see a new baby brother. When I asked how he had gotten here, I was told about the visitation of the stork.

Several years later, I asked how one could tell the difference between a boy and a girl. My parents looked at each other as if to say, "What do we say now?" After some hesitation, my father responded that a girl had a curl in her hair. The era in which we were raised was Victorian in many respects. No mention was ever made about biological differences between sexes or about reproductive processes.

I must have been 5 or 6 years when I was playing on the roof of a building attached to our barn when this building suddenly collapsed. My childhood memory is still vivid. An angel took me by the hand and guided me to safety. In my Sunday School class at my church, I often saw pictures of angels protecting children who were in some precarious situation so the appearance of an angel didn't seem unusual. When my startled parents inquired how I managed to survive unscathed from this collapsed building I casually told them of the angel's involvement. I also remember the look they gave each other. In my mind, the angel was just doing its job of protecting children.

We had no natural swimming areas but small lagoons that developed after heavy rains and often reached a depth of two or more feet. One afternoon, the neighbor girl, who was seven or eight years older than me, suggested that my brother and I join her for a swim at one of the lagoons located over the hill from our house. When we arrived, she suggested that we take off our clothes and go swimming—which we promptly did. When I asked her to join us, she said that she would just watch us. I had no idea then, or for that matter until I was approaching teenage years, how males were different from females. At this particular point, taking off one's clothes seemed like the most natural thing to do.

My father suddenly appeared on the scene. It didn't occur to me that he would be upset. He sent the neighbor girl home and gave my brother and me a spanking without explaining why. I was confused as to why we were being punished; I couldn't think of what we had done wrong.

Another early memory of my mother is that she was bedfast for what seemed to be months at a time. While my memory may not be fully accurate, I can only surmise that she was suffering from depression and arthritis that was partially related to her frustration and anger from her attempts to win her father's approval and at the same time stay loyal to her husband. My guess is that her feelings both toward her father and her husband were very mixed. Apparently, she was in a double bind. Her attempts to please both her husband and her father may have resulted in some measure of resentment toward them both.

The heavy burden that both of my parents faced in addition to the severe economic and drought environment in which they lived placed a heavy toll on their energies as they tried to merely survive. In addition, my father had not grown up on a farm. He apparently had to play a lot of catch-up in terms of developing farming skills.

Whether caused by the negative atmosphere, the Great Depression, the invasions of swarms upon swarms of grasshoppers, or his lack of farming skills, they faced great economic crisis during these drought-stricken and Depression years.

I once heard my father say that he had planted crops ten years in a row without getting a return—not even getting enough to replace the seeds that he had planted. I suspect that his lack of confidence in his abilities as a farmer must have reached crisis proportions. In many respects, I am similar in that I have often, particularly in younger years, experienced similar crises of confidence.

I recognize now that my father had little opportunity to develop parenting skills. He used the only model that he knew. He demanded total obedience. If he interpreted a look from us as defiant in any way, he would severely punish especially me and my younger brother. Black and blue marks on my body gave some evidence of the severity of punishment. Sometimes this punishment would be meted out with a belt or a piece of a horse's harness. When being struck, I learned to get as close as possible to his body so the swing of his arms would be restricted.

On some occasions, punishment would be delayed for an hour or two. We could only anticipate what was coming. I deviously planned to place my head in line with his blows and then pretend to go into convulsions. For reasons I no longer remember, I did not do this.

As the oldest, I should have been the one to confront my father. I was too intimidated by him to attempt to develop any strategy for this confrontation. My brother Claire, who is less than a year younger than me, was the first to challenge his strict behavior. He became quite a challenge for my father and his strict, authoritarian attitude. My two younger siblings appeared to benefit by my father's modification of his authoritarian behavior. My brother Merle appears to have a very different memory of our childhood environment and doesn't recall the harshness of my father's discipline.

While my father was often severe and dogmatic, I'm certain that he didn't intend to be cruel. He apparently believed the biblical statement literally that "if you spare the rod, you will spoil the child." He cared for us in the only way that he knew to care. In his way, he was a caring and principled man.

I didn't realize it at the time, but whatever self-confidence he had must have been riddled again and again with defeat. He had little status in whatever community in which he was a part, with the exception of the Pilgrim Holiness Church, which he joined in midlife. He must have experienced a significant amount of low-grade depression. As I have reflected on the burden that he must have carried, I think he functioned rather well, given the cards that he had been dealt.

It is quite embarrassing to share the following episode. One day my youngest brother, Merle, and I were playing around in a small building where an old gas-run Maytag washer was located. This is where my mother did the weekly wash. My brother and I became intrigued with the odor of gasoline. (I must have been six or seven years old or so, and he was about three years younger than me.) I must have convinced him to take the first swallow, and I planned to follow. I am not sure how much he ingested, but he became very ill and semiconscious. I'm not sure how my mother found out about his reaction. I didn't report what happened until after I was closely questioned. I was probably very noncommittal about what I had done. My mother attempted to get my father's attention (he was working in the field nearly one mile from the house) by waving a white bed sheet as a sign of distress. Unfortunately, my father didn't see the sheet. My mother, who didn't drive, really had no realistic option other than to hope for the best. My brother survived without medical attention.

As a footnote, the only time I visited a doctor during my youth was to have my tonsils surgically removed. Trying to alleviate any fears, my parents promised to get me some ice cream afterward. My brother Claire, who was ten months younger than me, had the same procedure at the same time. We spent the night on cots in the doctor's home, and I became upset later because no one told me I would have a very sore throat the following morning.

There was plenty of competition between my two younger brothers and me. Less than four years separated us. Two typically would form an alliance against the third. Such an alliance could change a number of times during any given week or, for that matter, during the day. Other than being in school, we rarely had contact with other children during the years that we were on the farm. Incidentally, my sister, Myrna, didn't arrive until I was in college.

My parents really sacrificed to give us our meager gifts at Christmas and developed the practice of giving gifts following the school Christmas program. Their idea was that we should have the opportunity to play with our toys during our entire Christmas vacation. On one occasion, my parents ushered us out of the room while they put the presents we were to receive on a table. We didn't have a Christmas tree. We then got into our car, probably a Ford Model A, and made our way to the schoolhouse for the Christmas play that would signal the beginning of the Christmas recess. As we were driving out of the yard, my father pointed to the sky, stating that he had spotted Santa and his sleigh. I, along with my brothers, strained to catch a glimpse of the jolly old fella. In later years, when I found out that Santa was a myth, I was keenly disappointed. While I never spoke about it to my father or anyone else, I felt betrayed by him, because I assumed at that time that he knew everything, and his word could be relied on, no matter what.

Years later, when our children were taken in by the myth, I made it a point to suggest that Santa was just a fabled person who symbolized the spirit of generosity and good will. I didn't want them to feel betrayed when they learned of the mythical nature of Santa Claus.

4

Rural School Days

My developmental skills were marginal at best when I entered first grade just before my fifth birthday. Kindergarten classes were not offered. The one-room school contained a tiny library and small cloakroom. A potbellied stove stood in the center of the classroom. When the temperature was zero or below, students hovered around this stove. The school was located on an acre of a cornfield, approximately a block away from the road. A barn a short distance away was provided for students who rode horses to school.

During the first year, I walked to a neighbor's house, where I would ride a horse bareback, clinging to the waist of a female eighth grader as we together rode the horse to school. The horse would be put in a stall until it was time to return home.

Since my eighth-grade classmate graduated after my first school year, my parents needed to find another transportation option for me. My father purchased a Shetland pony and a two-wheel cart. At age six, I would hitch the pony to that cart and then drive it to school. I'd unhitch the pony and tether it to a stall in the school barn. This provided the major means of transportation for me and my two younger brothers during my elementary school years. Occasionally, the cart would become temporarily nonfunctional. My brothers and I would then walk the two-plus miles to school.

During the eight years that we attended this school, the maximum enrollment for all eight grades was thirteen pupils. The student desks were arranged in three rows plus a recitation bench adjacent to the teacher's desk. There was an assigned period for each grade in each subject matter for the recitation bench ritual. For example, if the teacher called for fourth-graders to come to the recitation bench for their spelling class, every student in the classroom could hear the subject matter being discussed at this bench. It should have provided a wonderful learning environment. If a sixth-grader, for example, was weak in arithmetic, he or she could hear the class discussions on this subject at a lower class level.

The first day at school was traumatic for me. I urgently needed to use the toilet facilities, which was an outdoor privy. Unsure of how to ask for permission, I repeatedly asked the teacher for permission to go outside to play. Each time I made this request, she assured me that recess time was coming, and then I could go out to play. Finally, I could hold on no longer. I can still feel my acute embarrassment when the laughing students pointed to my wet trousers and the urine dripping from my seat.

This utter confusion and humiliation deepened when my parents anxiously inquired about my first day at school. I was embarrassed and didn't know how to respond to them.

The trauma during the second year in school was far more devastating. I'm not sure what I did to irritate my teacher, but she angrily told me that I was "dumb and stupid." I assumed that I was retarded and should have won an Academy Award for superbly playing that role for the remaining elementary school years and beyond. In effort, I dropped out for the rest of my elementary school years. For the most part, I was lost in my own fantasy world. I dreaded being called to the recitation bench because I had absorbed so little of the class material.

One particularly painful experience occurred on the recitation bench when I was in the sixth or seventh grade. The teacher asked me to recite the alphabet, a task that I should have easily mastered by this time. I responded that this task was "kid stuff." The teacher called my bluff by insisting that I complete it. When I failed miserably, I still remember her scornful rebuke. I was drowning in an ever-deepening sense of inadequacy and incompetence, lost in my own little world.

In spite of my miserable academic performance, I was passed on to the next grade level each year, not unlike today. I was asked to write an essay at the end of seventh grade. It must have been pathetic. Hoping for some small shred of evidence of validation, I asked my teacher, who happened to be my eighteen-year-old neighbor, about my performance on the paper. She stated that it wasn't good, but she had no choice but to pass me on to the next grade. I don't remember being stung by her remarks, so I must have been anticipating them.

A high school graduate could obtain a teacher's certificate by attending a summer session at what was referred to as normal training school. It wasn't unusual to have a teacher who was only seventeen or eighteen years old considered qualified. By the way, all the teachers during my first eight years of school were female.

As much as I dreaded the time in classroom, recess was even more terrifying. The school bully was the largest and strongest boy in the school. With only a dozen or so enrolled students, he amassed a great deal of power. I remember how miserable it was to try to play softball. He would pick one person to be on his team while the rest of us would be on the opposing team. The obvious result was the opposing teams were essentially pawns of this bully. He established the parameters of any activity on the playground, including defining the rules to his advantage. The rest of the students had no real alternative but to go along with his dictates.

If I had to walk home because the pony cart needed repair, I tried to lag behind. But my tormentor waited for me. I was terrified and felt helpless as he would chase me and threaten to harm me.

He likely knew that I felt inadequate and seemed to enjoy tormenting me. When I tried to stay in the classroom, the teacher would typically insist that I go outside for recess. I was to learn much later in life that this "bully" came from a family where the father was dictatorial and abusive. At that developmental stage of life, I had no tools to put this behavior in perspective.

Decades later, I had an opportunity to see both the teacher who dealt such a devastating blow by publicly announcing her assessment of my academic and social skills as well as the tormentor. They both attended a memorial service for my father, where I delivered the eulogy.

I was deeply moved when this teacher, who was then in her seventies, stated that she wished I would be in the area to deliver her eulogy. I'm sure that she had no memory of the devastating impact that her comments had on this six-year-old second grader six decades earlier. It is so important to give attention to the biblical admonition not to judge another. I also learned of the destructive environment she had experienced in her developmental years.

It also important to remember both the positive and negative impact we have on the lives of others. It is humbling when I learn, years after the fact, of the impact that I have had. Some of it has been painful and some has been healing. We are clearly fellow travelers. Without each other, we cannot survive!

5

Born to Work

I was somewhere around my fifth year of life when I milked my first cows. How surprised my parents were that I had enough strength in my fingers to perform this function. They soon assigned me the task of milking three additional cows morning and night. At first, this assignment was great fun. It felt good to have their approval and make a real contribution to handling the family chores. But when the novelty began to wear off and the assignment became permanent, the task became less exciting, especially when the corrals were wet and muddy in the spring. This muddy soil became mixed with the manure. The udder of the cows needed to be cleansed of the mud, even though there was no running water on the farm. Flies were often a problem too. When cows swished their tails back and forth, they often swatted me in the face.

Sometimes a difficult cow didn't want to stand still while being milked. Even though their heads were locked into place in the stanchion and their hind feet were hobbled, a restless cow sometimes kicked the bucket, spilling the milk. My father didn't scold us over spilled milk.

Several years later, my father apparently got tired of trying to coax my brother and me out of bed, particularly on cold, dark mornings, to do our milking chores before school. I became aware that my father was lighting a firecracker in our basement bedroom. I tried to pretend that I was fast asleep and that the explosion of the firecracker wouldn't awaken me. The explosion was so intense, however, that I sprang out of bed in spite of my intentions. My father found this incident very amusing.

I was six years old when my brother and I were given the assignment of herding cattle during the summer. This task involved five or six hours of being in the pasture, making sure the cattle didn't stray beyond the fences. Additionally, some farmers, although probably rare in number, would plant several rows of a poisonous cane that protected the corn from animals managing to negotiate the fences designed to contain them. These summer days were very monotonous, but one evening, the cattle became unmanageable and got away from us, going into the neighbor's field. Well over a mile from home and long after dark, but more afraid to go home without the cattle, I began crying. The sounds of my anguished cry carried through the night air, and a neighbor came and found my brother and me and took us home. I don't recall how my father retrieved the cattle, but I do remember the distinct surprise that he wasn't angry with us.

When I was in my seventh summer, I began driving a one-row corn cultivator pulled by two horses while my father drove a two-row corn cultivator that was pulled by four horses. Although I was too small to harness the team, I could drive the horses. The following year I graduated to driving a two-row cultivator that was pulled by four horses. There typically was a fence at the end of the row of corn. The trick was to get to the end of the row without plowing up the corn at the end of the row and still turn around soon enough to avoid clipping the fence that was the boundary of our property. I actually became quite skilled at this task.

Before the combines were in use, binders would cut the grain, wrap them in bundles secured by twine, and deposit them on the ground. It was necessary to stand the bundles of grain upright so the seeds of the grain wouldn't germinate as a result of their contact with the soil. In time, these bundles would be pitched onto a hayrack. The driver of the hayrack would pull up to the side of a threshing machine and throw the bundles into this machine. The grain would then be separated from the straw. I felt a great deal of pride the first time I drove the horses hitched to the hayrack that were filled with the bundles of grain that I had picked up from the field. After filling the hayrack, I drove up to the threshing machine and pitched the bundles into the receptacle of the thresher. I felt that I was on my way to validating my manhood.

During the threshing season, the men from the neighborhood would come together at the farm where the threshing event was taking place. It was simply understood that each farmer would be part of the work crew of those who had helped him during this threshing event and did not expect payment.

The wives of the farmers would prepare wonderful meals for the hungry men. It was truly a feast. The meals would consist of country fried chicken with potatoes and gravy plus lots of fresh garden vegetables. The best was the variety of pies—I rarely find a chocolate pie that comes close to the ones served at these work bees. It was more than a time to work; these times were truly community events.

Mechanization was rapidly changing farming techniques in a dramatic way. The self-propelled combines now gather the grain and thrash it in one operation. Initially, the combines were pulled by a tractor, and I drove the tractors that pulled the combines for several seasons. But soon the more costly self-contained combines took over. I never got the chance to operate a self-propelled wheat combine. I often drove the trucks that collected the grain from the combines when their bins were full and took the wheat to elevators in a nearby town for storage.

My childhood role models were men who could pick three wagonloads of corn a day. I would stand in awe when my father or the hired men would scoop the ears of corn from the wagon into the corncrib. As a very young child, I would accompany them to the cornfield. My ability to husk the corn by hand and throw the ear of corn into the wagon was limited. While my ability improved with age, the mechanical corn picker came along and dramatically changed how corn was harvested. Very soon thereafter, the corn was shelled as it was being picked in the field. Almost overnight, my model of how to become a man evaporated.

I was eleven or twelve years old when I first started working six days a week for a neighbor. Work in the fields started shortly after dawn and continued until dusk. While driving a tractor around the field hour after hour, I often watched the clouds form. I had heard sermons about signs appearing in the skies that would signal the return of Christ on earth to take the faithful with Him to the heavens. To be left behind would, according to the kind of theology that held this view, be catastrophic. I experienced a high level of anxiety, wondering whether I was prepared for the event that we were told to expect any moment.

On one occasion, the boss, who happened to be a devout Mennonite, was going to town for the afternoon and told me to do some chores around the farmyard instead of driving the tractor in the field. About four o'clock in the afternoon, I went to the house for a drink of water, only to discover that the boss's wife was nowhere to be found. I checked the baby's crib and found that it was empty. I cautiously peeked into the bedroom, where the woman of the house normally took a nap. It was empty, but the sheets were in disarray.

Convinced that the Lord had returned and that I hadn't been sufficiently prepared for this event and was left behind, in a total panic, I raced across the fields of uncut wheat and headed toward a neighbor working in the field more than a mile away. He was one of the identified sinners in the community, and I was going to notify him the second coming of Christ had just occurred and we both had been left behind. I was a short distance away from him before it occurred to me that the boss's wife and child might have accompanied him on his trip to the town that served as the business center of our farming community. Chagrined but terribly relieved, I made my way back to the farm where I was employed. My heartbeat soon returned to normal after this realization.

In many ways, I became a member of their family. If I was around the house and the baby's diaper needed to be changed, I changed it. After breakfast, we would go to the field and work until it was time for a hearty lunch that we referred to as dinner. After this meal, my boss and I would lie down on a hard wood floor for about a thirty-minute nap and then return to the field, where we would stay until dusk. Sometimes it was totally dark before we arrived at the house. Before harvest time, my primary task was to drive a tractor that pulled either a disc or a one-way plow. This disc had seven or eight circular disks that cut into the ground four or five inches. The plow would cut deeper into the ground. Much of the summer, I used one of these pieces of equipment. While we always worked long hours, the harvest was the peak work season, primarily because the grain, once ripened, became vulnerable to wind and hail and thus had to be harvested in the shortest possible time.

On one occasion, rain had slowed the harvest, and we couldn't get into the field until the wheat was dry enough to be threshed. The wheat field was about a mile from the farm building. My boss decided to hook up the tractor that was on the farmyard to be pulled by the truck to the wheat field. He had gotten angry because the tractor, which didn't have a braking system, coasted into the truck, causing a slight dent in the tractor's radiator. In a rage, he took off, towing me and the tractor along a narrow rural road at thirty-five to forty miles per hour. The horrendous dust kicked up by his tires hit me directly in the face. I was steering the tractor between deep ditches on either side of the road with my eyes nearly closed. It was a terrifying experience.

At one point, I considered jumping off, but I stayed on the wildly careening tractor down the road. When my boss realized the peril in which he had placed me, he slowed down as quickly as he could. It took some time to slow down because the tractor did not have a braking system. In true macho style, he never apologized. However, uncharacteristically, he quickly let go of his anger.

When summer ended and it was time to return to school, I received my first paycheck. It was a hundred dollars for an entire summer's work. I endorsed the check and gave it to my parents. It never occurred to me to keep the check, or even a portion of it.

When I was in high school, I worked for several summers for a farmer that raised Black Angus cattle. Much of the work, beyond the regular farm chores of caring for the animals, consisted of cutting hay. One of the skills that I learned was to sharpen the blades on the mower that cut the grass. When it came time to stack the hay, I took pride in being able to make a symmetrical haystack.

6

Our Family Shifts Directions

A pivotal moment in my father's life came when he was approaching his midthirties. It was clear that my father had little respect for his father, who had died in his early fifties. After my grandfather's deathbed conversion, my father had a reconciliation of sorts with his father. The night of his father's death, my father reported that he had a dream in which he visualized his father as being cleansed of all his transgressions. My father felt that God was calling him to preach the gospel following this dream.

From traditions of the church that he had adopted, this kind of calling was the most important thing that could happen to anyone. He hadn't finished high school, was financially devastated, and had little social standing outside the church that he had chosen—a church that had little status in the community. He took steps to affirm this call. Before taking this step, however, he prayed that God would give a sign. It was the first year in his farming that he had a bumper wheat crop that wiped out all of his debts. For him, that was proof enough. While my father would continue farming operations, he would move his family to the lights of the city.

Before my grandfather's death, I had attended only one funeral. Only four or five years old, I was mystified as to what would happen at a funeral. I thought that the deceased, an older farmer whom I knew, would be stretched out on one of the back pews at the church. While I didn't have this misconception about my grandfather's funeral, I experienced this first serious look at the facts of life and death as a mystifying experience.

My father continued to have unresolved feelings about his father, but he breathed an enormous sigh of relief that his father had been saved from the eternal flames at the very last moment. While he never shared a great deal with me about his relationship with his father, what he did share was mostly negative. I suspect that he didn't have the opportunity of working through at a deep emotional level his troubled relationship with his father. He did not have the tools to see his father's struggles as a strategy, however ineffective, for trying to discover and validate his worth as a human being. The writer of Ecclesiastes had noted that even though we cannot see God's purpose from beginning to end, even so God has planted eternity in our hearts. I sense that my father was attempting to tap into this sense of eternity.

We would move to Colorado Springs, Colorado, where his denomination sponsored an unaccredited bible school plus a high school academy. It was a major shift for my father to move from nurturing fields of grain to nurturing his mind and preparing to nurture the human spirit in others.

We rented a home situated on a hillside. While it was a modest home, it had a grand view of Colorado Springs. It was very different going from an isolated farming community to the bright lights of the city. I still have fond memories of exploring various parts of the city on my bicycle. I managed to secure a couple of jobs mowing well-manicured lawns in the elegant neighborhoods.

During this era, I was introduced to sights and sounds that I had never heard before. I went with my parents to visit a black church congregation. I think this was the first opportunity I had to rub shoulders with someone whose pigment of skin was different from mine.

Firmly planted nostalgic memories of this time include walking the well-established mountain trails that gave me a spectacular view of Colorado Springs and Manitou Springs. It was the time for developing a sense of autonomy that I hadn't previously known.

While I rarely have had the occasion of being in Colorado Springs as an adult, I have tried to reproduce memories of earlier years by revisiting the places I had known. Obviously, the city has dramatically changed, as have the circumstances in my life. Still, Colorado Springs will always occupy a special place in my memories.

7

The Scary Teenage Years

Utterly unprepared for high school and believing that I was incapable of the tasks ahead of me, I set myself up to fail. Actually, I attended two high schools. My first and last year in high school took place in a church academy in Colorado Springs, Colorado. In spite of my poor academic achievements, I was still the youngest in my class. My father, who had not completed high school, enrolled in this church-sponsored bible school. We attended classes in the same building during my freshman year. I decided that I was too young to be a high school freshman. My intention was to fail and thus delay my freshman year until the following year. While my father was a strict disciplinarian, he never seemed to notice my marginal academic performance until he became a student again. His newfound attentiveness resulted in instituting a no-nonsense set of rigid rules for my study routine. He effectively thwarted my attempt to fail the ninth grade.

I sensed that I wasn't mature enough or ready to be in high school. Academically, I clearly wasn't ready. My father told me that when he decided to drop out of school, his parents didn't object or show concern about his decision. He added that he wasn't about let me drop out or fail. So I managed to get back on track and take studies more seriously. And I felt much more accepted in this church academy than I would have in a public high school.

My sophomore and junior years were in the public school in Ogallala, Nebraska, and were the most painful for me. My grades were very marginal, but how startled I was at my first A. While it was only in typing, certainly not a demanding academic subject, it was my first indication that I might not be as dumb as I thought I was. I generally felt isolated from my classmates at school, although I felt close to the students who were from the church that my father served as pastor.

So uncertain was I about my abilities that I almost never volunteered to participate in class discussions. On one occasion, I had heard someone tell a joke that had amused me. In a rather awkward hope of getting some recognition and a laugh, I attempted to share this joke (the contents of which I no longer remember) with the class—probably in a clumsy way. The scornful look on the teacher's face and the anger in her voice stung me to the core. Not only did she rebuke me in front of the entire class but also cited this as an example of something that she never wanted to hear again. This message of rejection was internalized, and I resolved never again to take the risk of sharing thoughts or ideas with my peers. The scar was deep. Years later when I was a graduate student, I had some difficulty in getting involved in class discussions, even when I was certain that I had something valuable to share.

During this time, I was so shy, so afraid of rejection, that I avoided going to the downtown section of Ogallala, a city of three thousand inhabitants. I was terrified that I would meet classmates on the street. Now, I can't imagine how I could have messed up in saying a simple hello.

I had no intention of going to college because I thought I wasn't capable of doing college work. It is highly probable that my teachers wouldn't have disagreed with this assessment. I rather suspect that if my teachers at Ogallala High School had taken a poll of the student least likely to go to college, I would have been near if not at the top of the list.

During my youth, the option of farming was always open to students who were marginal performers. This, of course, dramatically changed as farming quickly became a high-tech operation.

While I operated a lot of machinery on the farm, my mechanical aptitudes were limited. I suspect that this paucity of mechanical skills grew out of the deep questions of uncertainty that I had about myself.

8

My Teenage Friends

While I can only recall a few names from my elementary school years, I maintained no significant friendships. Whatever limited associations I may have had with the students from my one-room country school days, the memories seem remote and unreal.

Even though there were several first cousins living within a few miles of our farm, I never felt very secure with them. The one exception was Kenneth Kornelson (now deceased), who was a year younger than me, minus one day. Several episodes stand out.

Ken was driving a stripped-down Ford Model A that was used to carry gasoline to the tractors in the field. One rather dark night, I accompanied him as he was driving down a field road. He had forgotten that his father had built a fence across the road. We hit the fence at approximately twenty-five miles an hour. Fortunately this "jitney" had a windshield that kept us from being decapitated. The front wheels initially left the ground for several feet before the fence broke. Ken was very worried about his father's reaction to this busted fence. We tried in vain to repair it.

Another time, Ken and I got into a water fight. Before it was over, we were throwing pails of water at each other outside the house, but eventually our friendly battle included the kitchen. While his mother wasn't exactly pleased at our delinquent behavior, she didn't lose her cool either.

We had limited contact during our adult life, but I kept in contact with Ken and his siblings over the years. Ken and I typically took turns calling each other on our birthdays, on September 12 or September 13—his or mine.

While my contacts with my high school peer group in Ogallala, Nebraska, were almost nonexistent, the one group of young people with whom I had a genuine comfort level was the church youth group. Actually, there were only six or seven teenagers in this group. I looked out the windows of our tiny church building, located next to the parsonage where we were living, waiting for these students who attended our congregation to walk down the street en route to school. I would pretend that I was casually on my way to school and just happened to be coming out the door when they arrived.

I assumed that people outside our church family would look down on us because of the super conservative religious convictions that we held. Our group held that it was necessary for us to be "separate from the world." They defined "worldly amusements" as movies, dances, card playing, sports activities, and so on. Of course, all these activities were strictly off limits.

I wanted so much to try out for the football team. I was looking for a legitimate "puberty rite" that would initiate me into manhood—and some morsel of acceptance that I desperately sought. The congregation, however, held that football fit the category of worldly amusements. My father didn't necessarily hold this conviction but didn't want to risk his standing with the congregation who, by the way, voted annually on whether to keep their minister.

At a student assembly, the principal made a strong pitch for everyone to go out to support the seniors that would be playing their final game for ol' Ogallala High. I was so moved by his speech that Don Molle, one of my closest friends from the church, and I slipped away without permission to attend this final game. We got caught. The Sunday evening services were a bit tense when we didn't openly confess our sins.

Dottie Wiseman and her sister, Bonnie Jean, were part of this church youth group. While I have had little contact with Dottie over the years, I remember her and our friendship fondly. We did have a brief romantic interest in each other but never really dated. Bonnie Jean would eventually marry my brother Claire.

By and large, this small group at the time bought into the rigid rules of the church. Several of us, hanging out downtown on a Saturday evening, were shocked to see people who called themselves pious Christians enter the local movie theater, an action that we had been taught would surely to lead to damnation. Movie attendance was a big no-no on the long list of forbidden activities.

It is probably a good thing that parents only belatedly learn what their offspring do in their growing-up years. My two close friends, Bob and Don Molle, and my brother Claire and I went to visit the Kingsley Dam, a few miles from our city of Ogallala. The lake itself was about a mile or so in width and several miles in length. We floated across the lake in inner tubes from automobile tires and came perilously close to the dam itself. We were certainly fortunate that we weren't sucked underwater. We made it to the other side of this body of water safely. I recently had a telephone conversation with Bob Molle, who remembers our foolish and dangerous endeavor well. His comment was that we are lucky to be here to tell the story. Incidentally, that was the first conversation that I have had with Bob in sixty years.

After we completed this feat, we went to the bottom side of the dam, where the excess water was being released into the river. We found that we could go where the water was splashing over the dam in considerable volume and be completely submerged and still breathe. For us, this was a liberating moment. I don't think our parents ever found out that we had participated in this activity. It never really dawned on us that this was risky behavior.

There was a reunion of these high school friends who were part of the same church youth group in the summer of 2006. I hadn't seen the Molle brothers for nearly sixty years. Bonnie Jean and her sister Dottie were part of this gathering as was my brother Merle. Don Molle's wife was also present. Lillian Harms, a first cousin, joined us in this celebration of coming together. It was surprising how well this group was able to come together in the twenty-four hours that we shared together.

Our church youth group actively participated in church activities. A blizzard descended on us one New Year's Eve, and the scheduled New Year's Eve services were canceled. Bob Molle and I decided that we would keep the vigil, affirming our commitment to be faithful to the church. It was a memorable evening, sharing this moment of religious commitment even as a blizzard was raging beyond the four walls of the church.

There was little formal or informal education about sexual development. No one would even use the word "sex" in a public conversation. As we reached puberty and our hormone levels heightened, my chums and I talked about the mystery of sexual involvement. We sensed that there was something wrong about the subject being so off limits with adults. We were very curious about masturbation and sexual involvement and envied, from a distance, those outside of our core group who dared to venture in this forbidden area of sexual activity. While we talked about sexual involvement, we were much too frightened by the subject to do more than talk. For me, this naïveté continued into the college years.

While we often questioned the strict rules of the church and fantasized about participating in forbidden activities like going to the movies, card playing, and dancing, we mostly followed the rules of the church.

9

A Couple of Close Calls

As my brother Claire and I approached our teenage years, we put a great deal of pressure on my father to get a gun. Most of our peer group already had a lot of experience with weapons. We were in the middle of pheasant season, and pheasants were plentiful on our farm. The really masculine thing to do in our part of world was to go hunting and fishing. My father disliked both. I remember him saying more than once that if he were given the choice to go hunting or fishing or putting in a hard day's work, he gladly would choose the latter.

Many of our peers talked constantly about their hunting exploits. Finally my father gave in and borrowed a gun from the minister. It didn't have a safety on it. None of us knew the first thing about guns. It was fall, and Dad was burning tumbleweeds along the side of the road. A pheasant suddenly flew into the air, and Dad, who just happened to have the gun in his hand, aimed the gun in the general direction of the flying pheasant and pulled the trigger. To his surprise, the bird fell to the ground. It may have been the first time he ever fired a gun. He commented that the pheasant must have died of a heart attack. In fact, we found no shotgun pellets in the bird.

Later the same afternoon, my brother Claire walked through the field for a short distance without scaring a pheasant out of its hiding place. My father was still burning the tumbleweeds that had accumulated in the ditch between the fence and the road. Claire came back to the truck. I was sitting in the truck bed, and he handed the shotgun to my father while he climbed into the truck bed. My father handed the shotgun back to him. Claire sat down beside me (about one foot away) on the edge of the truck bed and set the butt end of the shotgun on the floor of the truck bed. He was holding on to the barrel of the shotgun when it fired. No one had come close to touching the trigger.

The pellets of the shotgun shell tore through Claire's forehead. His face was covered with powder burn. He was bleeding profusely. Father raced the truck to a nearby neighbor's house, who took them to a hospital some fifteen miles away. When he returned from the doctor's office with his forehead in bandages, he looked like the wartime pictures of soldiers wounded in battle. Some sixty years later, the scar in the center of his forehead was still visible. This incident ended whatever enthusiasm we may have had for hunting. I don't think either of my brothers have hunted since. I fired a pistol on a military pistol range on one occasion, but have no real interest in firearms.

My younger brother, Merle, was also involved in a dangerous incident. He must have been around fourteen when he was driving a tractor that was pulling a machine known as a disc with large blades that cut into the ground three or four inches. Father had taken him to the field. The old Case tractor that he was driving had a clutch that engaged by pulling it toward the driver. Because the disc was engaged, the tractor needed a great deal of power to get started.

As Merle pulled back on the clutch, the tractor lunged forward. Merle lost his balance, falling back just ahead of the discs that could have ground him to pieces. The tractor was moving forward without a driver, and Merle was hanging precariously upside down on the draw bar. When Dad realized what was happening, he raced to catch the tractor and disengaged the clutch. Dad was not particularly athletic and could easily have missed his step trying to get on the tractor. He was literally risking his life in an attempt to save his son. Fortunately, Merle hung on until Dad was able to stop the tractor.

As I mentioned earlier, fishing was not part of our tradition, although it was a common activity among the families of our friends. My brother Claire and I managed to go fishing in a gravel pit that had filled with water on the edge of the city limits of Ogallala. I doubt that there were fish in the pit. Neither of us knew anything about fishing. We had a bamboo fishing pole with line wrapped around it and a fishhook attached to the line. When our fruitless efforts were about to end several hours later, Claire didn't realize that the hook needed to be attached to the pole. He had left it swinging free. As we were leaving, he swung the pole around, and the line with the attached fishhook caught me in the right eyelid. It was impossible for us to remove the hook. We didn't have a knife to cut the line. I was forced to walk all the way back to town, carrying his pole in front of me and still attached to the hook in my eyelid.

As we were nearing town, some dear soul had a knife and cut the line. My brother took both fishing poles and returned home while I looked up the first doctor that I could find who removed the hook from the eyelid. I didn't have money with me to pay for a visit to the doctor's office. The doctor had a great sense of humor while he was removing the hook. He asked that I pay the bill by sharing the fish that I caught, and he never sent a bill.

10

Turning Points

During these years, Bob Molle and I both felt the call of God to become Christian ministers. In many respects, it was a distorted call for me and probably for him. In this church environment, the most important thing that could possibly happen to a person was to hear the call of God. To hear the call to missionary service was the highest calling anyone could receive. The call to pastoral ministry was next in line in terms of choosing a vocation. It meant that such a person had received a special anointment from God. What could be more validating than that?

I feel certain that my deep desire to hear the call of God correlated to a frantic attempt to gain some sense of worth. This perceived call was pivotal in the new directions that my life would take in the future, directions that would ultimately take me places my wildest dreams wouldn't have anticipated. While I had no idea where my renewed interest in academic pursuits would lead, I was aware only that study would be necessary.

My freshman year, I enrolled in the church academy in Colorado Springs. At the time it was called the Colorado Springs Academy. This academy was to later merge with the church college in Bartlesville, Oklahoma, and is now known as Oklahoma Wesleyan University. It is a thriving liberal arts college. Then, the high school academy was actually attached to the unaccredited bible school.

What the school lacked in credentials, it made up for in a dedicated and caring faculty.

Colorado Springs was then a city of approximately twenty-five thousand people. The nearby military post was filled with homesick young soldiers who would inundate the city on weekends. Our church rented a hall in the downtown business district to have religious services on weekend evenings. While I don't clearly remember what transpired in these activities, I do remember meeting a number of teenage soldiers who were away from home for the very first time and often wandered into these religious services. By and large, they were uprooted, utterly confused, and bewildered.

Some Mennonite young men were serving in nearby conscientious objector camps. In lieu of serving in the military, the government assigned them to work on various projects, typically in the forestry service, although my cousin's husband, Lee Harms, worked in a psychiatric facility. They were serving under the same conditions as the military in that they were living in camps under forced conditions. For the most part, they received no pay. While they were away from home, they had the advantage of being with likeminded young men who had chosen this alternative to military life.

I vaguely remember being told that their church had to supply their clothes and food. Their only governmental subsidy, as I then understood it, was three cents a day to buy shaving equipment. Ironically, many wore beards as a statement of their faith.

My first real adventure in the world outside the familiar surroundings of my childhood came as a result of my association with Steve Emory, whose father was president of the school. Steve and I became newspaper boys at nearby Camp Carson; we sold the Rocky Mountain News. There were approximately thirty of us thus employed, and twenty-five or so were Hispanics. It was truly an initiation into the real world. I have never encountered racial differences before. The resentment that these young Mexican teenagers must have felt boiled over. We were dropped off in different places at the military post.

On several occasions, I was harassed when I happened to be the only gringo kid dropped off in a specific area of the military base along with a dozen or so Hispanic kids. It was quite intimidating to be forced to eat a crust of bread that had been lying in the dirt for several days. It was a shocking moment for a naïve farm boy from sparsely settled western Nebraska to feel firsthand the resentment of Mexican teenagers who, now looking back, had also been treated as second-class citizens. Many years later, our son Edward would also feel the isolation of being a minority member of the school that he attended for a few months in Rio Rico, Arizona.

I knew nothing about military etiquette. I typically went through the officers' eating facility, known as the mess hall, attempting to sell my papers. On one occasion, when going through the living quarters of high-ranking officers, I was thoroughly chewed out for being in the wrong place.

Again, thanks to the influence of my friend Steve Emory, I began selling newspapers on the street corners of Colorado Springs. One of the jingles that I got from an aunt went something like this: "Five cents, half a dime, keeps you reading all the time." It's hard now to believe daily papers sold for a nickel.

Since World War II was in full swing, there was considerable focus on security. Posters abounded, urging people to "keep their mouths shut" and avoid any discussions that could be remotely seen as connected with national security. I made an innocent but badly timed remark that nearly got me evicted from the post. I don't remember what the remark was, but I distinctly remember the suspicious stares I received from other passengers on the bus. If the way I felt was any indication, I must have looked guilty.

While my dad's permission was very reluctant, he finally did agree to my attempt to climb Pikes Peak with a number of young male teenagers whose parents were attending the annual church camp meeting taking place on the grounds of the academy. The person I would have thought had energy to spare was the first to turn back. We illegally climbed on the bed of the cog trail. We met several of the trains en route to and from the summit but received no admonitions to cease and desist. The trip up the peak took about nine hours, and the return trip took about three hours. It was one of the first tests of physical endurance that I had experienced.

I took a mountain path often, sometimes with friends, sometimes alone. On several occasions, my friends and I rode our bikes out to Manitou Springs at the base of Pikes Peak. Two friends often participated in these endeavors. One of these friends, Manuel Davenport, eventually became a professor of philosophy at Texas AandM. We shared a brief correspondence after becoming adults, but no real contact had been sustained since our school days. We had become part of very different worlds. On a recent cruise, I met some passengers who had been professors at Texas AandM and knew Manuel well. They felt strongly that Manuel and I would have connected immediately if we had met as adults. They reported how much loss they felt at Manuel's death.

While there was a great deal of rigidity in terms of what was considered "acceptable behavior," the time spent at the academy was crucial for me. There, I felt accepted. The final year was spent in the dormitory. Every student was given a task to perform. Mine was to milk the cow owned by the school that provided the fresh milk for the dormitory students.

One of the teachers lived in a small apartment located on the second floor of the primary school building. Dan Bursch, who had been a military pilot, had a worldview that seemed a bit broader than most of his contemporaries, including his spouse. He could be playful. On one occasion, I was delivering a quart of the fresh milk from the kitchen to his apartment. He saw me before I entered his building and suggested I throw the bottle of milk to him as he leaned out his window from his second-story apartment. My first throw was just out of his grasp. The second attempt proved disastrous, and the bottle crashed. He seemed to thoroughly enjoy his part in this playful act. Recently, I had the good fortune to meet Dan Bursch at a college reunion. We had a great time sharing memories of our time at Colorado Springs as well as sharing our military exploits with each other.

All the students in the school had come from families with

limited means. No one could afford to be extravagant. Even by our limited economic standards, one of our classmates was considered impoverished. One day I happened to notice that Morris's shoes had holes in the soles, and he had placed cardboard inside his shoes to give his feet protection. While my wardrobe was limited, I did happen to have two pairs of shoes and was willing to give him one of my pairs of shoes if they would fit his feet. In response to my question of what size shoes he wore, he replied with some desperation in his voice that he "wore anything from seven to eleven." He became the owner of my extra pair of shoes.

One of the most significant happenings in my life during this time was the invitation to join the male quartet while attending the academy in Colorado Springs. I had no idea that I would be chosen for this honor. While this group had little training or professional direction, we did a number of performances. When we sang in chapel for the first time, I was given the feedback that I was dancing from one foot to the other so rapidly that my face became something of a blur. Obviously, it was a nervous reaction. The big event for us was travel engagements to churches in Texas. During this trip, we got a glimpse of a Mexican border town of Laredo. We also sang at the church, where one of our quartet members, Wayne Quinn, had attended. (I had no idea then how important my Mexican friends would become. I was to develop a deep appreciation of their culture and have friendships there that began nearly three decades ago and will surely have a lasting importance for the rest of my life.)

While formal social activities were limited, high school seniors were allowed to have a sneak day. Planned far in advance and in utter secrecy, class members and the class sponsor would vanish from campus for one day. The juniors tried hard to decipher this secret. If they were successful, they would be permitted to accompany us on this special trip. The seniors, of course, were determined to prevent this from happening.

On that fateful day, the senior males shimmied down two stories of our dormitory by a rope that had been secured inside one of our rooms. Our class president, Paul McNall, who was later to become a superintendent of schools in Sharon Springs, Kansas, organized this escape. I'm not sure how the gals managed to escape from their dormitories without being detected.

Our class, with our advisor, then drove the seventy-five or eighty miles to the big city of Denver. The activities of that special day were not as well planned as our escape from campus had been. The boys went swimming at the YMCA. (I'm not certain what the gals did during this time.) With no skills as a swimmer, I had to be rescued when I went off the diving board and wasn't able to make it to the side of the pool. I still remember the panic I felt and how I was grabbing under the water for one person after another when they tried to rescue me. I knew at the time that this was counterproductive but was unable to stop grabbing the people who were attempting to assist me.

Thirteen of us were in the graduating class of 1946 from the Colorado Springs Academy. Many returned for the junior college and undergraduate classes in various biblical studies at the academy. Eight or nine of us got together to celebrate our fifty-fourth anniversary of graduation from high school in the year 2000—our first reunion. Three of us, including Paul McNall, Don Brown, and I, had ventured off to a bible college located in Owosso, Michigan, in the fall after graduating that spring from the Academy. Don died from a brain tumor some years ago, but his widow was able to attend our class reunion.

I had returned to work on a neighbor's farm during the summer. When I informed my parents of my decision to go with my friends to Michigan, Dad strenuously objected to this move on several counts. First, I hadn't yet reached my seventeenth birthday, and second, I had no funds. Michigan must have seemed like the other side of the world to him. On the matter of funds, I had given the money that I had earned to my parents, whom I assumed expected it, although they had not demanded that I do so.

I would not have dared to directly confront my dad head-on about my decision to join my friends in this adventure. I would return home on weekends that summer when dad would point out all the reasons that going to this bible college was an unthinkable choice.

Dad, in addition to farming, was serving a small congregation of a very right-wing, conservative church. The district superintendent, whose word was close to being law, had instructed my father not to allow me to go to this bible college because he was convinced that it was far too liberal. He told my father that I would be ruined if I came under the influence of that school. An institution that taught theology in any form was highly suspect if it didn't adhere in every detail to the rigid standards that this particular group considered orthodox.

My dad also expressed the fear that I would absorb a culture with which he wasn't familiar and reject my heritage. Specifically, he expressed the fear that I would marry some "Eastern girl" who wouldn't accept them. I doubt that I would have held my own in my encounter with my father if I hadn't made a commitment to two of my classmates in my high school graduating class at the academy to go to the bible college located in Owosso, Michigan.

As fall approached—the time to rendezvous with my friends— dad conceded at the last minute by stating, "I won't stop you, but I won't give you my blessing."

Seen now from the eyes of a father and grandfather, I understand his apprehension about my going that far from home at such a young age. He didn't have the funds to support this venture, and he was working in a setting that didn't allow much deviation from the party line. I don't think, however, that he had any idea the feelings of guilt that I would initially carry with me to my new setting as a result of not heeding his warnings. Seen from my perspective now, it was a truly crucially important decision for me to make, a decision that proved to be liberating.

Shortly after I arrived in Michigan, I began to develop boils on my body. While I never shared with anyone my doubts and fears, I secretly wondered if these boils were a punishment from God for daring to go against my father's wishes.

One vivid memory I will retain as long as there is memory: a couple of weeks before the time I was to meet my friends, Paul Mc-Nall and Don Brown, my boss had loaned me to work for another farm couple for a week or so. Their home was infested with bed bugs, an experience I was totally unprepared to deal with. When the family would ask me about the bites on my body, I was too embarrassed to tell them that it came from the bed in their home. I would avoid going to this bed as long as possible.

On one particular evening, there was a full moon. I wandered out into a nearby field and sat on the ground against a shock of wheat. The majesty of the evening was overpowering. I tried to imagine where my new adventure would lead me. I somehow sensed that my life was forever changing, although I could not possibly have imagined the twists and turns that my life would take. Something of an anchoring experience took place for me that evening. Since that evening, moonlight has provided deeply moving experiences and is a time when I am in touch with the mystical quality of being alive.

Part 2

Leaving the Nest

II

A New Beginning

I arrived in the city of Owosso, Michigan in September 1946. The population was about twenty thousand. With the very few dollars that I possessed, I was not in position to pay the tuition fees or my room or board. I don't remember even informing the college that I was coming.

As incredible as it now seems, I was admitted to the college without any kind of payment for either tuition or room or board. An unaccredited academic institution, it was anything but the liberal citadel that my father's district superintendent had warned about.

Upon arrival, my two cohorts and I arrived dressed in Western clothing, including cowboy boots, that we considered "going to meetin' kind of garb." Some were amused; some of the superconservative facility apparently had the stereotypic view that the three of us likely were "rowdies" and suggested that we be expelled before "trouble set in." Those who held a more moderate view felt it was important not to make judgments before the fact. The moderate group won the day.

Demands were made that every student accept every religious tenet without reservation. Military boot camps could have learned lessons from this institution when it came accepting without question the rules defining our behavior as well as our religious beliefs.

Even though the college was coeducational, any social contacts between the sexes were highly restricted.

Still, this college was a godsend for me. I was struggling with an intense sense of inadequacy in so many aspects of my life. I was still living out the pronouncement given years earlier of "being dumb and stupid." My social skills were clearly undeveloped. Had it not been for that perceived call to the Christian ministry, I could have easily accommodated myself to living a hermit kind of existence. It is also unlikely that at this time in my life I would have succeeded if I had attempted in enroll in a more typical educational institution.

In this setting, the instructors, most of whom had limited teaching credentials, were instrumental in helping me to begin to surmount the mountains of limitations that had plagued me.

I would rate one of these professors to be among the top professors that I have known in my academic career. Dr. Philo possessed a master's degree as well as a doctor of divinity. His charismatic style of teaching riveted the attention of the entire class. I remember signing up for two courses in philosophy that met from eight a.m. to noon, six days a week, a schedule that would normally be catastrophic in terms of holding the attention of students. Even though the subject matter was totally beyond my comprehension, Dr. Philo kept us spellbound hour after hour for six days a week for six or seven weeks. A bell would sound at the midpoint of this class session. I was so engrossed with the class presentation that the ringing bell would often startle me. Dr. Philo was indeed an educational giant.

I also will never forget another professor, Bertha Kienbaum. She could be stern and rigid. Still, she gave of herself in ways that left a strong imprint on a host of students fortunate enough to be part of her classroom.

With my lack of educational preparation, I certainly had no business signing up for twenty hours or so of academic credit during my first semester. This academic load included a class in beginning Greek. (I can't imagine any academic counselor allowing anyone with my educational background to enroll in this many classes, let alone a demanding Greek class.)

Miss Kienbaum, who may have held a master's degree, was our Greek professor. She decided about midterm that our class was coasting. Her body language suggested that the test the next day would be especially demanding.

In addition to my heavy academic load, I had procured a job working six hours daily for the newspaper known as the *Argus-Press*. When I returned from work, I studied late into the night for this "test of fire" that I was certain awaited us. After a few hours of sleep, I awoke in the early hours of the morning to continue my preparation for this test.

When the time arrived and the test was presented to us, I was utterly exhausted. In my mind's eye, I could even see page numbers of the textbook where the very items on the test were located. While I had studied diligently, my foggy mind simply couldn't reproduce what was being demanded. I gave up in despair and was the first person to leave the classroom.

When this esteemed teacher saw my abysmal performance, it obviously confirmed her suspicions that the "class was coasting." She projected the frustration she had with the class at large on me in front of the entire class. I left the class humiliated and deeply embarrassed.

I didn't share with her until years after I graduated from the college how much effort that I had in fact put into this exam. (I obviously had kept this carefully nurtured episode within my psyche for years and only shared it when she had come to visit me while I was stationed with the 82nd Airborne Division.) This sharing proved to be cleansing and healing.

She was keenly interested in my activities with the 82nd Airborne Division. Even though she was ninety years old at this time, she gamely boarded a military truck and was seated in the rear of that truck during the ride, taking passengers to see a military parachute exercise. She was thrilled by the sight of parachutes drifting from the sky. She was also pleased that her struggling academic student had made the grade.

Teachers at this college, who were less skilled than Dr. Philo and Miss Kienbaum, were people who also cared deeply about their students and attempted to draw forth what was waiting to be born within the student. While this unaccredited institution had its serious drawbacks, it nevertheless produced an exceptionally high percentage of graduates that eventually completed doctoral degrees. I owe these teachers and this institution of learning a profound debt of gratitude.

For me, one of the most fortuitous and surprising events at Owosso Bible College was my selection to be a member of the prestigious varsity male quartet. To say that I was both pleased and intimidated is an understatement. I viewed the other members of this group as far more sophisticated than I. I was the youngest member of this group and viewed myself as a hick from the sticks in this new setting. The familiar feelings of inferiority initially clouded my relationship with the team.

All three of the other members were military veterans. Wes Manker was a veteran with extensive military combat experience. Bud Brower had been a medic in the navy, and his military experiences had taken him to many ports around the world. Ed Doehring had been in the merchant marines and was the son of a prominent clergyman. (Incidentally, his father would one day perform our marriage ceremony.)

While I clearly felt over my head in this kind of company, it was a lifesaver in so many respects. I was extremely shy, and we were singing in front of groups, primarily churches, nearly every weekend of the year. In time, my stage presence and my social skills improved in a number of ways. This kind of personal validation also helped develop my academic skills.

A number of events contributed to the steep learning curve, some of which were painful. One such moment stands out in my memory. Our quartet was en route to one of the churches where we were to sing. We all wore matching suits. The other three members and our manager all wore top coats. I wore a mackinaw jacket over my suit.

Obviously embarrassed, one of the members pointedly asked, "Where's your topcoat?"

Chagrined, I never wore that mackinaw jacket again. I simply went without a coat of any kind.

In fact, up until that point, I had never owned a topcoat and couldn't afford one. When asked why I wasn't wearing a topcoat in subfreezing weather, I tried to hide my embarrassment by saying that the weather in Nebraska got really cold, and by comparison the weather in Michigan was so mild that a topcoat wasn't needed. As I remember, the weather at that moment was hovering around zero degrees Fahrenheit. It was a weak cover at best.

During the second year, two members of the quartet didn't return. Art Taylor and Vaughn Drummonds were the replacements. Ed Doehring, the third original member of our group, left to enter medical school. Bob Price was the replacement. This group bonded in a very special way; a close bond still exists nearly seven decades later.

While this college provided important maturational experiences for which I will be eternally grateful, there were obvious limitations. There was a strong Victorian atmosphere, where social contact between the sexes was, for the most part, verboten.

The first year that I attended (1946), the college was undertaking a brave new experiment. Males and females were allowed to study in the school library during evening hours at the same time. This new policy clearly specified that this procedure would be given a trial period. Both males and females had to be either in their dormitory rooms or in the library from the hours of seven to nine p.m. No exceptions.

I had chosen to study in my room one evening. It must have been somewhere between 8:30 and 8:45 p.m. when, in violation of this newly established study policy, I wandered from my room to the library downstairs.

A classmate, who happened to be the bass in our quartet, must have also been bored with the study routine. I found him examining the bulletin board near the library entrance. I was seventeen while he was a four-year navy veteran. For my classmate, the rigid rules of our college probably weren't all that different from what he had experienced in the military.

Contrary to my typical mode of a behavior that attempted to "fit in," I unexpectedly let my go of my usual controls. I gave a yell while running down the halls, pulled the fire bell that was only connected to that building, and then disappeared into the night. Since the study period was to be observed in absolute silence, my impulsive behavior was obviously seen as chaotic.

Caught by complete surprise, my classmate instinctively attempted to escape by going into a nearby, darkened classroom. Unfortunately for him, the place that the library monitor began his search for the culprit of this disruptive episode was the room that he had escaped to. He obviously looked very guilty. I'm not sure what explanation he gave, but to his credit, he didn't identify me as the real culprit. I'm embarrassed to say that I wasn't as generous to him. I climbed up the fire escape leading to my second-floor room and returned to my room, undetected.

Students of most every institution develop rituals of initiation. Among the male student body of Owosso College was a ritual referred to as the snipe hunt. This event would typically be held on a dark, moonless night. The naïve initiate would be taken to a remote setting and given a large bag and flashlight. He would be instructed to shine the flashlight toward the inside of this bag and patiently wait while other members would disappear into the darkness, purportedly to round up the "snipe" that would be drawn to the light and ultimately inside the bag. The initiate would be told to maintain absolute silence during his vigil. The supporting cast would then return to the dormitory to await his hapless return often hours later.

A beautiful cemetery just over the hill and across the street from the campus was a perfect get-away from the rigid rules of the school. Gorgeous, tall oak trees; well-maintained, grassy areas; and a small lake provided an idyllic setting. Students risked disciplinary action from the college to walk the lovely paths that were carved through the forty-acre cemetery with the one with whom they had a romantic involvement. I confess that I was among those guilty culprits.

Located at the far end of the cemetery was a mausoleum that contained a number of units or slots where families could choose to have their deceased buried aboveground rather than in the ground.

The unlocked but well-maintained mausoleum was not lit at night. A classmate discovered one unit that was empty with no door on the opening.

Though admittedly a bit gross, we planned to take a very naïve male student on his initiating tour to this site. One very dark night, a member of initiating team crawled into this empty unit, his arm extending over the edge. At the precise moment that the student being initiated entered the mausoleum with the supporting cast, the student inside the empty unit began to groan. Our terrified initiate bolted out of the mausoleum and ran back to the campus in record time. I hope that we didn't do irreparable damage to his emotional and maturational development.

While this prank was intended to be innocent and amusing, I feel sure that Dean of Men would likely not have seen the intended humor and, if he had learned about it, would likely have placed heavy restrictions on those who participated in this episode.

On another note, I did not have any financial support for these college years. My first job was with the local YMCA. My job was to interact and monitor the activities of elementary and junior high boys who were regulars at the Y.

I have never played the game of Ping-Pong. These ten-year-olds were rather skilled at the game and regularly challenged me to compete, a challenge that I initially lost badly. Repeatedly, I accepted the challenge to compete. These kids were instrumental in developing my skills in Ping-Pong. In time, I was able to participate in the citywide Ping-Pong tournament. It's a game that I now rarely play but still enjoy, thanks to the kids from the Y.

Some months later, I secured a job at the Owosso *Argus-Press*, the local daily newspaper. Here, I first met Don Elliot, who eventually would be the best man at our wedding. I also met Harold Cox, who is still a cherished friend.

My initial job was to operate the address-o-graph machine that punched out the names and addresses of new customers as well as changes of address. I was soon driving a motor route of more than ninety miles every day, except Sunday, delivering papers to local drug stores in nearby towns as well as to the paperboys in these towns and villages. I also delivered papers to customers in rural areas. This task required learning how and when to throw a paper while driving at sixty miles per hour and still have that paper land in a driveway or place where it could easily be found.

I took over the route from a fellow quartet member, Ed Doehring, who later became a physician. Ed had an engaging personality and was polished, particularly in his dealings with a given drug store owner, where he would drop off a batch of the daily newspapers to be sold over the counter. Periodically, the carrier would pick up the unsold papers from different drugstores.

I was clumsy, awkward, and unsure of myself when counting the unsold papers for the first time. The owner became verbally abusive. Using vulgarity, he shouted that he didn't have all day to stand around watching me count papers. Usually very passive and tentative, I shocked myself by softly responding, "The least that you could do is to be a gentleman." From that day forth, this owner was the epitome of cordiality.

Driving this route could be challenging. On several occasions, the entire route was under a sheet of ice. I was passing almost everyone on the road at thirty miles per hour or less. It wasn't unusual to slip off the road into the ditch or onto the adjoining field. Since I was driving a jeep with four-wheel drive, it wasn't difficult to get back on the road.

On one occasion, I noticed out of the corner of my eye some pheasants that were in a nearby ditch. The sound of the jeep was apparently different enough from other vehicles that the pheasants became startled. As I was passing, six or seven pheasants flew, crashing into my windshield and bumper as I drove by at about fifty miles per hour. I was startled but managed to keep control of the vehicle. I'm still surprised that they didn't break the windshield in this collision.

My first traffic ticket was disconcerting and disillusioning. I was driving an *Argus-Press* vehicle when I saw the flickering lights of the policeman's vehicle. I immediately glanced at the speedometer. I was exceeding the speed limit by three miles per hour. The ticket indicated that I was exceeding the limit at fifteen miles per hour and was traveling at dusk without headlights (which happened not to be true).

At age seventeen, I got my first lesson that the justice system is not always just. When I appeared before the judge, I asked if I had a right to dispute the ticket. He answered in the affirmative but immediately imposed a ten-dollar fine without giving me an opportunity to speak. For someone on an extremely limited budget, this was a huge fine. The heavier loss, however, was my loss of innocence regarding how inappropriately and unjustly the laws can be reinforced.

Financial survival was a clear priority. When there was an opportunity to work an extra job or by some means cut expenses, I was quick to do it. Don Elliott's father was a painting contractor and had been contracted to paint a wooden structure that was also the college church. This church was adjacent to a large industrial factory.

I was selected to wash down the dirt and grime on the outside of this church before the painting could take place. Actually this washing ritual frequently occurred even when houses away from the industrial area were to be painted. Don's father supplied the ladders that he used in his painting business.

The eaves of the roof must have been at least thirty feet above the ground. The roof extended several feet beyond the wall. If I placed the tall ladder on the roof, I was unable to reach the walls that needed to be washed. Placing the ladder on the wall just under the roof required that I put the ladder at a rather flat angle, which put a great deal of additional stress on the steps of the ladder.

I placed a bucket containing the strong solution necessary to cut through the grime and dirt on the top step, just under the eaves of the roof. Bracing one hand against roof, I was reaching out as far as I could with a brush in the other hand to scrub the wall. The force of my weight on the angle of the ladder along with my leaning hard to the right was too much stress on the step of the ladder. It broke. My body slipped down the ladder, but my elbows managed to catch the rung just below the broken step. I was not in a position to swing my dangling feet to catch the next rung, which was now above my chest. The bucket with the strong solution tipped and emptied into my face, including my hair. To complicate things, my ribs had been damaged as they caught the rung below. In a great deal of pain and overcome with exhaustion, I hung by my elbows as long as I could and then dropped the thirty or more feet to the ground.

The accident occurred on Labor Day. The watchman from the factory had witnessed my accident. He checked on my welfare and invited me to use the washroom of the adjacent factory building to wash the solution out of my hair. In the weeks that followed, I was to lose much of my long wavy hair, which never returned.

While I survived the fall without difficulty, my ribs hurt for weeks. I feel sure that they were cracked or broken, but I didn't go to the doctor to find out. In my family tradition, we didn't go to doctors unless things got critical. Funds were not available for luxuries such as medical care. While I didn't immediately go right back to work, I did return to finish the job the following day.

I returned to my Nebraska home for the summer. I worked on the farm owned by Dwight Softley, who had married my first-grade teacher. Dwight was a true workaholic who didn't finish in his shop until late into the evening. I tried to be of assistance but had no talent for tinkering. The dilemma facing me was to hang around the shop, feeling awkward and helpless, or to feel guilty about sitting in the family's living room and doing nothing during the evening hours. Desperate to please, I usually chose the first miserable option.

I learned, purely by accident, that my mother was pregnant. Pregnancy was not openly discussed in that time, at least not in rural western Nebraska. The rumor was that my mother had gone to her doctor early in her pregnancy and was told that she had a tumor. When the tumor began to grow dramatically, my parents in desperation finally sought a second opinion.

They were totally stunned when they learned that they were expecting a new arrival. I was told that my parents didn't exchange a single word as they drove to their farm home until reaching the last hill from their home. Dad purportedly began laughing while making the comment that this startling news was "the funniest thing I ever heard of." My mother clearly wasn't amused. There was a fourteen-plus year gap between their youngest and the expected newborn.

I learned that my sister had been born after I returned to the college that I was attending in Michigan. My new sister, Myrna, became my father's favorite and provided much company for our parents after their three sons had made their own way into the world.

Incidentally, I never returned to my Nebraska home for summer employment. After this first summer, I only visited my family home once every three years. I had indeed left home for good.

12

A Crisis That Wouldn't Go Away

A college friend named Bill Gilkerson, who later became a prominent pastor, rented a room across the street from the campus. When he got married, he asked if I would be interested in renting this room. With the owner's agreement, I accepted. While the room was not large, it was pleasant with a second-floor view of the street. It was to be my home until Leta and I were married.

A rather traumatic event with strong mind/body ramifications had occurred some months earlier. This story, while awkward to share, also *illustrates the destructive power of internalizing an agonizing conflict rather than finding an alternative strategy for dealing with it.* This and other personal development crises shared in the following pages left a powerful imprint on my psyche that impacted my later practice as a psychologist. A comment that I used to make to my psychology clients was that I would "keep their painful secrets in strict confidence," but added that if and when they fully resolved these crises, they "wouldn't care if this information was shared on a news channel."

When I was returning to college after my only summer of farm work in Nebraska, I chose to make the thousand-mile journey by a bus that stopped at every village from Ogallala, Nebraska, to Chicago. This journey lasted two days and two nights. The central bus station in Chicago seemed to me to be overwhelming and very confusing. With a couple of suitcases in hand, I was so anxious that I barely noticed how fatigued I was.

Suddenly, there was an urgent call from Mother Nature. I rapidly made my way to the men's room, only to find that I didn't have the correct coins to open the stalls leading to the toilet. One door didn't require coins. With great reluctance, I entered that stall since nature's call was demanding immediate attention. Believing in the old wives tale that one could get syphilis from a toilet seat, I attempted to hold myself a few inches above the toilet. However, the intestinal explosion was so intense that, in my fatigued condition, I lost my balance and sank down onto the toilet seat.

Haunted by the frightening consequences of this disease, I was deeply distressed that I actually might catch it. I was sure that no one would accept an explanation that a sexual indiscretion had not occurred. The very conservative religious environment of which I was then a part viewed sexual sins as the very top of the list that would offend the Ruler of Heaven and Earth. My perceived call to preach would clearly be in jeopardy if my worst fears had been realized. My closely guarded secret resulted in anguish and apprehension beyond description. I still managed to function normally. I don't think anyone suspected that an internal volcano was constantly erupting within me.

I soon began to notice pimples beginning to pop out in the buttocks area and on my scrotum. Panic set in. I would pinch these sores until my shorts and the sheets on which I slept became blotted with spots of blood. I was so embarrassed to have the lady of the house collect my sheets on wash days. These symptoms worsened over time. I thought I was doomed.

I became so desperate that I entertained fantasies of simply disappearing by going to some metropolitan city like Chicago to wait out the terrible medical consequences of the dreaded disease that I assumed that I had contracted in that toilet seat in that Chicago station.

With ever-deepening anxiety, I decided to contact a doctor, though I had no idea how. My only previous contact with a physician occurred during two childhood surgeries in a very small village, neither of which had resulted in a hospital stay. Actually I had spent the night in a doctor's office following a tonsillectomy.

With much apprehension, I showed up at the office of a physician that I had heard a friend speak of. It never dawned on me that appointments were needed. The waiting room was filled with patients. My first contact was with a teenage receptionist. She asked, in a voice loud enough to be heard throughout the waiting room, for the purpose of my visit. Deeply embarrassed, I awkwardly stated that I wanted a general examination.

Sneering, she responded with, "Yeah, I know why you are here." She was again loud enough for the people in the waiting room to hear.

I wanted to bolt.

Since I didn't have an appointment, I waited about four hours. When everyone in the waiting room had been seen but me, I assumed that I would be next. The receptionist seemed to take pleasure in announcing that the doctor was taking a dinner break and then would return in two hours. In a total panic, I left the office, never to return.

The next time I was to enter a doctor's office was about a year later, when I went to get the required blood test for a marriage. Plagued with deep fears that my bride to be would at last learn that I was a carrier of a venereal disease, I was certain that she would angrily say something like, "How could you string me along like this?" The time after the blood test was taken until the results were announced was a sheer hell.

When the medical result of the blood test came back normal, it was as if the weight of the world had been suddenly lifted off my shoulders. The long months, actually years, of vacillating between denial and abject fear were over. Interestingly, the bloody blemishes on my buttocks and scrotum literally disappeared in a matter of a few days.

In future years, when I would work as a psychologist, the lessons of these struggles were instrumental as I tried to assist clients who were fiercely holding on to deep, dark secrets that impeded their growth and development.

13

A Special Relationship

A number of friendships that developed during the Owosso College days remain to this day. None was more important than the relationship with Bob Price. It started through our mutual involvement in the varsity male quartet. We began to question some of the rigid rules as well as the theological dogma that the school held. It was strictly against the college's policy for students to question its rules and regulations or the doctrinal tenets of the church that was then known as the Pilgrim Holiness Church.

We were deeply troubled by some of the chapel services. While it was a time to be with our friends and enjoy the singing or the sermons, particularly from guest speakers as well as faculty members, we were often saturated by an attempt to manipulate students using guilt. At the end of these sermons, an altar call would be given. If a student responded to the speaker's admonition by kneeling at the altar railing, the first question was whether they were there to be saved or sanctified. This question presupposed that there were two distinctly different works of grace. The first work of grace was the forgiveness of past sins; the second was removing the root of sin that caused one to sin in the first place. This theological position held that, after one had received the second work of grace, one would be empowered to "live above sin." If one did sin, it was necessary to again experience both works of grace to gain a "correct" relationship with God.

We sensed that the evangelists, who were often the chapel speakers, engaged (however unintentionally) in a form of scalp hunting. Their effectiveness was measured by how many people would respond at the end of their sermons by coming forward to seek these works of grace. The student moved by the force of their sermons often came forward, sensing some spiritual void without being able say what that need was. When a person knelt at the altar near the speaker's podium, the first question the person who attempted to fill the role of spiritual advisor would ask was why the person had come. If they didn't know, it was assumed that they had come seeking the first work of grace.

Bob Price and I spent many evening hours discussing what seemed to us to be this well-intentioned but dysfunctional strategy in assisting a student with finding emotional and spiritual stability. To add insult to injury, we would hear faculty members discuss the lack of grounding for students who were "constant seekers," while these faculty members were part of the very system that fostered the confusion.

We also discussed the school's attempt to interrupt the normal development of relationships between the sexes. The school rules appeared to be driven by the fear that any contacts between the sexes might result in sexual fantasies or worse. The "rules" became, in our view, highly distorted. For example, if a couple became engaged, they could have a chaperoned date once every six weeks, although it was unclear how they could become engaged if they were not allowed legitimate contact. Incidentally, many couples snuck over to the large, lovely, well-maintained cemetery across the street. It featured rolling hills and a fair-sized lake. Other than the interesting tombstones, it resembled a large park that must have covered at least forty acres of ground.

Our discussions led us in many different directions far beyond our experiences at the college. We struggled with the meaning of our lives. Among other things, we looked at vocations, including the clergy. In the tradition of which we were a part, a minister found his way the best that he could. He or she (incidentally this denomination received women long before the old-line denominations did) hoped that they would receive a call to serve a given congregation. That congregation would then have a vote of the membership each year to see if that minister would remain at his post.

We sensed that many young ministers would start this vocation under very different, hard-to-survive circumstances. If he or she was considered successful, they might receive a call to a congregation with more status. As they approached the end of their careers, many would find that they were seen as less desirable. Often, their careers resembled a bell-shaped curve. We examined other professions. We sensed that many professionals lost their passion for their work somewhere around midlife. Even if they continued to do what they had been doing, their work became drudgery.

Over several years, we reached a rather astonishing conclusion as a result of these discussions. We both vowed that we would not allow ourselves to be caught in the trap of any given profession per se. Rather, we would risk change to maintain a sense of vitality both in our work and in our lives. This conclusion was to have a rather profound impact on the ways that we attempted to live our lives. I consider these discussions among the most important thought processes leading to life-altering decisions made during these formative teenage and young adult years. Bob Price and I have maintained our close relationship for more than a half-century.

14

An Unusual Mentor

Joe Uhrig is one of the most unique people that I have ever met. Among his many talents was being a suburb fund-raiser. Although his academic background was rather weak, he was a captivating speaker. This highly gifted person also had a troubling "shadow side" to his personality. (Let any person without a shadow side please stand.)

He was hired as the public relations person for the college. The male quartet traveled with him to various churches throughout the State of Michigan and surrounding states. He was so effective in this fund-raising role that many pastors hesitated to invite him to speak to their congregations. Even though the pastors were generally supportive of the college, their local fund-raising projects were often in jeopardy because of Joe's superb talents in raising funds for the cause that he represented.

Joe's gift to us was his ability to elicit new visions of what was possible. He shared that when he was discharged from the navy at twenty years old, he went to work in one of the major departments of Prentice Hall as a salesperson. He states that, shortly after his arrival, he became the top division salesman in the United States for six consecutive months. Purportedly called to division headquarters to explain how he had accomplished this spectacular feat, Joe was unable to give them a formula that culminated in this success-ful strategy.

In the several years that our quartet was involved with him, he demonstrated his talents again and again. His efforts to put Owos-so College on the map had moments of unusual success. Among his public relations activities was to broadcast the chapel services regu-larly on a local radio station, a first for the college. He performed this task exceptionally well.

Previously, most public relation activities had been confined to religious groups. Joe had our quartet performing before secular groups as well. Thanks to his initiative, we were invited to sing for a Republican Party banquet held in Owosso. One of the songs that we sang on this occasion was "Sleep Kentucky Babe." The song de-picted a black mother singing a lullaby to her baby.

Some of the more conservative students, who were even more to the theological right than most of the college students, got word of this event and were convinced that we had "compromised with the world," which was considered a weighty sin. They apparently assumed that we were singing about a sexy lady who was assumed to be seductive. They voiced their strong objections by organizing an all-night prayer meeting aimed at the erring quartet members, and of course, our leader, Joe Uhrig.

Joe's strategy was to give a sermon at the chapel that had a strong patriotic theme and appealed to the large number of vet-erans enrolled in the college. In his dramatic closing, he presented vivid pictures of the veterans who fought and died to preserve our liberties and family values. He had the bulk of the chapel audience in his hands.

The quartet was unprepared for the final drama of this episode. Joe had us come to the platform to sing "Sleep Kentucky Babe." At that moment, the tension was thick. The opening lines were "Skee-ters am a humming round the honeysuckle vine. Sleep, Kentucky babe..." The tension quickly melted, and the organizers of the pro-test were silenced.

I should add that the primary organizer of the protest was a highly articulate person whose religious conversation had taken place in a very conservative setting in the Deep South. In time, he would make major philosophical changes to his worldview and make a stalwart contribution to the professional development of future educators.

(It occurred to me while describing this drama of discord and protests that it comes close to describing today's polarized political climate. The telling question is how one gets past the tricky tendency to differentiate between "us and them" that ends up in attempting to inappropriately separate "the sheep from the goats.")

Still teenagers, the quartet members could be mischievous, particularly when we were traveling long distances with Joe as our leader. When these long distances turned into days of traveling, we could also become exhausted. On one occasion, we had performed at a church in Traverse City, Michigan. Partly as a result of fatigue, we became so amused when something unexpected happened during our performance that we broke down with laughter and couldn't continue. Joe, who was likely also fatigued, lost his sense of humor and in a rather abrupt way told us to take our seats. The resulting tension didn't subside until the following day.

Before we had gone on this trip, the administration had criticized Joe for spending too much money for meals during our promotional trips. He made the point that we would have to watch our spending for meals.

When we arrived at the restaurant, two of us had secretly decided that we would order one hamburger and then carefully divide it and loudly argue over who got the largest share of the hamburger. Joe was so embarrassed by our actions that he ordered full dinners for all of us. Mildly agitated, he then got in the car and drove away. We knew that he would return because we were singing in a local church in Sault Ste. Marie, Michigan, that evening.

We thought that it would be amusing to quickly eat our meals and disappear before he returned. We were certain that we would be able to find the location of the church without difficulty. Joe returned just as we were leaving the restaurant and running across an open lot. He wasn't amused by our prank.

On one occasion, we were traveling to various churches in West Virginia. We decided to hike the mountain trails. Bob and I decided to take a shortcut over the top of the mountain while the two other members wisely returned the way they had come. Predictably, Bob and I got lost. We could have been in deep trouble. Quite accidentally, however, we stumbled onto a very modest dwelling and found a girl who must have been nearing her teenage years. She was playing in the sand. My first thought was to seriously doubt that she had ever enrolled in school. We found a trail that was instrumental in finding our way back to town several hours after the two members of the quartet, who had stayed on the original path, returned. Joe and the pastor of the church where we were to perform that evening breathed an enormous sigh of relief.

We often stayed at the homes of parishioners after our performances. Sometimes, the accommodations left a great deal to be desired; at other times we had excellent accommodations and were royally received. On one occasion, several of us were being entertained in the home of an inventor in Columbus, Ohio. This person was in the process of getting a patent on a radar system that would guide airplanes that were landing in the fog. The time was somewhere around 1947. We thought it was an incredible invention— and indeed it was. I'm certain that this great invention would be seen by today's standards as being primitive.

Joe was eventually fired as the public relations director at the college in part because he was too good at it. As stated earlier, the pastors were afraid to let him come to make his pitch because he would do it so effectively that funds needed for other projects would be compromised. Still, his troubling shadow side was always lurking in the background. Joe was reassigned to Alexandria, Virginia, to a small downtown mission hall. Those who thought that he would hopelessly wither totally misjudged his capability.

A year later, he would move this hapless congregation from a small rented building to a lovely new building in an upper-middle-class neighborhood. The church's steeple featured a hand with a finger pointing to the sky, and he called the church the Hand to Heaven. As if this wasn't enough, Joe soon had a successful prime-time religious television program where, among other things, he would often feature well-known guests.

He once signed a TV contract for eight continuous hours on New Year's Eve. With no money on hand, he contacted Roy and Dale Rogers to be the featured guests (and I believe he also had the Sons of the Pioneers on this program). Roy and Dale didn't really want to spend the holidays away from their California home but agreed to come based on the promise that Joe would get them into the White House to see President and Mrs. Eisenhower.

When Joe called the White House to make the agreed arrangements for Roy and Dale's visit, he discovered that all appointments had been canceled, even with foreign dignitaries, because of the president's heart attack. Not one to take no for an answer, he found after some investigation that Ike's grandson, David, was having his twelfth birthday. What twelve-year-old wouldn't jump at the chance of having Roy and Dale perform at his birthday party? With a proud grandfather looking on, Roy and Dale did indeed perform at David's birthday celebration on the White House lawn.

Joe's shadow side kept catching up with him. Eventually he was forced to leave the churches that he had so successfully promoted. He was to create a number of business ventures that showed outstanding promise. After a dramatic start, these ventures would eventually fade away. He had a way of capturing defeat from the jaws of victory.

Joe was certainly not a mean-spirited person. On the contrary, he was generous, and it was a pleasure to be in his company. He did, however, have a major limitation in the way he handled his finances. The people who loaned him money soon learned that once the loan was secure, he tended to see the loan as a gift that would likely not be repaid.

It was a common saying among his friends and admirers that he was a genius at creating exciting ideas resulting in mind-boggling projects. These projects could have been realized if he would have allowed a competent accountant to manage and control his budget.

I was a young person from a very conservative background, and he opened up creative ways for me to view the world during my formative years. He was instrumental in challenging me to dream impossible dreams. For this very special gift, I will be forever indebted to him.

Part 3

An Adventure into Bliss

15

It Almost Ended before It Started

While my hair began to thin fairly dramatically following the ladder accident described earlier, I wasn't yet bald. On a fairly lengthy return trip to the college following a Sunday evening performance, all the members of the quartet decided to get a "butch" haircut, which was clearly not in vogue at the time. The decision was made while we were exhausted and bored on the long ride back to campus.

After Monday classes, I left for work earlier than usual to get the agreed-upon haircut. By chance, I saw Leta, whom I had invited to the banquet (the major social event of the school year) and casually asked how she would like me in a butch haircut. She quickly responded that she would not accompany to the banquet if I had that kind of haircut.

Amused, I continued to the barbershop and from there to my job. When Leta found out that I had indeed gotten the haircut, she wouldn't speak to me. At first, I was amused. No female was going to dictate my action, and besides that, there was no way that I wasn't going to keep the commitment that our quartet had made to each other, a pact that we had made.

Several days later, Leta still wasn't speaking to me. While we had not developed a serious romantic relationship, I was ready to leave it. I had ordered a corsage, which for me was a major expenditure. A close friend volunteered to take the corsage off my hands if the date didn't go through.

Since I invited her to be my partner for the evening, I felt that I had an obligation to ask what her intention was regarding my invitation. In a confronting macho style, I asked her if she was going with me to the banquet or not.

She responded rather meekly by asking if I wanted her to go with me. I curtly responded, "I asked you, didn't I?" Our early casual relationship survived a very close call.

When the big evening came, I was enchanted beyond expectation. Everything about her appearance was striking. Her beautiful gown, which I remember as being a pale blue, accented her lovely facial and body features. I did an about-face. Before the evening began, I would have predicted that our relationship wouldn't have lasted beyond the banquet. After that evening, I was prepared to take another look. Leta apparently had similar thoughts.

Before the banquet, I had no serious thought about romance. Just eighteen years old and barely surviving economically, I was living on a strict budget of a dollar per day for meals, a budget that I had maintained for several years. I would go to a favorite hangout that fellow college students frequented for a cup of coffee and a jellyroll for breakfast. It would cost fifteen cents. For lunch, I would go to a Greek diner next to the railroad tracks for the cheapest hot meal on the menu that would typically cost between forty-five and fifty cents. The evening meal was typically a bowl of soup for fifteen cents. (Nearly sixty years later, I met the owner of the restaurant, Alex Capitan, who was living in the same retirement city in which I now live. I shared with him that his diner had been a lifesaver for me during my college years.)

The rigors of that discipline left a deep imprint on my psyche. I still tend to look at the cheapest things on the menu, even though I now may make another selection. During my childhood and adolescent years at my home, I can't remember any family meals in a restaurant.

Whatever dating Leta and I did during the rest of the school went beyond school policy restrictions. We met on different occasions at the cemetery to walk the charming winding paths. Actually, the ambience of this setting was probably more romantic than any place in the city. While we didn't often break the rules by meeting in this setting, when we did, we would likely meet other couples who were also on a romantic stroll.

When the school year ended, we had more freedom to meet, although there was little time to rendezvous. Being enrolled in summer school meant I was working five or six hours a day. We lived a few blocks apart, so I would take a break from my evening studies to meet Leta for thirty minutes or so before returning to my studies. While our time together was limited, our commitment to each other deepened. The earlier ambivalence during the prebanquet event was gone.

It wasn't long afterward that I asked her to be my bride, although the initial proposal stipulated a date one year hence.

As ludicrous as it now seems, the Pilgrim Holiness Church, a denomination that my parents chose when they moved away from the Mennonite Church, took a strict stand against any form of jewelry, including engagement and wedding rings. This denomination held that jewelry was a show of false pride that was unbecoming to a person professing the Christian faith. To purchase rings would have put my career path in serious jeopardy in this denomination. Instead of a ring, I gave her an 1847 series of Roger's sterling silverware as an engagement gift. I might add that this silverware set is still in my home and is still used on special occasions.

When Leta was ready to give birth to our second child, I went against what I regarded as a silly rule to purchase a wedding band. I was then an army chaplain stationed at Fort Jackson, South Carolina. Eventually, the denomination relaxed this as well as a number of other ludicrous rules that apparently were a carryover from a long-gone Puritan era.

While we were engaged, I suggested that we consider moving up our original wedding date six months earlier than planned. Part of this decision was a result of institutional rules that now are seen as antiquated even by the denomenation mentioned. If someone married during the school year, they would automatically be expelled from school. Actually, these rules could technically have been levied after a new semester began. However, since I was a member of the variety male quartet that the college used for promotional purposes, the powers-that-be looked the other way.

Our finances were very limited, and I had been totally responsible for my survival when I left home just prior to my seventeenth birthday. Leta was no longer dependent on her parents and was working full time. While we were self-reliant in terms of our finances, we essentially had no financial reserves to meet unexpected crises.

Leta's sister, Beulah, had been in a TB sanatorium for a number of months. When Beulah was able to return to her home, she needed care. Leta's mother determined that it was the responsibility of the two unmarried sisters, Leta and Carol, to alternate in providing care for Beulah. Neither Leta nor Carol questioned this mandate.

Beulah; her husband, Glenn; and their son, then known as Sonny, lived on Stoney Lake, a small lake just off of Lake Michigan. I periodically made the trek of a hundred miles or so to visit Leta while she was the designated caregiver for her sister after her return from the sanatorium. Looking over Stoney Lake from their home, I would often hum at eventide bars from a song that was popular at the time. It was called "Red Sails in the Sunset."

Don Elliott, who was to be the best man in our wedding ceremony, accompanied Leta and me to Stoney Lake. Don had some romantic interest in Leta's sister Carol. We took the beautiful scenic drive along Lake Michigan, just north of Muskegon. There was a cold wind blowing off the lake, but that didn't stop us from parking the car and walking along the shoreline. When we started to leave, the car, parked just off the road, became stuck in the sand. It took several hours and considerable effort before we were able to maneuver off the sand and onto the road to continue the rest of our journey.

16

Wedding Bells

I spent the last night before the wedding with a close friend, Harold Cox. His father, who never lost his Texas accent, had a great sense of humor. He playfully attempted to talk me out of getting married. (I shudder to think that I was only a few months past my nineteenth birthday.)

As the wedding date approached, Leta flew to Grand Rapids with a private pilot who worked in the same dry cleaning company that she did. I think it was her first airplane ride. Her father was at the airport to pick her up. When the pilot offered to take him up for his first airplane ride, he readily accepted.

In light of the fact that he had significant heart problems, including having a major heart attack, Leta's mother and siblings experienced their private panic attacks. Flying was a new experience that seemed to them to carry great risks.

The wedding ceremony took place in Leta's farm home in front of a bay window in the living room. The wedding site was Leta's idea. I remember being mildly disappointed that the ceremony wasn't held in the church, but I did not verbalize my concerns.

Eddie Doehring, who had been a member of our quartet before enrolling in a premedical program, was the primary soloist. Leta and I sang the popular love song, "I Love You Truly," as a duet. The minister was Eddie Doehring's father, whom I knew well. I had been in their home a number of times while Eddie was in the quartet and felt as if I were a member of their family.

After the ceremony and a small reception, it was time to go. We would be going to western Nebraska in another couple's car with their three small children. What a breathtaking way to spend the first night of marriage, snuggled up in a car with five other persons, driving for twenty-seven hours and stopping only for gas and bathroom breaks! We would be driving through a winter wonderland of snow.

We planned to arrive at my parents' home in the wee hours of the morning. They were living in a church parsonage that only had a basement. (Apparently, the planned structure above the ground was never built because of limited church finances.) I'm not sure who was more anxious about this first meeting, my parents or Leta. Remember, one of my father's expressed concerns when I was leaving for Michigan prior to my seventeenth birthday was that I "would marry one of those Eastern girls who would not accept them."

I'm not sure when my parents were expecting us, but our early morning arrival clearly caught them by surprise. They had been processing the lard from a butchered hog that had been given to them. This processing ritual had left a temporary unpleasant odor that my parents hadn't had an opportunity to deal with. In addition to being very apprehensive, they were clearly embarrassed to meet their new daughter-in-law under these circumstances.

After introductions, our traveling companions continued their trip for their Colorado Christmas vacation but not before agreeing on a rendezvous for our cozy return trip to Michigan.

We were beginning our life together very naïve about sexual intercourse. It felt very strange when my father showed us which room was to be very first bedroom that we had together. Several evenings would pass before we relaxed enough to fully consummate our marriage. We simply were unsure how to undertake this mysterious adventure.

After a few days, we went to the village of Madrid, the community where I had spent the first dozen years of my life. One of my aunts arranged to have a reception for us at my maternal grandparents' home. Leta would have the opportunity to meet my maternal grandparents, uncles, aunts, and cousins. This would the only time she would meet grandparents as well as uncles and aunts.

We would also spend several days on the farm where I had spent my childhood years. My brother Claire and his wife, Bonnie Jean, were managing the farm. They just had a daughter, Sherri. It turns out that we were to leave hours before the blizzard of the century arrived with fury. It proved to be the storm of the century.

The Thornton family arrived at the prearranged time for our return trip to Michigan on the very day the menacing storm was to arrive. If we had left a half day later, it is likely that we would not have been able to leave Nebraska for several weeks. By the time we reached eastern Nebraska, the storm struck western Nebraska in all its fury.

My father later described blowing snow drifting so high that one could walk on top of a snowbank and unscrew the bulb out of the yard light on our farm. Mail couldn't be delivered to many of the rural routes for six weeks. A train was stopped near my hometown of Madrid by giant snowdrifts that formed on the railroad tracks. No snowstorm has approached this intensity since the 1949 blizzard.

The wife of one of my classmates from the rural elementary school was delivering a baby during this storm. I was told that a bulldozer carrying the doctor to the Kroeker home bucked huge snowdrifts, taking thirty-six hours before the doctor could arrive at their home.

My brother Claire and his wife and infant daughter had a very limited income and were forced to live hand-to-mouth. Hence, they had not stocked up on groceries. Moreover, there was little warning that the storm would strike with the force that it did. They lived for some time on the grain gathered from the granary and then cooked.

We were thankful to have barely escaped the impact of the storm by hours—just in time to begin our married life in earnest in our tiny apartment in Owosso, Michigan.

17

Beginning Married Life

One of our first activities was to straighten things up when we returned to Owosso. Our tiny apartment contained a small kitchen, a cracker-box-size living room, and a reasonably sized bedroom. We really hadn't had the opportunity to make the apartment fully operational before we left on our trip to meet my side of the family in the Midwest. The task of emptying boxes and putting everything in the right place had to wait until we returned from our honeymoon.

Our college friends found out that we had returned on the very day we arrived. They came to "shivaree" us. It was kind of an initiation custom, where tricks would be played on the bride and groom. They came to our apartment and left it in a chaotic condition. Furniture was haphazardly rearranged. Our dishes and kitchen utensils were either misplaced throughout the apartment or filled with water. They took me from the apartment, pretending to kidnap me. When they came back, it looked as if I had been roughed up. While I thought the whole act was hilarious, Leta wasn't as amused.

During the first year of our marriage, we didn't have a car. This meant walking to work, church, the grocery store, and wherever else. It was nearly a mile to the grocery store. Of course, the sacks of groceries had to be carried home. We took it in stride. Leta continued as an employee of Stoner's Cleaners, and I worked at *Argus-Press*. Additionally, I carried a full academic load at the college, rehearsed with the male quartet, and had scheduled performances with the quartet on weekends. Leta often went with us to these different events.

I would drive the vehicle for Glen Stone, who had contracted with *Argus-Press* for rural delivery routes. After driving the ninety-mile route, I would return the jeep back to the owner's home and then walk from there to our apartment. One day, Leta and I picked up some groceries before returning the car. The owner's son got very upset because we had used the vehicle for this task. When I returned the next day, the jeep was blocked in the driveway. The son showed his anger, from my perspective in a rather immature way, before allowing me to continue delivering papers that afternoon. If I had responded by quitting, he would have been in a difficult position because he didn't know the route. His father apologized on his son's behalf when he returned from vacation.

Our first car, a new 1949 Plymouth that was purchased with funds from the estate of Leta's grandparents, cost just under $2,000.

I graduated from Owosso College with an undergraduate degree in theology eighteen months after we were married. I continued to work at *Argus-Press* until graduation. I was planning to enroll in the psychology program at Taylor University that fall of 1950. We were expecting our first child and had not been able to save money on our limited budget for this addition to the family. We took the happenings in our lives in stride.

Joe Uhrig, being the salesperson that he was, convinced me to spend the summer following graduation singing with the quartet. While my salary was meager with *Argus-Press*, it was significantly more than the college offered. The quartet would spend the time traveling through Ohio, West Virginia, and Michigan, performing wherever we had the opportunity to do so, including at the general conference of the Pilgrim Holiness Church. This loss of income would place a heavy burden on our survival when we arrived at Taylor University in September.

18

Life on a New Campus

A compelling reason to attend Taylor University, located in a small rural Indiana village, was that it had excellent academic accreditation along with a high academic rating. Owosso College was not academically accredited. Taylor University would transfer academic credits for most of the classes taken at Owosso College. Like many of the academic institutions in the United States, Taylor University was supported and sponsored by founders with a Christian orientation. The same could be said of institutions such as Harvard and other educational institutions. Northwest University in Evanston, Illinois, for example, was founded by the Methodist Church and to this day has a United Methodist seminary located on their campus.

Bill Gilkerson, a classmate and close friend from Owosso, had chosen Taylor University and was certainly instrumental in my making a similar choice.

In the fall of 1950, Taylor University had a student population of five hundred to six hundred students. Transferring as a senior and married father of a newborn, I didn't get well acquainted with many of my fellow classmates. Our closest acquaintances were primarily limited to the residents of the campus mobile park, which incidentally used the toilet facilities, including showers and laundry facilities, at the university gym. (Obviously, the campus has radically changed in the seventy years since I graduated.) I got to know most of the students majoring in psychology, but there was little social interaction with classmates in my major. We were in a survival mode during the entire year that we were on campus.

Leta's parents loaned us the money to purchase a twenty-seven-foot mobile home, a place we called home during the academic year that we were at Taylor. We pulled that trailer behind our car for several hundred miles two weeks before Linda was to make her appearance.

I still vividly remember the first moments on campus. Leta was "great with child." We only had enough money to pay the first semester's tuition and the hospital bill but no funds for a doctor that we had yet to find. It was two weeks before the time Leta was scheduled to deliver our child. (By the way, the doctor that we did select was a kindly older gentleman who didn't seem to be concerned about when we would pay for his services.) We were living on the edge in every sense of the phrase. Leta never uttered a discouraging word, although there were many days when the skies were filled with ominous clouds of uncertainty. Linda was a trooper.

We attended the first football game primarily because it was free to attend at that time. After we got home, her water broke and the labor pains began. I took her to a hospital in the nearby city of Marion. After she was admitted, an older, buxom nurse told me in no uncertain terms that I was no longer needed on the scene and should leave the hospital grounds. Somewhat bewildered, I returned to our mobile home. I tried to call the hospital for a report on what was happening. My calls were unsympathetically seen as an anxious father who was making a nuisance of himself. In effect, I was told to buzz off. Fortunately, this unkind attitude would not be tolerated today.

Our firstborn, whom we named Linda Marie, made her grand entrance on September 23, 1953. Visiting hours were strictly limited, and mother and baby were required to stay for four or five days after delivery. The austere atmosphere of that hospital was probably typical for those times. Thank God that fathers are now able to be part of the awesome events surrounding birth. It was hard for me to wait for the day that we would be together in our own place.

After arriving in her new home, the baby would sleep as long as she could lie on her mother's chest. When Leta attempted to put Linda in her bassinet, she would awaken and cry. Leta was terrified that she might roll over in her sleep and harm the baby, but our little one would have it no other way. As every parent quickly learns, the new arrival has a lot to say about radical changes that take place in family life.

One of our friends, Bacchus (I have forgotten his first name), from the South American country known then as British Guiana, sang to Linda. He also attended Taylor University. It was a special moment when he would sing in his lovely tenor voice a song that was popular at the time entitled "Linda." He would cradle our precious Linda in his arms as he sang this song.

Six weeks or so after Linda was born, we made the trip to proudly show her to her maternal grandparents, who lived near Holland, Michigan—approximately two hundred miles away. It was Leta's first opportunity to drive since Linda's arrival.

She was following a Ford Model A with a rumble seat filled with bales of hay driven by a teenager who had several companions. Just before crossing a bridge over a small river, the driver looked back at the bales of hay, and while doing so apparently turned the wheel of his vehicle. The vehicle went off the road, just avoiding hitting the bridge abutment. It plunged into the riverbed that was nearly dry.

Before the days of seatbelts, Leta wisely decelerated our car so our baby, who was in a bassinet in the back seat, would not be harmed. As soon as the vehicle stopped, I ran back to the bridge to find that the vehicle was upside down in the riverbed. Fortunately, the passengers were not injured.

In the small village of Upland, jobs were nearly impossible to find. When students were able to find work that accommodated their class schedules, they tended to hold onto these positions throughout their time at the university. University scholarships at this time were rare.

Most of the year, I was unable to find work. While our funds had always been limited during our married life, during our stay at the university, they were clearly in the danger zone.

According to our calculations, near the end of the academic year, the money spent on food was approximately three dollars a week, half of which was spent on baby food. Occasionally we would find that someone had placed a dollar bill in our university post office box. Leta and I more than once held conference deciding whether we would purchase bread or milk.

The couples who also lived in the small trailer park next to the gym became a community, often intuitively sensing when a given couple was experiencing a dire situation. Sharing what one had was the model that each family subconsciously followed. No one (and I mean no one) ever, ever talked about what they needed. Everyone fiercely defended this kind of pride. I don't think that anyone ever contacted their parents for assistance. You can only imagine the embarrassment of one of the couples when they learned that their lass of three made a general announcement to all listening: "We don't have any food."

On one occasion, when returning home from church one Sunday, we found two cans of food in our doorway. It took several weeks to discover how it had arrived. One of our neighbors in the park had intended to invite us to eat with them and share the four cans of food remaining in their pantry. Since we weren't home at the time, they simply split the cans of food evenly.

All purchases, including fuel oil, were on a cash-only basis. I still shudder as I remember one subzero evening when the fuel man knocked on our door, inquiring if we needed fuel. I knew only too well that the fuel tank was nearly empty and that we had a baby a few months old in our home. I thanked the fuel man for inquiring and stated that we would not be getting fuel at that time. We didn't have the funds to make this purchase.

Leta performed a most difficult organizational task when my parents, younger sister, and an adult male who accompanied my parents stayed with us in our twenty-seven-foot trailer. My brother Merle, a student at Michigan State University, also dropped in for a visit at the same time. She managed to accommodate all of us, including our newborn. Her job was greatly complicated when a blizzard extended everyone's visit for several days more than anticipated.

It was the weekend when the University of Michigan and Ohio State, fierce competitors, played their final game of the year, a game that would determine who went to the Rose Bowl. The game was played in a blinding snowstorm, with more than a foot of snow accumulating on the playing field. Both teams consistently punted on first down. I don't remember who won but will always remember the circumstances under which that play was played.

Late in the school year, I heard of a job opening at a local foundry. Employment opportunities were scarce, and I quickly understood why this place was not being overrun with people looking for employment. The work hours were from 2:00 p.m. until 10:00 p.m., which left little time to study or complete term papers. The owner had come from Russia and had an Old World mentality when it came to managing a company.

There was no such thing as a ten-minute break. If an employee went to the restroom more than once during an eight-hour shift, the boss would become visibly upset. The boss expected everyone to work at top speed during the entire shift without any kind of break.

My job was to pour molten steel from a large vat into a smaller pouring unit that I managed. Then I poured the steel into small containers (molds) with long handles that were brought to me by another worker. When I would tip my unit into the pouring position, the weight of this molten steel would shift. It was a most difficult and tricky balancing act. I was under a great deal of tension while pouring the hot metal into this smaller container, with the men holding the container standing near my pouring unit. Everything had to work perfectly. It required a high level of alertness and muscle coordination. If I overfilled the small unit even by a tiny fraction, the hot steel would explode when it hit the ground, and the person on the end of the unit could be seriously or even fatally burned. This operation was repeated many times during the eight-hour shift. I shudder when I remember this process and the strain under which all the employees and I worked—without any kind of break. We worked under conditions that were a tragedy ready to happen.

I would return home literally covered with black soot from head to foot. I learned to leave my billfold with my driver's license and student ID at our trailer. On one occasion, I was stopped by the campus security officer as I was attempting to enter the gym to shower. Wearing heavily soiled work clothes, I became an immediate suspect in a robbery that had just taken place. While I don't think the security officer was being overtly discriminating, there was clearly racial profiling because at that moment, I appeared to be a black man. I was astonished and disappointed by the behavior of the security guard who was apparently trying do his job but with little finesse or cultural sensitivity.

Although I was majoring in psychology, I hadn't taken any psychology courses prior to my transfer to Taylor University because Owosso College didn't offer them. I ended up taking the basic course as well as the more advanced courses at the same time. Without a foundation, I had some difficulty grasping some of the more complex ideas in the more advanced courses.

I managed to get a bachelor's degree with a psychology major. No family member was present at the graduation, other than Leta and our nine-month-old daughter. (My parents were present years later for my doctoral graduation at Michigan State University.)

After my Taylor graduation, we drove to Nebraska to visit my parents. During the first ten years or so of our marriage, we never allowed ourselves the luxury of getting a motel. With limited funds, we drove without stopping for the night. Leta and I took turns driving. After a brief parental visit, we drove back to Taylor's campus. Instead of resting from our trip, we hooked up our trailer home and drove to Leta's parents' farm, arriving totally exhausted. I wonder now what we thought was so urgent that we didn't spend the night in our mobile home. I was to pay a heavy price for this decision.

19

In Between Times

We parked the mobile home in the yard at Leta's parents' farm. I came down with a heavy case of the mumps shortly after we arrived. I suspect that exhaustion made me vulnerable for this medical "bump in the road." The complications were very uncomfortable, and I don't remember if we contacted a physician. No remedies were taken, although one of my testicles swelled to the size of a grapefruit. I was immobile for nearly two weeks and felt weak for nearly a year.

Understandably, Leta, along with our daughter, who was now nearly a year old, would spend most of the time next door with her mother. The mobile home was so confining—and to have two people in this limited space all day long would have been close to intolerable. Leta periodically checked on me throughout the day. I'm sure I was miserable company. Yet I felt very alone.

When I was mostly recovered, I got a job on the midnight shift of a factory that produced the five-gallon gas cans for the military in Grand Rapids. I was soon to discover that my work ethic didn't fit the union model. I tried to work at top speed. I was the first person on the line making the first bend in the can. Unintentionally, I quickly created a logjam on the assembly line. Even though I was weakened by the aftermath of a heavy case of the mumps, other workers were not willing to work at the pace I was keeping.

The foreman of the unionized shop got on my case and told me to get lost for an hour or more at a time, of course, without seeming to be gone from my job. I found it absurd and boring to carry out his instructions. I felt fraudulent, as I would try to disappear for an hour—sometimes two at a time.

The summer was miserable. I hated the work conditions and felt uncomfortable about being in my in-laws' backyard. From my perspective, they viewed me as an inadequate provider for their daughter—especially during the difficult year of being financially strapped while attending Taylor University. I thought they hadn't realized or appreciated how crucial the year at Taylor University would be for my future professional development.

Early in the fall, we moved our mobile home to Owosso, where I had graduated the year before. The home really belonged to Leta's parents because we hadn't begun to repay the loan that we had from them. The quartet that I had been a part of had dreams of getting back together. The optimism that we had received earlier from Joe Urhig, the Owosso College fund-raiser, inspired us to believe that we might be able to do some touring—perhaps at some church rallies around the country and overseas.

I had the opportunity of becoming the pastor of a small congregation in the Ann Arbor area. I had some thoughts about enrolling at the University of Michigan in graduate courses but turned down this opportunity to pursue the dream of reforming our quartet. Obviously, the four years that we had spent together had left a significant impact on us all.

After I decided not to accept the position at the church, one of the quartet members backed out of the agreement that we had made together.

We were still feeling the financial impact of the days at Taylor University. After the plans to reorganize the quartet had gone by the wayside, there was little to do but get a factory job to keep bread on the table. I was reluctant to do this because I had seen a number of my colleagues get blue-collar jobs after going to school, only to succumb to incomes of blue-collar jobs and never return to carry out their professional goals. But there was little choice.

I took a job that ironically was located across the street where, years earlier, I had experienced rib injuries as a result of the ladder rung breaking when I was washing down the outside of a church building twenty-five or thirty feet above the ground.

Just as it had been in the factory in Grand Rapids, I was on the midnight shift in Owosso. I tried not to share that I had graduated from a bible college and a small but highly respected university. I tried to hide my identity, but I was soon called "Preach." Since I had lived primarily in a protected environment until this time, I had never heard such crude or vulgar language. Actually, I'm not sure which I resented most, the crude language or the utter boredom of the job. Driven by my strong work ethic, I worked as hard as I could. Again, the foreman of this unionized shop would ask me to get lost for an hour or more at a time. At 3:00 a.m., it was difficult to be invisible. The only redeeming thing about this job was that it put bread on the table. I couldn't imagine what it would be like to spend a career in this kind of an environment.

My close friend, Bob; his lovely wife, Flo; and their young son, Gale, had an apartment in the same place we had parked our mobile home. He was still taking classes at Owosso College. Our families shared interesting times together. Somewhat impulsively, both families left one Friday after I finished my hours at the factory to visit Joe and Arlene Uhrig in Alexandria, Virginia. While he had some flaws, including significant character flaws, Joe had a vast storehouse of ideas and for that matter, a storehouse of inspiration that he freely shared. Always the rescuer, among other things, Joe suggested that we could have a great future starting churches in the surrounding areas of Washington, DC.

As improbable and impulsive as it sounds, both the Prices and Friesens moved to Alexandria and shared Joe's basement. An important part of the decision for me was to escape the unpleasantness of the factory job as well as not allowing myself to be trapped in an unrewarding job. Leta deserves a great deal of credit for not attempting to block this move. It is important to remember the commitment that Bob and I had made at the beginning of our college days not to become limited by either career or circumstances to a deadening way of life.

While waiting for opportunities to open, Bob and I did some contracting jobs. We weren't very skilled at some of the tasks we undertook, but we proceeded on the assumption that we knew what we were doing. I cringe when I remember one of the cement porches that we built over a basement entrance. The porch was solid enough, but the forms that we had built for pouring the wet cement ended up sagging a bit.

Bob got the first opportunity to start a new church in Manassas, Virginia. I assisted Bob for several weeks while waiting for permission to start a new congregation in a booming suburb of Maryland. That project fell through, but an invitation came to take over a young congregation in Colombia, South Carolina.

20

The Trials and Tribulations of My First Parish

When I was invited to consider becoming the pastor of the newly formed Pilgrim Holiness Church in Colombia, South Carolina, I was told that I would be receiving a salary of forty dollars a week and that I could expect an attendance of seventy-five to eighty people. The district superintendent wanted to believe that this was so but surely knew that estimate was greatly inflated.

On the first Sunday, there were about a dozen or so children who had attended the Sunday school class, and most left before the worship service began. There were only six or seven people present for my inaugural sermon. I discovered that this congregation, or what there was left of it, was three or four months behind on their church building payments and had no money in the treasury. I refused to accept a salary until the payments on the church edifice were up to date. It turned out to be three months before I received a salary of any kind.

I attempted to drum up business by going door-to-door, trying to sell the folks in the Edgewood community of Colombia where the church was located. It was a tough sell. (Some fifty years later, I drove by this church. It was now a black Baptist congregation. I would love to have met the pastor, but he wasn't on the premises.) If I had been a neighbor living near the church, I doubt if I would have been interested in becoming involved in the life of this church either. There was little in the way of church programs to sell.

Most of the people who attended wanted to be picked up, so I would drive for an hour prior to services, picking up the folks who were willing to attend if transportation was provided.

One of the persons transported to church was a lady in a wheelchair who had to be carried down a dozen or so steps. She weighed at least 150 pounds, and with her wheelchair the weight must have been over 200 pounds. When I arrived at her home, my first task was to find a neighbor who was willing to assist in getting her down the steps and into the car. Sometimes an available neighbor was hard to find. If I had been in their position, I might have been hard to find as well.

While at the time I didn't know the first thing about psychosomatic medicine, I learned that she had broken or fractured her hips a number of years before and had never learned to walk. After speaking with her physician, I learned that she never allowed him to examine her hip. I was also aware that she moved her wheelchair around her house quite adroitly, but when she arrived at church, she became helpless and would ask someone to move her in the wheelchair even for very short distances.

The final straw came when I had gotten her wheelchair out of the car and had her in the chair. I was starting the search for a neighbor who would help me carry her up the stairs. A cell of rain clouds let go a mighty downpour of rain with little warning. I picked her up by myself, carrying her and all 200 or more pounds up the wet, rickety stairs without help from anyone. Right then and there, I decided that this would be the last time I would be part of carrying her up and down the stairs.

The following day, I called my wheelchair parishioner following a consultation with her physician. I informed her that the church would buy crutches for her and that the ladies of the congregation would help her learn to use the crutches. I further told her that no one would be carrying her up and down the stairs again. She responded with an angry, tearful voice, stating that no one understood her condition. I later learned that she made numerous phone calls informing people that her pastor had mistreated her.

While I did everything I knew to provide pastoral ministry, my efforts seemed to be ineffective. A lovely lady who lived across the street from the church was hospitalized. Even though she was a member of another congregation and I had no interest in persuading her to become a member of my congregation, I wanted to minister to her. As I reflect on it now, I needed to be needed.

Her hospitalization continued over some weeks, and I saw her regularly. She frequently commented that she enjoyed my visits. Maybe she was trying to be generous to a twenty-two-year-old pastor. I begin to sense that she was seriously ill and perhaps dealing with existential questions—questions of meaning and purpose. (I didn't know the meaning of "existential," but I had a sense of what it was about.)

With her husband in the room, I gently attempted to pose questions about her concerns about her lingering illness. Her husband became angry and ordered me out of the room, reminding me that I was not her pastor. I was totally devastated. I left the hospital feeling completely inadequate and certainly questioning my pastoral skills. I didn't sleep for several nights and constantly went over what I had said or what I should have said. I considered myself a failure of the first order.

When I learned of her death, I went to the funeral home to express my condolences and was very relieved when I discovered that her husband was not there at the time of my visit. I hastily signed the registration book and quickly escaped.

I dreaded the possibility that I would inadvertently encounter him when I was at the front entrance of the church. His front porch was easily seen from the church's front entrance. I didn't realize until much later how dependent he was on her. He apparently wanted to hold to the fantasy that his wife wasn't dying of cancer. More than that, I didn't realize how embarrassed he had been by his impulsive outburst.

Our meeting took place in a most unexpected way. We had a plumbing problem at the church. There was no money in the treasury to hire a plumber. I managed to get a black man to work with me digging the sewer lines. In 1952 in Columbia, South Carolina, it was untenable for a white person to work side by side with a man who happened to be black.

We had dug up much of the churchyard when the gentleman who had lost his wife walked across the street to speak to me. My first reaction was to panic. In those days, I attempted to avoid anything that resembled a conflict. While he didn't exactly apologize, it was clear that he had been troubled by his actions months earlier. His initiative to make this first step was an enormous relief to me.

Avoiding any situation that resembled possible conflict was a strategy that I was highly skilled in. I had great difficulty making hospital visits for a long time. I feared I might say the wrong thing—particularly if a person was seriously ill. While I gained a much larger measure of confidence as I learned pastoral skills, this episode may have had some subliminal impact on the choice that I would make years later to become a psychologist.

Art Taylor, who had been a member of our male quartet during the Owosso years, spent some time with us, living in our home and assisting with the activities of the church. On one occasion, Art was driving as several of us attended some kind of church event in Greenville, South Carolina. We came across a short stretch of the highway being repaired. There was one-way traffic for perhaps a half of a mile. It turned out that it was near quitting time. Art sped up so traffic from the opposite direction would be able to pass. A state highway truck was located at the end of this one-way traffic. A young black worker, apparently about to finish work for the day, rushed across the road from behind the truck and into the path of the car in which we were riding. Art's comments still echo in my memory as our car hit that worker: "I killed that guy."

We anxiously awaited the arrival of an ambulance. To see the lad's father hovering over the unconscious body of his son was both a moving and disturbing moment. In fifteen or twenty minutes, two ambulances arrived. The drivers carried on a casual conversation for at least five minutes. We were shocked to hear them say, "Suppose that one of us should be getting this nigger to the hospital."

We stopped by the hospital en route to our meeting to see if the injured young man had survived. A nurse informed us in a detached manner that "he was okay—just had a headache." Bewildered, we returned some hours later after the meeting. We wanted a leave a bouquet that had been placed on the altar at the church services as a symbol of concern. The nurse refused to accept the flowers on his behalf and coldly stated that we could leave some cigarettes if we felt it was necessary to leave anything. As far as we know, no police or investigative agency looked into this accident. Even though we had been directly involved in the accident, the police did not question us or get our vehicle registration. It was if an accident had not occurred.

I had heard of the "separate but equal" treatment of blacks, but it was a real cultural shock to witness firsthand what for the black person was an everyday experience. The equal part of this equation simply didn't exist. Hearing that blacks weren't welcome in the restaurants, restrooms, and even churches where "white folks" congregated was one thing; experiencing such a blatant act of discrimination was another. At the youthful age of twenty-two, I couldn't see what I could do. At that time, I didn't see myself in the role of an agitator for change, although I deeply sensed that the system wasn't working and needed to be changed.

I recall a mass outdoor meeting of a black church congregation located about six or seven blocks from where the church was located. On this particular Sunday afternoon, there must have been five hundred or six hundred people gathered in the courtyard of the church. They were having a mass baptismal service—baptizing everyone present by using the fire department's large hoses. Given the limited cultural experiences of a person with a very conservative religious background from a rural midwestern setting, I confess this scene startled me. I wish I then had the tools to absorb and appreciate some of the black religious traditions.

One afternoon, I was cooking something on the electric stove when a bolt of lightning struck the stove. While the stove virtually exploded in our presence, thankfully neither of us was hurt. The odor of burned electrical wiring didn't easily vanish.

We hadn't yet recovered from our extremely limited income while we were enrolled at Taylor University the year before. We were working for almost no pay—again, very difficult circumstances. We took out a loan on our car in a frantic attempt to make ends meet, but they really never did.

The director of home missions visited our congregation. He notified me that a tiny pane was missing in one of the windows and asked why it wasn't fixed. He had a hard time realizing that when I arrived, the congregation was months behind on making the payments on the church building and that I had refused to accept a salary for months—and he was worried about a windowpane. In the Pilgrim Holiness Church, ministers were often not very well cared for at that point in time. I'm certain that no one would be expected to function under those conditions today.

Leta didn't complain, although there was almost no money to meet even the barest of necessities. We later calculated that our income for a year had been about five dollars a week. Leta accepted our situation with much grace and dignity. While I never heard her complain, I confess I felt that I had been used by the system.

The Korean War exploded onto the world scene when I was a student at Taylor University. A number of students that I knew, at least casually, were either drafted or joined the service. I had brief conversations with my father about joining the service after I finished high school, but the war had ended at the beginning of my high school junior year. Involvement in the military had up to this point seemed remote.

Seeing some of my classmates go into service caused me to reflect on the possibility of serving as a military chaplain. There were a number of obstacles. My denomination at that time had never sponsored a military chaplain, in large part due to its limited size. Beyond that, military services required that candidates for the chaplaincy be graduates of both a liberal arts college and a seminary. The Pilgrim Church had no seminaries and was very suspicious of their ministerial candidates going to one. They were essentially afraid that the seminaries would be too liberal for their theology. Hence, the bulk of their theological students went to a bible college. These students were applauded if they received a bachelor of theology degree (which consisted of two years of junior college and three years of undergraduate biblical studies).

While I did have the BA with a major in psychology from Taylor University, I did not technically meet the requirement of four years of liberal arts college work and three years of seminary studies. In talking to the chief of chaplain's office of the army and navy, I was told that they would be willing to accept my undergraduate theological studies but insisted that I have a total of seven years of post-high school studies. My two degrees represented six years of undergraduate work. In essence, I would have met the requirement with an additional year of study.

I considered the option of the military chaplaincy closed, although I did regularly visit a friend who was a military chaplain at Fort Jackson, South Carolina. I also had some contact with a chaplain who, among other duties, was attempting to recruit new military chaplains. (Chaplains differed from physicians in the sense that by law, a chaplain could not be drafted while doctors were subject to the draft.)

I had been serving the little church in Columbia for eight or nine months when I was contacted by this chaplain recruiter (I no longer remember his name). He informed me that as a result of a shortage of military chaplains, a special board was being convened at Fort McPherson, Georgia, to select chaplains from clergy who met the requirement for ordination from their denomination but did not fully meet the military standard for selection to the chaplaincy. (During World War II, chaplains had been selected on a similar basis. The minimum standard during World War II was a BA degree.)

Part 4

Putting on a Military Uniform

21

An Impossible Dream Comes True

More than a little apprehensive, I showed up at Fort McPherson at the appointed time with thirty-nine other potential candidates for the chaplaincy. It was a thorough three-day evaluation with a wide range of tests at Georgia State University, including psychological testing, trial sermons in front of the ranking third-army chaplains, giving lectures that were videotaped, and observations by a team who would rank us on our social interactions in a number of different settings.

Twenty of the forty candidates were eventually accepted. I was thrilled to be among those who received a military commission in the grade of first lieutenant. This opportunity would release me from an untenable working environment.

More than that, it would open new doors for ministry. While Leta was conservative by nature and not prone to taking risks, I am so grateful that she never attempted to block my interest in exploring possibilities that most of my peer group would not have seriously considered. (I later learned that one of my female high school classmates had strongly objected when her husband expressed interest in the chaplaincy.) Leta's willingness to follow me, even though this would not have been her first choice, richly contributed to our life together.

When I received confirmation that I had been accepted for the chaplaincy, I was asked how much time I needed to complete my duties at the church and where I would like to be assigned. I suggested that I could be ready for active duty in about six weeks, and I requested that I be assigned to Fort Jackson, located on the outskirts of Columbia, South Carolina.

Since we could choose to live off post, I ended up renting a new home that had been built by Reverend Marvin Cockman, who had been my district superintendent. The house was located on the Old Highway 1 (now Interstate 1), several miles east of Columbia. It turned out be convenient to Fort Jackson.

Ten days or so after receiving confirmation of my selection to the chaplaincy, I received a congratulatory letter from the chief of chaplains in which he requested that I report to the nearest Signal Corps to have my picture taken in uniform. The picture would be kept on file at the chief's office. While I had purchased a military uniform and the appropriate brass, it dawned on me that I had no idea how to pin the insignia on the uniform. Based on some casual observations I had made on people wearing the uniform, I gave it my best effort.

When I put on the uniform for the first time, I felt very awkward, like somehow I wasn't entitled to wear it. Still, it was a dramatic moment. My intentions were to ask the military policeman at the gate for directions to the Signal Corps. It had never dawned on me that he would salute me. When he snapped to attention and gave a crisp salute, I was so startled that I knocked my bill-style cap into the back seat when I attempted to return the salute. My first salute must have resulted in raucous laughter when he told his buddies about this "really green" officer's clumsy attempt to retrieve his hat from the back seat.

The military personnel at the Signal Corps' photo lab assisted me in repositioning my insignia. The requested photo was developed and sent to the office of the chief of chaplains at the Pentagon.

On July 26, 1953, I reported to the chaplain's school, located at Fort Slocum, New York, a small island on Long Island Sound. It was the day that the truce was signed with Korea. It was somewhat ironic that after several years of seeking to enter the military chaplaincy, my first day of active duty was to fall on this date. Incidentally, the exploratory screening board at Fort McPherson never convened again. In fact, the need for chaplains would radically decrease when the Korean War ended.

I had taken my wife, Leta, and our daughter, Linda, to be with her parents in Michigan while I drove to Fort Slocum to go through the five-week orientation course. It essentially showed new chaplains, many with no previous military experience, how to function as clergypersons in this whole new world.

I was keenly aware that I did not fully meet the educational requirements of the chaplain selected in the usual way. Nineteen other chaplains must have had similar anxiety on whether we would measure up to the tasks at hand. I was also intimidated that I was the first representative ever from the Pilgrim Holiness Church, a church certainly not in the mainstream of religious life. I would be an overachiever in my efforts to prove myself.

As I got acquainted with these newly inducted chaplains, I found that these clergymen had a wide range of achievements, including a just-resigned president of a college who wanted a new challenge. It was the first time I was to rub shoulders with rabbis, Roman Catholic priests, and ministers from the reformed churches as well as other churches from mainline traditions. Most were considerably older. At twenty-three, I was one of the youngest to serve. I appeared older, which served to my advantage when we were to report to our permanent duty station.

While the timidity and feelings of insecurity that had characterized my early teenage years were still present, I was being introduced to a broader view of the world than I had ever known. I was still very unsure of myself and was more than a little frightened, but I knew that I belonged in this setting.

One of the instructors who left a lasting impression on me was a Roman Catholic priest who had made combat parachute jumps. Father Francis Sampson stated that when he was a new chaplain and was going through the orientation at the school, someone from the chief's office had stated that they needed a priest to serve an airborne unit. Not realizing that he would have to jump with the men, he volunteered, thinking that he was only volunteering to serve Mass to these jumpers. When he realized his mistake, he didn't have the nerve to back down and not accept the assignment. I doubt that I would have volunteered to become a jumping chaplain without his influence.

My roommate was a young rabbi who really didn't want to serve in the military but apparently was assigned by his rabbinical group to fill a quota. He acted out some of his authority conflict by intentionally making his bed in a haphazard way. I, on the other hand, had typically had a strong need to please authority figures. In my growing years, I had been terrified of displeasing my father, and this need would provide much of the energy to try to prove my worth in this new setting. While I was often anxious, I managed to disguise that anxiety to a considerable degree.

In my heart, I realized that I felt some discordance with my denomination; I tried hard to be faithful to its rigid rules even though I disagreed with them. I believed that I had an obligation to observe rules that I thought had little or nothing to do with religious life. Some of my chaplain colleagues and I attended the famous Broadway musical, *Porgy and Bess*. While I thrilled to hear the lovely voice of a female vocalist singing "Summertime," I was keenly aware of the rules of my church that prohibited theater attendance. I felt guilty in this theater, even while I was enjoying the performance. During the five years of active duty, I never saw a movie because of this highly restrictive rule that the denomination has long since relaxed.

I would have been hard pressed to verbalize my differences with my denomination at that time, in part because this kind of verbalization was so heavily frowned upon. I hadn't yet fully articulated to myself where I stood on given issues. Often, I knew I disagreed without fully knowing why. The church demanded full compliance to doctrine and procedures.

The chaplaincy gave time to explore some of these internal disquieting feelings that I harbored. Earlier in my life, I had tried hard to internalize the church's doctrine of sanctification as a second definite work of grace. I knew this primary doctrine didn't fit either my experience or my intellect, although I wasn't yet in a position to announce this discomfort with certainty. As a pastor of a congregation, I was expected to give sermons on this theme. In the military, I could choose other appropriate themes. Importantly for me, the military provided a freeing environment for me to examine my belief systems without fear of condemnation. It was the place where I became of age—a kind of professional puberty rite.

While the orientation at chaplain school had been helpful in a number of ways, the school curriculum had one major fault. Most young chaplains would be going to smaller units rather than to higher headquarters. Understandably, the instructional material often focused on the big picture. Many topics in our orientation phase wouldn't make sense until we had been at our duty stations for some months and had an opportunity to incorporate the concepts being presented. Still, it was a useful and productive time for clergy who were now functioning in a new sphere of activities.

One of the instructors, however, was rather compulsive in his teaching style. He explained in very vivid detail how one was to report to one's military unit at a smaller unit level. He made it sound that if his exact procedure was not followed, one's military career was in jeopardy. He stated that a chaplain should report to his (there were no military female chaplains or female infantry officers at the time) unit sergeant major with a copy of orders in his left hand. The chaplain should then ask to speak to the adjutant. He would salute the adjutant with the words: "Chaplain [last name] reporting for duty as ordered, sir." The adjutant would then arrange a meeting with the colonel.

I arrived at Fort Jackson on Labor Day weekend of 1953. The division had just passed a major inspection with flying colors. The general had given the entire division a four-day holiday. Since I was assigned to a division, later to be assigned to a training regiment, I reported to the duty officer at division headquarters. My orders were in my left hand. When I asked to speak to the adjutant, the duty officer gave me a puzzled look, asking why I wanted to see the adjutant. He told me to sign in and report in when the four-day weekend was over. It took me weeks to figure out that Chaplain

Luden had been speaking about reporting to a smaller unit when he gave his precise instructions.

Coming from a strong work ethic, I couldn't convince myself that I didn't have to return for four days. In my confusion, I wandered over to the division chaplain's office. While Chaplain Maxwell, a full colonel, was in his office, he had his feet up on his desk and was asleep. It was a holiday weekend, after all.

When I showed him my orders, his first comment was: "I heard that we had a Holy Roller chaplain assigned." I immediately became defensive and said that my denomination was not a Pentecostal church organization. He immediately took out a handbook of denominations and looked up the Pilgrim Holiness Church. It was listed under the Pentecostal listing, as if it were a subset of a Pentecostal body.

While Pilgrim Holiness Church members often became dramatic and ran up and down the aisles of the church "praising the Lord" and would express the exuberance of their faith by shouting their praises to their maker, they would immediately halt all proceedings if someone started to speak in tongues or an unknown language. I can understand why Chaplain Maxwell, a Presbyterian, expected that someone from an "off-brand" religious denomination would be "off the wall." I think his perceptions changed just a few weeks later.

I was assigned to a unit called a leadership school. It featured educational training in a number of specialist areas, such as Morse code, lineman, cooking school, typing, and more. The military personnel attending these schools had been through the first half of basic training. This training represented the second half of their basic training.

One of the required educational programs throughout the military at that time was the character guidance lecture. The chaplain's duty was to give these lectures. It was necessary to have a lesson plan, which was available to any inspector who happened to walk in during the lectures.

My first supervising chaplain was likeable, with a warm, friendly smile. But he was also quite unpredictable. He was known throughout the unit as the person to see if you received overseas orders and didn't want to go. He would often march a dozen or more soldiers to division headquarters and get them taken off the order list. The only problem was that other personnel would then be placed on the list to fill the quota.

I sensed that it was not appropriate to jump channels, as my supervisor was doing, but I thought this sense came from inexperience. The first time I attempted to do this, a wise officer took me to the side and gently told me how inappropriate this procedure was. It must have been the magic of his smile, but this good ol' Southern Baptist chaplain got away with it.

His unpredictability came through in another way—just ten days or so after I had been assigned to this unit. He was scheduled to give the character guidance lecture that morning. (I had never given one, although I had developed an outline.) He typically dressed in a freshly starched uniform when he gave lectures. On this Saturday morning, he was getting into this fresh uniform and asked me to assist him with buttoning his shirt. In the midst of his buttoning his shirt, the phone rang, stating that someone from Division G-3 (Plans and Training Office) would be there to critique the lecture scheduled to begin in about fifteen minutes.

The good chaplain suddenly remembered that he was to be somewhere else and asked me to take the lecture. I was much too naïve to realize that he was bailing out and leaving a brand-new chaplain to fend for himself.

The troops and the inspector arrived, and I began the lecture by telling a humorous story. The inspector laughed. The lecture was off to a good start. Then a platoon of troops arrived late, and there was nothing to do but to stop the lecture. I assumed that I was somehow responsible for the tardy arrival of the troops and thought I had blown the lecture.

With nothing to lose, I got into the subject matter proverbially "swinging from the heels." To my surprise, the inspector gave me the highest rating for any lecture on any subject given through the division that particular week. The only minor markdown was that my uniform had not been starched. The rating was circulated throughout the division. I think Chaplain Maxwell, the division chaplain, rested a bit easier about the quality of service that I could and would perform after receiving this report.

I had been at my unit assignment for about three weeks when I received word at the chapel that my father-in-law had been in a serious farming accident involving a machine that processed corn silage. I wanted to convey the message to my wife, Leta, personally. At the same time, I was attempting to solve crisis issues that involved some of the troops. I didn't arrive home for several hours. By then my wife's father had passed away, and the family had telephoned her. I experienced a lot of remorse that I had not been as available to her in my attempt to carry out my duties as I saw them on post.

We caught the first available flight home. Because of bad weather conditions, we had to drive to the Greenville, South Carolina, airport. I had flown very little up to this point and was more than a little anxious, actually terrified, during a rough flight. I didn't eat the meal that was offered. I would never then have guessed that I would end up as a pilot. I envied our three-year-old daughter, who would yell "Whee!" after the plane would take a significant drop in altitude during heavy turbulence. Children are truly our teachers. They have a sense of total trust when they experience radically different circumstances when they are with families they trust.

I kept a tight hold on Leta's arm as we viewed the body at the end of the service. I still held to a value system of not showing your emotions being a sign of strength. In my view, then, I had to be strong to modify her response to grief. I now hold that this belief system is contrary to the grieving process.

After returning to Fort Jackson, I worked hard to fulfill the role of a chaplain. I still had a lot to prove to myself and others. I was often uncertain about how I could relate effectively to the troops who would never attend my chapel.

When I arrived at Fort Jackson, the chaplains were stretched pretty thin, trying to be available to units who did not have a chaplain. I was trying to minister to soldiers who were detained in the stockade and at the same time had to be available for soldiers who dropped in at two different chapels located at opposite ends of the unit that I was assigned to.

Once, when I was driving from one chapel to the other, I offered a young soldier a ride. I asked the usual question of where he was from. His response was from Nebraska. I asked where in Nebraska.

"You've never heard of the place—it's near North Platte."

When I further inquired where his family home was, he replied with mild irritation that it was near Ogallala. Pressing him further, it turned out that his family home was north of the small village of Madrid—two or three miles from where my farm home had been located. It turns out that he was a classmate of my younger brother.

When Leta would come to the chapel for some reason, the on-duty military policeman would salute the officer tags on the car. Our three-year-old took great pride in returning the salute. She was to have her first multiracial experience here. When Sunday school classes were dismissed from the general assembly to go to their individual classes, Linda would wait for a black girl and take her hand as they marched off to class together. Neither her mother nor I discussed the racial situation with her.

It was Sunday, November 22, 1953. The doctor had predicted that our new arrival would come that day. Leta had stayed home from church that morning. I gave the sermon at the chapel. The colonel's wife was the babysitter in my office during the service. She was to give me the signal to cut the sermon short if she received a telephone call announcing that birth pangs were increasing. That call didn't come during the sermon. When I returned home, Leta had the noon meal ready.

Midafternoon, she suggested that it might be time to go to the hospital. After taking her to the base hospital, I returned to the chapel to conduct a hymn sing that was a regular feature at the chapel. This was a well-attended event, particularly by young men who had been active in their home churches. Cake and punch were served at the end of this event. It was a way to remind homesick soldiers of their church families at home.

After this event, I returned to the hospital just as Leta was being wheeled into the delivery room. Robert Arthur arrived somewhere around 2100 hours. Three or four days later, mother and baby were ready to come home. Our three-year-old daughter was very excited about their homecoming. She went with me to the hospital to escort them home. She very properly held her new brother. Her question to her mother just as we were entering the driveway was, "Mommy, do you still love me?"

Her mother wanted to weep. I imagine that most young children wonder about their place in the home when a new sibling has arrived.

—

There was political unrest in French Indochina, later known as Vietnam. After the French pullout, there was a growing US military presence. The soldiers sent to that part of the world were called advisors. The chaplains at the post would gather at the Red Cross building every Tuesday morning for thirty minutes or so for coffee, donuts, and fellowship. We would half-jokingly wonder if we would one day be meeting somewhere in Indochina. While full-scale fighting wouldn't break out for nearly a decade, we had a hazy premonition of what was coming. A chaplain from the Pentagon who was in charge of determining further assignments had greeted our class of forty-four chaplains with these words: "Congratulations, ninety-nine percent of you will be in Korea in six months."

That meant that maybe one chaplain of our group could expect orders for some other part of the world.

I kept watching the *Army Times*, which listed assignments for all officers. Every week, I would see the names of my classmates listed with orders for Korea. I kept waiting for word when I would be sent and wondering where in Korea I would be assigned.

Six months came and went with no orders arriving. I was really puzzled when nearly a year went by and still no orders. One evening I had dreamed that I would be receiving orders for Europe. I had so conditioned myself to receive orders for Korea that in that dream I was disappointed with this announcement. Within a week or two after that dream, I received the alert that I was being sent to

Germany. I think that there was only one other chaplain from that class who was also sent to Europe. Apparently, military units in Korea had become overloaded with young chaplains while Europe was being overloaded with the more senior chaplains.

22

Off to Europe

I left the family in Michigan, drove the car to the port of embarkation, and then reported to the military post in New Jersey I would be leaving from. The only duty I was given was to be a chaperone at a dance at a USO. This struck me as rather humorous because my denomination was in adamant opposition to dancing, and this was the first dance I had ever attended.

A few days later, we boarded the *USS Upshure* en route to Germany. The enlisted men slept on lower decks in bunk beds while the officers had rooms on the upper deck. Since our income had always been extremely limited, we rarely had a meal in a café. Here, we had waiters with tuxedos. I'm embarrassed about how little we tipped the waiter at the end of the voyage. In those days, a first lieutenant's pay was about $4,000 a year plus a housing allowance if you were forced to live off the post. While that was by far the best salary I had ever received, it still didn't go very far beyond meeting basic needs.

When we arrived in Bremerhaven, Germany, a personnel chaplain came on board the ship and gave me orders that would send me to the Second Infantry Division in Augsburg. I, with other officers, boarded the train, and we had the luxury of sleeping cars, a luxury that I had never previously experienced. Upon arriving in Augsburg, I was taken to the post where I was to meet the division chaplain, Chaplain LeRoy Raley. He was a real character whom I came to admire. That admiration seemed to be shared by all the chaplains in the division.

The Second Infantry Division had a regiment in Munich located about thirty-five miles from division headquarters. I was informed that I was to be assigned to this unit. The military complex in Munich was a former SS camp. Three thousand military personnel, plus their headquarters area, were all under one roof. The chapel, reportedly the largest chapel building in Europe, had been converted from a garage. It was beautiful in its simplicity.

During the mid-1950s, the Cold War was at its peak. The Iron Curtain was only minutes away by air. Each month, we had an alert that could come at time, day or night. Our unit had to be prepared to leave the post, fully armed for combat in an hour. This alert always took precedence over any other activity. When the alert sounded, often in the wee hours, I would usually help my chaplain's assistant to load our jeep for an extended stay in the field. Actually, the alert usually lasted for several hours, and then we returned to our regular routine.

Our regiment spent a considerable amount of time on military maneuvers under combat conditions. Often, the battalions would go on these exercises at different times. While I was assigned to the regiment, I would accompany the different battalions on their maneuvers that would usually last anywhere from one to two weeks — occasionally longer.

While I performed religious services on Sunday or whenever possible, the other chaplains and I would engage in what was referred to as "a ministry of presence." This meant that one would be with the troops on every occasion possible to share the same conditions that they would experience. I would try to find a platoon-sized unit and spend the night with them. At first, the personnel of these units would be uncomfortable with having an officer from a higher headquarters spending the night under field conditions with them. Most chaplains slept in the headquarters area during these maneuvers.

One evening when I dug a hole in a snowbank, I laid a blanket on the ground and then an air mattress and finally the sleeping bag and, after crawling in, I packed the snow around me as an insulator. The next morning when I zipped open the sleeping bag, I was greeted with a lot of fresh snow in my face. It had snowed nearly six inches during the night.

While I was involved in a lot of maneuvers under combat conditions, I was fortunate not to have experienced combat itself because my active duty time was between the Korean and Vietnam wars. Our training exercises under combat conditions at the height of the Cold War were designed to fully prepare for combat in the event that it took place.

I loved the combat story that a good friend, Chaplain George Lowery, shared. During the Korean conflict, on a moonless night, he found himself under enemy fire as he was attempting to get to one of the units that he was serving. He and his assistant were hunkered down for hours under a large log. He said, "I should have been praying, but the only thing that went through my mind during this time was the Whiffen Poof Song: 'We little sheep have gone astray. Ba! Ba! Ba!'"

One early morning when the temperature was below zero, I went to the outdoor unit kitchen, known as the mess hall. An officer friend of mine happened to have a tin cup of coffee. He passed it around to all of us. Until that time, I would have been reluctant to share a cup or drinking glass with anyone who wasn't a family member. It dawned on me that we were sharing communion in a nonliturgical way. Since that day, I have never hesitated to share a cup used in a symbolic communal sharing.

I remember another story of a chaplain from a very strict denomination where alcohol was forbidden. The chaplain was missing in combat for several days. When he finally rejoined the unit, one of the officers passed around a bottle of the hard stuff to celebrate the chaplain's return. The chaplain, who also recognized this as an act of communion, partook. In this very special moment, he recognized his connection to everyone in that unit in a new way.

This was the first time that I had been away from family and friends on such holidays as Thanksgiving, Christmas, and New

Year's. I don't remember much about the Thanksgiving that year, but one of the officers, who had arrived there the same time as I did, stated he planned to get so drunk on Christmas that he would miss the holiday. It was his way of trying not to miss his wife and children during these festive holidays.

An officer once invited me over on Christmas morning to watch his children open their presents. While I appreciated this gesture, this attempt at including me in their family tradition, I remember feeling very detached. My reaction puzzled me. Perhaps I didn't sense that there was a great deal of spontaneity on that occasion or that a deep sense of joy was present. The kids obviously enjoyed their presents, and the parents seemed to enjoy the moment. Still something was missing for me.

On New Year's Eve, I went to the officer's club and attempted to attend a party. In those days, officers tended to be hard drinkers; a policy discouraging heavy drinking would eventually emerge. I soon discovered that when my fellow officers were consuming a lot of alcohol, it didn't take long before their conversations tended not to track well. It was clearly the case on this night. This occasion was not festive. I ended up leaving the officer's club early that evening and going to my chapel office to take a spiritual inventory of sorts—and of course to reflect on my family that even at that very moment were on the high seas en route to join me. At midnight, I opened the windows of my second-floor office. Through the cold winter night, I could hear the voices of more than slightly inebriated enlisted soldiers trying to sing *Auld Lang Syne*.

I promised myself that in future years I would attempt to provide a celebration event on special holidays that would include those who no longer had close family members to share these moments. I have tried to live out this promise in a number of ways.

23

Leta and the Children Arrive

The evening before I had left the family at the home of my in-laws, I tried to figure out how to tell our three-year-old daughter, Linda, that when she woke up the next morning I would be gone. I eventually settled on telling her that I was going to get on a boat and cross a lot of water to another country. I promised her that I would look for a house, and when I found the right house, she and her little brother and her Mommy would come to live in our new house. I told her that she would also be on a big boat.

This explanation seemed to satisfy her. When Leta and the children received orders to come, they left for Munich on December 28 by train to New York. Military personnel met them and put on them on the Staten Island ferry en route to Fort Hamilton, where they would embark on a ship for Germany. After the end of the ferry ride, Linda asked, "Where's Daddy?" She had remembered that they would be on a big boat.

On January 8, 1955, the train pulled into Munich from the seaport town of Bremerhaven. I had moved out of the Bachelor Officer's Quarters into a military apartment at Perlocker Forest in Munich. It was some distance across the city from the chapel. I really didn't know my way across Munich very well, and I got thoroughly lost trying to get to the apartment from the train station. Leta was exhausted. Bobby, then thirteen months, didn't recognize me and wouldn't let me hold him. Linda, on the hand, was excited about her new surroundings and was eager to play catch-up on the happenings that had occurred since she had seen me.

Someone had loaned me a Christmas tree, and I had presents around the tree. I had purchased a lovely German coo-coo clock, which still is functioning. Originally, it played a German beer drinking song. (I didn't recognize the song when I purchased the clock. For a time, the rhythm of the song was off, and as a result, the song wasn't recognizable as a song. Efforts to find a clockmaker to repair the clock were initially futile. However, a highly skilled clockmaker by the name of Andy Gerrish, who comes from a long line of talented clockmakers, was able to restore the clock. When we return home after being away, one of the first things that I do is to restart the coo-coo clock.)

Within a few days of their arrival, our unit went to the field on combat-type maneuvers and, of course, I had to go with them. Military families quickly learn to adjust to these kinds of circumstances. Once, when I had come back from maneuvers for an afternoon to attend to some chapel business, I received a call from a frantic young mother who had just arrived, and her husband was on maneuvers. Her baby was sick, and the doctor on post had refused to see her. In his defense, he had been told to refer all military dependents to the health clinic across the city. This young mother had no transportation. I asked Leta to make that trip across Munich, a city with complex streets, to the clinic. Even though Leta had been in the country only a very short time and didn't know her way around, she courageously loaded up our children and this young mother and baby to drive across the city to the clinic. Unfortunately, the baby died. This crisis caused a change in health care policies.

I still feel a little guilty about calling the doctor to tell him that he had been derelict in his duties because he hadn't evaluated the medical condition of the child and had some responsibility in the child's death. I'm afraid I was overreacting to my anger. I can still see the tears in his eyes as he explained that he was new to the military and had allowed policy to override his oath as a doctor. The

German doctors, under contract with the government, had misdiagnosed the child's condition.

When military housing became available in an area just behind the post that I was assigned to, we moved. It was much more convenient. I could walk home for lunch, and Leta could take the kids for the short walk to the Post Exchange, although we still had to drive across Munich to get to the commissary.

I was the junior chaplain of the three assigned to this post. My two colleagues tended to compete for the commander's attention — or so it seemed to me. The Roman Catholic chaplain came from a strong Italian Old World Catholic orientation. He seemed to feel that he had special claims on the regimental commander, who happened to be Roman Catholic.

Since I was easily intimidated around high-ranking brass, I tended to avoid going to the headquarter units and spent the bulk of my time with the troops. One day I got word that one of the company-sized units was making a forced twenty-six-mile night march to the town of Dachau, where one of the infamous concentration camps was located. It was here that thousands of Jewish had been gassed and incinerated during World War II. Even though I was not in top physical condition, I volunteered to go.

The march started at about 2000 hours (8:00 p.m.). No one, including me, had any apparent difficulty in making the first half of the march. Most of the evening, I had been at the front of the group. En route back to the post, the muscles in my legs started to tighten. By the time we reached the halfway point of our return trip, I had fallen from the front of the unit to the rear and was having difficulty keeping up with the rear of the unit. I noticed that a sergeant in the unit was limping and was also at the rear of the line. When he announced that he was ready to go another twenty-six miles, I invited him to break ranks with me and start running. I recognized that pride was the only thing that either of us had going for us. We ran until we were well ahead of the front of the marching unit. In spite of the bravo attitude, we eventually fell behind once more.

When we finally arrived at the barracks around 0400 hours, I marched with the troops to the front gate. I realized that the back gate, which I would normally use to get to our apartment, would be closed. After watching the troops march through the front gate, I walked the long way around our military post until I reached our apartment. My leg muscles were so tight by this time that I found it necessary to rest every fifty feet or so. When I finally reached my home, utterly exhausted, I collapsed in a tub of hot water before going to bed.

Someone informed our regimental commander that I had been on the march with the troops. Until that time, he had barely noticed me, but overnight I became his favorite chaplain, even though I was the junior of the three chaplains assigned. I found the special attention he gave me to be both gratifying and frightening. His physique was imposing, and his voice was thunderous. I learned that he had been a wrestler at West Point. It is a massive understatement to say that I stood in awe of him.

—

When a party was held for the officers at the club, it was mandatory to attend. The colonel had a great capacity for alcohol. After he had partaken freely of spirits, he looked me up in the crowd of officers. Towering over me, he attempted to engage me in a friendly conversation. Most every officer there would have enjoyed this kind of attention. It frightened me. As he would buddy-buddy up to me, I would back away from him, only to have him follow my retreat. He reminded me of my father, whom as a youth I found a frightening, overpowering presence. I regret now that I was too inexperienced to recognize how lonely he was in his position as a commander and that I, in my own insecurity, didn't recognize this and other opportunities to be more emotionally and spiritually available to him. I heard from another officer who had contact with him in later years, long after he had retired from the military, that he would inquire about my whereabouts and make complimentary remarks.

We all have our doubts and insecurities. The senior chaplain during this period was an Assembly of God chaplain. He was outgoing and generally got along well with people. Like everyone else, he had his blind spots. At one of the officer's functions, he had imbibed freely of the champagne that was being served. When the prorated bill for the party was given, he objected to paying the liquor portion of the bill, insisting that his denomination took a stand against liquor. His refusal incurred the commander's anger. Even though I had not tasted alcohol, I paid the full portion of the prorated bill. (One of the battalion commanders with whom I had developed a close relationship saw the battle brewing. He didn't want me to get caught in the middle and had urged me to pay the full bill.)

The good chaplain stated that he felt betrayed by my action. He expected that I would take a stand with him against the commander. I didn't have the strength or courage to confront him with his inconsistent behavior of both imbibing and then claiming that his denomination took a stand against liquor.

While the concerns that soldiers brought with them to the chaplain's office varied, they often focused on concerns about home. Sometimes family members wrote to the chaplain, worried about their sons or daughters (though in Munich all of our soldiers were male). One letter from a family member requested that I give their soldier-brother a clip from the local paper showing his father being involved in a fatal car accident. I questioned at the time whether it was appropriate to present this newspaper clipping to this young soldier but decided to do so out of respect for his family's request. It was obviously a traumatic moment for this young soldier. With the help of the Red Cross, an emergency leave was arranged so he could be with his family. It was typically the chaplain's job to inform the soldier of a death or serious illness. The chaplain coordinated the emergency leaves with the company commander and the Red Cross. More importantly, the chaplain attempted to provide a ministry that would facilitate the grieving process.

Often a pregnant German girl and her mother would come to the office. Their mission was to be certain that the father of the expected child would follow through with a marriage ceremony. After a couple was engaged to be married, the German custom was for the couple to start living with each other at the time of engagement. It was apparently assumed that the engagement was in fact the life commitment to each other. The marriage certificate was merely seen as a legal endorsement of that commitment. Many soldiers took free advantage of this custom.

One time a soldier accompanied a young German lady and her mother, announcing that they both were expecting his child and asking for advice on which of them he should marry. Actually, one didn't really require the wisdom of Solomon to know that marriage to either mother-in-waiting wouldn't be on solid ground. Sometimes, there were marriages in the chapel or at some outdoor site. The one that stands out in my memory was a marriage ceremony on the grounds of a beautiful castle. The bride's family had connections with the owners of the castle.

A number of soldiers and their wives regularly attended chapel services. A deep bond developed among many of these folks, particularly the soldiers who were not eligible for military housing for their dependents. The couples that made the choice to be together, even though it meant living under hardship conditions, were especially close to each other and to the chapel family.

Leta and I had an ample supply of babysitters who would jump at the chance of watching our two-year-old and five-year-old. Some of the soldiers who had brought their wives to Munich, even though military quarters were not available to them, had rented apartments on the German economy that didn't have many of the amenities. Some of them had to heat water to put into a tin tub in order to take a bath. They would gladly accept babysitting responsibilities while staying at our modern but small two-bedroom apartment.

Sometime in the fall of that year, Leta and I drove through southern Germany and Austria to Venice, Italy. We had spent the night in a hotel in Verona that had been recommended by the military recreation group. We arrived in Verona in the early evening. We tried to ask local residents where the recommended hotel was located. Several Italian ladies, trying to be helpful, jumped in our car, giving us constant instructions in Italian as we drove. At every intersection, they would wave their hands frantically to indicate that this was not the place to turn. These instructions were both bewildering and interesting. Surprisingly, we eventually did find the hotel.

The next morning, as we were passing through what was then the small town of Vicenza, not far from Venice, we noticed US military policemen standing in the middle of the road, directing traffic. Puzzled, I asked one of the MPs what they were doing there. They informed me that a new military missile base was being opened there. We drove on to this military post and watched a parade of both US soldiers as well as Italian soldiers in their colorful uniforms. We got to meet some of the military families who were stationed there. They advised us to see Venice, which these new friends suggested could easily be done in a short time, and then return to a brand-new hotel to spend the night. This military post is still active nearly fifty years later.

We took their advice. We did ride the gondolas and visited St. Mark's Square and a few other tourist sites and returned that evening to the town of Vicenza. We had a full steak dinner that included a wonderful soup laden with cheese. When we went to pay the bill the next morning, the cost of our room, which included the meals from the evening before and breakfast, was under fifteen dollars. (How things have changed. In 2004, our male choir, the Sons of Orpheus, traveled to Italy. The costs have disappeared into the stratosphere since then. Vicenza has changed so much and has grown so large that I didn't recognize anything from fifty years before.)

We left early the next morning and hadn't traveled far before we had a flat tire. Thinking we should stop at the nearest gas station in town to get the tire repaired, we pulled off at the next exit. We immediately asked bystanders where we could get the tire repaired. These folks pointed in the direction of a courtyard. When we got in the courtyard, I sensed that it was a family courtyard and started to turn around. Before we could exit, the mother and father of the home in this courtyard streamed out of the home and welcomed us as if we were long-lost relatives. They literally pulled us out of our car and into their home and expressed their excitement (in Italian, of course) that we had come to visit them. While we were impressed by their reception, all we wanted was to have our tire fixed. Several hours later, he managed to take the tire apart and patched it with a small patch. He used a bicycle pump to inflate the tire. We were finally on the road again.

We were always conscious of our limited available funds when we were making purchases. We had planned to drive by Lake Como and then head over St. Goddard's pass. Because we were delayed for several hours in getting the tire repaired, we bypassed the lovely community of Lake Como. We started up St. Goddard pass, which we soon discovered was already blocked by snow. We were advised to put our car on a railway flatcar. We were also instructed to stay in the car. A number of people had already placed their cars on these flatcars.

They put chocks in the front and back of each tire, but the cars were not tied down. As the train picked up speed, we were rocking vigorously back and forth in our car through a long, dark tunnel. While I don't really know how fast we were traveling, it seemed that we racing down the tracks with incredible speed. While we didn't believe that we were in danger, it matched any thrill ride that I ever took.

We eventually ended up in the beautiful city of Lucerne, Switzerland. The pastoral scenes when driving through the mountains were awesome. We had to wait on the main road until a herder of cattle, who was taking his cows decorated with flowers and bells to another pasture, no longer needed the road.

We arrived back in Munich to check on whether the wives of soldiers, who were babysitting, had any problems with the children. We then drove to a town that bordered Czechoslovakia, where Leta's distant relatives had a chinaware factory that had produced excellent china before the war. The map I was using was somewhat sketchy. I was somewhat concerned that I might have accidentally strayed across the Iron Curtain border. As my apprehension was growing, I got a flat tire, the second one in a week. When I went to change the tire, I discovered that the tire that had been fixed by our Italian friend was also flat. How anxious I was until certain that we hadn't strayed across into Russia! As soon as the tire was repaired, we continued to the porcelain factory. Leta had letters of introduction from her mother, and we had a neat visit. The folks at the factory told us that US soldiers, who had used this factory as a hospital, had been excellent guests, and no porcelain was destroyed.

We didn't get to see as much of Germany as we would have liked, although we did visit the military recreational facility at Garmisch, an incredibly beautiful village, on numerous occasions. We also visited famous Linderhof Palace, the Neuschwanstein Castle, and the Herrenchiemsee Palace, located on a lovely island on Chiemsee. We also visited some of the festivities associated with Oktoberfest.

Rumors started to circulate that our entire division would be transferred back to the United States. Sometime in late summer or early fall, we learned that we would be exchanging posts with the 101st Airborne Division stationed in Fort Campbell, Kentucky. The senior chaplain was transferred shortly after his run-in with the commander over his refusal to pay the liquor bill. Several weeks later, a tall, lanky chaplain came strolling into my office asking, "Where's my office?"

I wondered what kind of character was joining our team. It turned out to be a chaplain from the Christian Reformed denomination. His name was Chaplain Dick Oostenink. I had a lot of reservations about how well we would work together.

It turned out to be a relationship that would last long beyond our assignments to the division. He would eventually become the librarian at the chaplain school where we would have contacts each year when I would return every summer to teach the psychological sequence on crisis intervention. (I had the privilege of visiting him in a retirement home in Grand Rapids in the summer of 2005. I felt a sense of loss when I heard of his death a few months later.)

Preparation for our unit's move to Fort Campbell began in earnest during the fall. We were scheduled to make the move shortly after the first of the year. An advanced party of both officers and enlisted personnel went to Fort Campbell to ensure a smooth transition. Some purchased homes in anticipation of the move. Incidentally, the 101st Airborne would be replacing us in Europe.

Rumor had it that an influential member of Congress was instrumental in the reactivation of the 11th Airborne Division that would be housed at Fort Campbell. We would be sent to Fort Ord, California, instead. It left some of our advanced party members, who had purchased homes, in somewhat of a lurch. Most of us were pleased about the change of venue.

24

A Trip to the Holy Lands on a Shoestring

Some of the chaplains who had visited the Holy Lands urged me to make this trek before our unit was sent back to the States. I was somewhat reluctant because I would be traveling alone. While I was receiving a salary, the salary for a first lieutenant at that time was considerably under $5,000 a year, although military housing was provided. With a wife and two small children, there weren't a great deal of dollars for extra things. So the trip to visit the biblical sights would be on a shoestring. It was well before the days of credit cards. I'm sure I possessed considerably less than a hundred dollars—more like fifty dollars.

I caught military flights on a standby basis, first to Frankfurt. I managed to get a navy flight to Naples. The thing that stands out in my memory about that flight was that the plane was not pressurized. Since we were flying over the Alps, the altitude must have been well over fifteen thousand feet. There was a young mother and her infant along. The baby was turning blue, so they were releasing some oxygen from a container in the baby's face.

A navy officer invited me to spend the night with a military friend who lived on a bluff with a view of the Isle of Capri. I woke up with a splitting headache, apparently caused by the unpressurized flight the night before. The following morning, we caught the train to Rome. I went directly to the airport.

That morning, I was able to get on a flight to Wheelus Army Air Field in Tripoli. We left in a driving rainstorm but were soon able to get above the weather. We arrived at Wheelus in the early afternoon, and I got a room in the bachelor officer's quarters. I decided to catch a bus to visit the nearby city. It was my first encounter with a city that had a predominantly fundamentalist Muslin population. It was intimidating for a person with my rural heritage from western Nebraska to see women who not only wore a veil but also had their entire faces covered with the exception of one eye. These women then held a fan in front of that eye so that no male, with the exception of their husbands, could see them. My fear was that I would inadvertently offend them. Since I was alone, I was really intimidated and returned to the safety of the military base.

The following morning, I caught a flight to Cairo, Egypt. I got acquainted with US military pilots and learned that they would be returning in about a week. A young Egyptian man, perhaps in his early twenties, was employed to carry their bags and whatever else. They called him Chico. He would prove to be a lifesaver for me when I returned to Egypt from my short expedition to Jerusalem.

I checked into a hotel that had been recommended to me and started to visit the nearby shops. As soon as I left the hotel property, I was immediately overwhelmed by at least a dozen entrepreneurs who were peddling everything from switchblade knives to whatever else. I tried to avoid them by stepping into a shop. The shop owner, who could spot a naïve tourist a mile away, used heavy sales tactics. I stepped back into the street, only to be confronted by the unwanted peddlers. In self-defense, I returned to the hotel without venturing into the marketplace.

I had applied for all the necessary documents for travel, including visas. Everything I needed had come back except the Jordanian visa. My military instructions were to go to the Jordanian embassy to obtain the needed visa. This was my first task the following morning. To my surprise, the officials at the embassy told me they couldn't issue the visa. When I asked why, they responded that I couldn't prove that I wasn't Jewish. Asking how I could supply that proof, they asked for a Christian baptism certificate. I was dumbfounded. If I hadn't been so taken off guard, I might have offered to demonstrate that I hadn't been circumcised. It never occurred to me that they were likely asking for a bribe. Furthermore, it never occurred to me to go to the US embassy and ask for assistance in this matter.

I then inquired what would happen if I proceeded without a visa. I still remember their laughter when they responded that I would not be allowed to disembark in Jerusalem. Naïvely, I boarded the plane without the visa a day or so later. The plane was a US military C-47 that had been the workhorse during World War II and was now in the process of being replaced. The planes had been purchased by a number of third-world countries. The pilots of this Egyptian flight were from the United States and were likely former military pilots.

While the primary language on board was Arabic, I heard some ladies behind me speaking English. When I told them how pleasant it was to hear my own language, they told me that their husbands were the pilots who had arranged for them to visit Jerusalem. In our continuing conversation as we were flying over the Sinai Desert, I referred to the biblical story of Moses who led the children of Israel out of Egypt and had been in the terrain below. They were fascinated. They had never heard this epic in the life of Israel and were eager to hear the stories found in the Book of Exodus. As the plane was landing, they invited me to join their tour that their husbands had arranged for them. My immediate concern was about my visa, which I didn't have. I left the plane, having no idea how I would proceed. As I was walking to the terminal building, I spotted a sergeant in the Jordanian military. (Jerusalem was still a divided city, and we were landing in the Jordanian zone.) I guessed that he might have served in the British army when the British were the official protectorate of this area. I told him that I was a US military chaplain and told the story of the refusal of the Jordanian embassy to issue me a visa purportedly because I couldn't prove that I wasn't Jewish.

He requested that I give him my passport. At the moment, it didn't occur to me how risky it was to give one's passport to a complete stranger. After the sergeant disappeared from view, I began to sweat bullets as I paced back and forth outside the terminal building where the immigration office was located. It was probably at least thirty minutes later before the sergeant returned. I'm embarrassed to think about it now, but when the sergeant returned with the passport, I was so relieved that I simply thanked him and took the passport with the newly stamped visa and went through the process of immigration. It never dawned on me to ask if he had to pay for the visa and to tip him. In my western Nebraska upbringing, people never expected to be tipped for assisting people. It was just the neighborly thing to do.

With the immigration and customs process behind me, I ran into the women with whom I had had the conversation on the plane. I accepted their offer to join their tour. They told me that our hotel was a place called the American Way, which, I was to learn, was very near to the dividing line between the Jewish and Arab sections of the city.

The first day of touring many of the places I had heard about as a child attending Sunday school, I was mildly depressed. The Holy Land didn't seem very holy to me. A particularly memorable place had a Muslim guide taking us to the very spot on the Mount of Olives where Christ purportedly ascended into heaven. He piously pointed to a footprint etched on a rock and assured us that this is the very place where our Lord ascended into heaven. I recognize that they were playing a role not unfamiliar to tour guides around the world.

Visiting the Church of the Holy Sepulcher was a major disappointment to me. The church was divided into four sections. The guardians from these sections were from the major ancient Christian traditions: Roman Catholic, Greek Orthodox, Russian Orthodox, and Coptic Christian. Each section aggressively (or so it seemed to me) sought donations as you entered their respective section of the church. As we descended by a series of steps, we arrived at the purported burial place of Jesus. Our tour group was entering the tomb. I was the last of our group to enter. As I was ducking down to enter the entrance, someone grabbed me by the collar and hurled me backward. I was startled, especially when I saw the angry look was from of one of the priests. It apparently was his time to carry burning incense into the tomb, and I inadvertently had gotten in his way. It likely didn't occur to this priest how contrary this action was to the spirit of Jesus. When he was finished, I was able to join my group inside the tomb. To say that I was thoroughly disillusioned is an understatement. The admittedly naïve image of what it was like to be in this place was shattered.

Before leaving on the trip, my colonel told me that he had been attached to the British forces during the time when they had been the protectorate of this area. He had told a story about a right-wing Jewish zealot group digging a tunnel under the line separating Arab and Jewish boundaries. This particular group intended, according to the colonel, to blow up some of the Christian sites such as the Church of the Holy Sepulcher. Someone detected some vibrations on the ground. An investigation revealed the tunnel had been haphazardly mined. My colonel said the decision was made to blow the mine rather than attempt to disarm the tunnel because of the irregular way in which the explosives had been laid. The colonel added the city would be evacuated because it was unknown how extensive the damage from exploding these mined tunnels might prove to be. He noted that this was the first time in two thousand years that the city had been evacuated. He told me that some of the significant structures were indeed damaged in the ensuing explosion.

During one of the tours, I asked my guide about this incident. I was startled when he told me that I was expelled from the touring group. Apparently, this surprise registered on my countenance.

He then asked, "You don't know what you said wrong, do you?"

When I said that I didn't know, he stated that I had used the word "Jew." He stated that the tourist board endorsed this policy because they did not recognize the Jewish state. He then stated that since I was unaware of this policy, he would permit me to stay with the group but warned that any further violation would result in my immediate dismissal from the group. For the most part, I asked no further questions. I had not anticipated this kind of tension and animosity.

Interestingly enough, on the third day of our tour, we visited a place called the Garden Tomb. I hadn't heard of this site before and had no idea what to expect. The Garden Tomb was so named, as I was to learn, by a British general named Gordon because it seemed to him that it resembled the garden of Joseph of Arimathea, the member of the Jewish Council who had given his tomb located in this garden for the burial of Christ.

When we arrived in the morning, the skies were overcast, and occasionally there was a light drizzle. We gathered around a tomb that had none of the elaborate adornment of the Church of the Holy Sepulcher and certainly didn't have a long history of Christians coming for centuries to celebrate the risen Christ. It had rather more of the feel of simplicity and authenticity with which a person with my religious tradition could identify.

The memory of the way that the priest with his wavering incense expressed his anger when I had inadvertently blocked his access to the entrance of the tomb located on the bottom floor of the Church of the Holy Sepulcher was still fresh. Here at this site, an Arab Christian lady who stood no more than five feet tall told us in a simple but compelling way the story of the life, death, and resurrection of Jesus. Mrs. Motar didn't attempt to prove that General Gordon's discovery was the authentic site of the crucifixion event or attempt to discredit the site at the Church of the Holy Sepulcher. My fellow tour members would likely not have identified themselves as very religious people, but they, like me, were deeply moved by her presentation.

After her presentation, I identified myself as a US army chaplain and expressed my thanks for her words that she had spoken with such conviction. To my surprise, she invited me to come to her home on the grounds and meet her husband that evening, after we had finished a day of touring.

As I was leaving our hotel to keep this after-dinner engagement, the evening manager of the hotel warned me to be cautious about returning. He reminded us that we were only a half block from the border and that if I inadvertently made a wrong turn and came up against the border at night, guards on both sides would direct hostile fire against me. This warning was on my mind throughout the evening. The sky was still overcast, which fit my mildly anxious mood.

The Motars were most gracious. One of the topics of conversation involved their children. They told me that most of their six children were studying at different universities in the United States. They also spoke of how pleased they were about being the custodians and spokespersons for the Garden Tomb.

Several times throughout the evening, I started to leave. Each time they would beg me to stay. I was too naïve to realize that this was likely an Eastern custom to invite a person to stay longer. While I enjoyed their home thoroughly, I really did want to return to my hotel, but at the same time didn't want to be rude. It was nearly midnight when I announced that I must leave.

They accompanied me through the garden of Joseph of Arimathea. The clouds had disappeared, and a full moon shone over the city. It was surreal to see the garden and the nearby city walls bathed in the moonlight. I spotted the entrance of the tomb that we had visited earlier in the day. It was silhouetted by the moonlight. Even though I was an ordained chaplain, it was the first time that the resurrection story came so vividly alive for me. I could imagine that I was in the very presence of the angels that made the announcement to the confused and weeping women. I could almost hear the words, "He is not here. He is risen. Come see the place where he lay." I still have a visceral memory of the rush of emotions that went through my body under that full moon. It was truly surreal!

I fully intended to keep in touch with the Motars, but we were moving back to the States shortly after I returned. Best intentions fell by the wayside. I had been their guest one month before the 1956 war. During the 1967 war, the Jews captured the city and the area surrounding the Garden Tomb came under heavy attack. The

Motars took shelter during the bombardment in the very tomb where they believed that Christ had been buried. Perhaps it is only coincidence, but they were confined in the tomb for three days with little or no food or water. On the third day, when the fighting seemed to have subsided, he went into the street to buy bread. He was shot and killed. Although I didn't hear of his death until sometime after it happened, it deepened my regret that I hadn't kept in touch with them.

The next morning, I caught the flight back to Cairo, Egypt. There were only several flights a week, and I had a rendezvous to keep with the US Air Force pilots, who were stopping before flying to Athens, Greece. I was surprised when I arrived at the Cairo airport. I was told by immigration that my Egyptian visa had expired because I had left the country. They let me into the country but confiscated my passport. Stunned, I wandered around Cairo for a couple days, waiting for the return of the plane. Again, it never dawned on me to go to the US embassy.

An acquaintance told me that he was staying in a large pension and invited me to join him. The evening meal had dozens of male waiters in long robes flowing from the dining area to the kitchen and back. It was truly impressive. The robes made it look like that they were indeed gliding across the floor.

At the pension, hordes of salesmen weren't waiting to descend on tourists, but I did meet one older gentleman the next morning who was very persistent. He kept telling me that "I was his first chance," and if he didn't persuade me to let him be my guide, things would not go well for the day. I was on such a limited budget that I had gone without some meals to make ends meet. The idea of getting a guide was simply beyond my means. But still, he persisted. Finally, I made an offer so low that I was sure he would reject it. But he accepted, and we were on the way to the famous national museum. He went through the exhibits so rapidly that I finally dismissed him.

The next day, I was to meet the air force pilots to catch a flight to Greece. Since I was without a passport, I had no idea of how I would proceed. My anxiety level was at its peak. I got to the airport very early. Eventually I spotted Chico, who was the "gofer" for the pilots. I was so anxious that I spilled my story of how my passport had been confiscated. Although he had no official position of any kind with either immigration or customs, he invited me to follow him to the immigration area, where no officials were present and started to rummage through unlocked drawers in the immigration office. He found my passport and gave it to me. I was dumbfounded but deeply appreciative.

I had hoped to be in Athens for a day or two to visit the Acropolis and a few of the ancient temples and then get home as quickly as possible. Friends had told me about the King George Hotel in Athens. I had given this address to MATS, the Military Transportation Service. While the hotel was not particularly expensive, it was threatening my extremely limited budget, so I moved to a less expensive place. It proved to be a false economy. MATS tried to reach me at the King George to tell me that a military flight would be leaving for Germany sooner than scheduled.

The expected flight had been canceled, and no regularly scheduled military aircraft was coming for another week. I kept hoping for an unscheduled one to arrive. Three of these five days, I hung around the airport, waiting for the "hop" that would take me home.

The airport was located on the sea. During my walks while waiting, I came across a young Greek person who was carrying buckets of water from the sea to a container on shore. I volunteered to help. While we couldn't speak each other's languages, he invited me to go with him on his boat to a nearby island. I didn't accept his invitation but appreciated his gesture. I was relieved when I was finally able to board the flight that would eventually get me to my home in Munich.

25

The Holidays Are Coming!

While I had been gone, Leta had had nearly twenty-five servicemen and their wives over at our home for Thanksgiving dinner. I had given the invitation to come to our home before I knew that I was making this trip to the Middle East. I obviously wasn't there to help her entertain this crowd. While the meal in the mess hall would be first class, the invitation that I had given before I left was eagerly accepted. Christmas Eve and Christmas Day were very special days indeed. Christmas Eve would begin by a number of chapel personnel going throughout our military residential community singing Christmas carols. Christmas Eve services at the chapel would begin at 2230 hours (10:30 p.m.) and end an hour later. We were accommodating the Catholic chaplain, who wanted the chapel during the midnight hour.

Following our services, about twenty of us accepted the invitation of a German Lutheran pastor to go to a mission service that was being held at the train station. It was a somber but moving moment. Many of the German people who had lost everything in the war were present. Some were missing limbs. They sang the Christmas carols in German and shared food. What impressed me most was that just that day, several people present had escaped from behind the Iron Curtain with only that which they could carry. They were present to celebrate their first day of freedom and to worship the

One who had come to bring peace. It was nearly three a.m. when we returned home.

Linda, age five, and Bobby, age two, were up at six a.m. It was Christmas morning after all, and they couldn't wait to open their presents. They tugged at us until we staggered to our feet—very sleepy-eyed. After the presents were opened and breakfast was served, it was time to get ready for Sunday morning services. After the services, nearly forty servicemen and wives gathered at our small apartment for Christmas dinner. For most, it was their first Christmas away from home. They were obviously homesick and would have preferred to be with their families. There was standing room only. The wives helped Leta get the final touches of the Christmas dinner ready. The dinner, which included turkey and dressing, was served cafeteria-style.

Everyone sat where they could find an empty space. Most sat on the floor to eat their meals. After the meal was finished, someone started a Christmas carol. When that was finished, they sang another and another and another. Leta remembers that someone had an accordion. They sang lustily until their voices could no longer sing another song. Singing every song that they could remotely remember, a wonderful bonding took place that afternoon. They moved past their homesickness and experienced each other as family. More than one said it was the best Christmas they had ever experienced.

The assistant regimental commander lived across the hall from us. We later learned that his family—and most every family on our stairwell—had opened their doors to hear the voices of these young soldiers and their wives sing. I think they may have been a little jealous. Chaplains were the only officers (at that time) who could invite enlisted men to their homes for a social event.

At about 1800 hours (6:00 p.m.) or so, most of us drove to the orphanage, where our Lutheran minister friend was the administrator. Each soldier and wife adopted a German child for the evening. When it was time to go, everyone was reluctant to leave the child with whom they had formed a special relationship.

26

California, Here We Come!

Moving time came in the first weeks of 1956. Military dependents had been sent ahead to Bremerhaven, the port from which we were to leave, three or four days before we would join them. We were preparing the post for the transfer to the 101st Airborne Division. Some of the enlisted men were being discharged shortly after their return to the United States. On the final morning, the battalion gathered by unit in the large gym. After final instructions and final words from the commanders, they filed out of the gym, waiting transportation that would take them to the train station. I stood at the doorway of the gym, greeting as many as I could while they were filing out. I recognized that I would never see most of them again.

We joined our families, who were already on board the ship that would carry us back to the United States. I'm not sure what the recreation officer was thinking about, but he had shown the film *Titanic* to family members the night before we arrived. It turned out that we did encounter a sixty-knot storm at sea. The ship's motion was significant enough that the propeller of the ship would come out of the water when the aft part of the ship was on an upward roll. It first happened at midnight. I heard a lady in a nearby cabin screaming that "we were going down like the *Titanic*."

I probably should have been a sailor. I thoroughly enjoyed the storm at sea. I would stare down at the fifty-foot waves from the top deck and delight in the sheer majesty and power of the sea. (Incidentally, Leta and I were at sea in January 2003 during a hurricane. We were not allowed on deck. The porcelain in the dining room and the community stores didn't fare very well, but both of us thoroughly enjoyed this adventure.)

The first time Leta had made the crossing, she had a three-year-old on a leash and a thirteen-month-old infant who was sick most of the voyage. She was grateful that I could be there to share in the responsibilities for caring for the children.

I tried to prepare Linda, our five-year-old, for coming into the New York harbor and sailing past the Statue of Liberty. I made up different lines like, "Tomorrow morning, we'll be in New York." "We'll see the statue of a famous lady." Then I added a melody with new lines that I tried to create.

Our car, which had been shipped ahead, was waiting for us. We were soon on our way to western Michigan to visit Leta's mother and siblings. We didn't know it then, but it would be the last time that we would see Leta's mother alive. After a few days with her family, we drove to western Nebraska to visit my parents before driving on to our new duty station at Fort Ord, California. It was in early February of 1956.

We left my parents' home on an early cloudy morning. It appeared to be a typical winter day. In midafternoon, someplace in the middle of Wyoming on the old US Highway 30, it started to snow. With a wife and two small children in the car, I started to feel some apprehension when the snow began to accumulate. It was then a two-lane highway, with long rolling hills in the wide-open prairies. Soon, the road was no longer visible. My only guidelines were the fence posts that were set back a hundred feet or so from both sides of the road. I would drive as fast as I dared down the hill and then the snow would slow my progress going up the next hill. As the snow was accumulating, the traffic was close to nonexistent. I did manage to follow the tracks of a truck for some distance, but soon they disappeared. One long rolling hill after another followed. By this time, we were really frightened. Although it was midafternoon, it was nearly dark. Leta was carefully following the map, but no towns seemed to be in range.

Suddenly, seemingly out of nowhere, a large filling station with a motel appeared. No other buildings were in sight. It was called Little America. I was so relieved that I would have given my last dollar for a room that night. As we settled into the room for the night, I noticed the legend on the wall of our room of how the dream of providing a shelter for travelers who were stranded in a storm. It seems that a teenager hearing of an approaching blizzard had gone to round up cattle on the range to bring them to shelter at their ranch home. The blizzard struck with force before he completed his mission. He huddled among the cattle for warmth that evening and made a promise to himself that he would provide shelter for those who, in the future, would encounter this kind of a storm. To us, it seemed that we were the benefactors of that dream. Whenever I pass one of the Little America hotels, I remember with gratitude this young man's making his promise a reality.

Our military home was in Seaside, California. At that time, it was a quiet village. (I drove through Seaside forty years later and couldn't find any familiar landmarks.) It was a beautiful area. I used to enjoy looking over Monterey Bay. It appeared to be always changing. I think I could have easily become addicted to the area.

Even though fifteen or twenty miles inland, the temperature would often exceed one hundred degrees Fahrenheit. We wore winter uniforms all year round at Fort Ord. The heavy fog would often roll in during the late afternoon and often hang on until midmorning. Our children often had colds and a cough in this setting.

The famous Seventeen Mile Drive was still accessible without charge, and we leisurely drove around the beautiful countryside when off duty. My brother Merle and his lovely bride, Delores, went with us to this lovely site during a visit in the time that they were stationed in San Diego.

Our division's mission at Fort Ord was to conduct basic training for new recruits. The draft was still operational. Every eligible young man, unless deferred for some reason, was expected to enter the military. I became increasingly aware that soldiers in basic training were rarely given permission to make an appointment to see the chaplain to discuss personal problems during training hours.

Basic training procedures are very rigid and demanding. If I wanted to be visible to soldiers during this time, I would try to show up when the recruits were on a ten-minute break. I volunteered to go through the infiltration course. During this exercise, live bullets were fired during the night exercises. When you are crawling on your belly as low you can get, the bullets still seemed to be flying just inches over your body. I learned these bullets were actually whizzing by several feet over our heads. Simulated mines are going off typically at the time you are trying to crawl under barbed wire. While this procedure was scary for most, it was a great opportunity for me as a chaplain to provide what is called a ministry of presence. I ended up going through it with a number of different classes. In fact, some sergeants and I would end up racing each other.

I think I was the first chaplain on post to announce evening counseling to allow recruits to look up a chaplain on their own time. I announced at church services that I would be available on Tuesdays and Thursdays from 1900 to 2100 hours (7:00 p.m. to 9:00 p.m.). I showed up about thirty minutes early on the first evening. I expected that one or two people might show up. To my astonishment, there were at least twenty-five guys waiting to see me when I arrived at 1830 hours. More kept coming in throughout the evening. I was both dumbfounded and wasn't sure how to deal with this kind of crowd. I have never heard of triage treatment strategies but I did develop my own kind of triage in trying to deal with this kind of crowd. Although I had very little psychological training, I did what I could, listening to as many as I could.

Many saw the chaplain's office as a place to go "to have your card punched." The notion was that a scheming soldier would try to get the chaplain involved in his case as a way that would get him off the hook for some unpleasant chore. Nearly all the young men that I saw were in deep crisis.

Some were in such deep personal disarray that it was difficult to see how they could get past the crisis. Some were deeply concerned about family members who were in crisis. While I did what I could, I recognized that I needed much more psychological training than I had. These experiences were the seed that eventually germinated in the decision to return to graduate school. I, however, had no plans of getting a doctorate in psychology at that time.

Years after I had been in private practice after getting a doctorate from Michigan State University, it dawned on me that what I was seeing in my chapel office was far more than young men, largely from southern California, going through personal anguish. I was seeing the distorted edge of what popularly was to become known as the hippie movement. Unbeknown to me and to everyone else, a major cultural shift (something like an earthquake) was forming and would have a profound impact that would forever change the way society organizes itself.

One morning before I left for the chapel, I answered the phone. It was one of Leta's sisters. She said that their mother, at the age of sixty-one, had a heart attack and had not survived. We made immediate plans to drive from California to Michigan. By the afternoon of the day of the announcement, we were on our way. We drove nonstop all the way to Nebraska, where my father served a small congregation as pastor. We made beds for our small children in the back of the car. We arrived at my parents' home in the wee hours of Sunday morning. After a few hours of sleep, I went to church. I can't believe that, at my father's request, I tried to give the sermon. I was so exhausted and my mind so cluttered, I'm afraid that I didn't make much sense in what I was trying to say.

After the noon meal, we were on the way again to drive nonstop to Michigan. In the middle of the night, we would take turns driving every thirty minutes to an hour. As I think of the trip now, I can't believe that we undertook this trip in this way. Air travel was expensive, and our finances were limited. We arrived at her family's place sometime on Tuesday afternoon.

I still had the macho idea that tears were to be avoided. In an effort to be strong for my wife's sake, I undoubtedly blocked some of her effort to grieve. I held her firmly while she wept, pausing at the casket, then led her away. I thought I was being strong for her. In a few weeks, we would be coming back that way. We were leaving beautiful California for a new military assignment.

27

Becoming a Paratrooper

As much as I enjoyed the Fort Ord area, I realized that I was at a crossroads in my military career. Even though I was terrified of heights, I decided that if I was going to be a paratrooper, it had to be soon. Back at the Basic Chaplain's Course at Fort Slocum, New York, I had been inspired by Father Frances Sampson, who would eventually become the chief of chaplains. I don't know why I was taken by this kind of adventure. It may have been that I had never been through a puberty rite that demanded total physical commitment. I realized that I would likely be getting overseas orders again in a couple of years. I rationalized that a chaplain should submit himself (women were not yet serving as chaplains in the military) to every military situation that other soldiers were asked to perform.

When we arrived at Fort Bragg, I was assigned as the division troop chaplain. I was in the same office as the division chaplain as well as the assistant division chaplain, who was Roman Catholic. The division chaplain, in my view, had crossed the line by attempting to be a line officer rather than a pastor. He may also have crossed the line in the use of alcohol. On the other hand, the assistant division chaplain was in my opinion clearly a pastor first, although he was well respected in his military role.

We arrived in the middle of September, and a few weeks lat-

Eugene W. Friesen

er, I would be going through jump school. Actually the first two weeks of training were simply called pre-BAC. I'm still not sure what the acronyms stand for, but it was clearly the most vigorous physical challenge that I had ever faced. In the hot October sun, training started at 1300 hours (1:00 p.m.) and lasted for four hours. The hours were filled with more push-ups than I thought I could count. Leg lifts that strained every muscle in the abdomen and fast-formation runs that would last for miles were part of the routine. I landed in one of the last platoons. The front platoon would set the pace. The farther back you were, the more difficult it was to keep pace. The rule was that if you fell more than two paces behind, you had to drop out. This meant if the person ahead dropped back a pace, you needed to fight your way around him to keep from falling farther behind.

If you dropped out, the jump school instructors assumed that you needed additional physical conditioning. In that event, you stayed for a fifth hour of physical exercises under their watchful and critical eyes.

The only accepted excuse for falling out of formation was if you physically passed out. An ambulance would pick you up if this happened. I remember one occasion where we were running a fast clip, and I was barely hanging on. I told myself that I could make it to the point where we normally would stop. When we reached that point, the platoon continued running. I dropped out for the only time in the training and was rewarded with an extra hour of very tough physical training. The irony is that the group stopped running in less than a hundred yards.

After the run, our heartbeats were way up, and we were overheated. We would be lined up near a fire hydrant, and the fire hoses would hit us directly in the face. It took your breath away. I understand that this procedure was later stopped when a soldier had a heart attack.

On one occasion, we were in the "lean and rest" position. This was essentially the push-up position on hold, a very difficult position to maintain for any length of time. The instructor told us that since we were resting, he would tell us a story. There were five

150

hundred men in the PT pit that day. I was the only chaplain in that group. Many hadn't been able to maintain this position and collapsed on the ground. I had several instructors watching for my collapse. Even though I was barely holding on, I didn't want to give the instructors the satisfaction of seeing me fall on my face. Eventually, one of the instructors lay on his back and scooted under me in such a way that his face was facing mine, although his feet were pointing in the opposite direction.

He smiled broadly and asked, "Chaplain, is the Lord helping you now?"

I didn't dare answer. I think the men thought I would get breaks because I was the chaplain. Actually, the cross on my helmet drew more attention from the instructors, and it often cost me dearly in terms of push-ups or some other physical activity. We were the last class to go through this extra two-week preparatory course for the jump school itself. While jump school was vigorous, it would not be as physically challenging as the two previous weeks had been.

When this preparatory course started, I would come home so exhausted that I didn't dare go upstairs to the washroom to clean up. If I did go upstairs, I knew that I wouldn't come back downstairs. So I ate something without washing, then took a shower and collapsed into bed. While I am not subject to nightmares as a rule, I did have nightmares about jumping. More than once, I awakened out of sound sleep, terrified.

In the morning, I would be so stiff that I could barely move. This didn't matter to the instructors at the school. We would begin the full regimen of exercises without any warm-ups. In a few minutes, we wouldn't recall how sore our muscles had been. In the jump school itself, we were only required to do an hour of physical training during the eight-hour day. We practiced the procedures of making what was called a PLF, a parachute landing fall, many times. This procedure called for rolling with the fall. This technique was so thoroughly taught that even to this day I automatically follow this procedure when I unexpectedly fall.

The greatest test for me was the required exits out of the thirty-four-foot towers. We would be hooked up to a harness anchored to a cable attached to the tower platform as well as to a set of poles some fifty or sixty feet away. The person exiting this tower would be picked up by the cables just before they struck the ground and then bounce down this cable to a mound of dirt at the other end. It was something like modern-day bungee jumping.

When it was time for me to make an exit from the door, I froze. If one freezes in the door, they are typically eliminated from jump school. I think I was given a second chance only because I was the chaplain. On the second attempt, I literally forced myself out the door. You were graded on each exit by an instructor on the ground. Before you could pass this phase of the training, you had to make five acceptable exits, which included eyes open, chin on the chest, arms on the reserve parachute, and feet together. Most of the student troopers received their five passing exits in fifteen or twenty exits. So great was my panic that it took me about forty or forty-five exits before I finally passed this phase of the training cycle.

One of the rituals most associated with the armed forces is the military cadence repeated while marching. The cadence chanted during the final week of training went like this: "In my throat is a great big lump, one more week till my first jump. If I die on the ol' drop zone, box me up and ship me home. Pin those wings upon my chest. Bury me in the lean and rest." The drill instructors made sure that we were singing this cadence with spirit and enthusiasm.

We finally completed our three weeks of jump school training. On a Friday afternoon, we were given the seating position on the plane when we were to make our first jump the following Monday. I was scheduled to be the seventh person to exit from our plane. For me, it was a long weekend, filled with a lot of apprehension.

When we assembled at the scheduled time at the marshaling area, we were issued our main parachute in one line and our reserve chute in the second line. When I went through the second line, the person handing out the reserve chute jokingly asked me why I needed the reserve chute. "Where's your faith?" he asked. I was too anxious to respond to the attempt at humor.

We filed onto the C119, known as the flying boxcar, according to the way we were listed on the manifest. Soon we were taking off.

You should have seen the expressions on the faces of these young troopers about to make their first jump. After we reached an appropriate altitude, the jumpmasters with a gleeful look on their faces took off the rear door on both sides of the plane and stowed the doors safely away. Some of our faces must have mirrored sheer terror as the doors were removed.

Normally, the red light comes on four minutes before drop time. That's the signal to begin the jump commands. We were at least ten minutes away from the jump when one of the instructors beckoned me to the door. He instructed me to hook my static line to the cable attached to the plane and stand in the door. All the other troopers were still in their seats. He told me to stand in the door. I moved very cautiously toward the door. He again told me to stand in the door, with my hands on the outside of the plane and the toe of my boot extending beyond the fuselage of the plane. I hesitantly followed his instructions. He then told me to look for the light on the boon. I didn't know what he was talking about, but I kept looking for it.

After I had been in this position for four or five minutes, the red light did come on, and I heard the jumpmaster give the routine commands that we had learned during the ground school phase.

"Stand up," he boomed, followed by the instructions to "hook up, check your equipment, and sound off for equipment check." The final instruction was to stand in the door.

I had already been in the door for eight or nine minutes by the time he issued this command to the trooper who would be in the opposite door.

I saw the green light come on and felt the jumpmaster slap me on my bottom. Jumping out the door on the thirty-four-foot tower had become so routine that I didn't think about it. The response to jump was automatic by then. I hadn't stopped to realize that the plane was traveling through the air at about 140 miles per hour. I expected to experience a falling sensation. Instead, I had a feeling similar to being in a recliner with my feet slightly higher than my head. I seemed to be gliding parallel with earth. I was so surprised by this sensation that I forgot to count one thousand ... two thousand ... three thousand ... four thousand as we had been taught. Just as the chute was opening, I remembered I had forgotten to count. Realizing I hadn't followed instructions, I called out "Four thousand!" although there was obviously no one there in the open skies to hear whether I had counted.

I looked around me. Other open parachutes were in the area. It seemed surreal. I had the feeling of being suspended in space. My first reaction was to wonder what I needed to do to avoid the displeasure of some instructor. It dawned on me that there were no instructors around, and that I should simply enjoy the view. I was surprised that I didn't have the sensation of falling to earth until I was about a hundred feet or so above the ground, and the ground came up fast. It was a good landing. The only feeling that I can describe was elation. I was scheduled and emotionally ready to make the second jump that same afternoon.

Five jumps occurred during a three-day period. A formation was held on Friday of jump week in which the commanding general awarded us the coveted wings. When the formation was dismissed, the assistant division Catholic chaplain rushed to me and took the newly pinned wings off my uniform.

"You can't wear those," he said with a smile. "Those are blood wings." With that announcement, he pinned a shiny new parachute badge on my uniform. I was moved by his gesture.

As an aside, the military provided an important catalyst in terms of bringing religious denominations, particular Protestant, Catholic, and Jewish clergy, together. We shared the same chapel. We got to know each of these clergy, as well as their families, quite well. When I was an instructor at the chaplain school in New York, I often got together with a rabbi who had been a fellow instructor. Sometimes the reunion took place in the officer's club; sometimes in his home.

When I was a jumping padre with the 82nd Airborne Division, Leta hadn't initially been pleased about my volunteering to be a paratrooper. I actually believe that she thought that this action might represent a secret death wish. While she hadn't said much, she didn't show a lot of sympathy for my aches and pains during the preliminary two weeks of training that involved a total after-noon of physical training in a hot and humid climate.

She took the kids and watched my third jump. From then on, she was a fan and rarely missed an opportunity to be at the drop zone to watch us glide to earth. On one occasion, the children were playing in the sand when she alerted them to the fact that "Daddy was jumping." They looked into the sky for a brief moment and said, "Oh." Then they went back to their play in the sand.

Most of the jumps were routine. One of the commanders had described parachuting as a way to get to work that required us to walk home. Several jumps, however, were somewhat unique. The first night jump won't easily be erased from my memory. It was the time of the new moon, when the moon is not visible during most of the night. The sky was clear, and stars beyond number filled the sky. There wasn't a light of any kind on the drop zone since we were simulating a parachute jump under combat conditions.

When I first exited the plane, I could dimly see other parachutes in the area where my chute had opened, but very soon, no para-chutes other than mine were in sight. I looked up at my open chute and could see stars through a number of the panels in my canopy. I assumed that I had a crippled chute. I thought of pulling my re-serve chute but then remembered that if one has a partially opened chute, it is necessary to catch the skirt of the chute as it is deploying and "shake it out" to ensure that the reserve chute doesn't wrap around a partially opened chute before it is deployed. Since it was so dark, I became concerned that I wouldn't be able to see the re-serve chute deploy. To avoid the danger of it further crippling my parachute with the blown panels, I decided to ride the open chute to the ground. I assumed that I was traveling down at a rapid rate of speed. I kept looking at the ground, but everything below was dark. It felt like I was falling into a sea of ink.

I waited and waited for a rough landing. After what seemed like a miniature eternity, I finally reached the ground so gently that I had to force a landing roll. In fact, the landing was so gentle that I could have easily made a standing landing. It was so dark that the only way that I could retrieve my parachute was to follow the risers attached to the chute. My chute was in perfect condition. I was later told that when a panel was patched, it was patched with a white silk covering and that stars were visible through a white panel.

Another memorable jump was also a night jump, and we were in the famous boxcar (C119) that used a jet assist, as I understand it, to get off the ground. I'm not sure what happened, but just as we were breaking ground, there was a strong gasoline smell in our cabin. If a gallon of fuel had been spilled on the floor, the odor couldn't have been stronger. A nervous young trooper started to light a cigarette. I never saw sergeants move any faster than they did that night. They literally pounced on that young man, crushing the match that was about to light the cigarette. I really thought we were going to go up in smoke at that moment. When the plane didn't blow up, I was half expecting that we would exit as soon as we gained sufficient attitude for the chutes to open. After the initial scare, the jump went off without a hitch.

One jump could have had serious ramifications. I was "sweeping the stick," meaning that I was the last one out the door. When the command was given to check equipment, the last person in line scheduled to jump checks the equipment of the person in front of him. This last person in the "stick" then turns around so that the person just ahead of him can check his equipment. (Usually twenty troopers are lined up on each side of the plane waiting to jump.) This specific command to check your equipment is a safety check to ensure that any excess in the static line is tucked into a loop located on the backpack of each trooper.

The Hispanic person ahead of me spoke Spanish as his first language, and his English vocabulary was very limited. I was aware that my static line needed to be tucked in, but I wasn't sure how to tell my examiner of my concern. Furthermore, I didn't think that the extra line was that excessive. This assessment proved to be wrong. As I exited out of the plane, the wind caught this extra static line and blew it in front of my neck, causing a rather heavy rope burn beneath the chin down to the lower part of the neck. This static line across my neck sent me spinning into space. The risers were twisted nearly all the way up to the parachute itself. After the chute opened, I spent a considerable time unwinding. I was fortunate indeed not to have sustained a broken neck. The rest of this jump was uneventful.

Another memorable jump occurred on the day that retired General "Slim Jim" Gavin, who had led the 82nd into combat during World War II, was there to watch a jump. The guidelines for wind velocity while exiting a plane in flight were that if the gusting winds were above fifteen knots, the jump would be canceled. On this day, the wind was gusting up to thirty or more knots per hour. The brass was reluctant to cancel the jump for a genuine hero and father figure for our unit. So we jumped.

There are four basic ways to land. One is that the movement pattern of the parachute is to the right; another movement is to the left, still another movement is backward. The final pattern is that the chute's motion is forward. (There could be variations of these basic movements.) I disliked the backward pattern and was fortunate to rarely land in that mode. Incidentally, one didn't make a choice on which movement will occur on a given jump. It just happens, and you deal with it. During the jump for retired General Gavin, I was moving backward. As I looked down from forty or fifty feet in the air (a no-no—eyes are to be on the horizon), it seemed to me that we were flying parallel to the ground. When I hit the ground at approximately thirty per hour or so, I did a backward flip so rapidly that I didn't feel my buttocks hit the ground. In the split second that there was slack in the rise, my feet flew into the risers. During this brief split second these risers quickly tightened, and I was hanging upside down with my feet caught in the risers as the chute kept rising in the air for ten or fifteen feet and then slamming back to the ground. I was totally helpless, alternatively being dragged through the sand at one moment and then being hosted into the air and slammed down to earth again. After a mile or so, someone on the drop zone grabbed the skirt of my chute, and it collapsed. I was able to untangle myself from the risers. What a relief!

On another occasion, I was the first person out of the plane. It turns out that we were given the signal to jump a second too soon. A communication truck was just ahead of the designated drop area.

As I was descending, I realized that I was heading right for the truck. The risers on the T-10 parachute were hard to manage. I just missed the tailgate of the truck by inches. As I hit the ground, I soon became entangled in the communication wires that had been temporarily laid on the ground. I had a lot of help that day getting untangled.

The G-3 (responsible for training) had planned a division-wide exercise in which we would have to carry everything that we would need for three days. Our backpacks were filled. We were all jumping with a lot of weight. It was a cloudy day, but the jump appeared to be uneventful. However, it started to rain, and the rain turned to snow. That evening the temperature dropped below zero. The discipline that these top soldiers were taught to follow fell apart at the seams. For example, when socks are wet, they need to be dried. If the only dry place to do it is under the armpits, then this is where they should be placed. It became obvious that the division was in serious trouble and the exercise was called off the next morning. I visited troops in the hospital who hadn't walked a step because of a bad case of frostbite on their legs.

A final jump story: many times a scheduled jump had to be called off because of the weather. Sometimes this call was made before we boarded the plane. Other times it was called off while we were in the air, waiting to jump. The jumping conditions on this particular day were highly marginal. We had made two passes at the drop zone, and each time we had gotten red smoke signal, which means no jump. On the third pass, we unexpectedly got the green smoke signal, which means to go.

I was standing directly behind our executive officer who was standing in the door. A captain, who allowed his weight to become excessive (he had had a heart attack the year before), was standing in the same position as I was but on the opposite door of the plane. It had been more than a year since his last jump. I truly think the captain was spooked by not having made a jump in a year's time. Just before the jump, he was gazing across the aisle of the plane when he suddenly realized the commander just ahead of him had jumped. (I suspected that he was very apprehensive and in total denial that the green light had come on.) Following the commander, he apparently made a lousy exit. I learned later that his risers were twisted all the way up to his chute.

The captain was slightly below me as I was drifting toward him. The T-10 parachute was hard to direct. I kept yelling at him to slip his parachute to the side. I was trying to do the same thing. I drifted on top of his parachute. The air pressure wasn't great enough to sustain my chute directly over his. I had a full field pack that was dangling on my knees. I was trying to walk off the chute. I kept sinking into his chute, even as my chute was collapsing. I had the feeling that I was walking in very soft snow up to my waist and moved with the greatest difficulty. I kept struggling to slip off to the side of the chute. I estimate we were eight hundred or nine hundred feet in the air when I was first landed on his chute. While I'm not sure of our height, I suspect that we were at four hundred or five hundred feet when I got free from his chute. He landed before I did. He appeared to be so shaken that he simply sat hunched down instead of springing to his feet to take care of his chute—as we had been trained to do.

I saw him while I was still fifty feet or so in the air and noticed that he had landed but was not moving. I was heading for the exact spot where he was sitting. I kept yelling, "Look out below. Look out below." All he did was to duck down in a crouched position. I landed in a sitting position rather than hitting him full force as I landed. It was a close call.

People often ask if anyone is shoved out the door on a jump. The answer is clearly no. At least this is true in combat simulated jumps. If someone blocked the door during an actual combat jump, it would probably be a different story.

A young Puerto Rican man, who did not speak English, had graduated from jump school but his unit didn't schedule him to jump again for three months, a serious mistake. On his crucial sixth jump, the military aircraft was a C123 instead of the C119. In exiting in flight, the C123 had a very different feeling than did the aircraft from which we had previously jumped. For example, this plane was much noisier, and the doors from which one would exit were off when the troopers entered the plane rather than being removed while in flight.

After we had gotten to jump altitude, this young soldier unhooked from his seat and went to the front of the plane. Knowing how terrified he was, I spoke to him, offering to jump beside him. Unfortunately, I didn't know how to speak any Spanish at that point in my life. When our unit returned to the barracks, he had already been shipped to what airborne troopers disdainfully call a "leg outfit."

I was on the same jump but not the same airplane in which our assistant regimental commander was hurt. It was a freak accident. One leg became entangled in the risers as the chute was opening. The colonel was hurt on the opening shock of the parachute rather than on landing.

I went to see him regularly while he was recuperating at the military hospital. While I went to see all troops from my unit in the hospital, the colonel and his family, which included their young sons, were regular worshipers at the chapel. One evening, he reported with a smile on his face that he was being discharged the following day.

About noon the following day, I received the surprising news that the colonel was in critical condition. I rushed to the hospital. As I walked down the hallway, I met his wife, who had been preparing to bring him home. Understandably, she was very bewildered and frightened.

We entered the room together. He was under an oxygen tent, gasping for breath. I had been in awe of anyone who held this high rank. It dawned on me that in a crisis like this, when life itself was at stake, it really didn't matter how much any person achieved or how much power, prestige, or wealth that person might have. In the next thirty minutes or so, I did my best to be in ministry to them both as we placed their futures in God's hands. The colonel survived.

A few new duplex homes, known as Caphart houses, became available to officers who were senior in their time in grade. These homes were given to a few first lieutenants, captains, and majors.

During the Korean War, promotions in each of these grades were over quota. After the Korean War, the military began to downsize. This process was known as reduction in force or by the acronym RIF. All the first lieutenants who had come into the army at the same time that I did weren't promoted to the higher grade for nearly five years because of this quota system.

As a result, I was one who had not reached the zone of consideration for promotion and hence was very senior in my grade. On this basis, I was eligible for a Caphart home. These new homes were much nicer than the quarters I had been eligible to have. They were located within a few miles of the new chapel facilities that I was then assigned to. Interestingly enough, I was promoted to captain a few weeks later. If this promotion had arrived several weeks earlier, the Caphart homes would not have been available to us because I would then have been a very junior captain. I guess everything is in the timing.

We taught the children to answer the phone in a proper military manner. "This is Chaplain Friesen's residence. This is Linda speaking." (Or Bobby, depending on which child answered the phone.)

On this occasion, Linda had just shared with her three-year-old brother that she had been introduced to the concept of capital letters in her second-grade class. Eager to impart this knowledge, she announced, "Bobby, you don't just spell your name b-o-b-b-y anymore. It's capital B-o-b-b-y."

Bobby was duly impressed. A few minutes later, I heard the telephone ring. Bobby rushed to the phone and answered, "This is Chaplain Friesen's residence. This is Capital Bobby speaking."

One Sunday afternoon, I went to the chapel to check on something at the office. I was surprised to see a bridal party waiting. I hadn't arranged for a wedding to take place. I looked around to see if some other chaplain was there to perform the ceremony. The groom had some of the men from his unit there to serve as groomsmen. The bride's mother was present.

I learned that the bride and her mother had arrived from Tennessee for the wedding. Normally, I wouldn't have performed the ceremony without prior counseling as well as the appropriate arrangements having been made. My first thought was that this couple was very naïve and that it hadn't occurred for them to make prior arrangements. The fact that the mother and bride had traveled a considerable distance was a major factor in my decision to spend an hour or so with the couple and then perform the ceremony.

As soon as the ceremony was completed, the groom asked if I could arrange a pass for him to spend time with the bride. I expressed shock that he hadn't had the foresight to ask for a pass prior to the bride's arrival. It turns out that he was on restriction and under guard. He had talked his guards into being his witnesses at the wedding. While his violation had probably been minor, I did not attempt to intervene to arrange a pass. I can only guess that the bride may have been in a family way, thus creating the hurried arrangements in the mind of the bride and her mother.

28

An Unusual Invitation

I was in my office at the chapel when I received a call from a close college friend and member of the college quartet in which we both had sung. Bob Price sponsored a religious television program in Philadelphia and was looking for opportunities to bolster his viewing audience. He told me that he was on a preaching mission in British Guiana and would be spending the final two weeks of his four-week tour in the southern interior of that country, visiting some interesting mission activities among the Amerindians. He excitedly spoke of meeting a real pioneer who had contacted tribal members who had no previous contact with the outside world. He then invited me to join him on this adventure into the interior of the country.

Admittedly surprised, I reminded him that I was in the army and didn't take off on whims to some strange part of the world without military orders. As our conversation ended, I agreed to check out the possibility of getting military permission for this kind of adventure. Permission to go to British Guiana, to my surprise, was actually easily secured.

A day or so after my arrival in Georgetown, Guiana, we boarded a C-47, the workhorse for the US Air Force during World War II. Our flight took us over areas that were largely uninhabited forest en route to our first stop at the Paramakatoi mission.

While the missionaries were well-intentioned people, I was turned off by their traditional model of providing mission services. For example, they thought it was important to "clothe the naked Indians" in Western-style clothing largely gathered from discarded clothes sent from US church groups. The missionaries made little effort to learn the native languages. They provided a school that taught subjects in English and provided basic health care. It was apparent to me that mission group had taken from the model that had been used by missionaries for centuries when much of Asia and Africa had been colonized. That focus attempted to build a small compound that remotely resembled the model of a Western community.

After several days in this setting, we flew to an even more remote mission site called Philippi to meet a very interesting and somewhat controversial person named Reverend Clifford Berg. He was the adventurous type who would have survived well on the American frontier. We were in awe as we listened to his harrowing tales of his contacts with Indians who had not previously seen Caucasians.

On one occasion, we observed a school in session, and the entire student body dispersed in a matter of seconds. I have no idea how they got the signal that there were javelins in the area. The male students didn't return for three days.

The mission house sort of resembled a house as we know it. (All the Indians were living in huts.) The house had divided rooms, although the walls were only four or five feet high. The Indians had given the Bergs a baby ocelot as a pet. I watched as this ocelot would crawl on top of the partial petition between the kitchen and living room. When they would fry meat, the ocelot would snarl. I commented to my mission friend that this ocelot still had strong instinctual behavior as it grew, and at some point it might be dangerous. In pages that will follow, I will relate the story of Reverend Berg's attempt to take this ocelot on a plane that I was flying out of this site to another mission site. It's something that I will never forget.

I vividly remember our last evening in this remote site. With no light pollution and no visible moon, it seemed to us that with not a cloud in the sky, every square inch of the visible sky was filled with stars. It's the kind of evening that will remain at some level of awareness in my psyche as long as there is memory. Bob and I spent several hours sitting on a fallen log, reflecting on our experiences. It had been a time when our view of the world had been stretched. I remember that we commented that while we wouldn't trade this experience for anything, at the same time this life wasn't for us.

The next day, we were off to Georgetown, which by comparison to the isolation of the jungle, was a major metropolitan center. We met the Gibbs family and spent a delightful time with them. Their daughter, Patricia, reported that one of her Guianese schoolteachers had insisted that the city of New York comprised the entire United States. When Patricia stated that she was from Michigan, which was in the United States but a considerable distance from New York, her teacher strongly rejected this explanation. After all, she was the teacher, and Patricia was only the student to be taught.

Life quickly returned to normal as I returned to my duties with the 82nd Airborne Division. I had been assigned, at my request, to the 501st Infantry Brigade. While we didn't go on maneuvers as much as we had in Germany, I still worked hard to be seen as the troop's chaplain. In addition to finding ways to be present at different kinds of military exercises, I tried to accept as many invitations as possible to jump with the different units within the brigade. Going out the back door of a plane in flight was a fascinating way to make a pastoral call. When you jump with someone, you have a special bond with that person, a bond that you have with only a few other people in the world. Units eagerly sought to have the unit chaplain accompany the troops on these jumps. Most of the jumpers were still teenagers and would find a measure of assurance to have their chaplain "go out the back door" of the plane with them.

I was deeply troubled by one episode that occurred in the unit that I was assigned to. A young second lieutenant had been asked to plan a party for our unit. Trying to be creative, he had several parachutes cut up and made into a canopy large enough to accommodate all the officers of unit, obviously in an outdoor location where the party was to take place. I heard our commanding officer commend the lieutenant for his creativity in planning this event.

A few days later, the inspector general's office heard about the parachutes that had been used in this manner. Legal charges were preferred against the lieutenant for destruction of government property. No one stood up for the lieutenant—not the commanding officer, not me, not any other officer. I didn't hear what ultimately happened to this young, inexperienced lieutenant, who at this moment was defenseless. I felt a deep sense of shame that I didn't confront our colonel to tell him that we all were somehow involved in his well-intentioned but mistaken behavior. I was surprised and disappointed that the colonel didn't support the young officer in his command.

Something similar occurred in a place called Mai Lai, but the consequences were much more serious and will forever be a black mark on our military history. As I remember the Mai Lai tragedy, only one junior officer by the name of Lieutenant Kelly was convicted. He took the brunt for a seriously flawed military operation that occurred on that terrible day in Vietnam. In my view, a junior officer who apparently blindly followed what he thought were orders from superior officers became the sacrificial lamb for senior officers who also bore responsibility for this tragedy.

When we returned home, both Bob and I assumed that the experience of the interior jungles was a thing of the past and we would pick up from where we had left off. That's not the way it happened. While neither of us were taken with the old, simplistic mission model that attempted to dress those who were viewed as "naked" in Western clothes and teach them Western ways of religious behavior, these missionaries were essentially good people who were carrying out their mission at considerable personal sacrifice. We enjoyed their company and especially admired the pioneer spirit of Reverend Berg. Still, we were haunted for months following our experiences there when we returned to live in the usual ways of doing things.

We were certainly aware of the criticism of some anthropologists, who, in my view, would fit the description of a hardline fundamentalist, only in their field of anthropology. They viewed any force that disrupted the life style of Indians as damaging. They included missionaries who, often enough, deserved their criticism. On the other hand, we had learned of how badly the Indians had been used when maverick gold and diamond miners had blatantly taken advantage of native people. While the traditional missionary was often blind to the cultural implications of rites, ceremonies, and activities, they mostly tended to follow through on their commitments for a number of years. Other groups, who had the accumulation of wealth as a major preoccupation, were both insensitive to the cultural values of native people as well as outright destructive in their interactions with the Indians and left when it was no longer profitable for them to stay.

Perhaps I was too sensitive to some of the limiting aspects of my developmental years. One of the issues that kept gnawing at me was that the Indians who grew up in the Indian environment had no choice but to follow their elders. While their culture had so many things to commend it, there were also significant restrictions. I felt strongly that every Indian child deserved the chance to learn the power of the written language as well as strategies of survival that went beyond the skills of hunting and gathering.

In the months after our return to the States, Bob Price and I contacted each other frequently. Both of us had been unable to shake the experience that had impacted us in ways that went beyond that which we had been conscious of during our visit. We began to dream of contacting Indians that hadn't had previous contact with the outside world, but not within the model of the denomination of which we had been a part and certainly not as career missionaries.

Occasionally, I had given passing thought of leaving the military to enroll in a graduate program in psychology. However, I was enjoying my duties as a military chaplain and was receiving the kind of feedback from my commanders that made it comfortable to remain in this role.

From every point of logic, it made no sense to leave the military to pursue a wild dream; it was downright foolish. Undertaking this task when having responsibilities for a wife and two young children seemed a bit irresponsible. Still, we were haunted by the intriguing challenge of contacting Indians who had never had contact with the outside world.

Bob and his wife, Flo, made a visit to our home at Fort Bragg, and we followed by making a visit to his home near Philadelphia. We tried to anticipate the barriers that we would encounter. There were many. Actually many of the obstacles that we anticipated didn't materialize, and many that we hadn't thought of caught us by surprise. It was in the wee hours, after months of struggle, that we decided to go for it. The pact was sealed. I would leave active duty. Both Bob and I would learn to fly.

Leaving the military was a big step. I simply assumed that leaving active duty was essentially the end of my military experiences. Actually, I was to spend thirty exciting years as a reservist. I never realized the role that the military reserves would play. More about that later.

While I was committed to go on a mission project to contact Indians who had no previous contact with the outside world, I was also determined to go to graduate school. I had a window of three years after leaving active duty to receive the GI bill. The decision was made to organize the expeditions to contact these Indians and then organize or arrange for medical, educational, and agricultural services during our time there. Assuming that we were successful, we would attempt to find a mission group that we considered to be most competent, regardless of denomination, and turn over the long-term project to them after we had completed the groundwork.

I had begun to realize that I could no longer stay within the restricted bounds of the denomination in which I had been ordained and be true to my conscience. The Pilgrim Holiness Church saw themselves as followers of John Wesley but generally felt that the Methodist Church had lost its biblical moorings. The theological issue that troubled me was referred to as the doctrine of entire sanctification, also known as the second work of grace. This church believed that following conversion, this second work of grace removed the very root of sin from the life of the believer, which in turn empowered the believer, according to this theological tenet, to live above sin.

Beyond that, I thought it a bit ridiculous that jewelry was considered worldly adornment and that even married couples were not allowed to wear wedding rings. Theaters, including movie theaters, were also considered off limits, although as television became increasingly common, this rule became more difficult to enforce. Ladies were not allowed to wear makeup. I realized that in twenty-five years, many of these rules would fall by the wayside. Meanwhile, I felt that I could no longer represent this kind of position with integrity.

I knew that I had to leave but had no clear idea which group I wanted to join. Bob Price, whose father was a pastor in the Pilgrim Holiness Church, was leaning toward the Baptist tradition, but this wasn't a good fit for me. When I was with Baptist friends, I tried to speak their theological language, but for me it was awkward and inauthentic.

Even though I was now committed to leaving active military service, I still needed to be endorsed by a denomination as a military reservist. I had no clear idea of what future denominational alliance I would be making. I didn't yet feel clear about becoming part of a mainline denomination. My explorations of more conservative religious groups did not prove satisfying. I perceived that they held many of the same kind of theological ideologies that I was attempting to leave.

As it turned out, I kept my official denominational affiliation with the Pilgrim Holiness Church, which later merged with the Wesleyan Methodist Church, until 1964. We met with this denomination and let them know of our plans to go to South America. If Bob's father had not helped in our effort, we likely would have been excommunicated from the Pilgrim Holiness Church.

29

Learning to Fly

As soon as the commitment to leave active military duty and go to South America had been made in the spring of 1958, I enrolled in a local flight school in Fayetteville, North Carolina. Initially, I was very apprehensive sitting in the pilot's seat with the instructor directly behind me. During the first few lessons, my eyes were glued to the controls. I didn't know where we were in the air. On one occasion, the instructor cut the throttle and announced a simulated forced landing.

"Where are you going to land?" he asked.

Taking my eyes off the instrument panel and looking out the window for the first time during this flight, I pointed to a field that I saw below. It was a little embarrassing when the instructor laughingly told me that we were directly over the airport.

The fear of heights still nagged me, even though I had learned to exit from an airplane with ease. After the fifth or sixth lesson, I asked the pilot when he was going to allow me to fly solo. It was my way of asking for feedback. I expected that he would say in five or six additional hours of training. I panicked when he stated that he almost "soloed" me that day.

The next lesson or so, when we were at the beginning of the runway after having taken off once, the instructor got out of the plane and told me to go for it while he waited for me. Every pilot will remember his or her first solo takeoff. My logbook indicates that I took the solo flight on July 19, 1958. It was an awesome moment.

The funds available to both Bob and me were very limited. We did sense the need to purchase an airplane. A plane would give us some credibility to our friends, who understandably had questions about the viability of our dreams or who questioned whether we were indeed serious about our intentions. We found a new Piper Super Club with a 150-horsepower engine that also had tandem wheels, a feature that would prove invaluable in the days that followed. The total price was about $7,000. Leta and I had managed to save several thousand dollars in bonds. Without hesitation, she concurred with the idea of cashing in these bonds to make the down payment on the plane. Brave, given we had no regular income since leaving the military. This purchase gave us an opportunity to get accustomed to our plane.

Part 5

An Irrational Choice That Changed Our Lives

30

It's a Go!

I had chosen to leave active duty on October 1, 1958. I managed to get the required sixty-five parachute jumps to qualify for Jump Master wings. However, I didn't think I should use my time away from my chaplain duties to go through the necessary jumpmaster's school, a decision that I came to regret. My work ethic got in the way. My later attempts to go through jumpmaster's school as a re-servist were never realized.

When my commander learned of my decision to leave active duty, he stated that he felt that it was my duty to stay with the troops. He was complimentary in his evaluation of my work in the 501st Battle Group of the 82nd Airborne Division.

As I was going through the processing procedures to leave, I met a young captain who had fourteen years of active duty. I asked him a question that reflected some of my doubts about the decision I was making and asked why he was leaving with only six years left for retirement.

He shared his story in a moving way. He stated that he had grown up in Eastern Europe and that in his childhood his family had titles of nobility. "Our servants were people whose children and grandchildren served our family. These attentive people anticipated our every need. We had never learned to take care of ourselves."

Then their fortunes changed. Communism took over. He said

that his family, in an effort to preserve what they had, stayed too long. They barely escaped with their lives when they left. They were fortunate to make it to a refugee camp alive. They lived there for several years before going to New York City. They had lost everything. Even though provision for their basic needs existed at the refugee camp, their world had been turned upside down. None of his family spoke the English language when they arrived in the United States. They lived their daily lives in this new environment on the edge of survival. He was then a teenager and adapted more quickly than his parents did. When he reached military age, he enlisted in part because of the promise of US citizenship if he joined the army. He would also be receiving a small but reliable salary. He had done well in the military and eventually went through Officer's Candidate School.

He ended his story by saying, "I learned a long time ago that there is no such thing as security." His story touched me deeply and seemed to validate my action of being willing to go with my dreams rather than opting out because staying was the more secure thing to do. From a practical viewpoint, our decision to go on this venture made no sense at all. With a young family of two young children and no visible means of support, this action may have seemed to many to border on the bizarre.

We temporarily moved into the basement of Bob and Flo Price's home in Media, Pennsylvania. When you live the structured life of a soldier, it is awkward to try to schedule your life around tasks that often seem nebulous. We tried to interest people in helping us carry out this mission that to most seemed farfetched. It was a formidable task.

I went with Bob to meet a family he knew who had healthy financial assets. There was a ten-year-old black child in the home of this Caucasian lady when we arrived. Bob had told her of my military background. Thinking that this child would be impressed, she said to him, "This man here has jumped out of an airplane sixty-five times."

The child eyed me rather skeptically and then commented, "Huh, I bet he had a parachute."

Leave it to a child to put an adult in their place.

One Sunday, we went to hear Dr. Donald Barnhouse, the pastor of a well-known Presbyterian church in Philadelphia, make a comment in his sermon that was to leave a significant impact on me. Speaking of the creation story, he said that it didn't matter to him if the Lord made the world in seven seconds, seven days, seven weeks, or seven billion years. The important thing for him was to acknowledge the Creator who was at the heart of creation. Having grown up and been educated in a tradition that held a literal view of the bible, this was a breath of fresh air for me. He further added that we never needed to be afraid of truth because God was the author of truth. I felt such a relief that one didn't have to feel that their faith was threatened by scientific evidence. It gave me a rationale for some of the theological perceptions that were beginning to develop in me that would not have been acceptable to the tradition that I had known.

The first real test of cross-country flying involved a flight from West Chester, near Philadelphia, to Michigan. A weather system was moving from west to east. I managed to get to some little town in Ohio when visibility from line of sight flying was too low. I waited out this system for several days while Bob anxiously awaited my arrival in Battle Creek, Michigan. When I finally did make it to Michigan, I landed the airplane in a field next to the home where Leta had grown up. Her family hadn't expected my arrival, and having an airplane in the field next to their farmhouse elicited considerable interest.

On another occasion when flying to Nebraska, I landed on a grass landing strip in Illinois. The snow on the strip was melting. It never occurred to me that my wet tandem wheels could lock into position because of ice that would form while I was in the air. When I landed on the runway, I had to hit a hard right rudder, and the plane was difficult to taxi to the terminal. I managed to get the wheel that froze solid off the runway and skid it along the ice that had accumulated alongside of the runway.

On another cross-country flight, I was near Chicago and was flying at an altitude somewhere around five thousand or six thousand feet when the windshield began to frost over. Only a very small portion of the lower left-hand corner of the windshield allowed any visibility. Since this was a line of sight flight, I became very apprehensive. Just before I lost total visibility from this frost-covered windshield, it began to clear up. To this day, I have no idea of what caused the plane's windshield to frost up or why the frost began to spontaneously clear.

On still another flight in the Midwest, the weather had been marginal for the kind of flying I was doing. I had been dodging heavy clouds, and as a result, my compass headings kept changing. My watch showed I should have soon been approaching the airport at Champaign, Illinois, where I intended to refuel. In a few minutes, I spotted a runway located on the southeast corner of town. Convinced that I had reached my destination, I folded my map and prepared to land. Since I didn't have a radio on board, I looked for the green light from the tower that would give me permission to land. It had been my experience that sometimes the light from the tower was slow in coming and sometimes didn't come at all. I stayed on course for landing. The expected light from the tower never came. Just as I was about to touch down, I could see military aircraft parked off to my right side. I had inadvertently made an illegal landing at Chanute Air Force Base. It turned out that Chanute was only a few miles away from Champaign.

The personnel at Chanute Air Force Base got quite a kick out of the fact that this "sky pilot" was lost. (A chaplain was often referred to as a sky pilot.) I spent the next hour or so signing papers that would allow me to exit from Chanute field. I was more than a little bit embarrassed.

Meanwhile, I had taken the written portion of the examination for a private pilot's rating. I thought I had passed easily. Before getting the results, I told Bob that I had dreamed that I had flunked the exam. The dream turned out to be prophetic. If one answered an earlier question in the wrong way, it influenced all the answers that would follow. I did get the hang of it the second time around.

I had stopped by to see another friend who had been one of the original members of the Owosso College quartet. Edwin Doehring was then a physician in Mount Clemens, Michigan, in the Detroit area. While visiting him, I went to a nearby small town, Romeo, where a rated instructor put me through the paces for my private flying lesson. I made a number of touch-and-go landings. When I started the aerial maneuvers, there was plenty of daylight. We kept going through the paces until dark. It was then an unlighted field, and the instructor had me land in total darkness. In the early evening darkness, we could see until we were about a hundred feet from the ground. From there, it was flying blind. I found some comfort in that the instructor knew the area. At the end of this ordeal, he signed off on my private pilot's license. My flight log indicates that the date was January 7, 1959.

Leta rode without hesitation as a passenger after I was officially licensed. Our daughter, Linda, who was probably nine years old when she first rode as a passenger, enjoyed the movement of the airplane and would ask me to put the plane in a steep turn. Our son Bob, who was approximately six years old, wasn't as enthusiastic as his sister about flying. I should have asked his permission before going into a stall maneuver. He turned ashen. However unintentional, I'm afraid that I am the cause of his lifelong uneasiness about flying.

When I invited my mother to go on a flight with me, she accepted only because she didn't know how to say no to her son. It was her first airplane ride. She was obviously mortified. I flew around the farm and would put the plane into a slight turn for her to get a better view. Her response was to lean in the opposite direction of the turn. She didn't want the plane to tip over. I loved her loyalty in accepting my invitation to fly with me.

Later, I had an opportunity to fly to Columbus, Ohio, to speak at the church where Reverend William Gilkerson was the pastor. Bill had been a classmate of mine at Owosso College. He arranged for me to give Sunday school kids from his congregation airplane rides on Saturday afternoon. I probably made a dozen flights with these youngsters aboard.

The following day I was invited to give a sermon to his congregation and tell them about our plans to go to South America. I said that the only thing delaying us was the fact that the plane was not yet fully paid for. After the service, a quiet gentleman asked me how much we still owed for the plane. I told him that a final payment of $2,000 was still needed. After I gave him this information, he disappeared. To my surprise, he showed up at the parsonage where I was staying with a check for $2,000. He instructed me not to cash this check for five days because he needed to get the funds to cover this amount in his bank account. My flight log indicates that I had flown to Columbus, Ohio, on February 15, 1959.

31

Time to Go

Given that I had stated that the primary thing preventing us from leaving for our mission was the amount of money we owed on the plane, I begin to feel a certain urgency to get on with our mission now that the plane was paid for. Even though we didn't owe anything on the plane, we still needed funds for the trip to Surinam. These funds simply had not been forthcoming. One day I said to Bob that it was time to leave. He agreed but quickly added that there was no money in our treasury. We had set up a nonprofit tax-exempt organization that was known as Door to Life Ministries. We were in a catch-22: we needed money to promote our cause, but funds were simply not available to demonstrate what we were about.

I proposed that we fly to Miami. En route, we would see several friends. We would say nothing about the need for money. I added that we would return to Philadelphia if we didn't have $500 in our pockets by the time we reached Miami. Bob agreed. Our cash on hand was about $25 when we announced that we were on our way to Surinam, South America.

We said good-bye to our wives and children. We each had two children as we began this venture of faith. Our first stop was to see Joe Uhrig, who was then the pastor of the Little Country Church located in Alexandria, Virginia. When we told him that we were on the way to South America, he invited us to speak at his church. He added that they rarely had church services on Friday evening, but that evening a church service was scheduled. An offering for our cause was gratefully received.

Next, we flew to a Richmond, Virginia, church, where Art Taylor, our former quartet member, was the pastor. He came to the airport to meet us, and with great reluctance, he accepted a ride in our plane. He hadn't been too impressed when Bob had bounced the plane on the runway several times before making a safe landing. He had a hard time believing that we had actually been awarded our private pilot's licenses. Art had us speak to his congregation on Sunday and another free-will offering was taken for our cause.

The next stop was to visit friends that I had left a few months earlier at Fort Bragg. Again, while we told our friends that we were en route to South America, at no time we did mention our need for funds. We would make a decision in Miami whether we would go or not.

From there, we stopped to see a former classmate, the Reverend George Farah, and his congregation at Troy, North Carolina. Our next stop was in Orlando, Florida, to visit with another classmate, Reverend James Kreider. Our final stop was in Hollywood, Florida, where we met another former classmate, Reverend Gene Osborne. He and his wife entertained us and invited us to speak at the church that he was serving as pastor.

We had left Philadelphia ten days earlier. When we counted the donations that we had received that Sunday evening in Hollywood, Florida, the total proved to be $503. The next day, we were to fly our tiny Piper Super Club over the ocean. Neither Bob nor I had yet flown over any significant body of water. To say that we were apprehensive is an understatement.

And we had plenty of reason to be apprehensive. Our navigational equipment was practically nonexistent, and our lack of flying experience, especially over water, was cause for concern.

Before flying over the water, we purchased a twenty-gallon gas tank that we put in the baggage area just behind the rear seat of the plane in case we ran short of gas. A wobble pump was installed, leading from this tank to one of the gas tanks, allowing us to pump gas into the tank while in flight. This decision turned out to be critical.

As we were filing our flight plan at the Broward International Airport, the person at the control tower told us to stay at least three miles from the coastline of Haiti, adding that we would be shot down if we got inside those limits. Papa Doc was still the heavy-handed dictator. This warning didn't do anything to quiet our apprehension.

We headed for Nassau for a refueling stop. Actually, we were putting the twenty gallons of gas in the extra tank in the cabin. (Federal Aviation Authority rules did not allow a gas tank filled with gas inside the cabin while in the United States.) After refueling, we taxied to a holding position just off the takeoff runway. We noticed a commercial airliner coming in, so we waited in our holding position and didn't call the tower to announce that we were ready for takeoff. When the airliner was perilously close to the runway, we received a frantic call from the tower. The man with a strong British dialect shouted, "N9362D, you are cleared for immediate takeoff, repeat, immediate takeoff!" With that startling announcement ringing in my ears, I pushed full throttle and hit a hard right rudder because I was still at a forty-five-degree angle from the runway. Even though we were heavily loaded, the power of the engine took us in the air in just a few hundred feet with the four-engine passenger plane landing behind us as we took off. Bob vividly remembers this event but insists that it took place at San Juan International Airport. We had some fun telling each other that the other's memory was faltering.

We were off to a small island called Great Inagua, located just an hour or so by plane off the coast of Cuba. It was a four-hour flight from Nassau. Only a few miles in circumference, the only town on the island was called Matthew Town. As we were approaching this tiny island, a rainstorm was moving in. We didn't have many options if this desolate airport hadn't been available to us. We managed to land just minutes before a heavy rain covered the area.

The airport radio station didn't open until 10:00 a.m. We were concerned that there might be a weather system, so we stayed on the island an additional day. We didn't feel that we could wait until 10:00 a.m. to get a weather report, so we left the second day for Puerto Rico without having a report of the winds aloft. We operated under the erroneous assumption that headwinds would be less at a lower attitude. So we flew much of the next five-plus hours at an altitude of three hundred feet. Bob was flying, and I was the navigator.

The coastlines of Cuba, Haiti, and the Dominican Republic were off to our right, about twenty miles or so away. While we could communicate with the tower when we were within a short distance from the tower, the severely limited navigational equipment was next to useless. When we were approaching a radio station that sent out a signal, we could tell only if we were getter closer or farther away from the beacon. It didn't provide any information about which side of that beacon we were located.

When we reached the last peninsula of the Dominican Republic, we would have no other landmarks in our line of flight for several hours. I figured out an azimuth heading that would take us to Puerto Rico. I kept a close eye on the map, even though we had been over water for several hours. I concluded that we needed to make a small correction of five degrees to the right, a rather risky thing to change azimuths with no landmarks in sight. Understandably, Bob, who was piloting the aircraft, resisted. I reasoned that if we were being blown off course to the left of Puerto Rico, there would no landmass in range of our flight capabilities. On the other hand, if we hadn't been blown off course and moved a bit too far to the right, we still could reach land, even if we weren't on a direct course to San Juan. Bob was finally convinced by my logic.

Meanwhile, both gas tanks on the wing of the plane were reading empty. Using the small wobble pump, I pumped the extra gas that we had stored in our baggage compartment into the wing tank. By our estimates, we should have reached land an hour earlier, and we had only enough gas left for one more hour of flying. We were starting to examine the rafts that were stored on board when we spotted land in the distant horizon. What a relief!

We followed the coastline of Puerto Rico. We weren't certain that we would have enough gas to arrive at the airport. When we were fifty miles or so away from the airport, we called the tower and requested a straight-in landing approach. The tower asked why we thought we needed to come straight in, rather than flying the usual pattern. When they learned that our gas supply was nearly exhausted, they kept in constant touch with us.

We were directly over the city of San Juan. It wasn't clear that we had sufficient fuel to make the remaining ten or fifteen miles to the airport.

The tower controller told Bob to look straight down. "You should be directly over a small naval airport."

We did indeed spot the runway. We were instructed to land.

Unfortunately, the naval station didn't have a facility for gas for civilian aircraft. We were given enough gas to get us to San Juan International Airport. It would have been interesting to find out how close to empty we actually were.

After spending the rest of the day in San Juan, we were in the air again. As we were taxiing to the runway in San Juan, we had an interesting conversation with the tower controller, who was commenting on the tandem wheels. It was the kind of casual conversation that one doesn't typically hear from the control tower.

The logbook indicates that the flight from San Juan to Antigua took three and a half hours. When we were near the island of St. Lucia, storm clouds covered most of the island. We considered landing along the beach, but as we approached the island, we noticed there was a small landing strip with a nearby hotel. We landed and waited out the rainstorm and then proceeded to the island of Trinidad, a three-hour flight from St. Lucia.

After spending the night in Trinidad, we proceeded to Atkinson Airfield in Georgetown, British Guiana (now called Guyana, after the country's independence from Britain). We were surprised to learn upon landing that we were required to make a large payment that was to be returned to us on our departure. We were further surprised to find that officials from the Pilgrim Holiness Church thought we had come to usurp one of their church missions. This faulty perception apparently occurred when we had met with the head of the foreign mission department to tell them that we were planning to get involved in South America, months before we had left the United States. Our purpose was to be up front with our intentions and to express the wish that we would be able to work cooperatively while not working for them.

The assistant secretary of foreign missions was a classmate by the name of Reverend Edward Jones. He happened to be at the airport at the time we arrived. He insisted that he had not been a part of this action and contacted the airport authorities to release the ban. We later learned that someone in the foreign missions department in Indianapolis had intended to have us banned from entering the country. This group hadn't realized that we had no intentions of locating in British Guiana but in the neighboring country of Surinam.

It was ironic that the Pilgrim Holiness Church mission plane had been confiscated that very day in an interior border town in Brazil. Their missionaries were in fact stranded until other flying arrangements could be made. In line with our earlier offer months before, we agreed to delay our journey to Surinam to fly emergency flights to their missions.

My logbook indicates that we flew to Paramakatoi on May 8, 1959, and then to Philippi on May 10, 1959. These were the mission stations that we had visited while Bob was on a preaching mission and I was still in the 82nd Airborne Division.

En route, we had flown over Kaeiteur Falls. While it is not a large body of water, its fall is greater than New York's Niagara Falls and the African Victoria Falls combined. There is a legend that in former times when a male Indian was no longer able to fulfill his responsibilities in the community because of the limitations of age, he would gather his clan to this spot, bid farewell, and climb into his canoe to go over these falls.

When we visited, it was time for Reverend Clifton Berg to go on furlough. I was going to fly him from the more remote mission of Philippi. The Indians had given him a baby ocelot whose mother had been killed. This ocelot responded in some ways like a kitten.

However, when meat was frying in the kitchen, it would snarl as it walked on the wall partitions that were only as high as our heads. Reverend Berg had decided to take this ocelot to the more populated mission station at Paramakatoi. He had the ocelot in a small woven basket.

The airstrip was a primitive short airstrip, and the ground was soft and unstable. On my first attempt at takeoff, I didn't like the feel of the takeoff attempt, so I cut the throttle to make another attempt. This time, I managed to get the plane off the ground just before coming to the end of the runway. The plane's ground speed was fairly slow, and there wasn't much room for error. Just at this critical point, the ocelot got out of its basket and was jumping around the cockpit in sheer terror. At one point, it was in the inside windshield area. I was fortunate enough to keep my concentration on takeoff while Reverend Berg finally managed to recapture the animal and put it back in the basket. As we gained altitude and were able to reduce power, the ocelot became calmer.

The time that we spent in British Guiana will always remain an important part of my memories. We couldn't have been received more elegantly than we were by the Gibbs family, who lived and worked in Georgetown. (In recent years, I learned that both Fred and Donna Gibbs had passed away. They were the salt-of-the-earth kind of folks.) This six-week delay hadn't been in our plans, but it proved to be a special part of our time in South America.

At one point during our six weeks of flying emergency flights in British Guiana, we ended up flying to visit the Wai Wai. Here, we were to meet Claude Leavitt, a missionary linguist who was to play a significant role in our activities in Surinam. While this group was a very conservative one, they did appreciate maintaining Indian cultural rituals and rites they saw as harmless. When I landed at the Wai Wai mission station, I was taken aback to see that all the women were bare from the waist up. I wasn't sure how to react. It was as if I wasn't supposed to be looking. In a few hours, seeing women's breasts seemed as natural as seeing their hands or face. I couldn't help but remember my experience in Tripoli, where I had seen women totally covered with the exception of one eye. I recognized how differently modesty is defined by one culture from another.

My logbook indicates that on May 26, 1959, I spent the day visiting Indian homes and observing their craft skills. Later that afternoon, we were paddling on very swift rivers in a canoe. We came near the heavy underbrush on the river's bank when Claude Leavitt spotted a hornet's nest. I'm not sure why he did what he did. He scooped up water with his hands and threw it on the hornet's nest. The logbook indicates that I was stung nearly thirty times. Even though I wasn't a good swimmer, I dove out of the boat in the fast-moving river. I managed to awkwardly swim to shore some distance downstream.

The log indicates that we spent a week with the Wai Wai Indians in the village of Gunoshin. We observed how homes were built, went on hunting trips, witnessed the Indians making a temporary shelter during a rainstorm, and were present at a ceremony commissioning the men of the village to go on a hunt to get food for a special festival they were about to celebrate.

While these Christian missionaries, in my view, had a very conservative and narrow theological outlook, they deeply cared about the material and spiritual welfare of the Indians they sought to serve. They tried to be sensitive to the Wai Wai tribal cultural perspective and make a real attempt to preserve their traditions. If, in their view, some ritual had negative consequences, they tried to supplement this ritual with another that would contribute to the cohesiveness of the tribe. These missionaries spent the majority of their adult lives with few material rewards to make significant contributions, particularly in the area of reducing unwritten languages to writing as well as contributions in the area of health and agriculture. I admire them and their commitment to their work and faith.

As I read my short diary notes from this period, I realize now how hard I tried to fit into their theological perspective. I also see from the perspective of forty years later that I was searching for a theological direction. I was very aware that my original denomination was not a good fit for me. I was to discover in time that the religious traditions represented by these missionaries that I continue to respect to this date, was not the direction I needed to go. To find a religious tradition I could follow in good faith proved a rather painful and lonely search.

32

Surinam at Last

We left for Paramaribo, the capitol city of Surinam, on June 15, 1959. Bob and I felt humbled and honored that Reverend Clifton Berg presented us with a gift of a hundred dollars just as we were leaving. His missionary salary must have been close to nothing. More than any person, Reverend Berg had been our inspirational model. Without this model, we might never have undertaken this project that seemed so foolhardy to many of our friends and colleagues.

We landed at the Zanderij International Airport, a ten-thousand-foot strip that had been built by the US military in World War II. It was from this airport that military planes would fly to Africa. We were told that the twenty-five-mile road into Paramaribo had been carved out of the jungles by the fires of the jelly gas bombs dropped by the US military during this time.

After a friendly reception by the immigration folks at Zanderij, we flew the twenty-five miles to the Zorg en Hoop airstrip on the edge of Paramaribo just before sundown. We checked in at the Lashley Hotel, primarily because of its modest prices. We had no idea that the proprietor, Miss Lashley, was the sister of one of the ministers of government. While her hotel was modest, important government officials stayed here. The meals were included with the price of the room. We were assigned to a table and told the hour the meals would be served. It was clearly expected that you be at the preassigned table at the designated time. Tea was served every afternoon at 4:00 p.m.

In our first weeks there, we were at loss as to how to spend our time. We had filed an application to work with the Indians, but that application was lost in the maze of bureaucracy. We visited everyone we thought might be even remotely helpful. We met with a Dr. Linahos, who was the director of an antimalarial campaign, and we met with the president of the congress, Mr. Kraag. We also met the director of the civil aviation program. All were cordial but unhelpful.

We had understood that various mission groups had sought permission to work with the Indians of the Interior but all of their applications had been denied, purportedly on the recommendations of the two major religious groups in the country. The Moravians and the Roman Catholic churches were nearly equal in strength and each denomination had about the same number of representatives who were members of government. The official position of these two religious groups was that providing religious coverage to the Indians of the interior was their responsibility. Given this history, Bob and I attempted to keep a low profile. However it is fairly easy for interested locals in a city of 150,000 inhabitants to keep track of us.

One day, Bob and I were in the center of the city, and a news reporter from the major paper in town found and confronted us. He wanted to find out who we were and what we were about. We thought that our project was going to be derailed right there. Incidentally, the head of the newspaper was a political opponent of the prime minister and took every opportunity he could to publish a story to make the prime minister look bad. This owner–editor saw himself as an advocate of the interior Indians.

We went into the interview thinking that this might be the end of the line. We tried to portray ourselves as persons who were interested in the educational, agricultural, and medical needs of the Indian people. When he asked what denomination we represented, we stated that we were nondenominational. When the story came out in the newspaper, in the Dutch language, of course, the news reporter pictured us as a philanthropic group from no special religion. Our friend, Reverend Walter Jackson, interpreted the article for us as he grinned from ear to ear. Indicating that we were nondenominational saved us from the typical interference from the two major religious denominations.

Two Dutch government officials, who had worked in Indonesia, were assigned to our table at the Lashley Hotel. They seemed disinterested in engaging in conversation. One evening, while trying to get a conversation going, I spoke to the person sitting next to me. His name was Mr. DeGroot. He worked in the justice department. I invited him to fly with us to get a look at the city of Paramaribo.

His response was, "I'm not a bit interested."

His companion immediately spoke up and said that he would be interested in such a plane ride. Bob took him in the plane for an aerial view of the city the next day. When he returned to the dinner table that evening, he was animated in his description of how much he had enjoyed the flight. Mr. DeGroot then causally mentioned that he might be interested in such a flight after all.

The next day, Mr. DeGroot came loaded with elaborate camera equipment and seemed to thoroughly enjoy his experience of his flight over the city of Paramaribo. At the table that evening, he said, "Tell me why you are here again."

We shared the story that we had tried to share earlier. His response was that he would attempt to find out what had happened to our application. He promised to assist us in any way that he could.

One afternoon, Mr. DeGroot stated that the original reaction to our request had been negative. To our surprise, he stated that the local church officials had had no objections, and the report from the Dutch Consulate in Philadelphia had been favorable. He discovered that a letter had been sent to officials in British Guiana, inquiring about our involvement there. We had mentioned on our application that we had flown emergency flights there.

On the strength of that information and Mr. DeGroot's recommendation, Bob flew to Georgetown, attempting to track down their response. I received a telegram from Bob when he was in British Guiana that no one there in government circles had known about a request from the Surinam government regarding our activities. A note in the diary dated June 26 states that the communication was strictly top-level, from the Prime Minister to Dr. Jaban, British Guiana's prime minister.

Bob ended up getting some very positive letters of recommendation from various British Guiana government officials about the emergency flights that we had provided for the mission groups there. Without Mr. DeGroot's inside help, it is doubtful whether our application would have been approved.

In the meantime, we met Mrs. Van Konten, who worked at the US embassy. She invited us to attend church services at the West Indies mission. There we met a young missionary couple: Walt and Marge Jackson. Marge's parents had been missionaries in China. At one point, when Marge was still a young student in a school for missionary children, the entire student body became Chinese prisoners of war. Both Walt and Marge seemed to be full of life and received us generously.

33

Miracles Do Happen

One evening, Mr. DeGroot said that he met with the prime minister's secretary, who really functioned like a chief of staff. Mr. De-Groot had served with him in Indonesia. He informed Mr. DeGroot that our application was going to be approved. He added, however, that as a condition of approval, Mr. DeGroot had to draw up some restrictions.

He took us into his room and looked at the map of Surinam. He asked, "What kind of restrictions would you like to have?"

We suggested that we be restricted to working in the southern half of the country, a restriction that Mr. DeGroot cheerfully added to his report. This report became part of the charter for Door to Life Missions, a charter that still remains in effect. Shortly after the charter was drawn and final approvals given, we had a chance to meet with the prime minister. My log indicates that it was a thirty-minute, very friendly visit that took place on July 27, 1959.

With that battle won, we moved out of the Lashley Hotel to a small house in a Hindustani community near the Zorg en Hoop Airport. The log indicates that the move occurred on July 3, 1959. A parenthetical remark indicates that the "house was small but comfortable in spite of the goats." Most of the folks here spoke one of the dialects of the Hindustani language; for some of the older residents, it was the only language they understood. Furniture was sparse, even by the standards of the community. We did have a small kerosene stove.

I went to purchase some matches at a very small neighborhood store that had almost nothing on the shelves. The proprietor happened to be Oriental. While I understood or spoke very little Dutch, I was certain that no one spoke Dutch here. Trying to speak in English would be fruitless. I tried to explain by using gestures that I needed matches. (Incidentally, the Dutch word for a match is "Lucifer.") I acted out striking the wall and using every other gesture I could think of that would resemble striking a match. The manager stared at me intently with the blankest look on his face. After ten minutes or so, he asked in excellent English if I needed matches. Was there egg on my face or what?

On the Fourth of July, the day after this move, we were invited to attend a party at the US consulate's home. We got to meet some of the movers and shakers of the community.

A young Hindustani man, who worked at the Zorg en Hoop Airport, had a wonderful smile and eagerly did everything possible to serve us. Without our asking, he would wash our plane and then refuse our attempts to tip him. One day I asked him if he had visited the United States.

His eyes lit up as he extolled the wonders of this faraway country, but then a cloud covered his exuberance. "It will never be possible for me to go."

I then learned that the farthest from the city he had ever been was to the international airport, twenty-five miles away. I recognized that so much of what happens to us is influenced by an accident of birth and remembered that one of the options that my ancestors may have seriously considered was to go to India. Instead, they chose the United States, apparently because of the land grant opportunities. My history would have been dramatically different had my ancestors chosen an option other than the United States.

We stayed in this place a short time until we had the opportunity to rent a larger home that would accommodate Leta and the children when they arrived. Our home was located at 26 Commewijnestraat, about two blocks from the Zorg en Hoop Airport.

We could see and hear the planes land or take off, depending on which way the wind was blowing. It was also near an elementary school, where Linda and Bob would be enrolling. It would be our home until we returned to the States. Our landlords were of Hindustani descent. It was a nice suburban area. The house was rather well built but in poor repair. One of neighbors was from the United States; another was Mr. DeGroot, who had moved from the hotel to be our next-door neighbor. It was to be our home for over a year. (Linda, her three children, and I dropped by to visit our former home forty or so years after we had moved back to the States. The current resident graciously invited us into the living room to reminisce about some of the events that had powerfully shaped our lives.)

Paramaribo was very much a third-world city. There were actually few cars, but that situation was changing fast. It seemed that everyone was learning to drive at the same time. I was somewhat amused to see an East Indian young man taking driver's lessons. There were four people in the front seat and at least that many in the back. The instructor was seated next to the driver. Apparently, taking driving lessons was an event to be shared with friends. (When we returned to Paramaribo for a brief visit in 2006, there were traffic jams everywhere. Cars were for sale at car lots. How things had changed!)

34

An Unexpected Invitation

A short time after we had received word that our application to contact the Indians of the interior would be approved, the director of aviation asked if they could use our plane to make some landings in the interior, where no airstrips currently existed. Our quick response was negative, but we added that we would be glad to make these landings with our airplane. An informal alliance was quickly formed between the Surinam government and us. While we would not receive any payment per se for our services, and we did not ask for any kind of reimbursement, the Surinam government would purchase the fuel for our cooperative work. From that time forward, we had access to their gas supply. It was a highly beneficial arrangement to all. With our limited budget, it would have been difficult to purchase the needed gas. On the other hand, our flying greatly aided the Surinam government in finding out what resources might be available in their unexplored interior. I remember one Surinam government official telling me that only five expeditions had ever reached their southern border in their history, the first being in 1899.

The first place that we would go as part of this new agreement was near a mountain resembling a table. Hence it was called Tafelberg or Table Mountain. Tafelberg became the name of the airstrip. Actually, one pilot had landed at this site before, but it was not developed in any sense of the word. Our first task was to make the Tafelberg landing strip accessible for planes not equipped for a rough, short-field landing. Located about ninety miles from Paramaribo, this strip would be instrumental for further explorations and landings in the interior. After this initial landing, Bob returned to pick up a helper provided by the Surinam government while I stayed and started to work on the airstrip.

This site didn't have the tall trees of the rainforest. Apparently, the soil in this area only supported small trees and brush, and the tall trees of the rainforest were only a short distance away. Several years before, someone had erected a little thatched shelter with an opening so small one had to crawl in. Bob returned before the day was over with the Surinam worker.

Surinam Airways dropped supplies by air that we would need, including tools and food. They also dropped a rather complicated incandescent lantern. Bob is more mechanical than I am. He was intrigued with the challenge of getting the lantern to function. On our first evening there, a full moon was shining. It was spectacular. I told Bob that it would be sacrilegious to have an artificial light with such a breathtaking view of the moon silhouetting Table Mountain. My comment didn't detour him from his preoccupation.

Mildly irritated, I walked up a small incline about a hundred yards away from our campsite and sat on a rock, taking in the awesome beauty of the evening. It was an evening to reflect and allow the stream of thought to flow as it would. I hadn't seen my family in six months, so of course they were much in my thoughts that evening. Suddenly, I became aware of a purring sound and noticed something that resembled a cat. Instinctively, I reached out to pet it. Then it dawned on me that there were no tame cats here. I jumped to my feet and stared at what I now recognized was an ocelot. I was afraid that if I ran, it might attack me from the rear. So we stared at each other for what seemed like an eternity. Finally, it slipped away, and I returned to the safety of the now-lit lantern. I later wondered if the ocelot would have allowed me to pet it if I hadn't become startled when we had so unexpectedly met.

We flew a number of flights to Tafelberg, stocking up on supplies that would prove crucial to deeper penetration into the interior. Gasoline was an important item. We would be loaded to the maximum when we had a full tank of gas in that plane plus twenty-five gallons in five-gallon cans in the baggage compartment. The US Federal Aviation Agency would not have allowed us to carry gas in the baggage compartment, but it was the only way to get the needed gas and supplies stockpiled in the interior.

Bob and I took turns flying in these supplies. On one occasion, another plane with official visitors was flying directly above Bob and taking photos of this event. What they didn't realize was that Bob was having an attack of diarrhea. His choice was to fly back to Tafelberg or continue on to Paramaribo. Since he was at the halfway point on the return flight, he decided to continue flying toward Paramaribo. The condition became critical. Bob took an emergency kit that was on the plane, emptied it, and then tried to position the bag under him while continuing to fly. The people in the other plane were taking photos. After Bob had taken care of the problem, he opened the door of the plane and tossed the bag out into space. Unfortunately, the side of the plane was splashed with feces. To add to his embarrassment, I was waiting for him at the airport with a close friend to take her on an airport ride over the city. He parked a considerable distance away so our friend Marge Jackson wouldn't see the plane covered with the remains of his attack of diarrhea. In years to come, Bob had fun embellishing this entertaining story with friends who roared with laughter.

Walt and Marge Jackson had been our good friends while we were waiting for action on our application to work in the country. Walt learned of a Wayanna Indian group living above the village of Maripasoula on the Lawa River on the French Guiana border. Farther south, the Lawa becomes the Marowijne River. Early on, we were able to spend several weeks in their village. Bob and I stayed in a hut that was the guesthouse for visitors from other villages. I awakened one morning to discover an Indian child staring in my face, apparently to see if I had awakened.

We examined the area for a possible airstrip in the Wayanna villages. The trees had been cut back, but heavy underbrush had taken over. It was quite a task to clear this land with only shovels, hoes, rakes, and axes. A number of tree stumps had to be dug out. A cane field was located near the end of what we hoped would be the runway. Arrows were made from the cane material. When we checked with Annapika, the chief, to see if it would be possible to move the cane field, he proposed that we angle the runway at a forty-five-degree angle halfway down the proposed airstrip to save this field, which played a significant role in their hunter–gatherer economy. When we convinced him that we couldn't develop the strip this way, he eventually agreed with our plan to relocate the cane fields, even though it would cause something of a hardship on the village.

The members of the tribe were friendly and typically welcomed us warmly. On one occasion, when we had been gone for ten days, we noticed that somehow the atmosphere was different. While the chief spoke to us, he seemed preoccupied and unavailable. We had observed the witch doctors gathering palm branches for much of the afternoon. While we didn't immediately know the reasons for this behavior until later, we sensed something was in the air.

We did learn that a village teenage girl was unconscious and was barely breathing. We thought that she had a respiratory infection, likely pneumonia. We were unable to pick up her pulse. Bob mixed up some penicillin that we carried in powdered form with water. He estimated the strength of the dose and then administered the shot to her.

When evening fell, an event took place that I had never experienced before in the many nights that I spent in the jungle. There wasn't a single campfire or light of any kind. It was an overcast night, and visibility was essentially zero. The tension in the atmosphere seemed to grow. We weren't able to put a finger on what was going on. The mosquitoes were very thick, and it was totally dark, plus we didn't know what else to do, so we retreated to our hammocks under mosquito netting.

Around eight o'clock in the evening, we heard the palm branches swishing in the hut next to ours. Soon the witch doctor began to chant, and the warriors began to march rhythmically around the hammock of the unconscious girl. Each held a spear in his right hand, pounding it into the ground as he stomped his right foot, grunting when his spear touched the ground. They were in perfect cadence with each other and with the mournful chant of the witch doctor. This ritual probably lasted six or seven hours.

I confess that I barely slept that night. I was aware of the tribe's perception that sickness was caused by evil spirits and by someone putting a spell on the sick person. I fantasized that we could be seen as responsible for her illness. I had read stories where the visitors suspected of causing the spell were killed. Fortunately, the young lady did recover. I'm not sure if their rituals or the penicillin got the credit.

35

A Spectacular Landing at Kayser

Things were now getting underway in earnest. We were laying the groundwork for the expedition to a tribe of Indians who never previously had contact with the outside world. One of the true flying dramas occurred at Kayser Airstrip. There was a very small clearing, less than a thousand feet, located on the slope of a hill. The only feasible approach was to land downhill. We had flown with the barest essentials to keep the weight of the plane as light as possible. We knew that rivers were in the area, so we took only a small amount of water because of weight concerns.

Bob, who was flying on this occasion, made six or seven approaches. We would be near a full-power stall position, which meant that the nose of the plane was elevated to just below the point of stall at full power. Then the plane would be turned sideways until we reached treetop level, with the wings dipped to literally slice through the air. At the last second, we would right the plane and chop the throttle just as we were touching the ground. It was a tricky maneuver at best, but it worked. There was a small tree at the end of our short rollout. Bob managed to ground loop around that tree in the middle of our landing path. We stopped fifty feet from where the forest began. Our tandem wheels likely saved us. The ruts were narrow but deep. I'm not sure that we would have remained upright when we hit these ruts without these dual wheels.

An ex-Polish military pilot, Vincent, who went by the nickname Vicki, was flying overhead. This cover was being provided by Surinam Airways, where Vicki was now employed. He had watched nervously from the air as we made these passes over the airstrip. I can still hear his words over our radio when we finally landed. "Congratalaluchyons!" he kept shouting in his broken English.

Our good friend, Walt Jackson, reported that when Vicki broke the news back in Paramaribo, Surinam's capital city, that a successful landing had been made in the interior, the local radio station broadcast bulletin-type announcements and repeated a number of times that Friesen and Price had made a successful landing in the middle of the jungle. This event also received broad coverage in the local newspapers. In fact, our activities were followed daily in the newspapers for weeks. When we later would be driving through the city, schoolboys would recognize our car and chant "Friesen and Price." For this small country, landing in the interior was big news, and it apparently meant for them that the interior was not the foreboding barrier that most of the residents of the city thought it to be.

When we landed, it was near midday. We had not anticipated the thick ring of brush from the very small clearing to the nearby rainforest. When we tried to use our machetes, we found that the growth was so thick and so high that there was little room to swing them. Because of this lack of leverage, our machetes were next to useless, and it was almost impossible to cut our way through to the nearby forest, where the trees were in excess of a hundred feet high. We worked for four or five hours in the hot and humid afternoon. Working in this environment about two degrees from the equator was exhausting. At the end of the evening, we had only penetrated fifteen feet or so into these heavy thickets. We were limited in how far we could see and were quite unsure how thick the band of this heavy brush extended before the tall trees were located and where it was easy to pass through the underbrush.

We were utterly exhausted and seriously dehydrated when evening came. We hung our hammocks under the wings of the airplane. Our only thoughts were of water. Bob awakened before I did in the early dawn. He noticed that there was dew on the plane. We began to lick the surface of the plane, catching every bit of moisture that we could. We knew that the sun would soon dry the dew. We should have used a shirt or other clothing to soak up the moisture. We instead used a chamois that we had used to filter out the moisture of the gas that we put into the airplane. Unfortunately, the vapors of the gasoline trapped in the chamois made the small amount of water that we managed to collect undrinkable. We tried without success to convert this precious water into coffee. The gas vapors were too strong, and we reluctantly poured out the coffee.

Bob felt the need to fly out of the very tight space to get further assistance and supplies. I felt that it was too dangerous to risk a takeoff. Water was a critical item, and we still were uncertain how close we were to breaking through the heavy brush. I tried without success to persuade Bob not to risk a takeoff. Driven by thirst, he insisted on attempting a takeoff.

We cut the tree around which we had looped on landing to give every inch of advantage needed should he manage to lift the plane successfully into the air without crashing into the trees.

My heart was figuratively in my mouth as Bob took off. He managed to clear the trees in very close to a stall position. We had agreed that if the takeoff was successful, he would gain altitude and then after circling would fly in the direction of the nearest body of water. Since I would be alone for the next day, attempting to hack my way the rest of the way through what seemed like an impenetrable thicket, it would be important to know which way to head to the river to get the badly needed water. It was nearly noon when I broke through this barrier of growth.

From that point on, walking through the light undergrowth of tall trees was relatively easy, even though I was dehydrated. It had been nearly twenty-four hours since I had had any water intake. I had been perspiring heavily during the previous afternoon and that morning before I managed to cut through the brush.

I reached the river within fifteen minutes after breaking through the brush. Words aren't enough to describe the relief I felt when I first saw the river. There was a steep embankment at the point where I encountered the river. I knew that a short distance away there had to be a river bend, where the bank was shallow. With my energy depleted, my first reaction was to sit on the steep bank and gaze at the water for fifteen or twenty minutes. While I was exhausted, to be in the presence of a moving body of water was truly a mystical experience. When I finally reached the shallow portion of the water, I plunged into it. It was like a baptism. My spirit was renewed, and my body was replenished. I stayed at this site for several hours. I would never again take for granted the life-giving essence of water.

When Bob returned the next day, we changed the direction of the landing strip so we wouldn't be landing downhill. The only tools that we had were axes and shovels. It wasn't all work, though. During the next few days, we would catch fish when we weren't working on the runway. Actually, all one had to do was throw a large baited hook in the water, and a fish that the Indians called the Anjamarrahs would take the bait. The first one we caught was about a yard long. Since this river hadn't been fished before, we could have caught as many as we wanted with very little effort. We could only eat so much of fish, and we limited our catch to two or three fish. In this same river, I would see a water boa snake that would likely have measured twenty-five or thirty feet.

Since this airstrip, called Kayser, would be a supply base in preparation for the next landing, we improved the strip to the point that the Surinam pilots could land with larger planes and bring in native Surinamers who would help to improve the strip.

After what was known as Operation Grasshopper, an operation sponsored by the Surinam government, was well underway, a three-engine Northrop was purchased from the US government. Less than twenty of these experimental planes had been constructed, and the US military decided not to mass-produce these planes. They were able to land in a thousand feet of runway while carrying several tons of equipment. Since the Northrop could not be licensed in the United States, the planes had to be sold outside the United States.

The Northrop eventually landed at the Kayser strip. It carried

bulldozers that had to be disassembled before they could be loaded on the aircraft. They were then reassembled after their arrival.
With this equipment, a sizeable airstrip was established. Prior to
the Northrop's involvement, it had been necessary to fly in all supplies by our little Piper Super Cub from Paramaribo. This was a
most tenuous task because of the cargo and space limitations of the
Piper. Both Bob and I flew a number of these supply flights.

Meanwhile, we were told that the Surinam government required a deposit of one thousand gilders in a savings account. We
didn't have the funds to do that. On September 12, 1959, a Dr. Es-
send, the minister of development, called Bob into his office and
congratulated him on our landing at Kayser. Then he stated that the
required deposit requirement would be waived as a result of our
involvement in the interior. What a relief!

After supplying the Kayser strip with the gas needed for further
flights, we began the task of looking for Indian villages. We would
fly at about five thousand feet, surveying the vast forests and looking for a clearing. It felt like we were looking for a needle in a haystack. After several days of flying, we finally spotted the clearing
where less than a dozen huts were located. We flew down to tree
level, opened the door of the plane, and dropped gifts—primarily
red loincloths. We later learned that they were terrified to see the
plane, and it took some time and considerable courage before they
dared to pick up the gifts. I suppose if we found a surprise package
from outer space, we might think that it was radioactive and would
likely exercise the same caution that they had when they first found
our packages.

We then began to look for a landing strip. Several people from
Surinam Airways accompanied Vicki, the pilot who had covered
our landing at Kayser, to look the site over. A few days later, we
arranged for Vicki to cover our landing at a savanna only a couple
miles from the Brazilian border. This was to be the site from which
we launched our expedition to the Trio Indians. When we arrived,
we flew around for thirty minutes or so, waiting for Vicki and the
Aero Commander that he was piloting to cover our landing in case
we got in trouble. Darkness was approaching, and we finally decid-

ed that we would go in for the landing without him being overhead to observe our landing. This time, we set down on an open savanna and didn't have to dodge the trees. My logbook indicates that the date was September 9, 1959.

We landed close to sunset. I never saw so many gnats. We were tormented until the mosquitoes took over after sunset. We weren't well protected. Unfortunately, our hammocks were supposed to be dropped by air, so we spent the night sleeping on the ground. Later, we built a shelter that consisted primarily of a palm branch roof in the forest near a creek. The insects didn't bother us as much as they had on the open savanna.

Some days later, we flew a chief from the Wayana tribe, Annapika, to this site. We considered taking him with us on the expedition to the Trios and took him to look over the terrain. Since my family was scheduled to arrive in a few days, we didn't have time to carry out the expedition. I think having a linguist and three Wai Wai Indians turned out to be more appropriate than Annapika would have been by himself.

Annapika and I spent the night in a shelter that Bob and I had erected just inside the tree line near an idyllic stream of water. Bob flew back to Tafelberg to pick up supplies. It was the night of the full moon. At this time of the month, Annapika would typically be leading his people in the traditional moon dances, when the women would be adorned with ten pounds or more of beads. It was the dress-up night of the month for the tribe.

Clearly, Annapika was caught up in the spirit of the dances that he would normally be leading. He was loudly singing his chants, dashing between his hammock and the one that Bob would have used if he had been present. His eyes appeared to be glazed over as his chanting became more intense. I became uneasy and wondered if the intensity that he was displaying might lead to violent behavior. I don't think I would have been as uneasy if Bob or anyone else had been present. In an effort to modify his behavior, I suggested that we alternate singing songs. While he seemed to tolerate my singing, my attempt to participate was undoubtedly more comforting to me than to him. The intensity with which he was engaging in his rituals didn't let up. He was in a sphere of being with which I was quite unfamiliar. Sometime after midnight, he became calmer and eventually fell asleep. The next morning, I was clearing out some trees while Annapika was making flutes out of bones.

36

A Major Setback

When we were returning Annapika to his village on the Marowijne River near Maripasoula, we were trying to avoid landing at an isolated strip in French Guiana, primarily because there were a lot of procedural hassles that we would go through to get permission to land. We had been there and done that. There was a small sandbar on the Lawa River, which formed the border between Surinam and French Guiana.

It would provide less than five hundred feet of landing space. The tall trees at the end of this space meant that the pilot, once committed to land, would not be able to gain enough altitude to get over the trees. As an aside, we were aware that we were having some problems with carburetor heat. Inasmuch as the aircraft mechanic back at Zord en Hoop Airport in Paramaribo didn't have time to deal with the problem, he assured us that if we cleared the engine well before landing, we would have no problems landing. I was at the controls. I had cleared the engine well and was coming in over the river at close to stall speed. Just before coming onto the beach, I felt the plane stalling and pushed the throttle fully forward. The engine did not respond.

Annapika, Bob, and I were on board when the plane hit the water. The plane overturned, and the tail of the plane landed on the beach. Bob, who was not strapped in, flew through the plastic windshield and through the props of the propeller that had fortunately stopped when the plane hit the water. His only injury was a minor bruise that had occurred as his shoulder made contact with the propeller. (Forty-five years later, Bob had some arthritic problems with this shoulder that may be traceable to this event.) I found myself strapped in the pilot's seat, upside down and completely submerged. Disoriented, I held my breath as I tried to figure out how to release the seat belt. When I found the release and came to the surface, Annapika was nowhere in sight. Bob and I both entered the cockpit under water and found Annapika in the baggage compartment, above the water line and holding his hammock so it wouldn't get wet.

Annapika had capsized many times when the boats in which he was riding had gone through rapids on the river. He didn't seem to be particularly startled by this accident. I forget how he phrased it, but he made some uncomplimentary comment about my ability to handle an airplane. My logbook records the accident as having occurred on September 15, 1959.

In hindsight, it would have been better to wait until the carburetor heat problem had been fixed or to have gone through the hassles of the government of French Guiana and gotten permission to land on the French airstrip. In actuality, the margins of safety were essentially violated on every landing and takeoff that we performed. If we had waited until everything was up to snuff, we would have been grounded most of the time. As I look at this incident from the perspective of more than four decades, I think I was too hard on myself. I really don't think the accident would have happened if the mechanical problem had been fixed.

We sent a wire from a village of Maripsula on the French site to Mr. Zaal, who was the head of Surinam Airways, to tell him of our plight. We had shared a number of experiences together, and he proved most helpful. He came to rescue us as soon as he could. Meanwhile, we went to the sand bar with two strong native blacks, who were known locally as Bush Negroes. The plane was disassembled and taken to Maripsula and then to the airport at a cost of 20,000 francs.

When we met with the district commissioner, Barends, who was equivalent to a state governor, he received us with real warmth. Commissioner Barends, himself a pilot, commented that every landing and takeoff had been a risk, adding that we had provided a real service for his country. He remained a staunch friend during our entire time in Surinam. The Jacksons and a banker and his wife named Widdapole were also important to us during this time.

37

The Family Arrives

This accident changed our strategy. Bob would return to Philadelphia to raise the money to get another plane. I took him to the airport, and then, according to my notes, hurried to pick up some furniture (mainly beds) before rushing back to the airport to meet Leta and our two children, who were arriving on KLM on September 21, Leta's thirty-fourth birthday. Linda and Bob eagerly tried to fill me in on all the details of the nearly six months that we had been apart.

While I was glad to see the family, I was struggling with some depression that I was trying hard to ignore. My notes dated September 29, 1959, read: "Lord, help us to rise above my sense of failure and realize your purposes are not limited by our apparent successes or failures."

The children would enroll in a Dutch-speaking school located about a block from our home, near the Zorg en Hoop Airport within a couple days of their arrival. While the classroom language was Dutch, the languages of the playground were different dialects of Chinese, Indonesian, Hindustani, and the local trade language called Talkie-Talkie. Bobby, as we then called him, who was a first grader, would be placed in kindergarten. Linda, a third grader, would be required to go back and do first-grade work since she was new to the language. We arranged for a tutor for her, which meant that every day after school, she would go to her tutoring lesson. She was required to complete every lesson normally required of a first grader before she could go on to second-grade work, even though she had gained competency of that grade level long before she had completed every lesson. After going to the second grade, she again was required to complete every assignment normally required of the second grade before she could eventually move to the next grade level. It was a lot of pressure to put on a ten-year-old, but she managed quite well.

On one occasion, I showed up after hours at the school where Linda and Bob were attending to chat with the principal. I was astonished to see the principal slapping a child, perhaps a second or third grader, so hard that the child was hurled from one end of the room to the other. This happened several times. The principal had seen me arrive, so there was no way that I could escape this scene. As he left the crying child, the principal approached me, saying, "That will teach that child not to flunk a test."

To say that I was totally astonished and bewildered is something of an understatement. I wondered what kind of learning environment I had subjected my children to and how this learning environment might impact their learning as well as their love of learning.

Despite the rigidity and questionable teaching practices, Linda and Bob gained competency in the Dutch language rather rapidly. They soon were comfortably speaking in Dutch with their friends. We learned that Bobby was having dreams in Dutch.

Without a refrigerator in our home, Leta ended up riding a bicycle to the market each day to purchase what was needed. She handled these duties like a champ. We did have a maid, who was a member of the little church we were attending, and a gardener that we really didn't need, but it was a way of sharing whatever resources we had with these folks who were barely surviving. We soon became accustomed to living as the natives did.

Our daughter, Linda, then ten years old, shared these words some forty-five years later about her perception of these experiences. "As a child, I never felt that we—and especially you—would be in danger during our adventure in South America. Now, as an adult woman, I have an added degree of respect for how Mom handled her supportive role and how challenging that experience must have been for a young lady with two young children from a conservative rural background in a third-world country where she was unable to communicate efficiently. I'm not sure I could have handled the experience with the same amount of poise and faith. Thanks for taking the leap of faith that led to our great adventure, a great adventure that I experienced with the confidence and faith of a child that all would be well."

Surinam has a rich and colorful cultural background. Creole women could balance heavy baskets and other materials on their heads and walk with great poise. Their garments were often very festive. East Indian men drove their ox carts right into the center of the city, causing massive traffic jams. The Indonesians, while a minority, represented a sizeable portion of the population. There were a number of Chinese people living there as well. Most people had arrived as indentured servants some generations earlier. If I remember correctly, there were seven or eight daily newspapers in the different dialects of the resident population.

I was asked to host a missionary who was arriving from the Netherlands for a day. I no longer remember his name, but he was considered a distinguished guest. He asked if I would take him to a Hindu temple. The priest at the temple received us with great dignity. After getting a photo of the priest in the temple, the missionary then started to tell the priest that he was lost and on his way to damnation unless he accepted Christ as his Savior—all in the name of proclaiming the Christian faith. I was ashamed and deeply embarrassed about the crudity of this missionary's behavior. In my view, he was not only insensitive but outright insulting. I was certain that he would show the slides of this temple and this priest to congregations he would visit in the United States and Europe to demonstrate that he was witnessing for Christ. That missionary missed an opportunity for dialogue with a rich religious tradition.

On one occasion, the Indians had given me a beautiful toucan that I had placed in the plane with me when I flew back to the city. We had a small building behind our house that served multiple purposes. The toucan shared that dwelling with several macaws as well as some chickens that a Hispanic lady from Ecuador had given us when the baby chicks became too large to be kept in her apartment. (She had entertained herself while her fisherman husband was at sea by learning to hypnotize these chicks so that they would maintain a position for hours lying on their backs.)

The toucan was clearly the ruler of the roost. It would eat first, and only when it was finished did the macaws and chickens dare to approach the food dish. Linda laid special claim to the toucan. She would put the toucan on the handlebars of her bicycle and go riding down the street with this large-billed bird casually taking in the landscape by slowly turning its head side to side.

We used to enjoy watching the toucan pick up a cherry and roll it up and down inside its long beak. At a given moment, the cherry would go down the hatch. On one occasion, the cherry went down the throat inappropriately, and the toucan choked to death. Linda shared her grief with her Surinam friends by speaking the Dutch language. Some neighbors from the United States who worked for the company that produced aluminum were visiting us. Linda burst into the room to share this tragedy with the neighbors by translating from Dutch to English. "My pet went dead."

As an adult, Linda has indicated how much she valued the toucan. She adds that she regards this pet as an important part of her childhood memory. In a recent e-mail in which she described her memories of this era, she made this comment: "Thanks for bringing home the toucan from the jungle. I loved that bird."

38

A Surinam Pilot's License in Hand

On October 7, 1959, I was put on standby flight duty with Surinam Airways. Vincent Faiks, known to us as Vicki, the Polish pilot who flew for Surinam Airways, and a pilot friend named Rudi Kappel were missing. (While Rudi was not involved in Operation Grasshopper, he played in important role in the earlier formation of Surinam Airways). The Aero Commander, piloted by Vicki, had crashed when they were attempting to deliver supplies to a site on the Tapanahony River. We called the site of the airstrip the Palomeu. It is now officially called the Vincent Faiks Vliegveld. "Vliegveld" is the Dutch name for "airfield."

With District Commissioner Barends, I flew a Surinam-licensed plane to the crash site to determine whether there were survivors. Just before I arrived, a message came through that both were dead. The Bush Negroes (a term by which these tribal people were known) had performed an outstanding feat, carrying the bodies by boat over rugged rapids and falls to a place called Stoelman's Island.

On October 10, 1959, on short notice, I was asked to fly to a new airstrip that was being carved out of the jungles on the Corantijn River that bordered Guyana to pick up Dr. Geyhes, the curator of the Surinam museum who had organized this expedition. A close friend of Rudi, he was flown out of this site to attend the funeral ceremonies for Rudi and Vicki. The strip was just being completed, and no one had yet landed there. I had no idea what the condition of the strip would be like. The diary notes indicate that I left at 10:15 a.m.

As on so many of the first landings, the internal tension was high. Because the approach had not yet been cut, I chose to make a downwind landing. It was successful, and I arrived back at Zorg en Hoop at 3:40 p.m. Both Vicki and Rudi were given a state funeral. It was purportedly Surinam's largest gathering ever. I was honored to be a part of the funeral procession.

On October 23, 1959, I was issued a pilot's license by Surinam's minister of public works and traffic, a license that is still attached to my flight log. (A copy of this license is pictured in the appendix.) On November 2, 1959, I made the first landing at the Palomeu with District Commissioner Barends aboard. He was also the official head of aviation in Surinam. He wanted to make an official visit to the crash site where our two friends were killed in the Surinam Airways accident. We approached the strip over the trees, toward the river. The trees on approach were at least a hundred feet high but were cut back for about a hundred feet. After I cleared the last tree, I began a sharp descent. As soon as I had cleared the last stumps of trees, I touched down as quickly as possible. I stepped off the actual length of the airstrip before we were in the water. The log indicates that it was 675 feet in length.

In the next weeks, there were numerous flights to the interior. My informal diary indicates that on November 5, 1959, an engineer named Mr. Fakkel flew with me to the Palomeu airstrip to determine the mechanical cause of the crash of the Aero Commander. This diary also indicates that I picked up food for the workers at Palomeu from the Tafelberg strip, adding that the weather was far from ideal.

Speaking of the weather, as the rainy season approached, pockets of showers that were scattered far apart from each other began to develop. As the rainy season progressed, the pockets of showers would multiply until they became a solid mass. Pilots tried to find openings between these pockets. These openings became increasingly difficult to find as the rainy season peaked. Since we were not doing instrument flying, I found it necessary to return to where the flight had originated on a number of occasions. I remember one time when I was debating about the best course of action and was ready to turn back. I slipped through a tiny opening that was closing fast. After getting through this opening, I was able to complete the rest of my journey. I managed to capture this scene on camera.

I remember another occasion when I was asked to fly a load of dynamite caps to the Palomeu airstrip. The other pilots had refused to fly this cargo. I accepted the task but didn't realize that I shouldn't have used the radio because of the possibility that radio signals could set off these caps. Blissfully unaware, I reported my position regularly during the two-hour flight. Fortunately, these radio signals didn't cause the caps to explode.

On November 7, 1959, I received word that a US pilot by the name of Meadows had piloted the three-engine Northrop to the Koeroeni strip. I learned that the nose wheel had hit a soft spot on this newly developed airstrip and had sunk into the ground, damaging one of the propellers. My task was to fly in a new propeller. My daily record indicates that I experienced poor visibility on the flight to Tafelberg—in fact it was so difficult that I had trouble locating the airfield. From there, I flew to Koeroeni strip, arriving at 11:15 a.m. It was a little unnerving to fly over the Northrop aircraft, with its nose wheel still lodged at the beginning of this short runway.

On the return trip from Koeroeni, an editor of an engineering and mining journal, Alvin Knoerr, flew with me back to Paramaribo. He seemed intrigued with our seat-of-the-pants flying operation.

On November 9, 1959, I received word that a new Surinam pilot had an accident at the Palomeu airstrip with the Piper Club that I had been flying. He wasn't accustomed to making short-field jungle landings. He made the mistake of trying to come over the river downwind and hadn't sufficiently reduced his speed. He hit the tree trunks at the end of the runway and overturned. He had had a shaky landing at the Koeroeni airstrip earlier. It was unfortunate that he hadn't had the opportunity to be better trained for this kind of operation. My close friend Mr. Zaal had promised that I could use this plane for contacts with the Trio Indians. It was to be another time of waiting.

We had waited for permission to be involved in the interior. Just when it seemed that the waiting time was over, we experienced the crash in the river, which had wiped out the plane that we had flown from the States. We had permission to fly the single-engine Surinam plane on a variety of missions. We would have access to fly this plane to take care of the logistical and organizational issues related to our planned expedition to contact the Trio Indian tribes, who hadn't had previous contact with the outside world. The plane that we had access to now lay damaged, upside down amid tree trunks.

Incidentally, during the first year of flying operation known as Operation Grasshopper, fourteen planes crashed, including the three-engine Northrop. Two pilots were killed. It was a risk that we all accepted. If we hadn't taken the risks, the process of opening up the interior areas of unexplored jungles would have been indefinitely delayed.

During the times of waiting, we developed a friendship with natives of Surinam both in and out of government as well as officials who were working in Surinam from Holland. We also got to meet a number of citizens from the United States who worked for mining companies or who were missionaries. As noted earlier, we developed a close relationship with the folks associated with the West Indies Missions, which in effect became our church home during our Surinam experience. Philo, originally from Aruba, was a delightful person who worked with the West Indies mission. She had a wonderful personality accompanied by a charming smile. She presented bible stories to the children of the neighborhood, which included our two children. We lost track of Philo when we returned to the States but learned that she had married and moved to Canada and become a mother. While we don't know the circumstances, we did hear that her husband murdered her after they moved to Canada. It left me with a feeling of loss to hear this sad news.

39

Getting Back on Track

I received a call from Georgetown, Guyana, on November 14, 1959, indicating that Claude Leavitt, a linguist with a mission group there, would be available to be part of the Trio expedition. He also said that several native Wai Wai Indians would accompany us. Demonstrating my impatience to get things moving, my diary on that date has this comment: "It's a pity that a plane isn't available at this moment." An added comment acknowledged that it was important to wait for "God's time."

The diary logs several contacts with Bob Price by ham radio. A note dated December 16, 1959, indicates that a Piper Family Cruiser had been purchased. Two days later, Leta and I flew to Albina and then took a ferry across the Marowijne River to St. Laurent, French Guiana, primarily to purchase beads that would later be used on the expedition to the Indians. At lunchtime, we managed to locate a restaurant. The menu was limited. They served great bread and a wide range of liquor but very little else. I didn't speak French or their local trade language. I had much difficulty in asking for the waitress where the restrooms were. She stared at me blankly as I repeated my rather urgent request for restroom facilities. My bladder had reached its capacity, and I did everything but point. Suddenly a look of recognition came on her face. She exclaimed,

"Oh, you want to pee." She led me outside and pointed to a sheet of corrugated tin. I gratefully accepted her invitation.

The Surinam government asked me to fly the workers back to Paramaribo. Under the leadership of Dr. Geyhes, they had carved what came to be known as the Koeroeni airstrip out of the jungle. It had originally taken the group six weeks just to reach this site. They had left the town of Nickerie to come up the Corantijn River with a number of boats loaded with equipment and food that would serve them during their construction of the new airstrip. Every time they reached a rapid in the river, they would have to unload their boats and drag their boats and equipment through the forests to the river above the rapids. It had been quite a feat. Now it was time for Christmas break.

I made a number of trips and logged a number of hours ferrying these workers home prior to the Christmas holidays.

During these approaching Christmas holidays, I was trying to make arrangements with the aviation officials to fly directly to the Wai Wai mission at Konashen in British Guiana. This would entail not going through the usual custom procedures and would also save hours of flying if I could ferry Claude Levitt and the Wai Wai Indian guides directly from their station into Surinam when the time was appropriate. On December 22, 1959, I flew to Georgetown, Guyana, with my friend Walter Jackson to present my case directly to the customs officials. My proposal was to fly to Koeroeni via Zorg en Hoop and Tafelberg to Konashen, Guyana. My notes indicate that I briefed Guyana's director of federal aviation, a Mr. Parker. He was very friendly. The following day, my proposal was accepted. Walter Jackson enjoyed our friends, Fred and Donna Gibbs. He was impressed with Georgetown and thought the Brown Betty, an ice cream store, was great. On the return flight to Paramaribo, we encountered difficult weather that had us dodging rain showers most of the way. Zorg en Hoop airfield was covered with clouds, and we had to circle north of the airfield for thirty-five minutes or so before we were able to land.

As the holiday season approached, the children received a

number of thoughtful gifts from our friends from the United States who were living in Surinam. We had a turkey dinner with all the trimmings with the Jacksons and with our friend Philo. In the evening, friends from the US living in Paramaribo visited us, filling out a wonderful day of festivities.

During the rest of the last week of the year, we were making active plans to get started on the Trio expedition. The local New Year's Eve celebration was unlike any other we have ever experienced. At about four o'clock in the afternoon, we began to hear fireworks. The volume kept building gradually. By 2100 hours (9 p.m.) the noise was so loud, we could barely hear each other speak. By midnight, it was deafening. The Jacksons told us that many native families would spend up to half of their year's income for fireworks for this evening. They further informed us that the purpose of this buildup of sounds was to "drive away the evil spirits."

My flight log indicates that I flew to Tafelberg and then to Konashen, Guyana, on January 17, 1960, to pick up the Wai Wai Indian guides. The next day, I flew to the Kayser Airstrip. My logbook had the following entry: "Returned to Konashen the same day to pick up another passenger." I intended to fly from Konashen to the Kayser Airstrip on January 19.

On this three-hour flight, heavy clouds developed as I approached the border of Surinam. I faced a dilemma. While the weather was clearer in the direction from which I had come, it was in the middle of the rainy season. There was no guarantee that the weather would not deteriorate if I tried to return. Previously on this same three-hour flight, I didn't spot a place I could make an emergency landing. On the other hand, I knew I would soon be flying along the Corantijn River, where I had earlier made several landings at the Koeroeni airstrip located on the river a month earlier. I chose the option of trying to locate and land at this airstrip.

I was flying in clouds as low as I dared to fly. Visibility ahead was zero-zero. All I could see was straight down. I followed the river at an altitude of less than a hundred feet. There were high banks where the river had cut into the earth as much as thirty feet or more. I wanted to be sure I cleared the highest bank and still keep the curving river in sight. Flying at a hundred miles an hour, I was afraid that I might fly past the Koeroeni airstrip and then have difficulty negotiating a low-altitude turn to return to the strip in case the strip came up too quickly to make a landing. Fortunately I saw the field in time and landed without difficulty. I breathed a prayer of gratitude to be on terra firma. To my surprise, thin bamboo shoots that weren't there just one month prior were a foot high on the runway. The jungles were rapidly reclaiming the space that had been cleared.

One of our guides, whose name I cannot now recall, had been one of the first to be ferried to the Kayser Airstrip several days before I could get everyone from our expedition group flown to this site. The Surinam workers who were upgrading this airstrip found this Trio Indian guide very entertaining. Through the linguist, he told these workers of a custom that his tribe had followed before the missionaries arrived. He described that when a child was born, the mother would present the child to the father, who would be surrounded by his fellow male tribesmen. The child would be lying on the ground. After examining the child, the father would decide if he wanted to keep the child. If the father made an affirmative decision, he would pick up the child and give it to the mother. By this act, he would confer tribal membership to this child. If the father decided not to accept the child, he simply left the child lying on the ground and departed with his tribesmen. The mother, who had no voice in the matter of whether the child was received, would then abandon the child in the jungle.

This Trio guide then proceeded to tell his audience that his father had rejected all the brothers and sisters born ahead of him. This procedure of taking an unwanted child to be abandoned in the jungles had been followed in every case. He then dramatically announced that when his father rejected him, his aunt picked him up and fled into the jungle, and by this act defied tribal custom. He then added that his aunt hid for a long time while nursing him. After several weeks had passed, she returned to the tribe. He then shared the story of his religious conversion by repeating his story again and adding that "when God saw me lying on that banana leaf, he picked me up and made me part of God's family."

The last evening that I was in Paramaribo before leaving on the expedition, one of the lower-echelon government workers that I had gotten to know fairly well pleaded with me several hours not to risk this contact with Indians. I knew that his words of caution needed to be considered. Just four years earlier, a group of five missionaries who attempted to contact the Auca Indians had been massacred. While the Aucas purportedly had had some hostile contact with Shell Oil Company workers, they essentially had been isolated. The missionaries had attempted to prepare the way for their planned contact with them by dropping gifts and pictures of themselves.

We realized that there were a number of similarities between the attempted contacts of these five missionaries and the contacts we had hoped to make. But there was one difference. We could find no evidence that this group had ever had contact with the outside world before. This would be confirmed when our actual contact was made. There would be other major differences. First, they had landed on a sandy bank of a river and waited to be found, while we wanted to be sure that we initiated the first contact with the Trios. Second, the missionaries contacting the Aucas didn't have any Indians with them—someone who looked and dressed like them. We would have three Wai Wai Indians guides.

I was aware that there were many unknowns, and the outcome was uncertain in this attempt to contact the Trio Indians. However, for us, there was no turning back. In the final day or two at home before the expedition was to begin, I tried to spend as much time as I could with the children. I specifically remember trying to help our five-year-old son put together a small model airplane. I was never any good at these kinds of projects, but I wanted to do something with him even if I had no real idea of what I was doing. If I didn't return from this expedition, I hoped that he would know that his father wanted him to remember this time as quality time spent together. (I was blown away when I recently saw the film *At the End of a Spear*, the film depicting the story of the five massacred mission-

224

aries in Ecuador in 1955. The pilot, Nate Saint, had attempted to spend quality time with his son by working on a model airplane.)

With all the members of our expedition together at the Kayser Airstrip, the next task was to ferry the five of us who would be on the expedition from the Kayser Airstrip to the Sipaliwini airstrip, the starting point of our expedition. Nearly twenty-five hours of flight time was recorded as we got set up to begin the expedition. The Indian guides were flown over the area that we were to walk. Hopefully they would pick up leads from the air that would be helpful when we were walking through the jungles with no identified trails. I'm not certain how useful this idea was. Indians were very skillful in picking up leads from the ground. They would be traveling over terrain they had never seen. They were phenomenal in their ability to pick up leads where we could see no sign of a trail at all.

By the evening of February 4, 1960, we were ready to go from the airstrip where we had made the first landing on the Brazilian border at a place we had called the Sipaliwini airstrip. We had food (primarily rice and some canned food) and other supplies stocked at the little shelter that we had made on the banks of a lovely stream. However, we would carry no food on the trail. We did have a gun that we used only for hunting purposes on the trail. Once on the trail, we did not stop for a meal at noontime.

40

We're on Our Way

The morning of February 5, 1960, five of us—three Wai Wai Indians from British Guiana, Claude the linguist, and I—began to go on the trails that neither Claude or I could identify as trails. I couldn't begin to know how our Indian guides, who had never been to this part of the world, would know the way. I could not have found my way without these skilled guides.

I was somewhat surprised when Claude, the old veteran of the jungle, stated that we would not stop for meals. While I didn't object, I had visions of being famished. To my surprise, that didn't happen. I was doing far better than I expected by the end of the day. It actually became a standard practice to not eat a midday meal while I was on the trail—even when Claude wasn't on the trail with us. The first day we did stop to munch on a small, tasteless wild pineapple.

At about four o'clock in the afternoon, Claude suggested that we make camp for the night. This would allow time for one of the Indian guides to hunt for some animal whose meat could be cooked over a fire. I was more than happy to have Claude making these kinds of decisions because of his considerable experience on the trails.

Just as we were looking for a temporary campsite, we heard the sound of running water. It was the small river that we had spotted a number of times from the air. We later learned that the Indians called it the Sipaliwini River; the name that would one day be given to the airstrip that we had just left. We wanted to discover the Indians rather than having them discovers us. Based on our observations from the air, we realized that the first Trio village that we were to encounter was only an hour or so walking time away.

We had walked about twenty miles on jungle trails that day. I vividly remember bathing in the shallow part of Sipaliwini River. As soon as the Wai Wais had bathed, they began to paint their bodies. Even Claude, who had been with them for years, wasn't aware of the significance of this action. It meant that our guides were dressing up for this occasion. They wanted to be seen as friendly visitors and not as the exploiters that their fathers had been.

As we prepared to go this last mile, we all stood on the far bank of the river for a moment of prayer and reflection. I remember clearly some of the words that I shared. "Whatever happens, may this be the day when the seeds of the gospel of love and hope are sown among the Trios." With these words, we were off for our encounter. I wasn't the only one with some apprehension. We learned that our guides were concerned that their fathers may have raided this village and taken the women as their wives. If this were the case, they were afraid that they would look enough like the villagers and possibly receive a hostile reception. The numerous warnings about the dangers of this encounter that I had received prior to our expedition were ringing in my ears.

When we got within a quarter mile or so of our destination, Claude spotted a hunting blind around a jungle fruit tree. He called out what he thought was a greeting. Two young men, one a teenager and the other probably nine or ten years old, stepped out from this blind. They were obviously terrified. Claude and our guides attempted to speak to them, but quickly discovered that their language was totally unknown to him. This encounter lasted only a few seconds. The young boys broke for their village on a dead run. With our full field packs, we ran after them. The first view that the villagers would have of us was chasing their children into their clearing. You might have some notion of how they must have felt if you can imagine how you would feel if green men from Mars, whom you obviously had never seen, were chasing your children into your yards.

The villagers were so startled that they were essentially immobilized. They didn't have time to go for their poison-tip arrows. We eventually learned that they thought we had come from the sky in our "flying canoe" (they had seen us flying over their village at treetop level some weeks earlier) to kill their men and capture their wives and children and transport them to our village in the sky. They further thought that we had magical power with which they would not be able to compete. Normally when a stranger comes into the village, the first thing that the women will do is to feed them. The food is typically presented a few minutes after the guests arrive. The assumption is that after being on the trail for some time the traveler would be hungry. Nearly an hour passed before the women collected their wits and provided this traditional welcome.

Since our linguist didn't initially decipher the language, the first few hours were awkward and tense. Claude was able to determine who the chief was and presented him with a machete. I confess that I was surprised at Claude's choice of a gift to the chief. All the other men were given fish hooks as gifts.

The first word deciphered from the Indian language was "naka," which meant "enough." Interestingly, when the translators put the previously unwritten language into writing and translated the New Testament, the word used for "amen" was "naka." It is an interesting way to end a prayer.

Initially, we really didn't learn how apprehensive our Indian hosts were. It took about ten days for our Wai Wai guides to develop enough rapport with the Trios for them to ask when the *pananakitties*, meaning Claude and me, were going to kill them. When the guides assured that we had no plans to harm but had come to help, some of the tension began to slowly melt.

I remember how apprehensive I was that first night. We slept in their huts with them. It was a customary thing for a guest to do. Beyond that, however, they could keep an eye on us. I don't know how well Claude slept, but my sleep was uneasy, and I confess that I didn't take off my old paratrooping boots.

I'm not certain whose idea it was for all of us to go to the adjoining villages some five or six hours away by trail after we awakened the next morning. I suspect that they were somewhat relieved to be with their comrades in another village. We had the advantage of having them introduce us to the local residents of that village. This initial contact with the second village didn't seem as tense as the first contact had been. I naïvely thought that the Trios were starting to feel more comfortable around us.

Claude's primary interest was in developing the ability to speak to their language. I was absorbed in finding a suitable place to build an airstrip. He decided that he wanted to stay for some days in the second village and sent two of the Wai Wai guides and some Trios to pick up supplies at the landing strip two days' walk away.

I can't believe that I left Claude to start for the third village with one of the Wai Wai guides. I couldn't understand Coffeeanni, but I trusted him implicitly. We were in the company with one of the chiefs. Being a driven person with established deadlines, I was eager to get started. It was noon or just after before we left. The route we were following could hardly be called a trail. I couldn't identify anything that showed someone had trod this terrain before us. Actually the average person from the Western world would have no clue about which direction to go. I'm still not certain how the Indians found their way—especially our Wai Wai guides, who had never been over this terrain before.

I vividly remember being with Coffeeanni on one occasion when he had obviously missed the trail. He stopped and retraced the trail by running his fingers through the air as if he were making a map without the benefit of a paper and pencil. After a few seconds of this kind of mental gymnastics, he quickly regained his orientation.

We stopped to spend the night on the trail long before sunset. With my agenda to get on with the task at hand, I was eager to get going the following morning. It quickly became obvious that the chief and tribesmen were in no hurry. They had a very different perspective of time than I did. Midmorning, they brought out the food. I happened to be seated near the chief, staring with kind of a blank look on my face and trying not to show my impatience. With machete in hand, he was cutting at something. I hadn't really paid attention until he handed me half of the item that he had been working on. It was a monkey skull containing partially cooked brains. I didn't know how to say no, thanks. There was no seasoning of any kind present. I made a valiant attempt to eat what was given to me, although everything within me was in violent revolt. Still, I didn't want to offend the chief, who was seeing a person with white skin for the first time only the day before.

We were finally on the trail again by late morning. It was about noon when we arrived at village three. This time, the fifteen or twenty residents of that village got a chance to see someone from the outside world for the very first time. I'm sure they had never seen a bald man before, let alone one who had a different skin color.

We had been there about thirty minutes when some of the ladies began to wail. It was the most piercing human sound I had ever heard. I would have given anything to ask my Wai Wai guide what was going on but I didn't know how to ask him in his native language. By the way, he didn't understand the Trio language either. I began to wonder whether I had inadvertently offended them in some way. The wailing went on and on for about six or seven hours. While I tried hard to remove any fantasies about being in harm's way, I was uneasy during much of the afternoon.

About four or five o'clock in the afternoon, I decided to go for a walk down the trail that we had taken when we walked into the village earlier that day. I had remembered crossing a stream that was fairly wide and perhaps three or four feet deep. Feeling increasingly restless and uneasy after listening to the wailing voices of these women for several hours, I waded into the water in the altogether nothing and was reflecting on what was happening back in the village. I began to wonder about the wisdom of not waiting for Claude, whom I wouldn't see for another ten days. I was aware that the expedition was scheduled to last no more than six weeks, and I felt the urgency to do something about locating a landing strip for the plane. Still, I remember feeling alone and isolated.

In the midst of my mind racing from thought to thought, I was suddenly aware that I wasn't alone. I turned around and saw six or eight women, who were also nude and who were bathing in the same stream. The wailing continued in the village, so I wasn't sure whether these women were part of the "wailing committee." I wasn't sure what do. So I stayed put in three or four feet of water. The women, who were obviously aware of my presence, didn't seem to be disturbed with my being there. After thirty minutes, perhaps more, they left. I noticed that they placed their hands over their genitals as they came out of the water.

I learned later that men and women bathed regularly together in the nude. Their standard of modesty was to have their genitals covered. When men were with men, the same practice occurred. In my early YMCA days, we were required to swim in the nude, but we made no effort to cover our genitals when we were out of the water. Of course, the sexes were strictly segregated during YMCA swimming events. Before the expedition was over, I became rather comfortable with this practice of covering my genitals whether I was in the water with men only or was in mixed company.

Much of what occurred during the days before Claude was to appear with our two other Wai Wai guides plus the villagers is somewhat hazy to me. I remember that I tried hard to find a piece of level land. All the land was covered by the tall, thick rainforest and was quite hilly. It was most difficult to get an appreciation for an accurate lay of the land in the midst of a heavily covered rainforest.

I was very relieved to see Claude when he did arrive. There were only about four weeks left before the expedition was going to be over—and my top priority was to prepare a place for landing the plane. I had searched for more than a week to find a suitable spot to carve an airstrip without much success. Claude joined me in the search. He wasn't any better than I was in finding a suitable location for an airstrip. We finally settled on a spot that was far from ideal—but we felt that we couldn't wait any longer to start creating the airstrip. The selected site had a fairly significant slope with a heavy dip in the center, but it was the best that we could do with our limited surveying skills. From this site, it was fifteen or sixteen hours of hard walking over mountainous trails to reach where we had originally landed and stocked a few supplies.

It was a formidable task to cut the giant trees, some of which were nearly 150 feet tall. The Indians often would clear the forest to plant small fields of cassava plants. (By the way, planting these plants was their sole agricultural enterprise. They were primarily hunters and gatherers.) They had a very clever way of accomplishing this task. They would notch the trees they wanted to cut lower in the trunks. A tree would then be cut, and when it fell, it would take the notched trees down like dominoes. The sound of these many trees falling at the same time made a tremendous sound— something like a jet flying at a low attitude.

After the leaves and branches had dried for several days, the fallen trees were set on fire. I was concerned that the fire would get out of hand and burn the surrounding forest. The Indians weren't concerned. They knew that the fire would be limited. It really didn't have much impact beyond the cut trees.

It seemed such a shame to not use these gigantic logs in a productive way. But here we were, several hundred miles from the nearest road. Some of the logs on the ground had such a large diameter, they came almost up to my chin. And our tools were so limited. Now it seems like a gross exaggeration to say that we only had four axe heads (we had to make our own axe handles), some shovels, and a few rakes that we had carried in over the trail of fifty miles. But that is all the equipment we had to do this enormous task.

Four of the strongest Indians would chop away at these mammoth logs with our four axes. Typically, it would take three or four days to cut through one log about five feet in diameter. Usually the length of the cut was twenty or twenty-five feet. Meanwhile, the shovels were used to dig out the enormous roots. When enough roots were removed, we would cut smaller trees to serve as runners.

At the end of the day, we would usually get everyone involved in moving the twenty-foot log onto these runners and then, inch by inch, nudging them off to the side of what was to become the runway. The task was so exhausting that we couldn't have managed to move more than one log a day. As I look back on it nearly sixty years after the fact, I am amazed as I think of how much was done with so little.

These Indians didn't have money as such. There was no such thing as a hired worker. We tried to have incentives. Loincloths and beads were given to the workers. As mentioned earlier, we had purchased the beads in neighboring French Guiana before we started the expedition.

We hadn't brought a food supply with us. We ate with the Indians and obviously ate what they ate. In a six-week period, I managed to lose thirty-five pounds. As Claude was gaining some proficiency with the language, I remember one day he suggested that if they brought some bananas, he would in exchange give them some beads. To our bewilderment, four of the hardest working young men took off and were gone ten days. We were astonished that they returned with four bananas. It didn't seem strange to them to have invested this much time to present such a limited supply of bananas. I'm not sure where they went, but am fairly confident that they had consumed all but the four bananas. In typical Western style, we were in a hurry while the Indians seemed to have little consciousness of time or sense of the urgency of time. As I look back on it now, I'm not so sure that their values were that displaced. Perhaps we could take some lessons from them.

Speaking of time, we tried to encourage all the men, including teenagers, to spend a sizeable portion of their day working at the site of the emerging airstrip. Claude invited one older man to be with us on the clearing, even though there wasn't much that he could contribute. On one occasion, this gentleman stated that it was necessary for him to rest that day because his wife was having her menstrual cycle. The wife, meanwhile, was carrying on with her duties without rest.

We learned in vivid detail how frightened the Indians had been when they had initially seen our plane come down to tree level and drop gifts, which consisted of loincloths and beads. The Indians were too terrified to pick up these gifts. I remember one of the Indians told the story how apprehensive he was when he eventually mustered up the courage to pick up these gifts. I don't think that they initially saw them as a sign of good will. It represented more of an unexplainable mystery that most viewed with considerable foreboding.

The Trios tried to decipher whether Claude and I were good or bad. A number of them asked us this question. On one occasion, Claude, who was becoming reasonably efficient in speaking to them in their language, assured the chief that we were indeed good. The chief's no-nonsense response was, "Good. I won't have to eat you, then."

We were jolted when we first saw this old man. He had a distinctive look, significantly different from the other Trios. He was the only Indian who looked old and was starting to lose his hair. I asked Claude, who had lived with Indians for decades, how old he thought this gentleman was. He responded that he might be forty-five years old. He added that it was rare for Indians living in these remote areas to survive beyond thirty-five or forty.

The reason for the double take when we first saw this man was that some of our friends in the Surinam government had told us of a US pilot who had left Georgetown, British Guiana, in the late 1920s in an attempt to fly across the jungles. He was never heard from again. The rumor was that he survived his forced landing in the jungle and was rescued by Indians in some remote area and possibly have taken up Indian customs. Several expeditions were sent out decades earlier to try to find this pilot, but they were unsuccessful. The rumor had persisted over the decades. Our Surinam friends had suggested that we be on the lookout for this downed pilot. His flight course would have taken him over the general area where we found these Indians. We soon dismissed the idea that this could be the long-forgotten flier.

On one occasion, a teenager and I were the only ones working on the strip. It took me a long time to understand what he was trying to say to me, in his language, of course. I finally figured out that he was asking if I had a son. When I responded that I did, it took me even longer to understand the next question. He was asking if my son was good. When I responded that he was good, he then asked his name. I was still slow in understanding his question, particularly in light of the fact that the Trios never used names, primarily because they were worried that evil spirits might be listening. When I responded that our five-year-old son's name was Bobby, he asked that I call him Bobby. He apparently reasoned that if I called him Bobby, the evil spirits, who might be listening, would go searching for Bobby and leave him alone. Every time I called him Bobby, he would grin broadly. The evil spirits would be fooled. I will share more about Bobby in later pages.

Traditional and conservative anthropologists usually took the position that these Indians who lived beyond the reach of so-called civilization were "happy children of the jungles." This dictum is somewhat equivalent to a far right-wing Christian announcing that their given dictum was the "Word of God." Their narrow view, in my judgment, totally missed the point that these Indians had deep anxieties and fears that dominated their lives. While they had lived in isolation from the rest of the world, their hopes and fears bore a resemblance to those who lived in a more mechanized society.

I remember crossing a river with muddy banks. The Indians took great care to make sure that their tracks were covered, explaining that someone might retrieve their tracks after the mud had hardened and use them in magic against them.

That magic would be used against them was a fear many of the Indians expressed. Sickness was seen as the work of magic of evil spirits. When we first arrived in the Trio villages, I had attempted to get blood smears for the World Health Organization. These smears would reveal how prevalent malaria was among these people.

The Indians were very reluctant to have us use hypodermic needles when we attempted to get the blood smears. In part, their concern was that we would be taking part of them to use in magic against them. We used various strategies to get these smears, including injecting the needles into our own arms in an attempt to demonstrate that the needles were harmless.

I remember seeing a man covered with ulcerous sores all over his body. These sores had a most unpleasant stench. I managed to convince him to allow me to give him an injection of penicillin in the cheek of his buttocks. We had a supply of penicillin in powder form and mixed it with water. I guessed how much powder to mix. (No one was going to accuse anyone of medical malpractice here.) Since neither he nor for that matter any other Trio Indian had ever been exposed to penicillin before, he responded dramatically to this injection. In a few days, all the open sores had been healed. The Indians apparently thought we were superior witch doctors. The scary part was that they were bringing their sick children to us in the middle of the night to perform the same kind of magic.

Plenty of Surinam government officials were concerned about our safety. One person was at my home until eleven o'clock in the evening before the expedition, trying to persuade us not to go. The director of Surinam Airways made me promise that we would return in three weeks to where we started the expedition so they could meet us. They wanted the assurance that we had indeed survived the initial contact with the Trios.

One of three guides on our expedition to the Trio Indians, Coffeeana, went with me to keep this rendezvous while Claude and the two other Wai Wai guides stayed and continued work on the airstrip and, of course, on decoding the language. I remember developing a rather intense episode of diarrhea on the trail. We had stopped for the night, and I consumed a package of pea soup. It apparently didn't agree with me. I had no sense that I was getting dehydrated and didn't feel that I was in any sort of real danger; I realized that if a real emergency had occurred, I would essentially have been helpless. Here Coffeeana and I were, in middle of the jungle, all by ourselves. I realized how vulnerable I was. We are confronted every moment with our vulnerability, whether or not we are aware of how fragile life really is.

On the appointed date, we arrived at the agreed place for our rendezvous with our friends from Surinam Airways. We eagerly waited for the plane to arrive. We waited for three days. When the plane didn't arrive after three days, we felt it was time to return to the site where we were working on the airstrip. We left a written message at the very temporary campsite that we had established informing Mr. Zaul, the pilot, that we had been there and gave him an approximate compass azimuth where we could be located.

On the return journey, which took three days, Coffeeana thought he heard a wild turkey, which the Indians called a *pow-wesee*, near the trail and wanted permission to take the gun and try to hunt it. This would have been a valuable addition to the Indian's meat supply at the camp. I suggested that I had all I wanted to carry and that he would have to carry the wild turkey if he managed to kill it. The turkey would probably weigh fifteen or twenty pounds.

As Coffeeana disappeared into the heavy jungles, I sat down on a log to wait. In moments I was surrounded by a herd of probably twenty-five or thirty *javelinas*. They seemed to be unconcerned about my presence. My only thought was that this would be a wonderful prize for the Trios if Coffeeana could be alert enough to make a shot when he returned. It never dawned on me that the javelinas could be dangerous. When I heard Coffeeana returning, I shouted, "Shoot!" The alarmed animals disappeared in a flash before Coffeeana realized what was happening. When I told this story to Claude upon our return, he stated that he would have been climbing a tree to get away from them. I had been close enough to touch them with my hand.

Several days after I had returned to the camp where we were building the airstrip, the plane that was supposed to have met us a week earlier flew over our base camp. They had read our message and followed the compass readings that I had given. What a welcome sight they were. We wondered why they hadn't kept the appointed date that they had firmly set before we left on the expedition. We later learned that they left some care packages, including a cake that had a hard time surviving the three weeks before I would discover it. While we couldn't communicate directly with our colleagues, we waved at them from the ground, and they were able to pass the word to my wife that we had indeed survived the initial contact with the Trios because Leta hadn't known what had happened to us for nearly a month. Obviously, it is more nerve-racking to be on the "not knowing" end of things. I might add that during this period of "not knowing," Leta had lost about twenty pounds. She carried the heavier end of things by giving the care and attention that our children needed and by supporting my activities unconditionally. Her gift to me and to our children was truly beautiful.

In the meantime, we had several weeks to move the heavy logs off the airstrip that we were trying to build and dig out the mammoth roots. It wasn't all work. We had opportunities to interact with the Indians.

While I didn't have linguistics training, I followed Claude's example of phonetically writing down each word that we heard and trying to guess from the context how the word was used and what its meaning might be. I was very proud when I had discovered, or thought I had, the word for "good morning." I still distinctly remember that word. It was *kabowharueme*. I used the word on numerous occasions as a morning greeting. The Indians, who were eager to please and agree with us, would nod. One morning, I greeted a woman using this word. I noticed she looked up into the sky with a wrinkle on her forehead and used the word *kanobo,* which I knew meant "rain." There wasn't a cloud in the sky, and she had made her statement in what I considered a very tenuous way. I suddenly realized that my morning greeting meant that the sky was getting dark rather than the sky was getting light.

Before the expedition began, Commissioner Barends, who knew that I had been a paratrooper, asked me to make a parachute jump during the dedication ceremonies of the new airport facility. He added that no one had ever before made a jump in Surinam and that a parachute jump would be a feature that would make this dedication of the airport an additional attraction for a number of local citizens. He stated that the featured guest at this event would be the president of the United States, Dwight Eisenhower. I told the commissioner that I would be happy to make the jump on the condition that he would get a parachute that had been approved by the US Federal Aviation Administration. He agreed to do that.

I told him that this scheduled event would come near the end of our expedition to the Trios. We coordinated the date when the expedition would be completed to match that of the dedication of the new airport building.

41

Cut off from All Human Contact

Six weeks after the expedition had begun, it was time to return to the landing strip that we had called the Sipaliwini. During our expedition, the plane had been flown back to Paramaribo to be used on the different Surinam projects. A group of Trio Indians accompanied me back to the Sipaliwini site while Claude stayed back at the site, now called the Alalapadu airfield, where we were creating the airstrip. Claude promised to have the trees cut on part of the runway that would be used to take off while I was gone.

The fifty-mile journey over mountainous terrain would normally take three days, but we managed, by really exerting ourselves, to make it in two days. The Indians were certainly not used to walking this far in a day but did so at my urging. I was eager to be there in plenty of time to greet the plane when it was scheduled to arrive the next day.

With my blessing, the Trios, along with a Wai Wai guide who had accompanied me, returned to the site where Claude was located on the day the plane was scheduled to arrive. From midmorning on, I went to the nearby airstrip several times, expecting the plane momentarily. I would then return to the shelter where I had hung my hammock to wait. We had constructed a temporary shelter roof of palm branches. By midafternoon, I began to realize that the plane might not come until the next day. There was still time to make the necessary preparations for the planned parachute jump—but it was cutting the time very short.

It got dark about six o'clock. While there was a small lantern, which frequently went out during the night, it didn't provide enough light to read. So there was nothing to do after darkness fell but wait and live with one's thoughts.

When the expected plane didn't arrive on the day that had been agreed upon before the expedition began, I assumed that the plane would surely arrive the next morning. After all, the commissioner himself was expecting me to do "my thing" at the dedication ceremony. I walked out to the airstrip several times, searched the skies, and waited for the familiar sound of the plane. I would walk back to the idyllic camp that we had created several hundred feet from the savanna inside the forest wall. There was a pleasant stream nearby. The trees of the forest were at least a hundred feet high. As the wind would rustle through the trees, I thought I would hear the sound of the plane. All day long, I waited. About four o'clock, I realized that the plane was probably not coming. There was nothing to do but go back to my primitive camp.

More than fifty years later, I can still feel the anxiety building that I felt then. I realized that it was highly unlikely that I would attend the dedication of the Zanderij airport. What had happened? Had the pilot crashed in the vast jungles somewhere? He was the only one, other than my friend Claude, who knew where I was located—almost three hundred miles from the nearest road at a tiny clearing near the Brazilian border. When darkness fell, about six o'clock, there was really nothing to do but swing in my hammock. I probably should have been concerned that there were jaguars in the area—particularly as the dim lantern typically went out during the night. My deepest anxiety, however, was related to being utterly alone without knowing when I would next contact another person. Years later, I was to be in charge of a hundred-bed psychiatric ward and was present among those whose illness totally closed them off from every other human being—even though people surrounded them. I often remembered these jungle experiences when I thought of them and their isolation.

While the expedition was at the core of why Bob and I had come to Surinam, I have to confess that I felt restless even though I had wanted to be there. We were in the middle of exciting stuff. While I'm certainly not a hero and had plenty of anxieties related to whether our mission would succeed, I had some ambivalence about being in a place that was so isolated from all with which I was familiar. I was counting the days when the expedition would be over. I certainly wouldn't have had the courage to make that admission at the time. Obviously, I was eager to get back to my family and ready to get back to the States and pick up my life where I had left off. I identified with being a pilot flying over unexplored terrain, even though I was frequently terrified. My restlessness was certainly related to being in the isolation of the jungle—miles from the nearest human being. These feelings of isolation were the most intense during the long evening hours, when even my meager lantern refused to stay lit throughout the night.

By this time, I had given up on my involvement in the airport dedication ceremonies. I then began to wonder when I would see the next human being. I tried hard to shake the oppressive feelings of being cut off and not knowing why. I started memorizing the fortieth chapter of Isaiah from which the classic religious musical, *The Messiah*, was taken. It is a chapter that I still can quote from memory. I would often mistake the sounds of the breezes through the tall trees as the sound of a plane. I began to distrust my memory. At the end of the third day, there was nothing to do but lie in my hammock as the hours of darkness slowly wore on. The hours of daylight also became deeply troubling.

In years to come, whenever I saw a brook in an idyllic setting, I would experience a wave of anxiety. There was indeed was a lovely brook near our primitive shelter, and it supplied the clean running water that I needed. Yet the anxiety I experienced here apparently was somewhere in the fabric of my unconsciousness.

On the fourth day, I didn't bother to go to the airstrip. Although I had a supply of rice and canned food that I could have eaten, food lost its attraction. I vainly tried to block out everything except my attempts to memorize thirty-one verses of the fortieth chapter of

Isaiah. In spite of my efforts to concentrate on the task at hand, I was frequently distracted, and my mind would wander.

Near noon on the fifth day, I heard the plane overhead. I refused to be "conned" one more time by the sound. I didn't move from my hammock until I actually saw the plane overhead.

42

The Plane Finally Arrives

My friend Zaal explained he hadn't come at the agreed time because he was afraid that my parachute wouldn't open if I made my scheduled parachute jump. He added that he wasn't able to tolerate the idea that I might not survive the parachute jump. In deep frustration, I responded that I had made sixty-five parachute jumps and felt that I was in a position to make that judgment by myself. But I understood his good intentions.

After nearly a three-hour flight, I was back in Paramaribo about midafternoon—back with my wife and two elementary-school-aged children. I was exhausted physically, mentally, emotionally, and spiritually. Within a short time, reporters were at our house, interrogating me in a friendly way about the contact we had had with the Trio Indians. They apologized for pushing me the way they did but stated the story was too important not to be shared. My mind didn't want to cooperate. It was like I was in a daze. The details of our contacts with the Indians were clear enough to me, but in my exhaustion, I had a hard time articulating these details. When night came, I tried to sleep. It was the first time that I remember being so exhausted—so empty—that I couldn't sleep.

About midnight, I gave up and read through the mail that had come in my absence.

My primary concern was about Claude. I knew that it was important for him to return to Guyana and to his home with the Wai Wai Indians who had been part of our team. It was also important for me to get him home now that we had made the first successful contact with the Trios. He had played a vital role in our contact.

When morning arrived, I went to the Zorg en Hoop airport and contacted some of my pilot friends for whom I had flown emergency flights on several occasions. I explained that my friend Claude was still at the airstrip that we had built and asked if they would be willing to fly to pick him up and bring him to the city. They declined, saying that they had dates that night, which happened to be Saturday night, and didn't want to get stuck in the jungle. Upon reflection, I think that they were intimidated by the vastness of the jungle. I was irritated by their response but didn't openly express these feelings. I simply stated that I would then fly this mission myself.

Very little sleep and all the tensions of being isolated in the jungle for those five days, plus that fact that I hadn't flown for the previous six or seven weeks, all pointed to an irrational decision. Yet I felt strongly that my friend Claude shouldn't be stranded.

So began the flight that was to prove so traumatic to me. After the flight of slightly under three hours, I reached the site. I couldn't believe my eyes. The airstrip looked so different from the air than it had from the ground. It seemed as if the tops of the tree on the side of the runway leaned at the top to form an umbrella over the airstrip. I was surprised that Claude hadn't cut the trees at the "fly-out" end of the strip as he had promised to do. Having the trees cut was crucial to attempt a takeoff. My better judgment told me not to land, yet I was so task-oriented that I couldn't turn back.

I found an opening in what appeared to be an umbrella covering over the airstrip and made a perfect landing. Once I landed, I should have remained and focused on cutting out that fly-out at the end of the strip. In my exhaustion, I made the flawed decision to take off. (I feel my heart beating more rapidly now as I write this story more than forty years after the event. Obviously, the anxiety of that moment is still stuck somewhere in the core of my psyche.)

I realized that I was expected back in Paramaribo that evening.

More than that, the idea of being stuck at this site for another night, particularly with all the raw emotions that were so close to the surface, seemed intolerable. The Pleaser subpersonality had played a dominant role in the urgency that I felt of getting Claude and the guides out of this jungle setting and back to their homes.

I piloted the plane down this crude, very short runway with one Indian aboard. I broke ground and almost cleared the last tree that should have been cut down. I tried to veer slightly to miss the tree. Whether or not I would have managed to gain the necessary feet to clear that tree if I hadn't veered ever so slightly was problematic. I was flying right at stall speed and smashed into the top of that tree, which was well over a hundred feet high. We crashed gently through the trees. Fortunately, neither my passenger nor I were injured. Claude came rushing to the scene, saying something about God having a plan in this accident. My response to him, with more than a hint of anger, was God wasn't at the controls, I was. While I didn't say that this accident would have been avoided if the fly-out had been cut as promised, I felt that he bore some responsibility in this accident. Instead, I heaped a ton of blame on myself. Incidentally, Claude never apologized or appeared to accept any responsibility for not keeping his commitment to cut the trees at the end of the runway.

On top of the exhaustion that I have earlier described, I was numb. Words fail to fully describe the depth of the rawness of emotions that I was experiencing. I felt like an utter failure—overcome by feelings of guilt. To make things worse, the plane I had been flying belonged to the Surinam government. That evening and for many days to follow, I questioned everything, including my ability to fly, even though I had flown a number of critical missions. Even though I wouldn't allow the words to escape from my mouth and desperately attempted to blot out the thought, I couldn't stop wondering where God was in this trauma at the very time when everything pointed to success. For me, everything seemed to turn to ashes.

It was sometime in the late evening, near midnight, that planes were flying over the airstrip. Claude and I tried to signal to the pilot that we had all survived, unlike an earlier plane crash where two of my flying buddies had died. While I wasn't certain, I suspect that one of the pilots who had refused my request to make this flight earlier that morning was piloting the flight—undoubtedly flying at the instigation of District Commissioner Barends, who was a close friend. By the way, the fly-out end of the airstrip was cut the night of the crash. Unfortunately, it was too late.

Ironically, the next day, the very pilot that I had requested to fly the day before was there to rescue us. When I got back to Paramaribo, my good friend Mr. Barends, the district commissioner, was there to greet me. I will never forget his words. He said something like this: "Every landing and takeoff that you have made has been made under critical conditions. We are deeply grateful for what you have done." The words were soothing indeed, as the wounds of the spirit were deep. I will always regard him as a special friend.

To say that I was experiencing a crisis of confidence is something of an understatement. My self-confidence was shaken to the core. I even went so far as to have one of the US pilots who had brought the three-engine Northrop into the country check out my flying skills. He said he would do so to humor me but added that there was nothing wrong with my ability to fly.

I acknowledge that I have often been anxious but rarely depressed for any significant period of time. This time, I experienced acute depression. I tried to shake my depression by walking all over the city of Paramaribo for hours on end for days. My wife, Leta, and my friends, Walt and Marge Jackson, did everything that they could think of to help me lift the depression. While I valued their presence and their words, my emotions were too raw to be comforted by words. Walt, probably overidentifying with my pain, wrote my colleague, Bob Price, stating that he had not been sufficiently supportive of me. At one level, I gave my unspoken support for the intentions of his letter, but at the same time I was aware that Bob was doing everything that he could to keep things on track through fund-raising efforts.

I remember one government official made some negative comment about the airplane accident that really stung. (He had not been sympathetic with our contacts with the Indians, whom he considered subhuman) The emotional rawness of this event would be with me for years. The mere mention of this crash would revive the emotional pain and block that memory. It took an event twenty years later to recognize that this memory had been largely healed. This event will be described later.

Years later, as an administrative head as well as the director of clinical services of a one-hundred-bed ward in a VA psychiatric hospital, I saw veterans who were chronically and profoundly depressed. While the intensity of my depression lasted only weeks, I was able to empathize with the pain that they were experiencing in a way that I probably wouldn't have been able to do without this jungle trauma.

While I didn't openly say so, I was eager to return to the United States. At the very outset, I had not planned to make a career of being a missionary but planned to get a graduate degree in psychology. The crisis through which I was passing deepened my desire to return. I was questioning the value of my being in Surinam at this point of time.

43

A Blessed Event Is Coming

Earlier in the story, I spoke of coming down with a severe case of the mumps, with all its complications, just a week or so after graduating from Taylor University shortly before my twenty-second birthday. It was clear that my sperm count was dramatically impacted by this event. We had been pleasantly surprised when our second child, Robert, came three years after our first child.

Seven years had passed since our second child had arrived. While we had hoped that another child would come, we had accepted the idea that it was not going to happen. As ludicrous as it seems, conception followed the intense experiences in the jungles— probably the night that I had spent in town just before the plane crash the next day.

We had initially planned to stay in Surinam until December of 1960 but decided to return in September, partly so the baby could be born in the United States. We also questioned the wisdom of returning in the middle of a Michigan winter with a child only a few weeks old. An unspoken cause for the early return was the restlessness I had been experiencing since the plane crash in March 1960. Although I had made it clear at the very beginning of the Surinam adventure that I needed to start graduate studies within three years of leaving active duty, I still felt the expectations from my colleague that I would stay and continue my tasks in Surinam with the Trio and Wayanna Indians.

A few weeks after our expedition to the Trio Indians ended, David Bergamini, the assistant science editor from *Life Magazine*, arrived unannounced in Paramaribo and called me by phone. He stated that he had heard of our Trio Indian contact through the Dutch consulate in New York and had come to investigate the story. We flew him back to the Sipaliwini strip and retraced our way through the jungles to the Trio villages. This time, the Trio Indians were not as terrified as they had been in our first encounter. Unfortunately, David contracted malaria shortly after we arrived. With a high fever, he had difficulty walking the many miles of unmarked trails, and the Indians who were carrying our supply of medicine got ahead of us, and we couldn't catch them. David was burning up with fever and had to stop to rest frequently. As a result, we had to stop for the night before we were able to reach the group who had gone ahead of us. I became very concerned that David might not survive before we could reach the people who were carrying some of David's pack, including the medicine kit.

Two Trio teenagers stayed with us on the trail. One was the son of the chief. They made a campfire and apparently stayed awake all night long, watching out for us as we slept. I vividly remember being awakened by these young men in the wee hours of the morning. They were shouting, *"Mataboo, mataboo!"* and threw the logs from the fire into the darkness. I later learned that jaguars were stalking us. I was grateful for the vigilance of these young men.

These same young men were puzzled as to why we weren't able to speak the Trio language. I remember that they selected several leaves from a plant that they apparently thought had magical qualities. After chewing it until it was thoroughly masticated, they took it out of their mouths and gave it to us with the instructions to swallow it. We were assured that if we did, we would know how to speak Trio. If we had had confidence in their remedy for our lack of language achievement, we might have followed their instructions.

The next several weeks and months are somewhat of a blur in my memory. I didn't attempt to keep a diary after the accident, although I now wish that I had. I had purchased an older French Citroen car from the widow of Vicki Faijks, the pilot who had covered our initial landing at the place that we called the Kayser Airstrip and who was later killed in a plane accident. We considered it somewhat luxurious to have a car of any kind. The left front wheel came off on a number of occasions as I was driving. One time, it came off in front of District Commissioner Barends's home. He happened to be sitting on the front porch and laughed uproariously as I chased the tire, which was rolling down the street without the vehicle.

Nearly three months after the plane accident, Bob returned with another plane. This time it was a Family Cruiser. He had recruited a missionary couple, Ted and Nancy Leper, and they had some missionary experience. He was a licensed pilot, plus had an AandE mechanics license, and she was a physician. While their credentials sounded great, they were in Surinam for a relatively short time.

Bob stayed in Surinam for three or four weeks before returning to Philadelphia. Our son, Bob, fell off the porch of our home and broke his wrist one Friday afternoon. He was about to turn seven years old. (Our daughter recently told us that they were pretending that they were paratroopers and were honing their skills by jumping off the porch.) We took him to the doctor but were told that we had to return on Monday. They didn't accept patients after 4:30 p.m. We knew for sure that we were in a third-world country when we got that news. Bob Price, who was more helpful than Dr. Nancy Leper, made a splint for his wrist. When we returned to the medical facility on Monday, his wrist had begun to set inappropriately and had to be rebroken to be reset correctly.

This medical experience caused us to wonder, at least momentarily, whether it was safe for Leta to deliver our child in this country. We were emotionally ready to leave. The delivery date gave us another reason to want to return to the States earlier than we had initially planned.

44

Homeward Bound

We left for the States on a KLM Dutch plane in the early part of September 1960. Because of flight connections, we spent the evening in the lovely Dutch island of Curacao. At that time, Surinam, Curacao, and Aruba were states of the Netherlands, much the same way that Arizona is a state within the United States. Thanks to the airline, we stayed in a lovely hotel located in the center of the city and connected with a flight to Boston the next morning. We had been living on less than $2,000 a year in Paramaribo, so this hotel seemed like the height of luxury. We were very impressed when the waiter served us roast beef that overlapped the large plates on which it was served. To our surprise and chagrin, both Linda and Bobby asked to be served peanut butter sandwiches instead of what to us was exquisite cuisine. (On a cruise in 2003, Leta and I visited the hotel where we, with our two children, had spent the night. While it indeed was a fine hotel, it didn't seem as glamorous as it had forty-five years earlier.)

After a stop in Boston, we arrived in Philadelphia the next day. It was good to see Bob and Flo Price again. The dream that Bob and I had that guided our actions now seemed to leave me somewhat jaded. I was still numb from the haunting memories of the plane crash. As stated earlier, it would take some years to put these phenomenal experiences into some kind of perspective.

Nearly two decades had passed since we left Surinam. It was 1980, and I was a professor at Louisiana State University. Leta and I and Bob and Flo Price received a surprising and delightful invitation to attend a ceremony celebrating the completion of the New Testament into the Trio and Wayana languages. The linguists had done a yeoman's job in translating both of these languages into written form. It had taken twenty years to accomplish this feat. To put this invitation into perspective, the Trio Indians had never seen a printed page of any kind at the time of our initial contact in 1960. Now children and adults were reading and writing in their own language for the first time. This was an invitation we couldn't refuse.

Our old friend, the district commissioner Barends, met Leta and me at the Zandery airport in Paramaribo. He made an interesting comment shortly after greeting us. He said, "There is a very small window of opportunity in the history of a country with unexplored interior when anyone will have the opportunity to pave the way in opening up the border. You had the opportunity to participate in this unique opportunity. That window is now forever closed." He continued by saying that when we made our first flights twenty years earlier, there were no landing sites, no network of communication in the interior, and no medical services available to Indian tribes. All that has changed, he added. It was wonderful to see him again and to recognize that we did play a pioneering role in the development of the interior.

Some years earlier, I was highly honored and very pleased when the Surinam government gave me an award honoring my contributions to the development of the interior—the only foreigner to receive this award. I feel certain Commissioner Barends was the driving force behind this acknowledgement.

When we landed for the ceremony, we were warmly greeted by a number of Indians. Both Leta and Flo Price were in tears as they saw the Indians who remembered us coming to the airstrip, welcoming us back. There was a lump in my throat when I witnessed this sight. In fact there is a lump in my throat even now as I recall this event. It reminded me again of how these Indians had impacted my life and how much we are a part of each other, regardless of our histories or cultural backgrounds.

One of the first things I noticed when we first arrived at the village was the number of children present. When we made the first contact twenty years earlier, it was rare to see more than two or three children in any given village. Now the village was filled with children. There were several reasons for this phenomenon. The tribal people were no longer practicing infanticide, so infants were no longer abandoned in the jungle. Also, medical care was now available to them. Beyond that, I'm told that the fertility rate increased after malaria was controlled.

I remember walking down a jungle trail early the morning after we had arrived at the village where the ceremony was to take place. In that quiet time, I was reflecting on some of my experiences when we were on the expedition that was to be the first contact of the outside world with these Indians. Unexpectedly, I came upon a group of teenage boys sitting around a campfire. Even though they had not yet been born when I was first here, they wanted me to know that they knew all about an airplane crash where I had been the pilot.

The crash, described earlier, was the one where my colleague had not cut out the trees at the flight-out end of the runway. I had crashed into the tops of the tall trees as I was attempting a takeoff. These Indian teenage boys made the sounds of the plane taking off and then crashing into the trees. After they made these sounds, they roared with laughter. I was able to laugh with them. Earlier I described in some detail how much distress and considerable situational depression over the crash I had experienced. I hadn't been able to talk about it for years. When I laughed with these boys, I knew that something deep in my spirit had been healed.

The return trip to the LSU campus was a time to reflect on our original decision to undertake this most unusual journey decades before. Our experiences in the Amazon jungle forever changed my perspective of the world, and the experiences changed me in ways that surprised me.

I remember going to a drug store in Media, Pennsylvania, the morning after we arrived. It seemed to me that the clerk "pounced" on me to ask me what I wanted. I was so surprised that I couldn't immediately say what I had come to purchase. It was indeed a cultural shock to be back to the States again. In Paramaribo, if you wanted to make a purchase in a major store, you would first select a given item and give it to a clerk. That clerk would take this item to the cashier after it had been packaged. When the item was paid for, the cashier would give you a receipt, and you would then take the receipt to another clerk, produce the receipt, and then receive the item. It easily took ten or fifteen minutes to purchase a simple item. Apparently, this system of checking and rechecking was a leftover from colonial practices.

I wondered if I would have trouble driving on the right rather than the left side of the road. I was able to adjust with ease to both the driving and other aspects of life that were quite different from the country from which I had just come. While we had been away only eighteen months or so, we had been so thoroughly immersed in a third-world culture that for a few days it seemed that we were reentering a strange and foreign world.

In a day or two, we were on our way to Michigan. We stopped by to see Leta's family in western Michigan before going to Lansing, where I would be enrolling at Michigan State University. We had few funds available other than from the GI Bill, which would prove most helpful. We had exhausted what savings we had during our life-changing adventures in Surinam. I had been ordained in the Pilgrim Holiness Church, a strong conservative theological orientation that saw itself as being more Methodist than the Methodist denomination itself. I had known for some time that I could not in good conscience remain in the Pilgrim Church.

I briefly looked at a Bible church that was searching for a student pastor. (We desperately needed funds.) I was asked to give several trial sermons, and fortunately for me, I flunked. Soon thereafter, I had contact with a Methodist district superintendent and served briefly as an associate pastor to a Methodist church in Lansing. This proved to be a happy association, although there was some discomfort in this change of direction. This assignment proved to be a lifesaver for me both financially and emotionally.

I had been the first-ever military chaplain to represent the Pilgrim Holiness Church and hence this denomination gave me significant amount of publicity. When I was in the process of leaving the Pilgrim Holiness Church, my changing theological outlook was suspect, and my former classmates kept an emotional distance. On the other hand, my new Methodist colleagues also tended to put me in a theological box because of my very conservative background. By and large, they were understandably cautious and somewhat uncomfortable about my joining their fold. To make this shift from the only church I had known as a youth and young adult was a very lonely experience.

While we were in Surinam, we had regularly taken medication to prevent malaria. We also slept under mosquito nets during our time there. Malaria was a risk in the capitol city of Paramaribo, but the risk was much higher in the southern interior of the country. I spent a lot of time in this mosquito-infested area.

I mentioned earlier that we had taken blood smears from the Trio Indians at the request of the World Health Organization. Every blood smear that we managed to get from the Indians indicated that all had been infected with malaria. I certainly had been aware of the risks of getting malaria and hence took the medication (I no longer remember its name) faithfully. What I hadn't been told was that we needed to continue taking it for a specified time after we returned to the States. I did what seemed to me the obvious thing to do: I quit taking the prevention pill after our return.

I remember that Michigan fall had been lovely, particularly in late September and in October. I had gone to a Michigan State football game with my very good friend from Owosso days, Harold Cox. It seemed that the ceremonies and rituals of the game showed the spirit of my country, and I was glad to be home.

Linda had reached her tenth birthday, and Bobby, as we then called him, was turning seven in November. In Surinam, they had attended very rigid, Dutch-speaking schools. The atmosphere of the Lansing schools must have seemed like a breath of fresh air to them.

Sometime in early November, just as the heavy, rainy weather of late fall had set in, I began to exhibit malaria symptoms. I went to a physician near our home in South Lansing and explained that we had been living in malaria country. I said I thought I had picked up malaria. He was a recent graduate of a medical school in Brooklyn, New York.

Typical of so many physicians of that era, he immediately told me in rather blunt terms that it was his job to do the diagnosis and my job to acknowledge his expertise. He then arrogantly began to tell me that I didn't have malaria but was having some difficulty in adjusting to a very different climate than I had been accustomed to in the last several years.

The expectation at that time was for patients to accept without question the authority of the physician. But I can't believe that I returned to him several times with the same symptoms that were getting worse. On the third or fourth visit, he stated emphatically that I didn't have malaria but that he would give me a test to prove his point. The test indeed came back indicating that no malaria was present. This procedure appeared to prove his point. I later learned that this particular test often presented a false negative.

A week or so later, I had developed a 106-degree fever and was close to being delirious. This same doctor ordered me to the hospital, where he did not permit me to get out of bed. After five days, he pontifically told me that he had finally figured what was wrong. He stated that I had malaria complicated with pneumonia. He never once acknowledged that I had repeatedly tried to tell him that because of my experience in Surinam. (Fortunately, a rapport is now beginning to develop between physician and patient, particularly where there is an implicit assumption that they are partners in the search for health.)

When I was released from this unneeded hospitalization—unneeded, that is, if my physician had not blindly pursued his course of action—I had no money to pay the hospital bill. The very first check I received from the church was sent as a down payment on the bill to the hospital. A day or so later, I received an angry letter from the sister who was the administrator, accusing me of being a minister who ducked out of financial responsibility on my hospital stay. Our letters had crossed in the mail. To say this letter stung — particularly in light of the medical fiasco that had just taken place — is an understatement. This was the first communication from the hospital after my release. Perhaps I should have taken the initiative to reassure the financial office one more time that a payment was indeed coming. I never received an apology or an acknowledgement of payment from the administrator of this hospital.

While it took a great deal of maturation on my part, I came to appreciate the importance of the doctor and patient making a team in terms of facilitating health care. It ultimately played a significant role in my conviction about holistic health. More about that later.

My hospitalization and the associated expenses had certainly been unexpected. But a child won't wait to be born. On December 12, 1960, Edward Alan Friesen made his entry into this world. His siblings would tease him about being born in a bird hospital. Actually, it was the Sparrow Hospital in Lansing, Michigan. Because of the seven-year gap between him and our second child, it was almost like having the second family.

In addition to this blessing, we also received an unanticipated second blessing. My brother Merle and his wife, Dolores, came to Lansing from their military base in Illinois, where Merle was a commissioned officer, and paid the hospital bill without telling us. We were unaware of their action until it was time for discharge. On a number of occasions, they have attempted to demonstrate their Christian commitment by acts of generosity to many different people. This gracious gift left a deep impression on us.

—

Dramatic changes have occurred in Surinam since we returned to the States in September 1960. The country is now independent of the country of the Netherlands although Dutch remains the official language of the country. The country experienced a major revolution described in Linda's account in the appendix.

The most notable change relates to mobility. In 1960 there were few cars, roads, as well as few people living beyond the city limits of cities and towns. There is a notable increase in the number of affluent homes. One suburban area that we witnessed now has homes that are likely in multi-million dollar price range. There is now an impressive bridge that crosses the Surinam river, that is high enough to allow ship travel, and serves as part of the land route that leads to the French Guiana border.

I was amazed at how young to middle-age residents know little of their history, particularly in reference to Operation Grasshopper, which began in 1959 and played a major role in opening up the interior of the country. When Operation Grasshopper began, there were not active landing strips in the interior. Beyond bauxite, there were no mining operations. Now there are a number of gold mines that have opened since that time. There are now towns that extend in what was then undeveloped jungles.

Claude Leavitt and I contacted the Trio Indians, who had never been previously been contacted by the outside world prior to 1960. While their language was linguistically sophisticated, there was no written language. Now the Trio and the Wayana tribes have a written language, thanks to the extensive effort of linguists who spent approximately twenty years putting their language into written form.

Now the tribal villages clearly show the impact of the change. The Indian tribes have for the most part gone beyond the hunting and gathering stage of development. The younger generation have lost many of the survival skills that their forbearers so carefully honed.

Now most villages have elementary schools that are conducted in the Dutch language. Some of the Indian students have gone to the capitol city, where they can take advantage of secondary schools, although it has been described as painful for them to leave the jungle environment to pursue these educational opportunities. I understand that plans are being formulated for students who want to attend education beyond the elementary to live together in a common community.

My daughter, Linda, described beautifully the wonderful way we were entertained in Surinam. I will not duplicate what she has described other than to say that I had intended on attending a Rotary meeting in Paramaribo. The meeting in Paramaribo got cancelled the evening we planned to attend. Our group did have an excellent meal at the restaurant where Rotary meetings are typically held.

Another major change has been the way that Surinam Airways has developed. In the 1950's the passenger was primarily restricted to the flight of one Aero commander with very limited seating. Surinam Airways has four commercial airplanes: a Boeing 747 and three Boeing 373 aircraft.

On the return leg of a flight from Paramaribo to Aruba, I was traveling on a Boeing 737. I gave my business card to one of the flight attendants and stated casually that I still was in possession of a pilot's license from the Surinam Civil Aviation Division; she gave my card to the pilot. He promptly invited me to the cockpit while the plane was inflight to Aruba. The pilot stated that he became part of Operaton Grasshopper after I returned to the States, adding that he had landed at some of the airstrips where I had made the first ever landing. We had a great conversation for about 30 minutes before I returned to my assigned seat.

Part 6

Developing a Second Career

45

Enrolling at Michigan State University

It was with a great deal of fear and trembling that I enrolled in graduate school at Michigan State University in January of 1961.

Earlier in the story, I spoke of the fear I'd entertained since childhood about my intellectual limitations. While this picture began to slowly change during my college years, I was awed and intimidated by entering what seemed like the "big time" to me, a Big Ten university. After all, it had been ten years since I had graduated from Taylor University. While my academic performance at Taylor had been average, I started by enrolling in only six credit hours in Michigan. I was being very conservative. I was pleasantly surprised when I received an A and a B. After surviving that first crisis of confidence, I took on a full academic load for the rest of my tenure as a graduate student.

In the meantime, financial survival became important. With the new arrival, our family now consisted of five. Perhaps the most important break came in June 1961, when I was assigned to serve as pastor for a circuit of United Methodist churches located in the village of Sunfield, Michigan, as well as two in rural communities while still holding my credential as a Pilgrim Holiness minister. This delightful assignment was to last four years. The congregation allowed me to be a graduate student and serve the three congregations as time permitted. There was little time left to be present with the family after trying to meet the pastoral needs of these wonderful folks and at the same time carry a full graduate load. Again, Leta never complained about my lack of availability and was fully supportive of my academic goals and me. The folks at the church couldn't have been more understanding. We still have strong friendships that date back to our years in this great community. More about that later.

When I left active military duty, it hadn't dawned on me that I wasn't giving up the military forever. I soon learned I would be starting a new and exciting aspect of my military career. After arriving in Lansing, Michigan, I heard about an opening in an artillery battalion for a chaplain. This opening would provide some needed income. I would be with this group for Saturday drills each week and as much of Sunday as I could possibly manage as well as spending two weeks for several years in the summer at Camp McCoy, Wisconsin. This position became an opportunity to develop a relationship with military reservists, many of whom were not active in a local congregation. It was very fulfilling to be present when a reservist was experiencing a crisis or a celebration in their lives or the lives of their families.

Of the many people that I had contact with during the next three or four years, one stands out: a university professor named Dr. Richard Featherstone. He was also a major in the same artillery battalion. We had several significant conversations during our weekend military drills and during our two-week summer field exercises.

With some embarrassment, I remember that I thought I needed to have a response to every question. I remember Dr. Featherstone asking me if I had read a book called *The True Believer* and if I could comment about it. While I acknowledged that I hadn't read the book, I was too insecure not to comment on what I thought was implied. I totally missed the point. He didn't seem to hold me in some kind of academic disdain for my clumsy response. Even after I was reassigned to another unit, we kept in contact. On one occasion, when returning briefly to Michigan from Arizona many years later, I telephoned his home to be informed by his wife that he had succumbed to cancer in the midst of a thriving academic career. I was shocked; I felt the loss of a valued friend. The Department of Education at Michigan State University established a foundation in his honor.

On the lighter side, I remember being on a military exercise in the upper part of Lower Michigan. It was a beautiful night, with no clouds in sight. It was fairly late in the evening when a young captain asked if I was going to set up a tent. My response was that I would take the risk of there being rain. I rolled out my sleeping bag on an air mattress under the open sky. The captain did the same. In the wee hours of the morning, a sudden thunderstorm descended upon us. We both took shelter under the front part of a two-and-half-ton military truck. I soon discovered that I had moved into a spot where the rain came through the hood and down to a greasy engine, dripping from there and hitting me in the face. The options were limited, but I made a slight adjustment in my location.

Soon, I received word from the appropriate military headquarters that I was being promoted to major. The position I occupied called for the rank of captain. A fellow chaplain who wasn't eligible for promotion temporarily vacated his position as regimental National Guard chaplain and accepted the captain position so I could accept the promotion in an authorized pay position. The understanding was that when he was eligible for promotion, I would vacate this spot. So for six months, I was in the National Guard rather than the Federal Reserves.

I am not sure how it happened, but apparently some chaplain in a supervisory position had informed the US Army Chaplain Center and School (a school every military chaplain has to attend) that I was soon to receive a PhD in counseling psychology. To my total surprise, I received orders assigning me to the chaplain school. I had two weeks to turn down this position, but I happily accepted. This was to be my military assignment for the next nineteen years. This teaching position would represent more than half of my total military service.

46

A Faculty Member at the Chaplain Center and School

My official title for the assignment at the chaplain school was mobilization designee, which meant that if I were to be recalled to full-time active military duty, I would go directly to the army's chaplain school. My first assignment was in the summer of 1965. The school had recently moved from Fort Slocum, New York, located on a small island in Long Island Sound, to Fort Hamilton, which was located at the very south end of Brooklyn.

All chaplains attending the career course had been through the basic course some years earlier. After a few years of active duty, many chaplains would choose to return to minister to civilian congregations and still remain active in the Army Reserve or National Guard program. These reserve chaplains were to be my students.

A number of these chaplains had received advanced degrees and were faculty members of a seminary or a university. It was always a most interesting mixture of rabbis, priests, and Protestant ministers from every imaginable denominational background. Many of these clergymen (at that time, all military chaplains were male) had stepped out of the box, so to speak, in terms of their usual clergy roles. I remember that one of the Baptist chaplains had lived for most of the year in a kibbutz in Israel.

While I didn't get to know many of the chaplains who were

266

going through my course as part of the career reserve training very well, I did get to know a number of the other mobilization designees. Most of the names of these fellow instructors have slipped out of my memory, but I can remember their faces. For example, there was a Southern Baptist chaplain from Florida who was the second ranking person in the Florida Baptist Convention. We shared a number of experiences together in Manhattan during the weekends. He was a true kindred spirit.

We both held the rank of lieutenant colonel at the time. He made a tongue-in-cheek comment on one occasion in which he suggested that when we were promoted to colonel and take the pledge not to be smart asses about our new status. In time, he took another assignment while I remained as an instructor at the chaplain school. Some years later, he made an official visit to the chaplain school. (By then we both had been promoted to full colonel.) I was surprised to see that he was part of an entourage of official visitors who came on very short notice to my classroom to make a formal presentation. Although we hadn't met for several years, we winked across the classroom as soon as we saw each other. We both had remembered his comment from some years before.

I fondly remember the name of Rabbi Stanley Dreyfus. He was a scholar in every sense of the word and a wonderful human being. I found him to be very personable. On several occasions, I had the opportunity to be his guest for a meal in his Brooklyn apartment, located on Prospect Park West on the fiftieth floor of a high rise. He and his wife were also my guests at the officer's club at Fort Hamilton on several occasions. Our times together were always memorable. (I had the opportunity of speaking with him by telephone in January 2005. It was inspiring to speak to him again after so many years. We agreed to contact each other again soon.)

I distinctly remember an incident that involved a Christian chaplain who was born into a Jewish family. He had become a member of a strict fundamentalist protestant denomination and took offense at something that Rabbi Dreyfus had said in the classroom at the chaplain school. He ended up making quite a scene in front of his classmates and later to the school commandant. The rabbi was a great storyteller and told an elaborate story that was both clever and humorous. I don't think that the young chaplain realized that he was not reacting so much to the rabbi's story as he was likely giving evidence that he really hadn't worked through his conflicts relating to his Jewish background and his conversion to Christianity. Rabbi Dreyfus was deeply concerned that this young man had totally misunderstood the point of his story. This young chaplain's anger surfaced in a way that was both destructive and embarrassing to many of us.

I remember another rabbi named Pinkus Goodblatt. His nickname was Pinky. He was excited about life. In our conversations, he would pick up on something that had been said during our conversations and enthusiastically proclaimed that he would make a point of including that idea in a future sermon. It was hard to get a word in edgewise with him. I once visited him in his home in California. What a delightful experience that was. I heard some years ago that Pinky had passed on. I was happy to have counted him among my valued friends.

During my summer military assignments to New York, my chaplain colleagues and I saw many Broadway and off-Broadway shows. I earlier shared the experience of attending a *Porgy and Bess* performance while I was attending the chaplain school then located at Fort Slocum, New York, in the summer of 1953. I attended with a group of chaplains from the school. I was certainly naïve about Broadway productions. More significantly, I was deeply conflicted because the Pilgrim Holiness Church condemned movies as evil, and I assumed that this denomination would also condemn theater performances. I felt that I had an obligation to observe the rules of my denomination even though I didn't agree with that position. (I seriously doubt whether this denomination, now known as the Wesleyan Church, would hold that position today. At least they have relaxed their position on a number of issues that were significant at that time.)

During one two-week period, I arranged for my good friend, Dr. Carroll Rinehart, to assist me in making holistic health presentations at the school. Some of the chaplains from the more conservative denominations thought our presentations were too "human-istic," meaning that they went beyond their theological boundaries. They became quite vocal and expressed their dissent to the admin-istration of the school. It was a minor bump in the road.

I was assigned to the Chaplain Center and School for nineteen years. I suspect I still hold the longevity record in terms of length of assignment. I probably would have stayed longer, but a new military regulation came out stating that no one was to be assigned to one unit more than five consecutive years. During those years, the Chaplain Center and School had moved from Fort Hamilton in Brooklyn to Fort Wadsworth, Long Island, and then on to Fort Mon-mouth, New Jersey. During the two weeks each summer (some-times I taught for four weeks), I watched the Verrazano Bridge be-ing built. Many nights, I sat on a bench overlooking the Narrows, the body of water that separates Brooklyn from Staten Island, and watched the ships coming into and leaving the New York Harbor. I also remember the impressive flotilla one Fourth of July that com-memorated this most important event in the annals of our nation's history. I will always remember the officer's club at Fort Hamilton. It was an old fort with walls that were nearly a yard thick. This of-ficer's club had a rich history and tradition.

Fort Wadsworth, located on the Staten Island side of the Nar-rows, was for a while the home of the Chaplain Center and School. During this period, it was the only military organization on this post. It is interesting that the New York Marathon began at the en-trance of this military post.

While I was never assigned to Governor's Island, I frequently stayed there. It was a very short ferry ride from the southern part of Manhattan. On one occasion, my wife was driving to our tem-porary quarters on this island when a whirlwind dust storm sud-denly materialized. We saw a lady walking who was engulfed by the storm. She didn't hesitate for a moment to get into our car when we offered her a ride. Who says that New Yorkers won't speak to strangers?

I also remember returning to Fort Hamilton from Manhattan on the subway near midnight. During the ride, New York had a severe power outage. While the subways operated on an emergency system, it was totally dark when the passengers emerged from the subway at the end of the line. I watched a lady that I judged to be in her fifties step out into the dark. I wanted to offer to walk her to her place of residence, but I felt that she would be more frightened to accept any offer to accompany her than to walk alone in the darkness.

My roommate, who happened to be a Roman Catholic chaplain, had also gone into the city that evening but hadn't returned when I found my way back to my quarters in the total darkness. I unwisely left the door unlocked so he wouldn't need to fumble for a key to open the door. It turned out to be a naïve decision.

Sometime in the wee hours, I had the sensation that someone was peering in my face. I vaguely remember being puzzled by this strange behavior and attributed it to my roommate before drifting back into a deep sleep. As it happened, he had unlocked the door when he came in without realizing that I had left it unlocked. The person who was gazing in my face was actually an intruder who came into the room after my roommate arrived and who made off with both of our billfolds. I laughingly confessed to my roommate the following morning that in my state of dim awareness, I had wondered if he was gay and was making a sexual overture.

47

Assigned to the Health Command

While I had no plans to leave my assignment as an instructor at the school, the new policy stating that a reservist could only stay in a given assignment for five years meant I had to take another position.

I accepted the opportunity to be assigned to the health command. The first two-week assignment was to the hospital at Fort Leavenworth, Kansas. Fort Leavenworth is an old, classic army encampment with a long and colorful military history. It was a pleasure to be assigned there. It was a laid-back, comfortable assignment. (Most people identify this post with the military prison, but it is in a separate section. I had the opportunity to visit the famous prison when Lieutenant Calley of Mai Lai was imprisoned there.) Earlier I had completed Command and General Staff College, located on the main post.

The following summer, I was assigned to the Fort Sarn Houston Military Hospital in San Antonio, Texas, as a mobilization designee. While my office was in a chapel, my entire day was spent counseling young soldiers, both male and female, who were training to become medics. Many of the clients were young, homesick mothers, many of them single mothers, who had volunteered for military service while other family members (often their parents) cared for their small children. The primary reason for their enlistment was to further their career opportunities by becoming eligible to enroll in a college or university, which was being offered as an incentive for them to join. (A number of these kinds of people would, in future years, find themselves unexpectedly involved in the Iraq conflict.) Many of them were experiencing a great deal of ambivalence at having chosen the military as their strategy to open doors of opportunity for both education and travel.

In the evening, I often went to the psychiatric ward of the hospital to see soldiers who had either made a suicide attempt or were hospitalized with a psychiatric diagnosis. It was a very full schedule, not unlike what I was seeing in my private practice as a psychologist in Tucson.

On weekends, I made it a point to get acquainted with as much of the city of San Antonio as possible—often walking fifteen or twenty miles. One of the points of interest was visiting the military headquarters area—quite some distance from the main post. In the past, it was where the famous Indian chief, Geronimo, had been imprisoned. I was surprised to see domesticated wild animals freely roaming on the parade grounds. These animals symbolized the history of the chief's imprisonment. He purportedly had refused to eat anything but wild meat. From that day forward, the military has continued to keep live "wild" animals on the parade grounds. Obviously, these animals have become very tame.

The final two years in the military, my reserve assignment was to Tripler Hospital in Honolulu. It was a pink hospital set on the side of high hill, facing away from the ocean. I was told both the color of the hospital and its position was a stipulation from the lady who had owned the property and presumably gave the property to the military.

The chaplain's office was on the back side of the hospital, overlooking the ocean. It was certainly a pleasure to take a break by going to the lanai, a large porch structure that extended out from the chaplain's office.

The hospital is a large facility that was undergoing major modification during the two years that I was assigned there. (On a visit during October 2002, we met hospital personnel who stated there were areas of the hospital that they hadn't entered and didn't know the layout.) I really don't know how common this perception was then, but I do know how confusing the hospital layout was for me, particularly during my first two-week tour of duty to this hospital.

I well remember my first evening there. I was the on-call chaplain for the entire night. On some nights, no calls were received. But on this night, I was busy all night long, responding to one emergency call after another. These calls came from different parts of the hospital, which presented quite a challenge in itself. Because of the major remodeling effort, it was not possible to go from one wing of the hospital to the next without a thorough orientation, which I didn't have. For example, I would receive uncertain instructions from one person to take the elevator four floors up, cross into a wing and then take the elevator two floors down, and follow another corridor for some distance before taking another elevator. There were few people in the corridors during the wee hours of the morning, which added to the confusion. I remember meeting with some of the offspring of an elderly person who was obviously dying. They appeared to have a great deal of difficulty with their mother's impending death.

Before our time together was finished, they were able to release their mother to God's care. She died later that night.

I had barely gotten back to the office when I got a call to go to the neonatal emergency room. (Tripler had three emergency rooms, all located in different parts of the hospital.) I did a lot of wandering around, trying to find this particular emergency room. I finally got there about 2:00 a.m. There were two doctors and two nurses on duty at this ER. When I arrived a young physician told me that there was a child twenty-four hours old who appeared normal at birth, but they had discovered the infant in fact had a major heart defect. He said that they were considering having the child sent to a New York facility that specialized in this kind of crisis.

He then told me that the parents had requested that the child be baptized. Under normal conditions, I would have spoken to the parents about the meaning of baptism. The father was a black soldier who had come from a Baptist faith tradition, where only adult baptism is practiced. His ability to speak in the Korean language was practically nonexistent. The mother was a Korean lady who spoke almost no English. I surmised that she might have come from a Buddhist tradition.

This young couple was obviously in crisis and wanted desperately to do everything possible for their infant daughter. The couple was brought into the nursing station, where the day-old infant was hooked up to a maze of life support apparatuses. When I first saw the child lying nude on the table, my first reaction was to wonder where I could place my hands, which had been dipped into the baptismal bowl, on this very vulnerable child. As I dipped my hands into the baptismal bowl and placed my hands to her tiny forehead, I repeated the words of the ritual: "I baptize you in the name of the Father, Son, and Holy Spirit."

At that moment, both doctors and nurses laid their hands on the very frightened parents. It was truly a profound moment, where all of us recognized that we were in the presence of God in a very special way—standing at that mysterious moment between life and death. I was so inspired by the response of the medical team. I think everyone was deeply moved by this moment. I suspect that one of the doctors may have been Jewish. At this moment, it didn't matter. We were one in the Spirit.

As soon as the baptism was finished, the doctor who had first described the serious medical situation told the parents that he wanted to examine the child one more time. I suspect that he made this decision during the baptismal moment. After examining the child, he put his stethoscope down. Speaking to the parents, he stated that this child was not going to live. He then suggested that the child be taken off the life support systems, wrapped in a blanket, and placed into their arms as long as the child lived. The parents numbly agreed.

As soon as all the equipment had been unhooked, the child was placed in the arms of the weeping parents. Doctors, nurses, and I surrounded the parents for the next thirty minutes. We had no higher priority than to be present to the parents as life slowly ebbed from this precious child. We shared this awesome moment when this child transcended this life into the hands of a waiting God.

During my usual routine for the two weeks of active duty, I would try to visit the different wards and intensive care units. I was surprised to find one of the patients to be a relative of a former parishioner in Sunfield, Michigan. I also attempted to meet as many staff as I could during the visits to these different units.

One day as I was finishing a counseling session, I was told that someone in the hallway was waiting to see me. I greeted him with the comment that he looked very familiar. It turned out to be my son, whom I hadn't seen in a number of years. For one thing, I had no idea that he was in Hawaii (he doesn't like to fly), and he had gained more weight than I had ever seen him carry. He didn't look the same way as I had remembered him. Still, it was embarrassing not to recognize my own son. We had the opportunity to spend a number of hours with Bob and his partner, Michael.

The officer's club at Tripler Hospital was on a hill overlooking the ocean. We could see the planes flying in and out of the international airport. I can easily understand why so many find this island so enchanting.

On several occasions, we drove around the island of Oahu (at least as far as the road went) as well as around Maui. We also had the opportunity to drive across the Big Island of Hawaii. The scenery is truly spectacular.

On one occasion, Dr. Bill Brooks arranged for us to use his father's condo on Maui. A close friend and colleague of over a half-century, Bob Price and his lovely wife Flo, accompanied us to Maui. We experienced a hurricane that wreaked a lot of damage on various islands of the Hawaiian chain. The condo was located on the beach. We attempted to tape the window to try to keep the lovely picture window facing the beach from disintegrating. We watched the progress of the storm until the electricity went out. On the news the next morning, we heard that a sailor had been swept off the deck of a ship about ten miles off shore. Miraculously, he was carried by the enormous waves and crashed on the rock-strewn shoreline. All of his limbs were reportedly broken, but he survived.

Leta and I were driving around some impressive hills in Maui during one Christmas season. We heard for the first time the song

Grandma Got Run Over by a Reindeer, which resulted in peals of laughter from us. Some years later, the male choir in which I sang, The Sons of Orpheus, included this song in their repertoire during several Christmas seasons.

I unexpectedly met Chaplain Gordon Schweitzer and his wife, Theo, on a Hawaiian cruise on the ship called the *Norwegian Wind* in the fall of 2002. We had gone through jump school at about the same time at Fort Bragg, North Carolina, forty-six years earlier. While we had met once or twice at chaplain conferences over the years, it had been twenty-five or so years since we had last met. What a celebration it was to spend a number of dinner hours sharing memories of our common experiences. We easily recognized each other. It added a special luster to this particular voyage.

48

Meanwhile, Back at the University

Having just returned from Surinam, I enrolled at Michigan State University. I was terrified that I might not be able to do graduate-level work. While my academic experiences during my college years steadily improved, I still had a poor image of my academic potential despite the unusual professional experiences in which I had performed rather well. We arrived in mid-October, and I enrolled at the university in January.

I was one of about fifty persons who had a clerical background to enroll in the counseling program. Dr. John Jordan had been instrumental in initiating this program, although many of his colleagues didn't share the enthusiasm that Dr. Jordan had.

I began to sense that I would be able to complete a master's degree, but I hadn't seriously considered entering a doctoral program. At the beginning of graduate studies, I would have been willing to state that I wouldn't pursue further training if I could have been sure of attaining a master's degree. I was surprised to receive feedback from several professors in response to the early term papers I had written that they had been impressed with my ability to write. I was taken aback by their response but obviously pleased. I had spent a great deal of time polishing these papers. My first drafts often have to be significantly changed. I typically would not volunteer a response to the topic being discussed in class primarily because I was afraid that my opinion would not be considered appropriate. I would realize after the fact that my response was not only appropriate but often insightful. I still didn't trust my ability to survive or compete in the world of academia.

After surviving the master's degree, I applied for the doctoral program. I took the graduate record examination plus one other screening test that purportedly correlated highly with the graduate record exam. My advisor told me that I did extremely well on one but not well on the other.

During the faculty interview that would determine whether I would be admitted to the doctoral program, one of the most visible and highly touted professors objected to my admission on the basis that it wasn't the responsibility of the university to train clergy, even though the master's degree I had just completed was in counseling and not in theology. As a result of his objection, I was admitted to the doctoral program on probation, which was lifted after a semester or so of my involvement in this program. Knowing that he had a hangup with clergy (I suspect that there was also some competition with Dr. Jordan that may have been involved in this professor's objections), I tended to stay at arm's length from him.

Two encounters with him were initially traumatic but turned out to be humorous. I had to take one of his courses because it was required for my degree. He announced that there would be no examinations and that the entire grade would depend on the term paper. He said that the best three papers (out of thirty or so students) would be identified and that these three students would be responsible for sharing their papers during one of the class periods.

On the day that he announced the three best papers, he read my name and asked, "Who is Eugene Friesen?" He expressed obvious surprise that I was among those he had identified as being the three best papers. His response was, "You mean you are Eugene Friesen?"

I was fortunate that he had only remembered my face and not my name.

Everyone in the United States who was at least ten years old on November 22, 1963, remembers where they were when they got the chilling news that President John Kennedy had been assassinated. I was on the campus of Michigan State University when I heard the news on that Friday afternoon. I was in the middle of doctoral studies. It also happened to be our son Bob's tenth birthday. Those who saw the drama unfold on television will never forget the events as they transpired during the weekend. It certainly overshadowed our son's birthday celebration.

Dr. Bill Kell, now deceased, was the teaching professor at the counseling center on campus who provided hands-on professional experiences for graduate students who were planning to be therapists. Bill's classes were both deeply experiential and theoretical. He shared himself in profound ways. Once, he referred to a shattering trauma that occurred in his life while he was a military officer stationed overseas without specifying what that trauma had been.

His response was to go into a deep depression that left him immobilized. He reports that his body became so rigid that he literally couldn't move. He sensed that he was in the process of dying. He describes a moment when, somewhere in the depth of his being, he was confronted with the choice of living or dying. In his mind's eye, he saw two doors. One was marked Life, and the other was marked Death. He remembers choosing the door marked Life. At that moment, everything changed for him. Life began to seep back into his body. He gradually regained most of his mobility. In time, he entered graduate studies and eventually became a professor.

When I retired, I gave away most of my books to various sources, including the local library. I decided that I would keep only the books with significant impact on my life or that I would most likely reread within five years. His book, entitled *Impact and Change*, remains in my library as a cherished possession.

Another professor that left a deep impression on me and influenced the way I saw the world was Professor Useem in the Department of Anthropology and Sociology at Michigan State. The classes that I took from him often had more than a hundred students — sometimes twice that amount. His classes were interactive, and he often called on students from the roster for their input. Drawing from the book entitled *The Ten Grandmothers: Epic of the Kiowas*, authored by Alice Marriott, he talked about the Kiowa Indian experience of cultural change and its implications for our rapidly changing society.

While I can clearly see the face of another professor, his name escapes me. He taught a course on the psychological testing instrument known as the Rorschach. Here, the entire grade depended on the term paper. The title of my paper was "The Color Shock of the Rorschach." Near the end of the term, he invited us to make an appointment to discuss our papers. I had a great deal of difficulty getting an appointment time. When I finally got the appointment, I was more than a little anxious. His primary evaluative comment to me was, "You spelled 'Rorschach' wrong throughout the paper!" My face must have turned red. I did get an *A* out of the course.

Another humorous moment involved Professor Fox from the statistics department. To set the stage, I entered college life with a very weak math background. The subject terrified me, and I made every attempt to avoid it. The doctoral program required some statistical background that would facilitate research programs. I would gladly have taken a dozen extra courses in my doctoral program to avoid this one in the stat department.

To say I was traumatized would have been a monumental understatement. Dr. Fox would write formulas that would filled entire blackboards. I would meticulously copy these formulas without having the foggiest idea of the point he was trying to make. Dr. Fox would examine these formulas and then began to invert parts of the equation. I was totally paralyzed.

On one occasion, the good professor was attempting to explain the theoretical foundation of certain concepts in such ethereal ways that he often lost even most of the statistic majors. On this day, he was waxing eloquent on the subject of "degrees of freedom." Realizing that he had lost the class, he thought for a moment and then announced that he knew what would make this concept clear. He began to describe poker hands. Before he began, however, he paused and asked, "Is there anyone here by chance who doesn't understand the basic composition of a deck of cards?" (Some ladies in the class wore bonnets. Their Mennonite background would have prohibited games of chance of any kind.) I had also grown up in a religious environment where playing any kind of games with cards was strictly forbidden. When I became older and no longer felt bound by this rule, I hadn't bothered to learn any of the games of chance.

I remember what happened next as if it were yesterday. Being one of the oldest students in the class, I was debating whether I should acknowledge this deficit in my education. After a fierce fifteen-second mental struggle, I reasoned that if he were going to use this illustration to illuminate the subject at hand, I had better acknowledge the embarrassing truth that I didn't know what poker was all about. I meekly raised my hand so that it was barely visible. Dr. Fox stood only a few feet from where I was sitting on the front row. He stared at me for what seemed like forever as if I had just arrived from Mars. I would have gladly fallen through the floor. When he finally spoke, he said, "Maybe you can find someone to teach you."

Totally humiliated, I left the class through the nearest exit as soon as the class was dismissed. I went to the drug store across the street from the campus to purchase a deck of cards in a vain attempt to try to figure out what the professor was talking about. When I arrived home that evening, my children took the cards and began immediately to play some game that is still a mystery to me.

When at least ninety percent of the course work had been completed, the awesome rite of taking what was termed "the prelims" would take place. The term "preliminary" obviously means something that occurs before a given event, but in this setting it was the final test. It is the most punishing test that I have ever taken. One could choose to delay the prelims, but this test was necessary if one expected to complete the requirements for the doctoral degree. There were two opportunities each year to take these tests.

Typically, students preparing for this ordeal would arrange to be involved in study groups. Our group of a dozen or so had been meeting for nearly six months when word spread like wildfire that everyone in the group who had just taken the test ahead of us had failed. A student could retake the exam only once, and if that student failed a second time, they were dismissed from the doctoral program. Our study group disintegrated. It took several weeks for three of us in the group to reorganize and commit to taking the exam regardless of what had transpired or what the risks were. We spent many hours researching the areas we might be tested. Most of our waking hours were spent concentrating on the exam. The night before the exam, I insisted on relaxing and going to bed early. I had remembered the painful experience in the Greek class during my freshman year at the Owosso Bible College when I came to the "test of fire" exhausted.

On the morning of this major test by fire, thirteen doctoral students showed up at the announced site where the writing marathon would begin. We learned that it was customary for us to be assigned to a professor's office for the eight hours of the examination. I felt some panic when I realized that I was going to be assigned to the professor's office who had attempted to block my admission to the doctoral program. Even though he had judged my paper to be among the three best term papers, I still felt ill at ease in his presence. Because my penmanship left a great deal to be desired, I, along with two others, had chosen to type our responses. While we were given code names that purportedly kept those professors who would be reading the papers from identifying us, I was somewhat concerned that my paper could be easily identified because only three of us were typing. What made matters worse, the professor repeatedly entered his office during the eight hours that I was confined there. I had fantasies of being in a compromised position. With the whole doctoral program at stake, I confess that I found it difficult to control my panic.

Four initial questions had to be completed in four hours during the morning session. One could spend as much time on any one question as one wanted. The doctoral candidate stationed in the next office to me said that she had barely read the questions and hadn't had time to reflect on how to proceed when she heard me beginning to type. She said that she was aware of the sound of my typewriter through the ordeal. My typing persisted during most of the eight hours. She added she didn't dare to stop writing long enough to relieve the cramps in her fingers or long enough to ponder her response to a given question.

We had an hour's break for lunch before returning to the professor's offices where we had been secluded for the day. All four hours of the afternoon were devoted to one question. I remember staying at my station, typing until the very last moment. When time was called, we were numb with exhaustion. Typically the faculty took their time to read the papers.

Six weeks would pass before we heard the results. For me, nightmares were not uncommon during this period, and I suspect others who underwent this "baptism of fire" must have had similar experiences. In my dreams, I lived through crushingly disappointing scenes where I had been informed of failing the exam. Apprehension was high during this period, and it was hard to focus on the other tasks I needed to do. I remember the utter relief I felt one evening at the end of this lengthy time of waiting when one of the professors from our department called me at home to say that I had passed. It was possible to get a conditional pass. Any one of the thirteen who took the exam would have settled for a conditional pass. I remember asking Dr. Costar if this was a conditional pass. It was truly an exciting moment when he said that all of us had passed with flying colors. I think the faculty may have had second thoughts about "flunking" everyone in the previous session to ours. As I now look back on this kind of ordeal, it doesn't strike me as a real evaluation of achievement other than it forced us to organize the material that we had been exposed to during our graduate training. It was an excellent exercise, however, on how to experience and process stress.

49

A Needed Retreat

I served as pastor of the Sunfield United Methodist Church during my doctoral studies. This community was so accepting of my family and me. Many happy memories remain from this period of our lives. We will always value the friendships of the Fleethams, Gilberts, Rarieghs, Smiths, DeLands, and many more.

One of the parishioners, Bruce DeLand, had asked about designing a retreat for couples in their middle years. My response to him was my first priority was to get ready for the "big exam." However, he had my full permission and support to organize this event in any way he chose to do. Quite honestly, I hadn't expected a great deal to come out of this event, but I wanted to support his efforts. It was to take place at a lodge in a national forest with a lovely stone fireplace and sleeping facilities. This retreat was scheduled to start the evening of the day of the big exam. Shortly after I arrived home from the university that Friday afternoon, Leta and I drove the forty or fifty miles to the retreat. I would rather have gone to bed or had some place to simply relax. Initially, I went to this retreat event out of a need to support my parishioner who had organized the event. It turned out to be a place of high energy and spiritual renewal.

The evening meal and a communion service right after kicked off the retreat. The timing was somewhat ironic in the sense that every meal where people are gathered for a common purpose is a communion event. I hadn't done the scheduling, and besides, I was so fatigued by the ordeal I just completed at the university that nothing else really mattered.

The communion seemed uneventful. I had expected an evening of socializing to follow the communion ritual. Instead, the folks gathered (primarily couples) around the huge fireplace after the elements of communion had been served. It was around seven o'clock. No one said, "Let's gather around the fireplace." No one had indicated that this was to be a time of silence. It just happened. Not a word was said. No one stirred. For the next several hours, there was total silence. The silence truly became hypnotic. Out of the corner of my eye, I could see that tears were present. I noticed that couples were snuggled close to each other. As I now remember it, around ten o'clock couples began to slip away to their rooms without saying a word. It remains one of those moments where we experienced in an unusual, unexpected way an Unseen Presence. A bonding took place that evening that was truly remarkable. Nearly a half-century has passed since that event. Whenever we meet, which is rarely, there is still that bond that continues to be valued.

Earlier, I described how in the church tradition that my parents chose after leaving the Mennonite community, the most important calling that a person could possibly receive was God's call to the ordained ministry. I also attempted to explain how my perceived call was likely distorted because of a very shaky journey through childhood and adolescence. This calling, however distorted, proved to be a godsend. While I am forever indebted to this beginning in the Pilgrim Holiness Church (now known as the Wesleyan Church), particularly during the years at Owosso Bible College, it was also a rigid system that allowed little room for searching and questioning. In that setting, it would have been a form of professional suicide if one had attempted to raise questions and doubts about the dogmas of the church. The experience in the chaplaincy was another godsend in that it allowed me to explore the areas that I previously did not have an opportunity to explore. After five years as a military chaplain representing the Pilgrim Holiness Church, I realized that I could not in good conscience remain in this church. The sense of fellowship at this retreat and in the local Sunfield United Methodist Church was truly a godsend. I had come a long way on my search for a church, but the search wasn't quite over. More about this later.

I attempted without success to find a theological home in other denominations labeled evangelical. My colleagues from the Pilgrim Church had a strong bias against the Methodist church primarily because they felt that most Methodist churches had strayed far from the doctrinal teachings of John Wesley. When my mother eventually learned that I had become a Methodist, tears welled up in her eyes as she pleaded for me to "get right with God again."

50

Finding a Home in Sunfield

Sunfield, a small village of several hundred people located about twenty-five miles from the campus of Michigan State, proved a very satisfying assignment. The parsonage certainly didn't meet the standards the Methodist conference had established for clergy parsonages, but the people were very generous to my family and me. The people there were truly the salt of the earth. I can't begin to say enough good things about the four wonderful years that we spent in this community.

Several events stand out. One day I was working on a theme paper for a graduate course while keeping an eye on our son, whom we then called Eddie. He was about three years old. Somewhere around noon, he came to the room where I was concentrating on developing my term paper. He asked if it was time to get his brother and sister from school. Not really listening, I apparently mumbled an affirmative response while continuing to type. Thinking he had my permission, he slipped out into the cold snow without a jacket, crossed a busy street where cars tended to travel at high speeds, and ended up on the front steps of the school several blocks away. A high school student from the church recognized him and asked him what he was doing there. Eddie responded that I had given him permission to come. Her call to the parsonage shook me out of concentration on the term paper. I went quickly to retrieve him—

feeling very guilty about my negligence and terribly relieved that he hadn't been hurt crossing a very dangerous road.

A small grassy piece of land the school owned served as the football field as well as a track. I would take my kids jogging with me. This was long before jogging became a craze. While I never heard this comment, I suspect that my neighbors saw me as the eccentric Methodist preacher who insisted that his kids go jogging with him. Even our youngest, age three, insisted on going with us. I usually ended up carrying him most of the way around the track while I jogged with his older sister and brother.

We had been jogging for some months when the football coach showed up with his team during the first football practice of the season and had them jog around the track. Our daughter, Linda, was in good enough shape that she was able to outrun the entire team on their first day of practice. The coach didn't let these young bucks forget that they had allowed a "mere" girl beat them.

Around this time, I decided that spanking generally wasn't an appropriate disciplinary strategy. I also felt that there should be some way to creatively demonstrate the often-used parental statement to their children that "this hurts me as much as it hurts you." I created a system when an infraction of some kind would result in a certain number of push-ups or running a given distance. I told my children that I would also be doing push-ups or runs along with them. I tried to work out a formula that I considered a fair ratio between us. For example, with Bob, who was ten years old, I would do three times as many push-ups or three times as many times around the track. I also said that after this infraction had been satisfied with the assigned number of push-ups, they were free to assign me push-ups or runs if they felt that their assignment of physical exercise had been unfair. The catch was that they would have to proportionally match the appropriate number of push-ups they assigned to me. I don't remember that they ever chose this option.

If we were traveling as a family in our automobile and the kids got to arguing and the decibel levels became unacceptable to their mother or me, I would warn them that if this behavior continued I would stop the car and all of us (their mother excluded) would be doing push-ups alongside the road. We only exercised this option once. It was so embarrassing to them that the mere mention that this action was possible was enough to have an immediate impact on their behavior.

Our son Bob often disagreed with this strategy of discipline. On one occasion when we were running down a country road, he was lagging behind. I told him that if he hadn't caught up by a certain landmark, an additional mile would be added. He called to a neighbor who happened to be near the road and said that his father was trying to kill him. Right on the spot, in earshot of the neighbor, I assigned us the privilege of running an additional mile. While I continue to think this was a creative idea, I don't think Bob, even as an adult, would agree. On the other hand, Linda seemed to take it all in stride.

When she became a high school freshman, she discovered she was the only girl jogging. She found this to be embarrassing. Having some sense of how important it is for a teenager to try to fit in, I agreed to her request to stop jogging. Just a few years later, jogging was the "in thing" to do.

Once, as I was walking out the door to go to the university, I got a telephone call from an older parishioner. She said, "Preacher, get over here right away and serve me my last communion."

I, of course, went right to her home. She appeared to be in appropriate health for her eighty-five years or so. I asked whether she had some sort of intuition that she might be dying soon.

Her response to my inquiry went something like this: "You know all my family, and they're all doing well. While I'm getting around okay, I am fairly crippled. I know and you know that it is all downhill from here. I know what I'm doing. Go ahead and serve me my last communion."

I saw her logic and responded to her request to serve her communion.

A few days later, she was hospitalized. Responding to her family's concern about her health, she stated, "I know what I'm doing" in no uncertain terms. When her physician and family still tried to keep her alive, she responded, "I can wait you all out."

Finally both doctor and family members understood that they couldn't keep her alive in any meaningful way without her cooperation. They not only dropped their objections, but also affirmed her choice. She died peacefully a few days later. I conducted the memorial service shortly after her death. She had taught her family, her doctor, and me an important lesson that a person has rights even during the final moments of their life.

On a humorous note, I remember a wedding held at the church on a hot humid Saturday in June. The church had neither an air-conditioning unit nor a telephone. The bride had just graduated from high school, and she was marrying one of the younger teachers from the high school.

The bride had ordered an elaborate wedding gown from a major department store in Lansing, Michigan. This rental service included delivery and a person who provided a professional fitting. This person was scheduled to arrive an hour before the wedding.

The appointed hour came. No dress. Thirty minutes before the wedding ceremony, the dress had still not arrived. The Irish father, known to have an explosive temper, went to the parsonage to call the department store that had rented this service. The only person in the bridal department was a teenage girl who responded that her boss was delivering dresses, and she didn't have her schedule. The father was furious.

The hour for the wedding had arrived. The church was packed. The organist played her preplanned numbers; the soloist sang. The entire wedding party was waiting in the basement of the church for the issue of the bride's dress to be resolved. The distraught father instructed his daughter to "get married in your damn street dress." The bride was calm and unmoved, stating that she had always planned to have an elaborate dress to wear at her wedding and wouldn't get married without it.

Suggestions were coming fast and furious from the wedding party. The bride rejected all of them outright. Meanwhile, a very puzzled congregation waited without the benefit of knowing what was going on. Had one of the parties backed out? What was the holdup? The organist just kept playing the organ. When thirty minutes had passed after the wedding should have started, someone in the wedding party suggested that we have the reception first, followed by the wedding. The bride bought this idea. It was my job to explain to the congregation what had happened and invite them to come to the reception in the basement of the church.

The cake was cut. The food was served. The wedding gifts were opened. About 4:00 p.m., the person showed up with the dress. Apparently, she had been confused about the time of the wedding. The bride got into her dress. The congregation filed back upstairs. The wedding ceremony finally took place. Brides have rights, too!

It was a wonderful four years in this very rural Michigan village. While I had tried to serve the people with the limited time available to do the work of a pastor, they generously served and loved my family and me and had become family to us.

I began to feel at home in the First Methodist Church I served in Sunfield, Michigan, even though this move was not made without some apprehension. I was still ordained in the Pilgrim Holiness Church and was considered a local pastor by the Methodist District Conference, which had the status of a pastor who had not yet completed seminary, which in effect stated that I was on a kind of probationary status. This group was concerned that I had not completed a graduate seminary. At one point, one committee member suggested that I abandon my doctoral program and enroll in Garrett Theological Seminary, the seminary from which our son Edward and his wife, Micki, eventually graduated. It is interesting to note that I had already served on active duty as an army chaplain and had been involved in organizing and expedition of contacting Indians who had never seen anyone from the outside world. I had pastoral experiences that none of the clergy serving in that conference could match or would ever have. From their perspective, this suggestion may have had some merit, but to me it was totally ludicrous.

Of the fifty or so clergy who signed for the doctoral program at Michigan State University, only two or three chose to keep their clergy credentials alive. When I completed my doctoral program, I assumed that there would be no further official involvement with the Methodist Church. Still, it was important to keep my ecclesiastical endorsement for my military commission. If this one remaining concern had not been present, I might have joined the majority who chose solely to focus the remaining of their professional career in psychology.

I explored the possibility of becoming part of the Presbyterian clergy. I met with the appropriate bodies of this denomination in the Lansing area. I explained that I had three years of theological education but that this education took place at an unaccredited bible college. Their comment was that this biblical education probably had a greater focus on scriptural studies than their seminaries would have provided. They were pleased that I had attained a doctoral degree. This group fully endorsed my application. They stated that the only action to be taken was the endorsement of Dr. Eugene Carson Blake, who was the clerk for the denomination. They expected this endorsement to be routine.

However, when their recommendation reached Dr. Blake's desk, he ruled that since the denomination from which I was transferring didn't have a formal correspondence relationship with the Presbyterian Church, it would be necessary for me to be reordained. This solution was unacceptable to me, and I was becoming reconciled that my future was going to be solely in the field of psychology.

Charles Nessett, now deceased, was pastor of an Evangelical United Brethren Church near the village where I was serving a Methodist church. He was enrolled in the social work program at Michigan State. We formed a carpool to the university campus for several years. When he heard what transpired about my application for clergy status in the Presbyterian Church, he urged me to apply to transfer my clergy affiliation with his denomination, commonly known as the EUB. I, with a considerable lack of enthusiasm, agreed to meet with their board of ministry to discuss this possibility.

I was a little surprised to see that this body had about thirty members. I have to confess that I had a chip on my shoulder when the meeting began. I explained that endorsement from an ecclesiastical group was necessary to maintain my commission as military chaplain. Someone asked if I would be willing to undergo a probationary period, assuming that I would be accepted for transfer. My response was that I had undergone many professional puberty rites and that one more seemed a little ridiculous, but that I would be willing to do it one more time. Most chuckled, though I did hear one older pastor ask what a puberty rite was. The result was that I was received in full status. This relationship proved to be a very happy one, with the exception of the first appointment.

With the knowledge and consent of the superintendent, I had accepted a full-time position as a psychologist with the Veterans Hospital in Battle Creek, Michigan. I was assigned to a church about thirty miles away, near the community of Three Rivers.

One or two families who tended to see this country church as their private club dominated the church. Others were invited to support it financially, but they were expected to remain on the periphery in terms of church leadership. It was a difficult time for my family. The community seemed to be insulated and didn't easily receive strangers. Our children, particularly Linda and Bob, found that it was difficult to be assimilated by the church family as well as in their school in nearby Three Rivers. It was such a contrast to the way we had been served and loved in Sunfield.

I decided to take on the self-appointed church rulers. While I didn't mind facing their hostility, I felt that some of the folks in the inner circle played dirty pool. When they discovered that their anger toward me was largely ineffective, they began to target our children. I was deeply troubled by this action. I might add that the folks on the "fringes" of the church family received us well, but I was relieved when an opportunity came to serve another congregation.

—

When I left home in my early teens, I returned to my parents' home about once every three years. While I cared for my parents, I felt out of touch with them. When I did return, I didn't understand why I felt so restless and could hardly wait to leave. I would want to stroll over the landscape that I had known as a boy. My dad would be puzzled about why I seemed eager to get out of the house and would suggest that I take the truck and drive to where I wanted to go. I felt hesitant to describe my restlessness and desire to walk the terrain that I had known so well as a boy. Actually, I really didn't know where these feelings were coming from.

Some years later, a colleague and I were discussing these feelings, and he said something that struck a resonant chord with me. He stated that, in many respects, I had never had a childhood. In a family where one's identity was determined by how hard one worked, there was little sense of play or celebration. He suggested that this intense desire to roam the fields of the farm was my attempt to find my childhood.

On one particular visit, my brother Merle and his lovely wife, Dolores, and their children were also present. It was one of the rare moments when my siblings and I were to be together. This had been an enjoyable visit. The morning we were leaving, my father had us form a circle in the yard for morning prayers that he described as the family altar.

I still vividly recall the scene. As my father was leading the prayer, he openly wept. His prayer was that the family circle would not be broken in heaven. It was as if he was visualizing his tribe gathered in one place in that heavenly realm. He obviously was expressing deep concern that his children might not be fully observing the high spiritual standards required to gain entrance to this celestial city. While my spiritual understanding was significantly different than his, I remember feeling a deep sense of appreciation of his concern for his family.

As we got into the car to return to our home a thousand miles away, I remember our daughter, Linda, who was about to enter high school, being puzzled by her grandfather's prayer. Her question was this: what was Grandpa so shook up about? I recognized in a new way how different her family environment had been from the one I had known.

The following year, I was invited to serve a pastoral role in two rural churches near St. Johns, Michigan. I was to meet with the pastor and parish committee who had come to a district conference meeting in another city to interview me. As I began to reflect on the fact that these two churches had been served by a full-time pastor for many years, and I would be keeping my full-time psychology position at the VA hospital, I began to question the appropriateness of this assignment. It would mean a commute of more than an hour each way. More than that, I realized that this congregation would likely expect the kinds of services that they were used to having from a full-time clergy person. I told the district superintendent that I decided against accepting this assignment. He said that the pastor and parish committee had traveled some distance for this meeting, and it was important to meet, but added that I could share my decision and the reasons for it with them.

One of the first questions that one of the older members of the committee asked was whether I could handle both my job at the VA and the job at the church. I jumped on that question and said that he had made an excellent observation, adding that a person who could devote the time they had come to expect might be more appropriate. The other members quickly assured me that my limited availability would not be a problem. I still did not intend to accept this assignment. I searched for other limitations that they might encounter should I come to their congregation. I presented several scenarios that might cause concern. They assured me that none of the issues I raised presented problems for them.

In the end, accepting this opportunity turned out to be an excellent choice for me and my family—and I believe for the church family. In the four decades plus that have transpired since we left St. Johns, this community has had a special place in our hearts and lives. During the period I served this congregation, the Evangelical United Brethren and the Methodist merged into one denomination. This time it was official. I was a Methodist—actually the new name of this merged denominational body became known as the United Methodist Church. Many exciting and happy events transpired during our four-year stay in rural St. Johns, Michigan.

51

All Done but the Dissertation

Dr. John Jordan, a former classmate at Owosso, had completed his doctoral degree during the ten years that I had served on active military duty and was a bush pilot in Amazon jungle. When I was admitted to Michigan State, he was appointed as my advisor.

While we had known each other during our undergraduate studies at Owosso College, it was at best a causal relationship. Now that he was my advisor, I took great care that I would only contact him in this professional role as advisor. This professional distance lasted for approximately three years. He was the one to break the ice by causally suggesting that this professional distance wasn't necessary. I was well into my doctoral program before there was any degree of social contact.

Dr. Jordan had a talent for developing grants that funded various programs at the university. I really didn't have any idea at that time how competitive professors could be in terms of attempting to get control of grants once the granting authority had provided the funds or, for that matter, how much professional jealousy professors often harbored.

After several grants, Dr. Jordan had developed a significant grant designed to create scholarships for rehabilitation counseling. I, along with a number of other graduate students, had received one of these grants. I was invited to pursue my dissertation topic on an attitude study toward physical disability, which was going to be part of a much larger study for which Dr. Jordan was the grant advisor. My dissertation focused on a comparative attitude study toward physical disability between four different groups of people: 1) those who hired persons with disabling conditions, 2) those who worked with persons with disabling conditions in the workplace, 3) regular classroom teachers, and 4) special education teachers. I was to compare the responses of a questionnaire given to these four groups of people from Peru, Colombia, and from a sample previously collected in Kansas.

Because of his interest in the larger study, Dr. Jordan invited me to accompany him on making a number of professional contacts in various countries of Latin America. The first stop was one where I invited him to accompany me to visit the Trio Indians in Surinam. When we arrived in the interior of Surinam, Claude Leavitt greeted us. He had been the linguist on the initial contact with these Trios. He and his wife ended up spending over two decades in this area. His five children were to spend their developmental years in this setting.

During the five years that I had been away, Claude had managed to translate a significant part of the Trio language into writing, a feat that had never before been accomplished. He had brought in a gas-driven generator to provide electricity to several areas. It was truly a spectacular sight to see Indians of all ages hovering around the three light poles that been erected, all learning to read and write.

While Claude was part of a very conservative religious group, they had a liberal component in that they had a deep respect for cultural traditions that was a part of tribal life. For example, they did not insist that the Indians wear Western clothing. They understood that doing so would create a host of problems, such as how to replace and launder this newfangled clothing. The school program was designed to enhance their tribal language.

When they did feel that a change in their cultural behavioral was needed, these missionaries sought to understand the role that this behavior played in culture. Claude understandably felt that infanticide, the practice of selecting which newborn would be admitted into the tribe and which would be abandoned in the jungle and left to die, was unacceptable.

Dr. Jordan suggested that we look for grant money to carefully study the process of how learning to read and write was assimilated into a given culture. Unfortunately, we never got around to applying to the institutions that would be interested in funding this kind of educational research.

I recognized a number of the Indians from our initial contact five years earlier. It was a moving experience to meet the young Indian who wanted me to call him Bobby. Claude was by now fluent in the Trio language and translated Bobby's greeting to me. In great detail, he told me how frightened he had been on our initial contact some five years earlier. In his own words, he spoke of the importance that his introduction to the Christian faith had been. He stated that he was no longer terrified of what he had earlier perceived as malignant spirits that he then thought were haunting him.

Several days later, as we were leaving, my Trio Indian friend Bobby presented me with a bow and arrow set, saying we would always be brothers. Claude told me that he had carved the bow with the jaw of a javelina. That bow and arrow set, until recently, occupied a prominent place in our living room for nearly forty years.

The first stop after Surinam was Belem, Brazil, where we were scheduled to change planes for Recife, Brazil. We arrived about 11:00 p.m., only to discover that the airline for which we had reservations was going out of business at midnight. We frantically searched for an alternative flight and managed to find an airline that used old US military C-47s. That plane had been a workhorse for years in the military. Even as a former bush pilot, I was a bit unprepared for the adventure ahead. The plane made a number of stops at runways surrounded by thatched-roof villages en route to Recife. I could tell by the uneven performance of the engines, including sounds of backfiring, that this was going to be an eventful journey. At very short runways, we would barely clear the tops of the huts at the end of the runway. It was certainly disconcerting to see aircraft identical to the plane that we were on had crashed and were simply put off to the side of the runway. I can't tell you how relieved I was at the end of this eight-or-nine-hour ordeal.

While the flight had been perilous enough, I was even more intimidated by the taxicab ride into Recife. The driver broke every rule of the road, at least as far as I understood driving behavior, and drove at high speeds, dodging whatever happened to be in his way. He obviously had skills that I didn't possess. Much to my relief, we arrived at our hotel without mishap.

While in Recife, Dr. Jordan had arranged to meet with one of the top educators in Brazil. His name has slipped from my memory, but I remember the sense of awe that I experienced being in this gentle man's presence.

The next stop was really for rest and relaxation. It was my first introduction to the famous Rio de Janeiro. I don't remember meeting with any professional during this short stay of two, possibly three nights. The first view of Rio is the large impressive statue of Christ overlooking the city from a nearby mountain. We stayed in a hotel on the famous Copacabana Beach. It was one of the first times that I had played in the surf. We had an opportunity to see the very poor sections of the city and enjoyed an outdoor café. I still remember a street entertainer who was very skillful in performing his routine.

The next stop was Buenos Aires. En route, we landed at the Montevideo airport. We were on a German Lufthansa plane that came close to overshooting the runway. In my imagination, I can still smell the smoke of the tires, which penetrated the cabin as the pilot hit the brakes hard. We were at the very end of the runway that had a steep drop-off before the plane was able to stop. I was unnerved by this episode and wondered whether the tires of the plane were up to another takeoff and landing.

We met with several professional people in Buenos Aires, including a party with a number of psychologists. We were also treated to a street theater performance that had been set up by actors years before to bring professional theater to the ghetto.

While many of the memories of this stop have been erased by the passing of four decades, two memories stand out. The modest hotel room wasn't air-conditioned. Both the outside temperature and the humidity were probably in the nineties. Fans were rented separately for the rooms, but all the fans were taken. So we experienced a very hot and humid night as we tried to sleep.

I sent a postcard to my wife, Leta, describing the high January temperatures. (It was summertime in Buenos Aires.) She later stated that she had shoveled snow from our Michigan residence for several hours to get the car out of the driveway, just to drive to the post office to get the mail. She wasn't at all sympathetic when she saw my description of how hot our room had been that particular evening.

We got up at about 4:00 a.m., after having attended a social event with a local psychologist that lasted until 1:00 a.m., to catch a flight to the university town of Cordoba, which was, as I recall, about an hour and half by air from Buenos Aires. It turns out that the airlines were on strike. But the strike was unlike anything I had heard of before. The airline personnel would work for an hour or so and then go on strike for thirty minutes and then come back to work for an unpredictable amount of time. While flights were taking off, their schedule became erratic. We finally arrived at our destination four or five hours behind our scheduled time. When we finally got to Cordoba, I was totally exhausted and would have preferred to have found a place to sleep.

A university professor was there to meet us and told us that he had invited a number of people to join us for lunch. I later found out that when a person who is considered a dignitary came to town, he was expected to demonstrate his importance by hosting as many "celebrities" as her or his status would merit at the luncheon. Our host apparently worked hard to get some thirty or forty people to attend this event. The two of us thought we would be meeting with a professor or two. While served the best steak I've ever tasted, the surprise was that the persons considered celeberties were expected to pay for everyone's meal. It made quite a hole in our limited budget.

From there, we flew to Lima, Peru, with a brief half-day stop in Santiago, Chile. Here, my work on my dissertation began in earnest. As stated earlier, my dissertation was to be part of a much larger study that Dr. Jordan had initiated on attitudes toward physical disability. The questionnaires had to be translated into two versions of Spanish—the kind spoken in Lima, Peru, and the kind spoken in Bogota, Colombia.

Dr. Jordan and I were to spend about ten days in Lima. We were staying in a small downtown hotel and meeting with our Peruvian colleagues, who were administering the questionnaires for us. About halfway through our stay, I asked John if he had ever stayed in a pension. (I was remembering that a friend I had met on a flight decades earlier convinced me to stay in a pension in Cairo, Egypt, and it had proved to be a most interesting experience. This particular pension catered to young people from all over the world.) Dr. Jordan reluctantly accepted my suggestion that we try a pension in Lima. We went to a lovely suburb known as Mira de Flores. This pension proved to be a delightful family-oriented pension.

Just as we were checking in, I saw someone who looked familiar. I mentioned to John that I thought I knew him. John was very skeptical. It turned out that we had served together in the 82nd Airborne Division. He was a helicopter pilot, and we had briefly met during one my visits as a chaplain to his military unit. Truly a small world! (On a cruise to Lima several years ago, we were in Mira de Flores, now an elegant suburb of Lima.)

Our final stop on this month long trip was in Bogota, where we were to repeat the research routine that we had just completed in Lima. Again, our hotel was modest but very nice. We learned from our colleagues firsthand about some of the violence that this troubled country had known when revolutionaries would cause havoc in the small villages by maiming the villagers. We were told that it was not unusual for these revolutionaries to cut off a limb or injure someone permanently—apparently to put political pressure on the existing government. These professionals said that the government had been forced to create a number of rehabilitation programs to meet the urgent physical needs of those who had been tortured.

Both the professionals in Lima and Bogota promised to ship the completed questionnaires (some were to be completed after we left these countries) to us. The questionnaires would be ana-lyzed by putting the responses into the computer—which were still at a primitive stage of development. The questionnaires ar-rived promptly from Lima. Well over a year later, after repeated correspondence and telephone messages, the questionnaires finally arrived from Bogota. Completing my dissertation was essentially hostage to the tardiness of the professionals from Bogota who had not kept the arranged time schedule.

52

The Veterans Hospital Connection

I had completed all the course work for the doctoral program and had completed the major prelim (described earlier). The proposal for my doctoral thesis was accepted, and I had completed the trip to get the data for my dissertation by the time I arrived at the VA hospital. It housed twenty-five hundred or so veterans with a psychiatric diagnosis. As a psychologist, I was assigned to various hospital wards and conducted individual and group counseling as well as psychological testing.

The chief of psychological services was a most interesting gentleman named Dr. Stuart Armitage. He was clearly respected by the twenty-some psychologists in his section of service. He could be professionally aloof, but at the same time very concerned about the welfare of his staff. When I first joined the staff, I found him to be somewhat intimidating but came to value both his professionalism as well as his friendship.

The first hour of the day consisted of having all the psychologists on staff meet in the psychology conference room with no special agenda. In the beginning, I felt quite insecure and relieved when the hour was up and each psychologist went to the wards that they were assigned to. It tended to be a time of who could best play the game of one-upmanship. Most of the time, I maintained an awkward silence. I felt quite comfortable with most of the psychologists on an individual basis, but when the group dynamic was at work, I felt immobilized.

As the Christmas season approached, the secretary showed up in the conference room with the names and addresses of all of the psychologists. It was assumed that each psychologist, including the psychologist who happened to be Jewish, would send Christmas cards to every person on the list. When I returned home that evening, I asked my wife where our Christmas cards were located. As it turned out, we had only the cards produced by the United Nation's Children Fund, known as UNICEF. These cards had drawings made by children, but there was no Christmas greeting. If these cards were sent, one would have to create their own message.

My first response was to purchase some regular Christmas cards. Then it occurred to me to write each psychologist a positive message that described at least one thing that impressed me about them. I was totally dumbfounded by their responses. They assumed that my individualized message held some hidden form of hostility that I hadn't expressed openly. I remember one of the psychologists asked me privately what I really meant by the Christmas card message. Another highly verbal psychologist, who tended to dominate the morning group sessions, told a close friend of mine that he didn't know how to respond to the message I had written on his Christmas card.

Without really thinking about it, the Christmas card episode was reflecting my changing perspective from a model that focused on symptoms to one that focused on potential. The dominant model of psychological practice then was the medical model of identifying the symptoms and the professional working to alleviate these symptoms. The focus was on the pathological, and a primary assumption was that health was in some way the opposite of illness. Dr. Carl Rogers and others were presenting another model that focused on human potential. This model was seen by many psychologists of this era as being inferior. My changing perspective often caused my ministerial colleagues to be concerned that I was becoming too humanistic.

I had been working at the VA hospital for seven or eight months, waiting for the data from Bogota, Colombia, to arrive. I had written the introductory chapters of the dissertation, but there was little that I could do without the data for which I had been anxiously waiting. When the data finally arrived, I could begin analyzing the data and proceed with writing the dissertation. Dr. Armitage, the chief of our section, freed me from all duties and stated that my job at the hospital was to work on the dissertation for eight hours a day. As I remember, it took about six weeks of writing. I worked on a typewriter that sat on a regular desk. I developed severe shoulder and neck cramps that eventually required some medical intervention, but the motivation was so intense that minor discomfort and pain was a formidable obstacle. This is the first and only time that I devoted an entire workweek to writing—eight hours a day.

There was a small glitch in retrieving the material that I had given to the hospital print shop, which was primarily a workstation for patients. The supervisor had enthusiastically taken on the task of printing the material—probably forty or so pages. At the end of nearly eight months, only a dozen or so pages had been printed. With all the diplomatic skill I could manage, I approached the supervisor and said that I realized that they were overloaded with work. I suggested that I could relieve their workload by retrieving my material. The following day, I was called into the office of his supervisor, who angrily demanded to know why I had placed so much pressure on the supervisor of the print shop. I was really taken aback by this response. I realized that the hospital could be very bureaucratic, but this episode pushed that boundary beyond anything I had imagined. I still can't think of a way in which I could have more been diplomatic in requesting that my material be returned.

I found a commercial print shop that printed the requested material in a few hours. It was now time to defend the dissertation with the doctoral committee. It was an exercise in frustration trying to get the committee together. The candidate was responsible for finding a time where everyone on the committee could meet.

Since my research dissertation was part of a larger study of my doctoral advisor, the design of the study was fairly well known to the committee. Nevertheless, the questions of the committee were demanding and somewhat intimidating to me. Only minor changes had to be made. It was official. From that moment of getting the blessing of the doctoral committee, I could officially be addressed as "doctor." It took quite a while to get used to that title.

Dr. Armitage, the head psychologist, soon assigned me as chief of one of the psychiatric wards. This position had been largely re-served for psychiatrists in the past. However, there was a shortage of psychiatrists at the VA hospital, so they were used as consultants rather than administrators.

From the beginning, I attempted to have an open-door policy for patients. I soon discovered that, in addition to the therapeu-tic programs, the administrative responsibilities were awesome. I found myself writing all the extensive admission reports as well as the discharge summaries. Ironically, these reports were signed by physicians who never changed a word in these summaries. I sus-pect that these physicians barely skimmed these reports and sum-maries before signing them, as if they had produced these reports and summaries. In effect, we were responsible for the medications given to patients, although these legal responsibilities were dele-gated to physicians. While the psychologists were very careful not to attempt to prescribe medication, the physicians who served as consultants typically gave our suggestions and recommendations about medications serious consideration. Every psychologist who was the head of a ward came to know a great deal about medica-tions and their contraindications so that we could be fairly knowl-edgeable about what was being prescribed to the patients.

On one occasion, I asked a patient who was an artist to create an "in and out" sign to be hung on the office door. I assumed that it would simply have the words "in" and "out" with some artistic de-sign on it. The result of his creation was both amusing and telling. He drew a picture of my bald head barely appearing over a huge mound of paperwork with a sign indicating that "The doctor is in." He had obviously sensed that the administrative demands on my time were enormous. The reverse side of the card simply read: "The doctor is out." He pictured me flat on my back, covered with the paperwork. It's now five decades later, but I still have this sign that once hung over my office door.

I was both the administrator and in charge of clinical programs of this ward. In addition to scheduled group therapy sessions, I saw people in one-to-one counseling sessions. A patient once asked about forgiveness in a way that brought me up short. It caused me to realize that I had unfinished business with our teenage daughter.

At this time, we had moved from Three Rivers, Michigan, to St. Johns, which was located seventy miles away from the hospital. We lived in the church parsonage, and I commuted to the VA hospital. I often stayed over one night and then returned home for the next night. One Sunday evening, we were having a dinner at the church when our daughter, Linda, innocently asked a question of a parishioner who, unbeknown to her, was seeing me in a counseling relationship. Her question made it sound as if we were discussing her therapy issues around our dinner table. I was furious.

When we got home, I lambasted our daughter for her insensitive remarks. She had no idea what I was so angry about. I wasn't about to tell her I was seeing this church member in a counseling relationship. When she tried to defend herself, I intensified my angry response. I was so angry that I didn't see how confused and hurt our daughter really was.

I went to bed that evening feeling fully justified with my angry response. The next day, I held a group counseling session and had a chance to examine my response to our daughter from a new perspective. A group member had no idea that he was asking a penetrating question that had implications for the previous evening's encounter with Linda. I thanked this group member for his question and shared with the group that I had alienated my daughter, whom I loved very much. I told them the context of my response and announced that I would seek my daughter's forgiveness when I returned home the following evening. I followed through on that promise. While I still couldn't share with Linda that I was in a counseling relationship with that church member, I could share that her innocent remarks had triggered my angry response. I also said my anger had been an overreaction and asked her forgiveness.

My friend, colleague, and former doctoral advisor, Dr. Jordan, heard of an opening in one of the university educational departments and encouraged me to apply. I did and was accepted. I'm certain that my emotional blinders were on as I interviewed for this position. My duties were fairly vague, and I soon realized that it was not a fit for me. Some level of discomfort was there before I took the position, but I didn't pay attention. While I loved the university setting, I became intensely uncomfortable with the task. I had difficulty in understanding what the function of this position was. When I tried to inquire about the intended function, the supervisor suggested that I produce a document that made very little sense to me. It seemed like busywork to justify my position. I felt like a fraud.

Even now, I remember with discomfort and anxiety how much I looked forward to the end of the day when I could escape from this environment. When Friday evening came, I would feel a great deal of relief but a growing cloud of anxiety would roll over me as the weekend began to evaporate. It was the only time that I remember having both dreaded and intensely disliked my work. After several months of anguish, I vividly remember one Friday afternoon reading in the lines from Gilbran's essay on work in the daily university paper. The lines were these: "If you can only work with distaste, it is better that you leave your work and beg alms of those who work with joy." That statement released me. Never again would I allow myself to work in an environment that imprisoned my spirit. I immediately gave notice and returned to my work at the VA hospital.

A patient, who was on the psychiatric ward where I was the administrator was a total loner. His emotional isolation seemed all-encompassing. I called him into my office for a friendly visit. He was terrified. His eyes literally darted around the room like he was a cornered animal. I discovered that he hadn't left the hospital grounds in over twenty years. I offered him a pass and offered to find him a fellow patient to accompany him into the nearby city of Battle Creek. The idea totally immobilized him. His security, as he saw it, was to remain in the safety of the hospital wards. It was at this time that questions about focusing on mental illness rather than mental health took a giant step forward. While pathology couldn't be ignored, its focus in terms of someone getting in touch with their potential was missing. This experience was to significantly influence the direction in which my professional growth and development would take in the future.

As I worked at the VA, I observed the new employees. I noticed that many left after a very short time of employment. While I never pursued my hunch, I began to suspect that many of these new employees expected that there would be a wide emotional gap between themselves and the patients who were institutionalized at the hospital. But they soon discovered the differences were not as great as they had expected, and the patients had the same dreams and aspirations, giving them more in common with the patients. I guessed that they left in panic when they made this discovery.

Several experiences are still vivid in my memory. One had to do with a patient named Norm. Norm was heavily medicated and had the dual designation of being committed and incompetent. The first designation meant that he was confined to the hospital. If he left the hospital, an alert would go out to all the law enforcement agencies that would attempt to apprehend him. The designation of incompetent meant that he had a guardian who was in control of both his finances as well as any legal decisions. Norm had been hospitalized for ten years and had had no visitors in years. He had scored in the low normal range on an IQ test that I had given him. The most optimistic assessment of his future was bleak at best. He had made three serious suicidal attempts. The chief of our department had written a note in the progress report that predicted that Norm would one day take his own life.

One day Norm requested that I put him on the ward that was locked twenty-four hours a day. He stated that he was feeling "shaky" and wanted the security of a locked ward. I agreed with his request, adding that I would be visiting him frequently and would have him immediately released from the locked unit on his request. Several months went by. One day, he asked to return to the ward that he was regularly assigned to.

Shortly after he returned, he stopped by the office and asked for a pass to go into the nearby city of Battle Creek. He said that he wanted to go the post office and apply for a job. I gave him the pass and asked him to report on the results of his interview. In effect, I told him to let me know when his application was denied. My intention was to assist him in dealing with this rejection. To my utter surprise, I got a call from the post office stating that they wanted to hire Norm. In total panic, I gave them a highly guarded prognosis, citing Norm's long period of hospitalization and his past suicidal behavior. They stated that they wanted to hire him even in light of his psychiatric past. I was stunned.

The words of the chief of psychological services that Norm would one day commit suicide were haunting me. I was certain that my colleagues would think that it would be completely clinically irresponsible to even consider this request. Yet in my heart, I knew I could do no other than give Norm this chance, regardless of the risks. I knew that if I said no, Norm could sink into hopeless despair.

Norm had no funds available to him. His guardian apparently made certain of that. A number of logistical problems arose immediately. For example, how would Norm negotiate getting the ten miles to work and then get back to the hospital? Bus service was not available from the hospital to the city. He was scheduled to work from 2:00 p.m. to 10:00 p.m. The solution was shaky at best. He would ride a bicycle the ten miles on a busy freeway in all kinds of weather. His return trip to the hospital would be at night. Remembering his three suicide attempts and the prediction by the chief of my service, I was very nervous. When I arrived at the office on the morning of Norm's first day at work, the first thing I did was to go to his dormitory room to check to see if he was there. I can't tell you how relieved I was when I discovered Norm in his bed, fast asleep.

Norm got excellent reviews at work. I initially approved a twenty-eight-day pass. This meant that he could come and go as he wished. After the first twenty-eight-day period had elapsed, I approved the second twenty-eight-day pass. After he had received several paychecks, Norm requested permission to move off the hospital grounds to an apartment near his work. I gladly endorsed this plan. The next step was a ninety-day trial visit that was repeated several times. The last action I took before leaving this post for another job was to discharge him. This discharge broke his commitment status as well as his status of being considered incompetent. I didn't want to risk someone who took my position after I left recalling him to the hospital after reviewing his records. The last I heard, Norm was doing great.

Dr. Armitage supported me in a number of ways. Unsolicited on my part, he contacted the head psychologist of the Veteran's Administration in Washington, DC, and recommended that I be considered for the chief psychologist position of a VA hospital.

To my surprise, I received a letter from the chief of VA asking if I would be interested in becoming the chief psychologist at the VA in Tuscaloosa, Alabama. I was told that this hospital had a large staff of psychologists. While I was flattered by this tentative invitation to consider this opportunity, I was more interested in the southwestern part of the United States and wanted to be involved in different kinds of programs.

When I was in the process of joining a mental health center in Lansing, Michigan, I was truly honored and humbled by the farewell party given to me by the patients on the ward at the VA hospital where I had administered. These patients, who by and large had so little, exerted a great deal of effort to make this occasion a success. It was deeply moving. It stands at near the top of any farewell ceremonies that I have experienced. I will always be grateful for the role that these patients, some of whom had been hospitalized for decades, played in my life. In many respects, these people, whom most people called patients, were truly my teachers.

The graduation ceremonies at Michigan State University during which I received the doctoral degree took place in June 1966. Because of the large number of graduates, only the doctoral graduates were given their diplomas individually. Vice President Hubert

Humphrey was our speaker. As he was introduced, a number of protesters for the Vietnam War walked out. However, their protest was peaceful. This was the first protest that I had witnessed. In the next months and years, the protests would dramatically build, and our nation would truly be in crisis.

Several parishioners from the Sunfield Methodist Church attended the graduation ceremony and the celebrations that followed. Bob and Flo Price also attended. Bob was certainly one of the most influential persons in my life during the important years as a college student and young adult. You will remember that we both shared in the dream of contacting Indians in the Amazon jungle—a dream that left an indelible mark on both of our lives.

My parents came from their Nebraska home to attend the graduation ceremonies. Father had initially protested my leaving home to attend school in Michigan twenty years earlier. I was the first person in our family to attend a college or university. I showed him my doctoral dissertation. He looked at it for a few minutes and gave it back with this comment: "I don't understand anything about this, but I'm proud." I was moved by his affirmation.

The following week, we were to move to St. Johns, Michigan. The afternoon of the graduation, we drove with my parents to look at the area that was shortly to be our home. They would be leaving for their Nebraska home the next day.

53

A Very Special Place

At the beginning of my doctoral studies, I had never seriously considered surrendering my clergy identity. My experiences as a military chaplain had been a vital anchoring life experience for me. These experiences opened up new horizons in terms of how I viewed the world, while most of my colleagues in the doctoral program who had backgrounds in the clergy surrendered the clergy credentials in favor of their newfound role as a psychologist. While I was finding my identity as a psychologist to be exciting, it was important for me to maintain my role as a military chaplain. Earlier I described the nineteen very satisfying years as an instructor at the U.S. Chaplain School. One has to maintain the endorsement of their denomination to function as active military chaplain. My transfer to a denomination where I could in good conscience function had now taken place.

I was given an opportunity to become the pastor of a congregation in an interesting setting while still working as psychologist at the VA hospital. I was given the opportunity to meet with the pastor/parish committee of a church in St. Johns, Michigan. Several members of the parish pastor committee had met at a district-wide conference meeting at the request of the district superintendent, primarily to interview me to become their pastor. If I accepted this invitation, I would be working full-time as a psychologist at the VA hospital some sixty miles away while serving two congregations that had been served by a full-time pastor for over twenty years.

The more I thought about this arrangement prior to the interview, the more my better judgment suggested that I should not accept it. It seemed to me that it would very difficult to meet the congregation's expectations and still continue my full-time employment at the VA hospital. When I shared this assessment with the district superintendent, he suggested that since this group had traveled some distance, we should still meet, and I could share my decision with them.

One of the first questions the panel asked during this meeting dealt with the very issue that had been concerning me: Would I be able to handle both positions? I told him he had an excellent point that needed careful assessment. I thought that this would be my opportunity for an early exit.

Other team members quickly stated that they didn't see my limited availability as a problem. I then initiated other concerns that I thought might get in the way of my appointment. It was the immediate consensus that they saw no obstacles for every issue I presented. I was soon out of excuses.

This move, which I so hesitatingly accepted, proved to be one of the most satisfying experiences of our lives. This congregation received with so much joy.

After my first sermon, Jim Cornell sauntered up to me with the comment that they would like to replace me in the pulpit the following Sunday. I was taken aback until he explained that the following weekend, a number of them would go to Lake Michigan for a weekend away, and they wanted me to come with them. About 150 members of this congregation would spend the weekend together at the lake. It was truly a time of celebration. It was a yearly ritual that we had the opportunity to experience several times.

I had and have been a confirmed workaholic and rarely took time to participate in any sporting activities. Now, in the precense of these parishioners, I was attempting to ski for the first time in my life in Lake Michigan. I was terrified. A person who was to become a very close friend, Howard Williams, had a powerboat. I was in chest-deep water with the ski rope in my hands. I tried to get to my feet. Most of the group had given up on my successfully standing up on the skis—but not Howard. After most people had left for other activities, he persisted in coaching me. His boat had a powerful motor. On each attempt, he would give full throttle to the engine, and the boat would lunge forward while I desperately clung to the ski ropes. After dozens of attempts, I failed to reach a standing position. I remember frantically hanging on to the ski ropes after I had failed to get up on my feet. Howard didn't let up on the throttle. I remember going fairly deep into the water before I had presence of mind to let go of the ski ropes. (This is an interesting metaphor about hanging on to things that we should release!) After several hours of trying, the miracle happened. I got to my feet; I had little trouble in successfully skiing.

It was fun to watch young teenagers who were reluctant to try to ski. If they didn't find the courage to try then, it would eventually happen—perhaps the next year or the next or possibly the next.

I remember one New Year's Eve. The decision had been made to have a church family celebration that would conclude shortly after midnight. It was a wonderful evening. The teenagers went snowmobiling while the older people made it a point to play games with the preschool and early elementary children. The middle-age couples were very much present to each other and the larger church family.

The young people returned from their outdoor winter wonderland adventure in time for a potluck meal. At the stroke of midnight, we celebrated communion. It was an exciting way to begin the New Year.

Earlier I had shared my memory of New Year's Eve 1955, when I was an army chaplain in Munich, Germany. I had gone to the officers' club early in the evening, but most of the officers became intoxicated fairly early in the evening. I left the club early and went to the chapel. At midnight, I opened the office windows, even though the temperature was near zero. I could hear the intoxicated voices of soldiers in nearby barracks trying to sing "Auld Lang Syne." I knew these young men, many away from home for the first time, longed to be part of a community. I promised myself I would attempt to create that community for lonely people—especially on special holidays.

Our home in St. Johns had been a wonderful refuge for our children, particularly for Linda. Now fifteen years old, she was accepted for a summer exchange program, Youth for Understanding, in Rotterdam, Holland. She had barely gotten acquainted with her new peers from St. Johns before she had to say good-bye for the summer. One of her newfound friends, Dee Gill, accompanied us to the airport in Detroit, where Linda was to meet an entire planeload of kids headed for placement in Europe. An hour or so after we arrived, the Youth for Understanding personnel said that it was time to say "good-bye to your little darlings." After an embrace, Linda, along with other participants, entered a room that we didn't have access to. I will never forget Linda's look as she passed through the door. She turned for a backward glance. I interpreted the look as a mixture of apprehension, uncertainty, and anticipation. This was her first extended time away from her home.

Linda and her newfound friend Dee would remain close in high school and then enroll in the highly respected Presbyterian-related Alma College, where they would be roommates, both majoring in Spanish. They were to share a host of life experiences, including pulling a large U-Haul trailer with all their belongings behind a car that they hoped would get them to their new home in San Francisco and eventually to a career in the airlines. This close bond remains after a half century.

As an aside, Dee and her husband, Allen, and Linda and her husband, Paul, would later join me in a trip to Surinam, South America, where I spent time as a bush pilot in the Amazon jungle and where Linda and her brother, Bobby, as we then called him, attended Dutch-speaking schools.

I had sensed when Bob was still in elementary school that he was struggling with the question of who he was. He was extremely bright but seemed to feel unsure of his relationships. When I first had begun my doctoral program, homosexuality was still classified as a medical and psychological illness. This diagnosis did have a code name in the diagnostic manual. The predominant etiology or cause was thought to be related to an overpowering mother and a weak father.

I cringe now when I remember how I frantically tried to present a strong image. I tried to borrow some technique I had been exposed to in the airborne military units as an attempt to present a strong masculine figure. My clumsy efforts to provide a role model probably led to his feeling a great deal of isolation from me—and perhaps from his peers.

He ended up getting a lead part in "Brigadoon," the school's play. Initially he didn't tell us about it. In one scene, he played the part of an intoxicated person and seemed genuinely disappointed when the church members weren't shocked. In fact, they congratulated him on how well he acted out his role.

Still, his time at St. Johns was valuable, as were the friendships that he developed. Both Linda and Bob participated in the Belize adventure. Their little brother, Eddie, was on this thirty-day venture—ten days traveling to Belize, a ten-day work project there, and ten days return on the bus.

I was delightfully surprised at how many of the ideas I had for church programs were so quickly adopted in this very conservative community. For example, my recommendation that we provide an international work experience for our young people was quickly endorsed. The plan entailed driving a caravan through the Mexican Yucatan peninsula to the small country of Belize. Belize's primarily ethnic population was black, whereas the citizens of St. Johns many years before had created a "lily-white" town. No one remembered any black families ever having lived in St. Johns. It was reported that one family had tried to locate in this city but were purportedly told in no uncertain terms that they were not welcome.

I had some concerns that the youth of the church would be turned off by an effort that would entail them working side-by-side on a project in Belize with youth who were primarily black. But my concern proved to be unfounded. The youth were actually enthused by the opportunity to interact with the black youth of Belize and upon their return eloquently spoke of their new black friends in Belize.

I was very impressed with the members of the St. Johns church who volunteered a month of their time to be involved with this trip. Howard Williams, Jim and Geneva Cornell, and Bob Peck all provided vehicles for this journey and ten full days of driving each way. Geneva was a skilled nurse, and both Howard and Jim had excellent mechanical skills. Howard drove a converted school bus, and Jim and Bob both had vans. Twenty high school students were part of this venture. It was truly a life-changing experience for all who participated. Some fifteen or twenty years after this event, these young people, now married with their own families, had a reunion and shared the memories of this powerful experience in their lives.

I feel certain that these experiences impacted Howard Williams, who incidentally led a second work team to Belize and then got involved in many work experiences in rural Haiti that have lasted several decades. Several hundred people have been involved in these work projects in Haiti over the years, primarily as a result of Howard's influence and example. While all of our friends living in St. Johns have been important to us, we seemed to gravitate to Howard and Eleanor Williams. We have often been guests in their home and they in ours. While they have different political and philosophical outlooks than I do, they are numbered among our closest friends. They are warm, nonjudgmental, and caring people. Truly the salt of the earth!

The two rural churches near St. Johns were located only four miles apart. Each had been established before the twentieth century. In that time, two churches located that distance apart was appropriate enough. But times had changed. The grandparents of some of the old members of the congregation had been instrumental in creating these churches and not to continue this time-honored tradition was, in the view of some, a matter of disrespecting the founder's memory. A pastor had been assigned to serve both of these churches for many years.

It became clear after some months in this community that their desire to maintain these churches as separate entities was counterproductive, but if they combined their energy into one congregation, they could become a vital force in the area. The youth of these congregations enthusiastically endorsed the idea. The middle-age couples, who for the most part had been part of the church all of their lives, were also in favor of the merger, but there was some ambivalence. The seniors of the church were largely opposed to the merger. The tradition of keeping things as they were ran deep in their thinking.

While I felt that merger was clearly in their interest, I also felt that it was important that this be their decision. After months of dialogue, it was time to vote. I insisted that all the folks who were in Florida for the winter receive an absentee ballot. On the other hand, I insisted that young people had to be present when the vote was taken for their vote to count. I wanted them to see that this was a painful decision for the older folks, including, in many cases, their grandparents. I also insisted that the decision was to be based on a two-thirds approval. It was a big-time gamble, but I felt strongly that a favorable vote had to be decisive.

When the vote was counted, including the absentee ballots, one couple had written their thoughts rather than making a direct vote. Since it was difficult to interpret their comments, the folks counting the ballots asked their two sons separately to interpret the vote for their parents. One son thought the parent's comments represented a negative vote and the other son thought it was a positive vote. One negative and one positive vote were cast for their parents. When the final tally was in, the favorable vote was exactly two-thirds in favor.

After the vote, one of the parishioners, who had been very vocal throughout this process and had voted in the negative, gave me one of the finest compliments I have ever received. He looked me squarely in the eye, shook my hand vigorously, and proclaimed, "Preacher, you beat us fair and square."

The now-united congregation built a lovely church building after I left for other duties. The congregation, as I had predicted, is truly a thriving congregation four decades after that decisive vote. It was a privilege to have led them through that process.

They purchased land for the new church located midway between the two churches. One of the first actions was to build a new parsonage. We had lived in the older parsonage that had served many clergy families. This parsonage was located on an unpaved, picturesque, narrow rural road. However, during snowstorms, it could be difficult to navigate. I remember one winter when our roads were blocked with massive snowdrifts. While the storms were raging, the children and I had a great time playing in the mounting snowdrifts.

We were the first clergy family to move into the lovely parsonage that was located next to where the church would be erected a few years later. Malcolm Williams had a sod farm and provided the sod for the large yard. It was a real treat to have a lawn like this.

We had a Siamese kitten that the children named Misty. It had been given to us by one of my favorite professors at the university, Dr. Bill Kill. We followed his recommendations to have this kitten declawed. It was strictly a house pet. One summer day, the kids took Misty outside. She was experiencing the feel of grass on her feet for the first time. It was fun to watch her put down her paw on the grass and quickly retrieve and examine her paws. The sensation of grass on her paws obviously surprised her. We all forgot to bring Misty inside. She hadn't developed any survival skills and was unfortunately killed by a passing car. I wanted to use this moment to teach the kids about the reality of death. We had a burial for the cat, and I insisted that our children take part in this ritual.

54

A Fledgling Mental Health Center

We had already moved to St. Johns before I left the VA hospital. A colleague, Dr. Paul Kreider (now deceased), told me about the Ingham Community Mental Health Center, located in Lansing, Michigan. I applied and became a psychologist on staff. It was a rather small staff of about ten or twelve therapists. I was pleased that most of my time was spent in a therapy relationship with clients rather than with administrative duties.

We were located on the third floor of a wing of Ingham Medical Hospital. Dr. Stanley, a physician with a kindly grandfather image, was the chief medical officer. Ed McCree was the hospital administrator. My hours were fairly predictable. Beyond the forty or so hours at the center, I was able to spend a fair amount of time fulfilling my obligations to the Bingham and Bengal Evangelical United Methodist Churches. (Sometime after, the EUB merged with the Methodist church; the merged congregation was later to be named the Pilgrim United Methodist Church.)

Some nine or ten months after my arrival at the center, I was surprised to see an announcement on the bulletin board that I had been promoted to chief psychologist. This prospect hadn't even been discussed with me. It came shortly after Dr. Kreider decided to leave the mental health center to join the staff of the Lansing Community College. (He later became president of Mt. Hood Community College in Portland, Oregon.) I suspect that the promotion was designed to give me a raise and assure that I wouldn't be another professional leaving for another program. The title didn't carry with it any specific responsibilities since our staff was so small.

I became increasingly concerned about the large number of people who were on the waiting list to be called for a counseling opening. We soon discovered that many on this waiting list stated they were no longer in crisis when we informed them there was now an opening.

I came to realize that it was counterproductive to place people on waiting lists. Crisis intervention theory suggested that most people tend to solve their own problems within six to eight weeks after a crisis occurred. While most of the staff therapists weren't yet ready to change the model of seeing patients only when there was an opening, I began to place people whose names were taken off the waiting list directly in group therapy without screening.

This new strategy meant seeing new clients in groups every day until the waiting list began to shrink. I assured those who came to the group that I would be available on an individual basis should a crisis arise that demanded immediate attention. I went so far as to give these new clients my home telephone number and assured them that I would make every effort to respond.

The reaction to this effort of bringing people who were on the waiting list into a group therapy mode was mixed. Some groups quickly bonded and continued for a number of weeks. Other groups fell apart quickly.

I vividly remember one group that formed a bond. After one especially powerful session, I reflected for some time on the question of why this particular group had functioned so well.

While none of these group members would have thought of themselves as being particularly religious and, as far as I know, none of them were active in any religious system, it dawned on me that the following dynamics had been present. There had been confession, repentance, forgiveness, and reconciliation. I further realized that while these terms were considered theological terms, the church did not by any means have an exclusive claim on these terms. There were clearly related to the healing in whatever discipline the healing arts were practiced.

I further came to realize that these processes were sequential. That is, confession, the art of squarely facing a given issue, preceded repentance or the process of changing behavior. The next step in this process was forgiveness of one's self as well as dealing with issues involved in deviant behavior. The last step was reconciliation.

Dr. Carroll Rinehart, now deceased, was a nationally recognized teacher who empowered students, primarily in the elementary grades, to write and produce operas. He would assist students with no musical background with writing, and many students leaped over learning hurdles in remarkable ways.

Carroll and I coauthored a book entitled *On the Journey to Wholeness*. The chapters attempt to reflect this progression of the healing process.

I was caught by total surprise when Dr. Jose Llinas, the director of the Tri-County Mental Health dropped by to see me on one occasion after our director of the Ingham Mental Health program resigned. He asked if I would be willing to consider being the director. My reply was that I was happy in my role as chief psychologist, where my primary duties were still primarily focused on being a practicing psychologist.

He responded with these words: "You have no choice. You're the new director of the Mental Health Center."

On January 1, 1970, I assumed this new role. I'm fairly sure that I was the first psychologist to become the director of an established mental health center in the State of Michigan.

There were about a dozen therapists on staff, and they were as shocked as I was by my new appointment. I had moved from being their colleague to being the boss. Predictably, several of the therapists pushed the limits apparently to check out how I was going to respond. It was an interesting time. Some years later, after the center had become very successful, Dr. Llinas, who had appointed me to this position, admitted he wasn't sure that I would survive in this new role.

Several key staff members at the center were excited about the prospect of applying for a grant for mental health staff made possible by President Kennedy's initiative in the area of responding to the mental health needs of those who could not pay for psychological services.

Dr. Rom Kriauciunas, who became the chief psychologist, did the majority of the work of writing the grant. Dr. Ed Oxer, who became the assistant director of the center, and I played instrumental roles in guiding these grant proposals through all the potential political hazards.

Another mental health center in the community wasn't eager for this proposal to succeed. For some months, it was touch-and-go in terms of the proposal being approved. The last hurdle was cleared in an unusual way. A major player, who shall remain unnamed, in the mental health programs in the Lansing area was essentially an opponent who apparently wanted to appear supportive by putting a favorable motion on the floor of the council making the final decision whether to approve our application. She apparently miscalculated in that the opposition that she seemed to have fomented didn't materialize when the motion to approve was on the floor. The chairperson, knowingly or unknowingly, didn't follow her script. The plan was approved. Based on this approval, the National Association of Mental Health granted the request for two million dollars for new staff.

The staff would grow from a dozen or so to seventy professional and support staff in ninety days. The rapid growth was due largely to the fact that the parameters of the grant required instant implementation. It was a bewildering time for most of the staff who were present before the grant was approved. The attendance at the weekly staff meetings grew so rapidly from week to week that the original staff was outnumbered by nearly five to one. It was a time of adjustment for everyone.

In the grant proposal, we had promised to develop a new network of services that ranged from consultation to the community:

twenty-four-hour emergency services, outpatient counseling services, and inpatient hospitalization. Prior to the grant proposal, outpatient counseling service was the primary service that was provided.

It was one thing to describe new services on a grant proposal and quite another to develop those promises into a viable and more comprehensive network of services. There was now a new layer of administrative services. I insisted the directors of each new service also keep actively involved in providing clinical services. Even though it meant that I would work as much as eighty hours a week at this Center, I also put myself in the position of needing to keep active clinically. It was a demanding and creative time. It meant that we had to be innovative in our approach. There were times when the administrative staff would be in meetings for six or seven hours a day as we sought to implement the new programs.

The same policies that applied to a much smaller staff no longer fit the staff of seventy. As a group, we decided that before we added a new policy, we would eliminate an old one. We often had lengthy discussions over which "older policy" to eliminate.

Crisis intervention theory suggests that people resolve their life crises in a fairly short period of time—anywhere from six to eight weeks. That so many on our original waiting list stated that they no longer needed our services when their names came up on the list seemed to prove this point.

Soon we adopted the crisis intervention model for the entire staff. Each therapist on staff would be assigned patients from this list on a rotating basis. Earlier on, most of the therapists on staff were typically more interested in seeing patients (I preferred the name "clients") in their private offices. The therapists tended to keep seeing the clients with whom they felt comfortable and appeared to be making some progress in working through the issues that had brought them to the mental health center. This comfort zone for the therapist was one reason there was slow movement getting to the people who were on the waiting list.

While I had singlehandedly tried to solve the waiting list problem in the early days of my involvement, it would now be the policy of our center not to have waiting lists. A client who made an appointment with our center would be seen immediately, guaranteed a weekly appointment for eight weeks, and then be placed in a group therapy setting. If a therapist strongly felt that more time was needed to work with that client, they could extend the time for another eight weeks. However, the therapist still would be required to accept, on a rotating basis, new clients that came to the center and would be responsible for finding time in the schedule to keep seeing the client who had exhausted their eight weeks.

One of the requirements of our staffing grant was that we provide a program of inpatient hospitalization. I had remembered the days at the VA hospital, when there were long periods of inpatient hospitalization that often lasted for a number of years. We felt that there had to be an alternative. We were aware that if a patient in a major emotional crisis were placed on a locked ward of a psychiatric unit, this patient would regress in a significant way. We felt they would be responding to the major stimulus around them. On the other hand, if this same patient were placed in a setting where the stimuli with which they are surrounded are healthier, then this patient would predictably improve much more rapidly. We had several visits from the representatives of the National Institute of Mental Health (NIMH) who were uncomfortable with our position on this issue. Our position was that we would attempt to hospitalize patients in crisis on the regular medical wards rather than a psychiatric ward. NIMH personnel eventually went along with our position, although with considerable reluctance.

In addition to being the director of the mental health center, I was also given the title of associate hospital director. This title was given primarily so I would have a direct voice in the hospitalization of patients with a psychological diagnosis and would have access to the medical wards. Ed McCree, the hospital director, was most generous in his support of this idea, although there was some resistance by some of the traditionally trained nurses.

The first patient to be hospitalized under this plan was a person who was clearly psychotic. It was noon, and all the other therapists were at lunch. I had chosen not to eat lunch the day that this patient arrived at the center by himself. He stated that he was Jesus Christ. After a short conversation, I suggested that he be hospitalized. He quickly agreed. Our center was attached to the hospital. Rather than taking the shortcut through a series of basement tunnels that connected the mental health center with the hospital, I chose to lead him outside and through the front entrance of the hospital. He paused along the way, examining blades of grass on the lawn and trying to remember how he had created the grass and flowers that he saw.

When we got to the hospital elevators, he noticed the crack between the ground floor and the elevator itself and was reluctant to cross that line. I held the doors to the elevator open until the alarms began to ring. I then gently assisted him across the line, and we were on our way to the fourth floor.

He was assigned to a room that held a man with a medical diagnosis. His family was called, and they were to stay with him until he could be medicated. Instead, they chose to leave. Before the medication could be given and take effect, he had crawled in bed with the other patient. The nurses, who objected to the whole idea of placing persons with a psychiatric diagnosis with persons with a medical diagnosis, were sure that he was making a homosexual advance toward the other patient. It turns out that this patient, who thought he was God, was responding more like a frightened young child in a thunderstorm who was attempting to get in bed with his parents. Admittedly, this was a snafu but only a temporary one. He was soon heavily medicated and participated in our program, known as the Activity Center.

For this patient, and every patient who was hospitalized in this program with a psychological diagnosis, we used the hospital much like a hotel room. These patients would spend the day at the mental health center and would be involved in a series of exciting programs that included such things as cooking gourmet meals, participating in bowling in the community, and many other activities. There were also therapy sessions in which the clients had an opportunity to work through the concerns that were part of the crisis resulting in hospitalization.

The interesting thing is that this patient, if he had been hospitalized in the VA hospital where I had previously worked, would likely have been hospitalized for a number of years. The delusional patient was hospitalized in our program for less than three weeks and was then seen on an outpatient basis. He modeled beautifully the idea that if a crisis were solved early and effectively, a person would be in a much better position to solve future crises. I might add that all the psychiatric hospitals, including the VA where I had been assigned, have changed significantly in recent years—particularly in the ways services are delivered.

After I left the program, the department of psychiatry took over the inpatient program and unfortunately, in my view, insisted on a psychiatric ward. While having organizational controls in place would have seemed to simplify the management issues, it was a step backward (in my opinion) for developing health rather than a pathological mentality in the delivery of services.

I thought it would have been interesting to provide short-term emergency care in a nonhospital setting. While it would not have been politically feasible, I would have loved to have presented the idea of contracting space in a hotel with a pool to provide a "time out" space for people whose lives had been overloaded. With this kind of an arrangement, it would have been important to have a therapist with counseling skills as well as a physician to provide medication. In my view, it would have provided health care in a healthy environment.

Now deceased, Dr. John Aycock had carried out the duties of developing a twenty-four-hour health care emergency service in a most creative way—and with great humor. As in the other counseling services, the focus was on identifying the positive aspects of the behavior of people in crisis. This program became a valued part of the regular hospital emergency services of Ingham Medical Hospital. I developed a close friendship with John, who incidentally was a former priest, and was in frequent telephone contact with him during the final days before cancer claimed his life.

A number of interesting and exciting stories could be told about the clients with whom we worked. These folks, often in severe crisis, became our teachers and had an impact on the way we experienced and saw the world.

I will share only one more story at this point. One of my patients, whose fictitious name is Jane, had a history of extended shock treatment and long periods of hospitalization. A pastor who had acted as a spiritual advisor, who obviously had deep emotional and spiritual needs himself, had had a sexual relationship with her. Following this sexual indiscretion, he gave Sunday sermons strongly condemning adultery. She assumed that she had been the tempter that had led him astray and accepted all the guilt associated with this relationship.

During the four years that I saw her in a counseling relationship, she never evidenced one shred of hope. There was only profound despair. Everything I tried seemed to have little impact. One day she appeared in my office and announced she intended to drive into a tree at a hundred miles an hour on the way home. I offered her every option I could think of, including a temporary period of hospitalization. She refused everything. Out of seemingly nowhere, I received an inspiration. I essentially told her that if she chose this option, I would feel a great deal of pain because of the concern I had for her and her spouse and two preteen age children. I also told her that I would not sleep well for several nights if she took this kind of action, but eventually I would recover. I further shared my belief that one of the very special gifts from the Creator is the gift of choice. While her choice of ending her life did not fit my value system, I would support her God-given right to make that choice.

It was a freeing moment for me. I had previously worked with many suicidal patients and accepted a great deal of responsibility in blocking their suicidal behavior. I now knew in my very depths that I did not have the power to force anyone to choose life. It forever changed my responses to desperate people. I still attempted to be compassionate in every way that I could think of but recognized that ultimately the choice was theirs. Jane had been my teacher in a profound way. This was the first moment where I was witness to Jane's therapeutic movement during the four-year period in which we were working on her life issues. While there is more to this story, the last I heard of Jane was that she was completing junior college.

The idea of consultation was new to most therapists. While we never reached the goal of devoting 50 percent of our time toward consultation rather than direct services, we did make a conscious effort to do so. We consulted with pastors, police academies, educational organizations, and other groups to teach skills in reducing stress in high stress situations.

When a clergyperson, for example, would refer a parishioner for counseling, we would attempt to involve that clergy in the counseling process. If the patient needed to be hospitalized, we attempted to involve the clergy in the inpatient treatment program. The goal was also to empower teachers. In short, we attempted to give our skills away to professionals who touched the lives of people.

We thought about housewives who were natural healers. While untrained, they were often good listeners over a cup of coffee in their kitchen. We thought about identifying a voting precinct and then identifying the women within that precinct to whom other women naturally turned to when they were facing a crisis. Unfortunately, we didn't get around to trying out this intriguing idea. It was still another way that we tried to switch the primary focus from pathology to engaging the potential within each person.

During the days that I worked at the VA hospital, I realized that a large percentage of the patients were diagnosed with what was then termed the inadequate personality. This term typically described those people whose social skills were inadequate. These patients faithfully carried out their assigned daily tasks and presented few if any behavioral problems on the ward.

A former therapist from the mental health center returned to his home state in Virginia where he became the assistant commissioner of health in charge of mental health (I'm embarrassed to admit that I cannot remember his name). He called me one day to say that he could rent a three-hundred-bed hospital for a dollar a year and asked for recommendations. I responded by suggesting that he convert the hospital into a dormitory-like atmosphere and then fill it with people who were capable of carrying out work assignments but lacked social skills. I further suggested that he contact one of the larger factories and make a contract to provide low-skill jobs for these candidates and that he provide transportation to and from the converted hospital. It would be important, I suggested, that we schedule the evenings and weekends with activities that would naturally build social skills. While he apparently wasn't able to carry out this ambitious program, I thought it was an interesting model to explore.

When the osteopathic college first moved to Michigan State University, we developed a program in which all osteopathic medical students would do a clerkship at the mental health center. For the first year of their existence at Michigan State University, all new medical students would spend a significant amount of time at our center. Our staff was intrigued with medical students getting hands-on experience. They were, however, reluctant to integrate the demands of nearly forty medical students with the demands of their heavy clinical assignments. A result of this reluctance, the clerkship for every osteopathic medical student changed to accommodate fewer students.

Our center also developed a formal relationship with the Department of Psychiatry at the Allopathic (M.D.) Medical College. As a result of these relationships, I was given an adjunct associate professor position in the department of psychiatry as well as in the college of osteopathic medicine.

For some time, I served both as the pastor of the church in St. Johns and the director of the mental health center. After becoming its director and after having received the two-million-dollar staffing grant, the demands of this center increased dramatically. It was time to choose between serving the church or the mental health center. While we were very happy with the church assignment, I felt the challenge of developing the center took priority.

We moved out of the parsonage to a rented place in St. Johns so Bob could finish his senior year in St. Johns. We then bought our first home on a manmade lake, called Lake Geneva, on the edge of the city of DeWitt. As the crow flies, this was four miles south of the Lansing, Michigan airport.

The thing that really caught our eye when we looked at the just-completed home was the fieldstone fireplace. It was truly impressive. It had three bedrooms upstairs and a full basement downstairs and was fully air-conditioned, somewhat unusual for Michigan at that time. We could look down at the lake that was just across the street from our home.

While we were there, Linda, who was then attending Alma College, took a semester of her work at the University of the Andes in Bogota, Colombia. The time in Bogota had left a deep impact on her. She decided to go back to Bogota, where she had been promised a teaching position. It seemed to me that this offer was at best nebulous, and I encouraged her to get a firm contract. Linda felt comfortable with the arrangement and wasn't to be easily deterred. We took her to meet her plane and watched her plane fly into the sky just as the sun was setting.

I realized that our little girl had become her own person and was making her own choices. I suddenly remembered that some two decades earlier I had said good-bye to my parents, who felt a great deal of apprehension about the choice that I was making. The baton had passed from one generation to the next. Leta and I returned to our home on Lake Geneva with few words between us that night. We were each lost in our thoughts.

The first home we owned was to be our dwelling place for only two years or so. We celebrated our twenty-fifth anniversary here. It was a very nice occasion when our children and Leta's siblings would join us at our home for this event. We recognized that our immediate family would rarely all be in the same place. In fact, in the next thirty years, there would only be two occasions when our children would be in the same place. We would meet in California when Linda was introducing us to Kent and then again on our fiftieth anniversary.

While we looked forward to the future, it was hard to leave our beautiful home. We would also be leaving our two oldest children. Bob was then attending Western Michigan University and Linda had graduated from Alma College. The year 1974 was just beginning.

The decision to leave the position of director of the mental health care center was made when the center had achieved the major goals set forth in the grant from the National Institute of Mental Health. The center had grown from a dozen or so employees to approximately seventy. The position as director was highly desirable and many considered my decision to leave puzzling, if not foolhardy. In fact, as I was in the process of leaving, I had many questions as to the advisability of my choice. I remember the mixed feelings that I had at the time of a farewell party given to me by the staff that I had directed.

The decision to leave was prompted, in part, by the questions raised by a middle-aged couple that I had seen in a counseling relationship several years earlier. They were struggling with the issue of leaving a secure job to go where they really wanted to be but had no promise of employment. It was a question of staying with what seemed safe and secure on the one hand and responding to something that might be regarded as an inner calling. I reflected on the issues that we had discussed over the sessions that we had together. I feel sure that these questions that were raised in the counseling sessions with this middle-aged couple were being processed in my own psyche.

I distinctly remember the time that I was driving through South Lansing, Michigan. It was as distinct as if I had heard a voice posing two questions. The first question focused on whether or not I was satisfied with my job as director of the mental health center. In answering my internal question, I remembered thinking that this position had been fraught with many uncertainties and considerable anxiety, but it had succeeded beyond my wildest dreams. I had a great deal of visibility in the community, including often being featured in the daily newspaper as well as having adjunct appointments as an associate professor in both medical schools. My answer to myself was that I did enjoy my job.

The second question that raced out of my subconscious startled me. Is this where you want to be ten years from now? I was aware that if I stayed in this position for that amount of time, I would likely stay until I retired. I remembered the commitment that my close college friend, Bob Price and I had made to each other. Without really understanding this commitment made in college years, we decided to go with what we felt would enhance life qualities. This included career decisions. I became keenly aware that I stayed simply because it was easier to stay rather than risk leaving, and something within me would grow stale. Something akin to the question that the couple whom I had counseled faced regarding staying at place where things were going well or going to a place where their dreams were guiding them struck a chord in a new and powerful way.

I wasn't sure where to start or what to do next. A number of months passed without any action. Another event got my attention. It was wintertime, and this particular morning was very cold. I had just purchased a Sears diehard battery for one of our cars. The second car wouldn't start. On one of the car batteries, I wasn't able to distinguish between the positive and negative poles of the battery. I hooked up the jumper cable on the recently purchased battery because the positive and negative poles were clearly marked. When I attempted to start the second car, the new battery exploded in my face. My eyes were filled with liquid from the exploding battery. I wasn't certain whether or not I was blind. With my eyes closed, I slowly made my way to our utility bathroom. When I washed away the liquid from my eyes, I opened my eyes and could see. (I later met a gentlemen who had the same accident but with very different consequences. He was blind.)

I realized that if I had become blinded in that moment, my options would have been significantly limited. In that moment, the decision to move to Arizona was sealed. I realized with greater clarity than I had ever known before that security is essentially an "inside job."

Still I was uncertain how to implement this decision. There were no job openings that I knew about. A physician friend, Don Lipsey, was also a pilot. We talked about Arizona and decided to fly out and look around. We stayed at the Rio Rico resort, where we had purchased a lot on the spur of the moment during our first visit to Arizona some years earlier. We checked out various job possibilities.

Because I had worked with the college of osteopathic medicine, I was interested in the fact that there was an osteopathic hospital in Tucson known as Tucson General Hospital. The most interesting contact was at the drug and alcohol treatment center that was connected to the hospital. Dr. Richard Reilly, who was the founder and director of this program, was the first person to encourage me to come to Tucson.

There were very few psychologists in private practice at this time in Tucson. Because of the location and the warm winters, the city was overcrowded with physicians. Psychology positions were almost impossible to come by. Still, I chose to accept Dr. Reilly's encouragement to come. In the waning months of 1973, I submitted my resignation as director of the hospital and intended to leave on the first of January—exactly four years after I had become the director of Ingham Medical Community Health Center. I was surprised that my decision to leave was headline news of the second section of the *Lansing Gazette*.

The staff gave a very nice farewell party for Leta and me. I remember the heavy feeling that I had of leaving a place that had become a significant part of my life. I think that I also played a major role in the evolvement of the center. I tried to dismiss the questions that were surfacing within me as to the wisdom of this decision. I felt that something within me was being torn from me and I was again questioning the prudence of this risky decision.

I wanted to give the staff a farewell party as a way of expressing my appreciation to them. Leta and I intended to give the party at our Lake Geneva home. As mentioned earlier, it had been the first home that we had owned, and we had been the first owners of that particular house. (We knew that we would be doing quite a bit of downsizing when we moved to Arizona.) The afternoon before the reception, Leta had worked hard to provide a great spread for the staff. She had gone to the next-door neighbors to borrow some items the day before and fell on the ice that covered the driveway.

She had broken her ankle. So instead of attending the reception party, she had surgery. Our move was delayed for several weeks. I extended my time at the mental health center for several weeks as well. When our very good friends, Howard and Eleanor Williams, heard of Leta's accident, they volunteered to come with us to Arizona and drive one of the vehicles, which consisted of a U-Haul truck and our personal vehicle.

Part 7

Arizona, Here We Come!

55

Getting Started in Private Practice

The month of January was nearly over when our two-vehicle caravan left Michigan. We weren't at all sure that the weather would cooperate, but we managed to escape without being confronted with heavy snowfall. We spent the first night at my sister and her husband's home near St. Louis. Myrna was born after I had left home to go to the Owosso Bible College in Michigan. As a result, I had rarely seen her—perhaps a dozen or so times in my life. These limited times together with her and her husband, Dennis, have always been a celebration.

We arrived in Arizona on February 1, 1974. The gas crisis had reached a fever pitch. We had chosen Rio Rico, a one-hour drive from Tucson, primarily because Leta had the promise of a job in the restaurant at the resort. We initially reasoned that the job was to be a factor in Leta's developing roots in our new community as well as provide some extra income while I was trying to establish a private practice in psychology. While we had no debts, our total financial reserves totaled only $3,000—not a huge resource given the uncertainties of our income.

Initially it was difficult to get started. Beyond the gas crisis, it seemed foolhardy to be commuting seventy miles, particularly in light of the fact that Leta's broken ankle ruled her out of the waitress position.

Shortly after we arrived and during the time that my anxiety about our survival had reached a fever pitch, I remember walking on a nearby golf course in the moonlight, totally lost in my anxious thoughts. I suddenly realized that a mother skunk, with her three kittens trailing behind her in lock step, was just a few feet to my right. It was at the same time a tranquil scene and a startling one. A mother taking steps to protect her brood. I stopped dead in my tracks, jarred into the present moment. It was my good fortune that I wasn't seen by, or didn't upset, the members of this passing parade.

I began to feel a great deal of panic about our survival. Had I had made a very unwise decision to leave my position in Michigan? I fretted because I had not taken a leave of absence rather than resign my position at the mental health center. The anxiety was intense enough that I explored whether or not it was feasible to return. It didn't take long to realize that one can't really go back once one has left.

Our youngest, Edward, went to a three-room school in Rio Rico during our five-month stay there. The pupils were primarily native Hispanics. Suddenly a number of non-Hispanic students began to infiltrate the school. The Hispanic students did what those who are in the majority typically do—harass those who are in the minority. It's a sad commentary on the behavior of people around the globe. At any rate, Ed, who had reluctantly left his friends in Michigan, felt isolated and unhappy in his new surroundings. These early months were difficult for him—as well as for his mother and me.

I tried several experiments in terms of building a private practice. I wanted to represent the value of focusing on the whole person who needed help. My first idea was to see patients in a physician's office and have the progress notes that I would write be a part of the medical records of that office. While this idea had merit, it turned out to be quite awkward trying to schedule one patient in one office and then in another office across town. The perfect solution evolved. I was invited to rent an office in Tucson General Hospital by the hospital administrator. All the osteopathic physicians had privileges there. My office was just around the corner where the doctors checked in at the board indicating their presence in the hospital. It provided a great deal of visibility. But I'm getting ahead of the story.

Sometimes an event occurs that serves as a benchmark. This one occurred just before I rented space from Tucson General Hospital. I was going to a physician's office and introduced myself to a young physician who had just become part of that office staff. His response to my introduction went something like this: "I have heard about you. I hear that you used to be a Methodist minister."

I wasn't sure what to expect. Before I had a chance to respond, he stated that he had rebelled against the church of his youth and had become something of a hippie in college. He added that he had been involved in environmental causes in the years of his medical school. While these activities held meaning for him, he announced that he was trying to find his way back to the church. This conversation took place in the first few minutes of our first meeting.

I was taken aback and didn't want to over respond. I might add that this physician, Dr. William Imboden III, is still a valued friend and, until he retired in 2016, was our personal physician.

I cautiously suggested that it might be useful if a few interested physicians form a luncheon group during which we might discuss existential issues. To my utter surprise, a group of a dozen or so physicians, plus their wives along with Leta and me, formed a bible study group within a couple weeks of this encounter. We met without fail for the next two years. This group went far beyond discussing the "there and then" of some biblical text. There was a great deal of passion and searching for spiritual direction and how we could live out our lives with meaning and purpose.

One of the first patients I saw in my hospital office was a nurse named Sally. She stated that while she wasn't feeling well physically, something was missing in her life, and she wasn't sure what it was. I began to sense that she was searching for meaning and a sense of purpose. As a way to get at this issue, I asked her about her about her church family. She said that she had been to church three times in her life—once to a wedding and twice to a funeral.

I told her about the bible study that the physicians had formed.

She quickly expressed interest in attending. Some of the physicians were initially somewhat hesitant about her joining the group because they saw this as an occasion for "docs" to get together. Her naïve questions about faith issues were especially a turnoff for some. The objections quickly subsided. A turning point occurred shortly after she joined the group. She told the group that she had heard that some religious groups observed the ritual of laying on hands.

She added that she had no idea what this ritual was about but asked, in light of her physical concerns, if the group would do to her whatever it was. Everyone present, including me, became immobilized. Sensing that the group was very uncomfortable, her eyes searched around the room as she inquired, "Did I say the wrong thing?"

A female physician, who happened to be Jewish, had heard about the bible study and had dropped in out of curiosity. Sensing Sally's anguish, she rushed across the room and threw her arms around Sally, stating, "I don't know what it is either, but let's do it."

At that point, all of us gathered around Sally and placed hands on her head and shoulder and offered a prayer for her healing.

In another six months or so, Sally was confined to her bed. When I visited her in her room, she asked if I thought our group would be willing to have their next weekly meeting in her room. Of course, we all came. I was surprised that this group of physicians engaged in small talk. It seemed surprising that these members of the healing profession found it so difficult to communicate what was in their hearts.

Finally, my anxiety reached a point where I had to act. I began with these words: "Sally, I know that you won't be with us very long. I want to tell you how much I love you and how much you have meant to me."

The floodgates of emotions for all of us opened. It was a powerful hour of sharing for all of us. Just before we left, Sally prayed a beautiful prayer of benediction and wished God's blessing on all of us. It was the last time we were to see Sally alive as part of our group.

Several days later, I went to see Sally in one of the Tucson hospitals. By now, she was barely able to breathe. She stated that she had arranged for her cremation and had planned the memorial service. She made a final request: "Would you guys be there for my final service? Will you share with those who attend about how we prayed together, laughed together, and cried together?"

Speaking for the group, I quickly affirmed that we would be there.

The memorial service was on Saturday, the day before Easter 1975, which, incidentally, would have been Sally's fortieth birthday. Everyone from our group was there. What a powerful celebration of her life! When members of this group have an occasion to see each other, we have often spoken of Sally and her impact on our lives.

The idea of attempting to provide psychology services in different physician's offices fit my philosophy of being a part of a model that provided integrated care. It, however, presented some unworkable logistical problems. I was very relieved when the hospital administrator offered to rent space to me in the hospital.

For the first year, my anxiety level about building a private practice was high. During the first six months, I wasn't at all sure that I would be able to survive financially. I ended up teaching some psychology courses at Pima Community College as a way to supplement my income. After my first year in private practice, the demands for my services had dramatically increased. After the second year, I no longer accepted the teaching duties at the college.

Soon, a number of physicians invited me to do inpatient hospital consultations and then provide psychological services after the consultation. Many of the consultation requests related to the psychosomatic elements of the physical symptoms that resulted in the hospitalization of the patients.

I remember getting one consultation request to see a lady who was in her sixties. She had had a number of hospitalizations in the same year. Her symptoms simply wouldn't go away. I requested, on several occasions, to see her husband of forty years. The husband was very reluctant to be a part of the consultation. After a week or so of my repeated requests, he finally showed up for a joint interview that included his wife. To my dismay, neither the husband nor the wife would speak one word. My questions were drowned out by utter silence. Finally, the wife responded to one of my questions. Her remark seemed innocent enough to me. As soon as the words left her mouth, he bolted out the door. She explained that they had not heard each other speak for over twenty years. There was total silence in their home—even at mealtimes. It was as if he panicked at even the simplest of verbal exchanges. Interestingly enough, neither apparently was willing to consider leaving the marriage. Apparently, neither was willing to change. I began to sense that her repeated hospitalizations reflected the inner pain and barrenness of their lives.

On another occasion, a surgeon referred a woman who was about thirty years old. The surgeon stated that she had a history of intense abdominal pain. He reported that he had performed several exploratory surgeries but had not found the cause of her pain. Before he operated again, he wanted to determine if this pain had a significant psychosomatic component. Hence his referral to me.

In the first few sessions, nothing much happened. I was aware that some of her responses seemed emotionally remote and my early efforts to get at the source of this emotional detachment weren't going anywhere. In response to my question about her dreams, she denied remembering her dreams. I suggested that she give herself permission to remember her dreams.

At the next session, she reported that she did in fact remember a dream. In this dream, she and her mother were pushing a baby carriage across a well-traveled street with light traffic. She described a car making a left turn at a busy intersection at a high rate of speed. Both she and her mother barely managed to get out of the way of this speeding vehicle, but the baby carriage was struck and the baby was killed.

After describing the dream, she quickly added that she had no idea what the dream meant. I asked her to role-play each person in the dream. When she started to role-play the baby, she became agitated and stated, "I know who that baby was. It was my father."

The story quickly unraveled about how her father had continually sexually molested her from the time she was just reaching puberty. Her attempts to resist were met with reassurances by her father that this behavior was appropriate. When she attempted to report these sexual episodes to her mother, her mother berated her and stated that she "shouldn't spread these kinds of terrible lies about her father." For several years, she felt trapped in this kind of a relationship.

While the surgeon had no idea of these kinds of family dynamics, he was right to wonder whether the presenting symptoms were reflecting a deep emotional pain. The surgery was canceled, and the focus shifted to psychotherapy.

I remember another physician referring a patient who was deeply entrenched in her Jehovah's Witnesses faith. The doctor made the mistake of informing her that I sometimes used hypnosis in my therapy sessions. Her first statement in the counseling room was that her faith tradition held that hypnosis was the work of the devil. I tried to reassure her that hypnosis was merely a tool occasionally used and then only with the patient's permission. This assurance was not sufficient for her. During the counseling session, she would repeatedly ask whether I was hypnotizing her. I repeatedly tried to assure her that I seldom used this tool and then only with the patient's permission.

The reason for her referral was that her husband had died of cancer, and her twenty-seven-year-old son had cancer with a poor prognosis. Her responses to these life crises were emotionally blunted. It was as if these events had been blocked out and had not occurred and were not occurring in her life.

I was attempting to find where the emotional blockage was occurring. I asked her to remember her marriage ceremony and the feelings of excitement that she may have had. She responded that she remembered her wedding day well but didn't recall any feelings of excitement. It then occurred to me that her marriage may not have been very satisfying and that she may have felt some relief regarding his death that she may have been suppressing.

I then began to ask her about the feelings that she may have had when she held her son in her arms for the first time following his birth. Her response was that she remembered this occasion well but couldn't recall any feelings of excitement.

My response went something like this, "My dear lady, you have been very concerned about whether I was trying to hypnotize you. The truth of the matter is that you have been in a trance for most of your life. My job is to break the trance so that you can start feeling again." During the remainder of the therapy sessions, she never again questioned whether I was trying to hypnotize her.

One of the situations where I did use a form of hypnosis was for patients shortly before surgery. During this time, I would ask them to imagine that they were instructing their bodies to prepare to welcome the surgeon's knife as a friend and to fully cooperate with the operative procedure. I further asked them to imagine that they would instruct the blood vessels to bleed only enough to cleanse the wound. I would then attempt to have them experience a deep state of relaxation.

I remember receiving a call from a physician who had made a number of referrals to me. He himself was going to experience back surgery and requested that I hypnotize him. He was the last person that I expected to make this kind of a request primarily because I had seen him as a person who didn't allow himself a great deal of access to his feelings. He later reported that because of our work together, his hospital stay was significantly reduced.

Malpractice insurance was a fact of life for every physician and every psychologist in private practice. I was insured for a million dollars per client. I suspected that, with our society's orientation to legal liability, I would one day be sued. Since I dealt with a heavy caseload of people who were suicidal, I assumed that one day one of my patients would commit suicide, and the family would sue me for not taking what they considered appropriate action to prevent this behavior.

I am aware of only one client that actually committed suicide. He was a school principal whom I initially saw when he was on sick leave. He appeared to make progress through the summer, but when he returned to his old job, he was unwilling or unable to make the behavioral changes that would help him confront the work-related issues that were causing him anguish. When he did return in an agitated state, he refused hospitalization. In attempting to provide a structure for him, I urged him to return the next day for another appointment. He promised to come but chose suicide instead. His family asked that I be involved in the funeral ceremonies.

The person who sued me was a person I had never seen. His claim was that he had been injured by one of my clients, who occupied the bed next to him in the hospital. The story that he told in court was bizarre. He said that he was having a nightmare that a huge monster on Mars was strangling him. He stated that when he awakened my client in the next bed, who happened to be six feet seven inches, was choking him. He further stated that my client was out of control and had gone into a psychotic state as a result of the hypnosis that I had purportedly used. He added that, with his knowledge of martial arts, he was able to hurl this purported intruder through the air to land on the very bed that the intruder had vacated to begin strangling him. He stated that in this process he had injured his back.

The case was obviously thrown out. I was so disillusioned that a lawyer, with a well-appointed office and apparently some standing in the community, would handle such an obviously fraudulent case. Incidentally, we were in the courtroom on a Friday. The hearing began at 9:00 a.m. and didn't end until 9:00 p.m. Typically, on such petty complaints, insurance companies would settle out of court because it is far cheaper to settle than to defend their client from the lawsuit. Apparently, the lawyer expected to settle out of court for this relatively small claim. I felt that this lawyer had been willing to "sell his soul for a pot of porridge." While it was uncomfortable to go through this grueling process, I feel that the insurance company was right in its willingness to challenge the cases that were so obviously fraudulent.

I was the first psychologist to gain privileges as a consulting psychologist at Tucson General Hospital. It was an active hospital that later fell on bad times and was eventually sold. The chair of the credentialing committee, who shall remain unnamed, initially attempted to block the approval of my application. He apparently thought psychologists were not appropriate candidates for consulting staff privileges. Another physician, Sanford Berlin, who later became a psychiatrist, wrote a minority report to the decision makers that suggested that I be granted these privileges. Dr. Berlin's report was accepted rather than the chair of the committee.

An amusing incident occurred several years later that involved the physician who tried to block my application. I had given a psychological test known as the Minnesota Personality Inventory to one of his patients. He saw the raw data before the test was scored, and until it was scored, the data was meaningless. When I inquired tongue-in-cheek what he was observing on the sheet containing the raw data, he attempted to make some interpretative comments. It helped me understand why the staff had accepted the minority report on my application rather than accepting his judgment.

As mentioned earlier, Dr. Richard Reilly, a general practitioner, had started an alcoholic and drug treatment program that was known as West Center, which was a branch of the osteopathic hospital. Dr. Reilly was the patron saint of this program. He was the first to give me encouragement to come to Arizona when most thought this venture was foolhardy.

It was my privilege to do literally hundreds of consultations at West Center. In many cases, Dr. Reilly asked me to do the follow-up counseling with clients who were typically in residence at the center for a month and participated in a full range of programs at the center.

Unfortunately, this program and Tucson General Hospital no longer exist. My nearly two decades of affiliation with this hospital were for me an important setting in which to practice psychology.

During the first six months of my private practice in Tucson, it was far from certain that I would succeed. I was keenly aware that I was close to the borderline of survival. My income was largely based on how many patients were referred to me. As mentioned earlier, I rented office space from the hospital. My office was just around the corner from the doctor's directory. There was a place for them to press a button, which lit up their names on the directory board, indicating that a given doctor was on the hospital grounds. The referrals from a number of physicians began to dramatically increase.

By the second year of practice, I would come to the office by 7:00 a.m. and typically wouldn't get home until nearly midnight. Saturdays I would be working until 5:00 or 6:00 p.m. and then spent much of Sunday afternoon in the office. In addition, I was often called to the emergency room in the wee hours to see a patient who had attempted suicide. My job was to determine whether this patient should be admitted or whether it was appropriate to develop a treatment plan before the patient would be released. This pace continued for several years.

I considered taking a partner in practice but wasn't certain enough about the future to take action on this idea. While the patient load was heavy, my appointment book was rarely filled for more than two or three weeks at a time. I remembered from my days at the mental health center that patients solve their immediate crises in a fairly short time.

Several years after having my office located in the hospital, the administrator informed me that a physician had applied for office space in the hospital. When his request was denied, the physician asked why I had had office space in the hospital for several years and his request was denied. The administrator then adopted the policy that hospital offices would not be available for rent. I was given several weeks to move.

Meanwhile, several psychologists and physicians had purchased a house located a couple of miles from the hospital. Our intention was to create a holistic health center. Dr. Vaughn Huff, Dr. Harmon Myers, Dr. Carroll Rinehart, and others were involved in this program.

I remember chatting with the medical director of Tucson General Hospital sometime during the mid-1970s. I shared with him that, in my opinion, 80 percent of the patients in the hospital that evening could have as easily gone home and returned the next day for whatever treatments they were receiving. (To implement this strategy, however, would have meant significant loss of income for the hospital since hospital stays were typically paid without question.) I then suggested that, since they were in the hospital anyway, the patient's clothes be returned to them. They could eat meals in a cafeteria, and we could arrange for a band or a combo of some kind to play festive music. The medical director gave me a stunned look and commented, "What would Blue Cross say?"

Interestingly enough, Blue Cross eventually started evaluating how critical inpatient hospital stay was to needed patient care. The pendulum probably swung too far in the direction of releasing patients too soon in the name of cutting costs.

In less than two decades, the implementation of health care systems was to radically change the way that medical services were delivered, including for my practice of psychology. Health maintenance organizations, meant to dramatically reduce the cost of medical services, impacted the health care delivery system.

56

Blessed Be the Tie that Connects and Blesses

Shortly after moving to Tucson in 1974, we became active in the First United Methodist Church. Both pastors, Larry Hinshaw and Doug Bobbitt, became close friends. A special bond also developed between Leta and me and two other couples in the congregation: Dr. Harmon and Edith Myers and Dr. Carroll and Marilyn Rinehart. It is a bond that has lasted for nearly three decades.

This relationship began shortly after we arrived in Tucson. Growth groups, sponsored by the church, were the initial catalyst for this bonding. We have since celebrated each other's birthdays and anniversaries and have had season tickets to the Arizona Theatre Company for thirty years. New Year's Eve will likely find us together sharing food in one of our homes. Each couple was married within one year of each other. We have all celebrated each other's fiftieth wedding anniversary. Each event was planned very differently and was a real celebration. This network of relationships has been rare in our mobile society and is deeply treasured by all of us. Carroll, Harmon, and I have also shared psychosynthesis workshops in the past.

Over the past thirty years, Carroll Rinehart and I have shared ideas that have stimulated and challenged us. I think it has left a significant impact on the way that we see the world. I remember

351

sharing with him an experience that I had at the mental health center in Lansing where I had served as a director. I had facilitated a number of different short-term group counseling sessions. Some groups bonded quickly while others had some difficulty in forming the bonds of trust that are necessary for a group to come together.

I was sharing with Carroll how a new group bonded quickly. (Part of this story was shared earlier.) Powerful dynamics were in evidence on their first meeting. I reflected for some time on how this had happened and what made this group so distinctly different. Several days after this particular group meeting, it dawned on me that a series of dynamics had occurred. While this was not a group that would have considered themselves in any way religious, confession, repentance, forgiveness, and reconciliation had occurred. This process is profoundly psychological as well as theological. It further occurred to me that this process was sequential—that is, confession or owning who you are must come before repentance, which is essentially the process of changing one's behavior. Forgiveness becomes a crucial step before healing can occur. The thesis of *On the Journey to Wholeness* is that if these steps are not followed, then the process of healing will be short-circuited.

In this book, we both used our experiences—he as a music educator and me as a psychologist—to illustrate the steps of healing. All of the steps with their psychological subtitles became chapter headings.

The book was in process for nearly two decades. A close friend and colleague, Dr. Vaughn Huff, a retired psychology professor at the university, spent countless hours editing these writings. The many revisions over the years reflected the changes taking place in our lives and an evolving perspective of our worldview.

57

Time to Shape Up

During the years that I was working one hundred hours a week or more, there was precious little time for anything else. My meals were sporadic, at best. If I took time to eat, it was usually in the doctor's dining room, where I would have a chance to interact with physicians from whom the bulk of my referrals came. When I would arrive home in the evening—usually somewhere around midnight—I would indiscriminately eat what was in the refrigerator. I was usually so fatigued that I was barely aware of what I was consuming. Not the best strategy for keeping healthy! The bind was that if I didn't accept the referral requests of physicians, the source of referrals would dry up. I would often see the newly referred persons after a long day of seeing my regular patients. It was as if I were running as fast as I could but still falling behind.

Consequently, there was little physical exercise with one exception. When I would go to the different floors of the hospital, I would take the stairs rather than the elevator unless I was accompanying a patient or engaging a person in a conversation while walking through the hospital.

Soon, the weight began to accumulate. A chance conversation with a pediatrician by the name of Dr. David Leopold sparked a change. David had just run a complete marathon. I suddenly realized that this was not some impossible dream as far as I was concerned. I began running in the complex where I lived, and soon I was running faithfully five miles a day or more. I hadn't realized how important stretching was, and soon my groin muscles became so sore that I had difficulty walking. Still, I was reluctant to stop my early morning runs. Dr. Leopold, who informally became my coach, advised me to let the muscles heal and then introduced a stretching routine. Soon, I was back on track and was running ten to twelve miles per day.

When it was time to sign up for this daunting twenty-six-mile run, Dr. Leopold, a pediatrician, followed me throughout the run. I kiddingly stated that he "babied me to the finish line." Near the twenty-mile point, my leg muscles tightened to the extent that it was difficult to continue. The good doc had some salt tablets that got me through that first crisis. The solution worked for several miles. From there on, it was mind over matter.

Four other marathons were to follow, one in Tucson, one in San Diego, and two in Honolulu. The final two marathons in Honolulu were memorable in so many ways. The first time was on December 7, a special day in history for Honolulu residents.

We had gone to a large park across the street from Waikiki Beach the morning prior to the race to pick up the numbers that we would wear on our T-shirts. Both runners and their friends flooded the park. I didn't know a single person gathered there other than my wife. I was quite surprised when an older lady inquired how fast I intended to run the race on the following morning. Trying to be cute, I replied that I would make every effort to beat all the eighty-year-old ladies. With a smile that quickly put me in my place, she responded that she was running and that she was seventy-nine years old.

We had been instructed to show up by five on the morning of the race. The gun, in this case a military cannon, would announce the start promptly at six. Some twelve or thirteen thousand runners were in place at the start time. The faster runners were placed near the front of the line, while the plodders, like me, were placed near the back of the line that stretched for several blocks.

When the cannon fired, my adrenaline was high, and I wanted

to start. It took several minutes before I or the runners around me could take a single step. The faster runners at the front of the line obviously took off at full speed at the sound of the cannon, but those of us who were further in the line couldn't take a step, let alone run, until those in front of us began to move. The several-minute delay was maddening. When the line began to move, it was only a very slow walk. It seemed to take forever before we could break into the pace that we were going to set.

What impressed me most about the race was the attention given to those who didn't consider themselves professional runners. I was also impressed with the celebratory nature of the run. The residents gathered in great numbers to not only watch the start and finish of the race but also line up along much of the twenty-six-mile route that we were to follow.

At the beginning of the race, several runners (I don't remember whether it was six or eight persons) were harnessed together and dressed like reindeer. They were singing a familiar jingle to the crowd as they ran: Santa Claus is coming to town.

The marathon became an exciting time of social interaction. I noticed one couple, apparently from Japan, who wore T-shirts announcing that they were just married. I was told that several hundred runners had flown in from Japan to participate. I remember running beside a young girl who was eleven or twelve years old and desperately trying to finish. She stated that her older brother was one of the faster runners and that her father was an official in the race. She obviously wanted to have their approval by performing well. I remember one man at about the twenty-mile mark who, until that point, had been ahead of me. He stated that he was eighty years old and had come all the way from Chicago for this run. Another runner took some time out at about the halfway point to get a quick cup of coffee. Still another runner had a beautiful Great Dane that he held on a leash while running. At the midpoint, his wife met him to pick up the dog and bring another that apparently was born from the same litter. The runner's explanation was that no dog should have to run more than thirteen miles.

I remember running through a residential section located between mile twenty and mile twenty-three. Many of these residents were holding hoses of running water, inviting anyone who wanted water poured on their bodies to run under the hoses. Many held signs of encouragement. The sign that I don't think I will ever forget simply read: "Gut it out!"

One young lady, who was part of the support staff, acted as an enthusiastic cheerleader at mile twenty-five, admonishing everyone to "hang in there" for the final mile. Although my muscles were extremely tight and I was struggling, I had no intention of dropping out. A mischievous streak didn't prevent me from suggesting to her that I might not make it.

She practically fell to her knees, pleading for me to finish. While I was amused at her response, I did feel slightly wicked for playing with her wonderful words of encouragement.

As I remember, there were slightly more than eight thousand finishers. Nearly seven thousand had crossed the finish line ahead of me. As we approached the final two hundred yards, I was so surprised and inspired to see that a group of people formed a corridor from our final sprint area to the finish line. They were excitedly cheering us on, as if we were winning the race. At the final line, lovely Hawaiian young ladies placed a wreath of seashells around our necks as we finished.

Leta and I briefly wandered around the park before taking the bus back to our hotel. The streets in the center of Honolulu tend to be one way. Since I didn't know the one-way street going back to the hotel, I misjudged, and we ended up getting off the bus some ten blocks before reaching our hotel. By then the muscles had set, and I was struggling to walk a few feet let alone ten blocks. After stopping to rest a number of times, I noticed a family restaurant. While I wasn't the least bit hungry, I decided to get a milkshake and rest. As we entered the restaurant, a lady about fifty years old asked me if I had run in the marathon. Since I was still in my running outfit with my number on the front of my T-shirt, I was amused by her question. She then asked if I had finished. When I responded that I had, she placed a kiss on my cheek, gave me a carnation, and then simply disappeared. I was so moved that I wanted to weep. Part of my reaction may have been related to the chemical changes that had occurred in my body, but I felt that I had truly been touched in a profound way by a total stranger.

Much of the rest of the day was spent in our hotel room. I tried to find relief alternatively in a hot tub of water and collapsing in bed. We had heard that there was to be a documentary of the marathon shown on a local TV station that evening. The documentary was well done. Again there was little mention of the winners but rather the focus was on a number of human-interest stories. The story that stands out was of a seventy-two-year-old who reported suffering a stroke during the last year. Following her recovery, she announced to her startled family members that she intended to run the marathon. She reported that they had warned her of the possible dire consequences and urged her to reconsider this foolhardy decision. I will never forget the shot that the camera technician took as he caught her response to her family members. With a toothless smile, she said, "I told them, 'What have I got to lose?'"

I had been in Honolulu before this marathon. To me, it seemed much like any other sprawling city. This time I had experienced the friendliness and warmth of its people and my perception of Honolulu changed. It became for me a very special place.

Every parent should be blessed by having an offspring work for the airlines. Our daughter, Linda, has worked for Delta Airlines since 1979. Following the marathon just described, we took advantage of Delta's offer that allowed the parents of Delta employees to fly from Honolulu to Fiji. Reed and Violet Berrett, parents of Linda's husband, Kent, joined us on a short visit to Fiji. We stayed at a lovely resort for several days on the beach. The beaches were wonderful. My leg muscles were still rigid from the marathon. I still remember the incoming waves gently washing over my feet as I slowly walked along several miles of wonderful beaches. I could visualize my very sore muscles beginning to relax and let go of the tension. One of the many islands that are a part of Fiji was less than a mile away. I became aware of both the incoming and outgoing waves and soon noticed that my breathing was matching this motion.

357

I also remember how the native Fijians loved to sing. Every time a car or a bus would arrive at the front entrance to the resort, the employees seemed to congregate out of nowhere to sing a song of welcome. When guests departed, they would sing songs of farewell. I have found nowhere in the world where singing seemed to be so spontaneous. I still regret that we didn't find time to accept the invitations so freely given to join them in their village homes for the evening. The natives seemed so cordial—so willing to share themselves.

Back in the saddle again in Tucson, I planned to run the marathon the following December. While my daily schedule was extremely busy, I found time to run and stay in shape. Some days, I would run as much as ten miles without walking. I often found myself silently chanting mantras that went something like this: O Lord, how wonderful is Thy name in all the earth.

I would often not be aware of the repetition of this or some other phrase for miles. It was almost like this chanting had occurred in my subconscious mind.

During this time, I was going through the reserve phase of the Command and General Staff College. Completing this course was a necessary condition for promotion to full colonel, although going through the college was not a guarantee that this promotion would be forthcoming. This particular phase was to be taken at Fort Sill, Oklahoma. The final phase was at the headquarters of the Command and General Staff College, located at Leavenworth, Kansas.

While attending this demanding school, I still managed to run forty miles each of the two weeks I was there. When the course was completed, I stopped by the farm in western Nebraska to visit my parents. The military language for this side trip would have been a "delay in route." My father was eighty years old but regularly rode a spirited horse. He suggested that I ride the horse to bring the cattle from the grazing land to the corral for the night. I had grown up on horses as a child but hadn't ridden much as an adult. This task seemed simple enough. I got on the horse and went through several gates. Just before going through the final gate that led to the pasture, the horse bucked. Up until this moment, there was nothing to suggest the horse was going to buck. I had been very relaxed. The buck of the horse threw me up in the air six or more inches from the saddle. Before I had settled back into the saddle, the horse bucked again. I began to rein the horse in to gain control. At the same time, I had a vague awareness that I was falling off the horse. Although I didn't feel the pain, my body went into total shock. I had passed out before I had fallen to the ground.

My sister-in-law, Bonnie, who didn't like this horse, had gone behind the barn to assure herself that the horse was behaving. She spotted me lying on the ground. She called my brother and father, who got me in the car and were taking me to the nearest hospital — still unconscious. I came to just as we were nearing the hospital, which was some twelve miles away from my parent's farm. When Dad told me that I had fallen from the horse, I began to wiggle my toes and other parts of my body to see if I still had movement. I did. I expected that I would be able to get out of the car without difficulty. I was very surprised to find that I couldn't walk.

While no bones were broken, the bones in the pelvic area are normally flush with each other but had been separated by well over an inch. As a result, I lost a lot of control of muscles that I had used most of my life. It was a humbling experience to realize that for the first time as an adult, I couldn't even manage to take care of my own toiletry.

With very limited mobility, I began to explore various options of getting back to Tucson. I eventually arranged for my brother to drive me and my rented car to the Denver airport, some 225 miles away. He left me off at the Delta terminal, where our daughter, Linda, was waiting for me. I was wheeled into a first-class seat on the plane en route to Tucson. I didn't dare to drink beverages of any kind because I couldn't move without a wheelchair and hence wouldn't have access to a restroom for the entire flight.

The Tucson airport was not yet equipped to disembark passengers on a Jetway ramp. So I had to be carried off the plane on a stretcher. I was transported directly to our car, and Leta took me immediately to Tucson General Hospital, where I was admitted as a patient.

Dr. Roger Grimes, an orthopedist and good friend, attached a rigid metal frame (that resembled an erector set) to my pelvis by six screws. The purpose was to force the separated pubic bones back together. After this surgical procedure, I remember struggling to use a walker to get a few feet across the room. After forty-five minutes or so, I managed to travel six or seven feet. This effort was exhausting, and I was perspiring profusely.

Dr. Grimes stated that he was prescribing pain medication. My response was that I had worked with many patients on pain control and said that I wanted to avoid pain medication if at all possible. He reluctantly consented but stated that pain medication was on order at any time I might request it. I managed not to use any pain medication during this entire hospital stay.

After trying to use a walker with little success, I asked Dr. Grimes to refer me to physical therapy to see if I could learn to use crutches. While he was somewhat skeptical, he scheduled this evaluation. To my surprise and his, I was able to use crutches with some success.

I was to remain in the hospital for another week. A number of physician friends dropped by to see me. They kidded me, observing that this metal frame attached to my pelvic bones resembled an enormous erection when a sheet or blanket covered me. Dr. Vigorito, an internist who was in the same office as I was, asked if I wanted to work up a consultation. The patient came to see me in a hospital while I did a clinical referral. I dictated my report from my bedside phone.

I had approximately six weeks of rehabilitation at home, where I slept and spent a good deal of time in a recliner in our living room. While I could move around with crutches, the pins attaching the metal contraption didn't move. Any movement of my hips meant that the pins would be tearing at the flesh. My choice was to either accept this consequence or not navigate. I wanted to be as mobile as quickly as I could, so I doggedly pushed myself despite the discomfort and the irritation when the metal pins were attached to my thighs.

I remember one event during the rainy season when the sun was shining between the clouds. I decided to go for a short walk outside. I hadn't realized that storm clouds were building. As I was walking with the aid of crutches, I had almost reached the street when there was an enormous bolt of lightning, followed by thunder. At that moment, I became very acutely aware that the metal contraption was attached to my body. As quickly as I could, which wasn't very fast, I did an about-face and headed for the safety of our townhouse.

When this contraption was taken off some six weeks later, the pelvic bones were still separated by nearly an inch. This meant that my gait would be forever changed. I limped badly and recognized that I could easily limp permanently until I willed it otherwise. I began to focus on walking without a limp. This felt very artificial in the beginning. While I am conscious of going into a slight limp when I am exhausted, I don't think that even close friends have noticed that my gait has changed.

I was scheduled to be in Honolulu during the time of the annual marathon run so I signed up to run just for the fun of it. I hadn't run a single step for well over a year. I reasoned that I might be able to complete three or four miles of the twenty-six-mile marathon. Although I set a slower pace than I did on the marathon the previous year, to my amazement I finished the entire race. When the race ended, I was surprised to discover that my muscles weren't as tight as they had been on the previous marathon.

As before, what I found empowering about the Honolulu marathon was the focus on enabling as many runners to finish as possible. This running experience also became a wonderful social event.

I could have become a casualty in the early moments of the race. From my starting point, it was several minutes before the line started to move. The race started at 6:00 a.m. because the heat and humidity at midday tended to be intense. As the runners started to move, I attempted to pass a runner by stepping over a curb. I stumbled and fell to the ground and was fortunate that I wasn't crushed by the rush of runners around me. I managed to get to my feet before that happened and only suffered minor bruises on one arm and my face.

I was disappointed that a TV documentary, like the one shown following the first Honolulu marathon, hadn't been created to capture the drama of the ordinary runners who invested so much energy to participate.

58

The Jesuits Help Me Get It Right

A valued friend, the Reverend Douglas Bobbitt, then the campus pastor and associate pastor of the First Methodist Church in Tucson, learned that the Jesuit School of Theology at Berkeley was offering a doctoral program designed to enhance the pastoral skills of Catholic clergy and nuns. He inquired whether Protestant clergy would be admitted to this two-year study program. While the faculty would be sent from Berkeley, the classes would be conducted at the Regina Cleri Center in Tucson.

Seventeen priests, four sisters, and three Protestant clergy were admitted to this program. While I was in full-time private practice as a psychologist, I had still retained my status as ordained United Methodist clergy. This two-year program ended up being one of the most exciting educational experiences I have ever had. While the PhD from Michigan State University was the foundation of my academic work credentials, the Berkeley program impacted my clinical practice as well as my worldview as much or more than the doctoral program at MSU.

I found two requirements impressive at the beginning of this program. The first was that we needed to have an inventory battery of tests that attempted to evaluate both the emotional and spiritual dimensions of our lives. I had given many psychological tests and written many psychological reports. The impressive factor was that the same battery of tests would be given to us at the end as well as the beginning of our academic experiences in an attempt to measure how we had evolved in both our emotional and spiritual development. The second was that we were required to have a support group consisting of a dozen people to participate with us during the entire two years. At the end, they would evaluate our "change statements" and write a report of their evaluation of the progress we had made as they saw it.

The entire design of the program was determined by consensus. The first consensus-building effort, lasting several days, focused on what the participants wanted to experience and learn from our two-year project. Then, daylong consensus meetings were held prior to each of the nine major units. The final segment was to be in essence a summary section in which each student would attempt to integrate what he or she had experienced.

Each of these nine segments consisted of ninety hours, beyond the consensus sessions, that would be equally subdivided into three categories. The first thirty hours were to be invested in reading. Once a subject area had been identified, the facilitators of this program from the Jesuit School of Theology at Berkeley would then select outstanding faculty members for a given segment. This person could be drawn from anywhere in the United States. The person(s) selected as faculty would select a number of books that were required reading. The seminary sent these books, along with the appropriate bill. The students would be given approximately six weeks to read them.

The second segment of the program, also a thirty-hour unit, was the instructional phase in which the selected faculty would be sent to the Regina Cleri Center in Tucson. This consisted of six hours of instruction per day for five days.

The third thirty-hour segment involved the support group. The students were required to present a summary of our readings as well as the week's instruction. This would occur on ten different occasions. Our support group, which consisted of four physicians in active practice, several educators, and several people from the local congregation, was required to design a project that would crystallize both the readings as well as the academic week. This proposed project that Douglas and I wrote was submitted to the instructors who had to give their approval. Once approval was received, the project had to be written up on its conclusion and approved before the unit could be considered complete. More than once, we had to rewrite the project proposal and/or its conclusion.

Douglas Bobbitt and I, both United Methodists, were allowed to have a common support group. Each support group member had to be willing to invest three hundred real-time hours during the two-year program. I don't remember anyone missing any of the many sessions involving our support group. The project designs were often long and drawn out. After one particular lengthy debate on the given project, I remember one of the support group members, Dr. Lee Scott, said he had a new appreciation of what Thomas Jefferson had purportedly said as the constitution of the United States was being written: "I would be happy to write the whole damn thing myself."

One project vividly stands out in my memory. We had focused on this statement from one of the professors during one of the segments who was commenting on the scriptural statement that unless we become as children we cannot enter the kingdom of heaven. His comment was that many had never really had a childhood. Some of us had come from families so focused on work and survival that we had never been children. The project was to design a play-style questionnaire.

The group decided that perhaps we should go to a park and observe children at play in an effort to grasp the significance of play. With some apprehension, we gathered in the park that evening. We weren't sure where or how to begin. It was a most exciting and invigorating process.

Our introduction to psychosynthesis occurred during the first lecture week. During my graduate training, I had never even heard of Italian psychiatrist Roberto Assagioli, who originated this concept. He was an admirer as well as a contemporary of both Freud and Jung. Assagioli developed his own thought about human personality. He felt that Freud was right to focus on what Assagioli referred to as "the basement" of the human psyche but felt that the concept of repression dealt with far more than the tendency of human nature to repress that which was socially unacceptable. He felt that humans too often repressed the "sublime" within us. That is, we were frightened by the awesome potential that resided within us.

Assagioli developed a fascinating mantra about the mind, body, and emotional relationships. It declared that while we have amazing bodies with a miraculous function, we are more than our bodies. We have powerful emotions that add so many important dimensions to our lives, but we are far more than our emotions. While we have minds that are immeasurably complex, we are far more than our minds. At the integrated center of our being we are part of the energy of the universe. This integrative core of our being does not have agendas other than synthesizing the different aspects of our selves known as subpersonalities.

A major premise of his system was that the core of who we are is connected with universal energy. While I'm not aware that he used the term "God" or the theological phrase that we are made in the image of God, this implication was implicit throughout his writings.

The subpersonalities of which he speaks reflect the process of socialization and apparently are influenced by our genetic history as well. These subpersonalities can be thought of as our "internal children," who are important members of our internal family, but like children, cannot give direction to the family itself. There is often sibling rivalry between these subpersonalities. For example, the internal child that I have named the "workaholic" doesn't get along very well with the "playful child." When the playful child wants to play, the one devoted to hard work is disdainful of the one who wants to recreate. Likewise, the part of me that wants to play it safe gets very uneasy around that one that I have named the adventurous one. While these and other subpersonalities play an important role in my life, they do not know how to give direction to my life. That job of coordination belongs to the aspect that has been labeled the center.

When we lose touch with that center, the internal children compete for leadership. That competition often becomes distorted and confused. I well remember one of my clients who had grown up in grinding poverty in a single-parent family. He had a job in a factory at a very young age, thanks primarily to a sympathetic owner and CEO. This young boy stayed with the company and eventually became the owner. His workaholic tendencies had served him well. The only problem was that when he was forced to retire decades later, he became a lost soul. He had lost touch with his center, and the workaholic had taken over the coordinating role. The workaholic didn't know how to provide meaning and direction to his life. Now in his eighties, and with all the money that he could possibly want, his life became empty and meaningless. While his workaholic aspect had played a vital role, it didn't have a clue about how to tap into the energy of the universe and give purpose to the closing chapter of his life.

Back to the question of good and evil. There is a sense that what is typically described as evil can be thought of as a distorted good. An issue closely related to this question is the issue of intentionality of behavior. This system taught me to distinguish between the behavior and the intentions of a given behavior. For example, I worked with many clients who wanted to stop smoking. Initially I used techniques that would result in a repulsive reaction to smoking. While these techniques sometimes were effective, I was drawn to exploring the initial intentions of that behavior. I discovered, for example, that many in my age group had begun smoking as a way to validate their sense of autonomy as well as winning the approval of their peers. As time passed, this strategy had not served them well. It was then important to find new behaviors that met these intentions in a more creative way. I often told clients that it was very important for a two- or three-year-old to learn the art of coordination by riding a tricycle. If that person was still riding a tricycle at age twenty-two, then the maturational process has gone awry.

What we term evil often comes from the distortion of subpersonalities that have attempted to take over the center. I remember when I was perhaps ten years old, I heard a sermon on Jesus's admonition to the rich young ruler to sell everything that he had and give it the poor. Apparently, I was very moved by what I heard. After the sermon, I attempted to convince my parents to sell our farm and give everything to the poor. I couldn't understand why they were so unresponsive to the passionate way that I wanted to literally follow that teaching. Obviously, I had stepped out of my role as a young offspring and had attempted to take the role that appropriately belonged to my parents.

Much more could be said about this system of thought. It's enough to touch on some of the aspects of this system that left so deep an impact on my life.

59

Partners of the Americas: Michigan and Belize

One of the major components of President John Kennedy's foreign policy with South America was labeled the Alliance for Progress. A people-to-people corollary of this policy was known as the Partners of the Americas. Under this program, different states were matched with South American countries or parts of the country. I was privileged to be part of two different programs, one that matched Michigan with Belize, Central America, and the Dominican Republic and the other matching Arizona with the states of Durango and Oaxaca in Mexico.

My friend and colleague, Dr. John Jordan, played a major role in these relationships and was particularly active in areas of health and rehabilitation. While I was primarily involved with the states of Belize and Durango in Mexico, I was a part of a seminar in Oaxaca. I made a dozen or more visits to Belize. The purpose of one of these visits was to lead a mental health seminar that included staff from Ingham Medical Hospital. Prior to this, we made a brief stop in Costa Rica, where I gave a lecture at the university. En route from Costa Rica to Belize, the plane stopped in Teguicigalpa, Honduras. Even though we had confirmed flights to Belize, we were taken off the plane and told, after a considerable delay, that we would have to exit the flight and take a flight the next day. Apparently someone

369

outranked us. Our group was somewhat disgruntled, so when we arrived at the hotel in the late afternoon, we went to our rooms to rest. I decided that there was plenty of time to rest later and went to explore the city.

I found a craft shop with incredible handcrafted articles for sale. It was near closing time, but I urged her to keep the store open until I could rouse my colleagues. I ended up purchasing a lovely hand-carved coffee table as well as a piece of wood that could have multiple uses, such as a folding seat or a footstool. It was beautifully carved, a single piece of mahogany that folded into several positions. Both grace our living room. On several return trips to Belize, we intentionally chose to visit this unique city.

In all, I had the privilege of visiting Belize over a dozen times. Our groups often had meetings with the prime minister. On several occasions, I was surprised that he called me by name when a delegation of which I was a part was visiting.

Several towns formed a sister-city relationship. Delegates from the city of St. Johns, including the vice mayor of our city; my wife, Leta; and several young people, went to the village of Stand Creek for ceremonies celebrating the establishment of a formal document mutually declaring that a relationship had been indeed been formed. As with many other sister-city groups who formed this relationship, it is difficult to maintain this status unless there is at least one person who will take the responsibility to sustain this effort. Neither side found the person who would carry this torch.

When I arrived in Arizona in 1974, I discovered that the Partners program had lost its energy and not much was happening. I volunteered to organize a group to go to Durango, Mexico, for what would prove to result in a number of different exchanges.

After coordinating with Guadalupe Razo, the chairperson of the Durango part of the partnership, I got together a group of volunteers primarily from the church of St. Francis in Tucson to be a part of this group that would explore if new life could be breathed into this partnership. Twelve or thirteen people agreed to go for ten days or so. We found that we could take the very inexpensive train ticket to the seaside city of Mazatlan. We were fortunate enough to secure Pullman cars on railroads that got very rough before we reached our destination. Through a car rental agency in Houston, I had arranged for three late-model rentals to drive over the high Sierras. When we got to the car rental agency in Mazatlan, where the rental cars had purportedly been arranged by the agency in Houston, we discovered that we were assigned two Volkswagen Beetles that were thirty years old plus a newer station wagon. It turned out that the Beetles functioned perfectly while the newer vehicle became disabled on the return journey from Durango to Mazatlan.

It took longer than we had expected to get the cars from the rental agency and begin our journey to Durango. Unbeknown to us, Guadalupe had arranged for us to have a meal with the Rotarians. She had told them a group of Rotarians was coming. Actually, I was the only Rotarian in the group. We arrived somewhere around nine o'clock in the evening—several hours later than we had anticipated. We hadn't stopped to eat and were all very hungry. When we discovered that we would be going to a Rotary meeting, our group was less than enthusiastic. But Guadalupe was very insistent on our going. After we made introductions, they were surprised that there wasn't a Rotarian other than me in the group. Guadalupe apparently had made an unwarranted assumption. A wonderful meal was served following the introduction. Even though I was the only Rotarian, this was a very important beginning as far as future Rotary contacts were concerned.

Guadalupe was a marvelous host, and we were introduced to many aspects of Durango's cultural history. While the members of this initial group did not return to Durango, they played a role in the kind of relationship that would develop between the citizens of the states of Arizona and Durango.

On another occasion, a group from Arizona was taking a Spanish course in Durango provided by one of the active members of the Partners. We were in a building not far from the city center. On a break, several of us walked around the block and discovered a Methodist church. This discovery resulted in a number of cultural visits to Durango from the Church of St. Francis in Tucson and the Community Methodist Church in Green Valley.

Kenneth Darg, now deceased, was president of the American School, which has had ties to the US State Department, for ten years. He later became president of the Methodist Schools for a time and also served as the head of the US subconsulate office in Durango. Several leading Rotarians in Durango heaped high praise on Ken Darg. Ken would play a facilitating role in future cultural exchanges that would take place between the Durango and Tucson area.

In the first decade of my involvement with Durango, I experienced three programs as overlapping and touching each other: Partners, Rotary, and the Methodist Church. While the Partners of the Americas was an important part of my early involvement in Durango, that involvement became less important after I left the position to become president of the Arizona/ Durango-Oaxaca Partners. Dr. Macario Saldalte, who was chairperson of the Mexican-American Research and Study Center, followed me as president. We had a great relationship and had an opportunity to attend a Partners function in Oaxaca together. This was a special time for both of us.

60

Rotary in Durango, Mexico

While Rotary was not directly involved in the Partners program, Rotary International was involved in programs for those who were mentally challenged. It was certainly in tune with the aims of Partners programs.

Gard Pierce, a retired army colonel and a past district governor of Rotary, was directed by our then-current district governor to find a project in Mexico that all the Rotary clubs in our district could hopefully support. I was invited to be part of this task force. Two clubs were visited, one in Torreon and the other in Durango. Durango was selected primarily because some of the club members were involved with a program for the severely retarded. Several club members had children that fit this category. Close friends developed with the members of both of these clubs. Our Rotary club in Tucson ended up inviting about a dozen high school students to be exchange students. Our club in turn sent about seven or eight students who would spend the year in Durango. Leta and I hosted four students.

One of these students, Mari de la Parra, would spend an entire school year in our home and then return a year later to spend another three or four months with us. We would have a number of contacts with her and her family over the intervening years, including attending her wedding and attending the christening of her

373

first child. We also visited her and her husband, Luis, and sons in El Salvador, Guatemala City, Buenos Aires, and Lima in Peru, where Luis had a management position with a large firm. On our frequent trips to Durango, Leta and I stayed in the home of Mari's parents, Andres and Carmen de la Parra. They have also stayed in our home in Tucson. This wonderful friendship has now lasted more than two decades. In 2008, we had a delightful visit with Luis and Mari and their two sons in Buenos Aires, Argentina, where Luis had been transferred by his company to take a management position.

Our Tucson Old Pueblo Rotary club also developed a special relationship with a club in Torreon and had one major exchange between the two clubs, where a number of club members and their spouses spent a weekend in both Tucson and Torreon.

Our closest friends in Torreon were Celso and Patricia Reyes. On one occasion when I was their houseguest, Patricia took me for a ride through the part of Torreon, which, at one time, had been her father's farm. I found the sentiments she expressed during this experience very moving. When Patricia was in the final days of her life, I wanted Leta and me to drive to Torreon and spend ten minutes with her to say a prayer for her and to say good-bye. She died the Tuesday before I had planned to leave.

Celso, who owned an office supply and computer store, was very interested in psychosynthesis, a psychological system that had been at the core of my private practice for the last fifteen years. We had a number of contacts over the years. Their Rotary club's major project was to sponsor the equivalent of our county fair. This project brought in approximately $300,000 a year that either went to enhancing their facilities at the fairgrounds or went directly to service programs in the community. It was my privilege to witness this program in action.

I was surprised and delighted when Celso invited me to his son's wedding in the spring of 2003. It was a high honor for us to attend. It was wonderful seeing Celso and his family again as well as to be welcomed by a number of his friends and Rotary colleagues. In 2006, we were honored by the invitation to attend his daughter Patricia's wedding. It was truly an elegant event, with eight hundred guests from many parts of the world attending. We also had an opportunity on this occasion to see a number of people that we knew.

Among our close friends in the lovely land just south of our border are Jesus and Paula Cerda. We first met them in Durango, where Jesus was an active Rotary member. They later moved to Torreon and then to Mexico City. We have had the honor of entertaining them in our home on several occasions and to be their guests in Mexico City. I had the privilege of attending their daughter Veronica's wedding. The wedding reception was the most exciting reception that I have ever attended. An orchestra played classical music, and a band played popular music, most of which I didn't know. I had never seen such vibrant dancing by people from every age group. I was envious that I had never learned to dance. Dr. John and Eloise Westover from Tucson were also present. We decided to return to our hotel at 2:30 a.m. Our hosts were shocked that we would consider leaving so early.

As a footnote, when I returned to the hotel, there was a message waiting that my father had passed away. He had requested, obviously before his death, that I conduct the memorial services. Instead of going to the language school located in San Miguel de Allende, a three-hour bus ride from Mexico City, as I had initially planned, I flew back to the States the following morning.

Jesus and Paula Cerda, along with Dr. John and Eloise Westover, attended the celebration of our fiftieth wedding anniversary on December 21, 1998. We had requested that there be no gifts other than anyone interested was invited to make a contribution to Habitat for Humanity in celebration of our anniversary. Paula had brought with her a lovely painting of a peasant that she had painted. We couldn't say no to this beautiful gift. This picture currently hangs on our living room wall.

In early 2004, Jesus and Paula, along with Dr. Francisco and Claude Delgado and their two daughters, met us in Puerto Vallarta to spend a week in a time-share exchange. Francisco was in practice in San Miguel de Allende but had been given offers to join the medical facility of Vanderbilt as well as the medical school at the University of Indiana. Actually we had several days with Jesus and Paula before all of us flew to Puerto Vallarta.

Dr. Delgado has done residencies in both internal medicine and infectious diseases and now serves with an internal medicine group in the Indianapolis area. In the spring of 2009, we spent an evening with him and his wife and their three charming daughters.

I first joined the Rotary club primarily because of Dr. Carroll Rinehart's invitation. I have to confess that it wasn't the idea of attending a Rotary that had my primary interest. It was rather an opportunity to have lunch with Carroll and his friends once a week. I could have easily fallen by the wayside as far as Rotary involvement was concerned. When Carroll became president of the Old Pueblo Rotary, he invited me to be the chairperson of the international committee. In this role as well as the Partners of the Americas role, I became interested in the various programs in which I eventually became involved with Durango. In the spring of 1987, Leta and I attended the International Rotary convention held in Munich, Germany, as the incoming president of the Old Pueblo Rotary Club.

We were excited about returning to Munich, the city where I had been stationed from the fall of 1954 until the beginning of 1956. Among the many memories of that era I was to personally witness how much Munich had experienced in terms of massive destruction during World War II. I remember hearing the estimate that 80 percent of the city had been destroyed. Ruined buildings were seen everywhere. I remembered a church that still stood while all around it the buildings had been destroyed. In the mid-1950s, massive cleanup efforts had been in evidence. I had been puzzled that the debris from these bombed structures had been deposited only a few miles away from center city. (In my Nebraska farm setting, debris was always taken to an isolated place where it was invisible and in a place that would prevent soil erosion before being dumped.) When I asked why the debris was dumped not far from the city's center, neither my military colleagues nor my German friends seemed to know. When I chanced to meet someone who had been in Munich, I would inquire about those mounds that rose several feet in the air; I typically got a blank stare.

When we arrived at the Olympic Convention Center where the International Rotary convention was being held, I saw those huge mounds of debris that I had witnessed in the 1950s. They were now lovely hillsides covered with grass. I suspect that only a handful of the twenty-nine thousand Rotarians registered at that conference realized that these lush, grassy hillsides actually contained the debris of war. For me, it became a resurrection story. In the midst of the chaos of war, death, and destruction, there was new life.

The highlight of the convention for me was the address of Wilhelm Schmidt, the former chancellor of West Germany. I'm not certain if he was or had been a Rotarian or had simply been invited to speak as a dignitary. One line in his speech was that, in his view, Rotary was the most effective nongovernmental organization in the world working for world peace. In that moment, I knew why I was a member of Rotary. I knew then I was a Rotarian for the duration. It summarized in a single line what I wanted my life to represent.

61

Rotary Group Study and Friendship Exchange in Thailand

While I was a member of the Casa Adobes Rotary, I was chosen to be the group study exchange leader to Thailand in 1995. This was one of the defining moments of my Rotary experience. Four professionals who were not Rotarians were selected to be part of the team. Pat Koester was the owner of a newspaper in Tombstone, Arizona. She had lived in Thailand for six years as a Peace Corps volunteer and later as a director of the USO for the military. Christopher Niccum had a career in landscaping and had worked in a management position for a major resort in the Caribbean as well as in Tucson. Pauli Amornkul was a physician in a resident program at the University of Arizona. She was born in Thailand of Thai parents but had spent all but her first years in the United States. Patty Kelly didn't begin her formal academic undergraduate education until she was forty-four years old and then earned her certificate as a teacher.

This group spent a number of hours preparing for this exchange, including nearly thirty hours of Thai language study. As with every GSE exchange, the purpose is to experience another culture and share aspects of our culture with our hosts. The goal is to create understanding between people whose cultures are very different from each other.

We were to spend a month in northern Thailand. After an overnight in Bangkok, we flew to Chiang Mai, which is Thailand's second largest city and is "bursting at the seams" with growth. From there, we would travel with representatives of the Thai Rotary GSE to a number of clubs over a number of miles. We were kept busy from morning to late at night by visiting schools at every level, government officials, farms, and factories. We were introduced to many places of interest in this beautiful country.

Among the many social events, I remember one occasion where our hosts dressed us up in traditional Thai dress at a party given in our honor. Chris and I had a different look with our unique headdress. The ladies of our team were dressed in elegant formal dress of another time period.

It is difficult to capture all the sights and sounds that we experienced. I remember that we were in Mai Sok on the border of Myanmar (Burma). One of the Rotarians was an outdoor restaurant owner on a small lake. It was a delightful setting. Prior to dinner, different Rotarians were having cocktails. Most of the English-speaking Thais had gathered around our team and were speaking English. I noticed a table where a group of older Rotarians had gathered. I guessed that they didn't know a dozen words of English among the five or six people who were at this table. I decided to join them. Conversation stopped immediately. Everyone seemed uncomfortable, including me. Finally, one of the Rotarians asked a question in Thai. I understood enough of Thai language to know that he was asking how old I was. While my ability to speak in the Thai language was very limited, I did answer this question in Thai. That group exploded with laughter. Suddenly the language barrier was gone. They were patting me on the shoulder and back. Someone rubbed my stomach as a gesture of friendship (a custom that caught me by surprise). In our orientation, we learned that in the Thai culture, two questions are typically asked. The first is how old are you, and the second is how much money do you have? It was their way of determining how much honor and respect that they should give the respondent.

A number of friendships developed as a result of this exchange as well as a number of visits. Dr. Suthep Nimpitakpong, who owned a 150 bed state-of-the-art hospital with a large outpatient service in the city of Phitsanulok, was one of my hosts. He arranged for our group to visit a former communist training camp during the years before and after the Vietnam War. More importantly, he took us to a very rural village where we met with the teacher in charge of the school. It was a one-room classroom with no desks. There was only a crude conference table. The teacher introduced us to a child that I judged to be ten or twelve years old. We were told that he had been a normal child but had contracted a waterborne infection that had severely incapacitated his learning system and left him profoundly retarded. We learned that the village did not have a water purifying system.

Before leaving for this GSE trip, Past District Governor David Hossler, who was the chairperson of the district 5500 Rotary Foundation, had suggested that I look for a project that would qualify for a matching grant where the international organization of Rotary would match grant monies that had been raised by Rotary clubs of the district. David Hossler and I would return to Rotary District 3360 in Thailand to evaluate different projects and select the most viable project among the possibilities that I had suggested. This project, of bringing clean water to the village, easily beat out the other possibilities. The local club in Phitsanulok did a great job in overseeing this project once it had the formal approval of the Rotary International office located in Evanston, Illinois.

Three water towers, a smaller version of water towers one might find in towns in the United States, were erected. Water from a nearby river was chlorinated, filtered, and then stored in these towers. They bore the name of our Rotary district and the Thai district in both English and in Thai. Past District Governor Rad Fisher and his wife were the first to visit the completed project. Leta and I were there to visit this site in January 2002.

A year later, Leta and I were entertained for five days in the home of Dr. Suthup and his lovely wife Dr. Ni (Thai tend to use their first names along with their professional titles). It was a true celebration to be with them. The Phitsanulok club had custom-made jackets for every member. Leta and I were honored to be presented with our own jackets with their club's emblem.

We were also the houseguest of Dr. Surapong (Pong) Lerdthusnee, a professor at Chiang Mai University, and his lovely wife, Dr. Kumsuma, who is an internal medicine physician. Pong and I had had a number of contacts over the years. When we go to Chiang Mai, we love to visit this wonderful family. Pong took us to the elephant camp, where Leta had a chance to take a thirty-minute ride on an elephant.

About a year before the visit just described, a Rotary group primarily from Green Valley went to Thailand on a friendship tour. Our club president was Herb Morgan. When invited to go on the trip, he responded that it was a great trip and a real bargain with an outstanding itinerary but added that it came at the peak time of the year for his jewelry business.

My response to him was, "Herb, in a short while, you won't really know how much you gained or lost in your business during these two weeks that we will be gone. Besides that, you haven't seen your daughter (who lived in Thailand and had married a Thai citizen) in seven years. Maybe you should consider that as your priority."

His wife, Mary Ann, quickly agreed, and they both went on this trip. It was an exciting reunion with his daughter and the son-in-law, whom he had never met. I suggested to Herb that his daughter and husband come with us on our visit at Chiang Rai, where we would be spending two nights in a resort hotel. Even though they had been married for about two years, they had never had a honeymoon. I had suggested that he pay for their airfare, and I would pay for the hotel out of the funds I had collected. During the day touring near Chiang Rai, we had made a visit to Myanmar (Burma) and returned to our hotel in the late afternoon. When we returned, Herb called his daughter's room after he had showered. She answered the phone, stated that she was on her honeymoon, and hung up the phone. We learned that she had conceived for the first time on that very weekend.

Upon our return, Herb went with me to a presentation of the

trip at the Rio Rico Club. He was animated when he spoke about his experiences. Within days of our return, Herb had a stroke and never recovered. Mary Ann was so grateful that he had had the reunion with his daughter.

Another person on this Rotary Friendship Exchange program was a Tucson attorney, Michael Drake. He was my roommate during this Friendship Exchange. Later, we served on one of the Rotary committees that selected members for the group study committee. Michael was to become the Rotary district governor and has played a dynamic leadership role in our Rotary district. (I was honored when he nominated me for the prestigious Service Above Self award and I was selected by the Rotary Board of Directors International to receive this award in 2011.)

Aey, Dr. Suthep's daughter, was our delightful guide during the Friendship Exchange when Michael was a member. She accompanied us to Phuket as well as to a number of cities in northern Thailand.

Several years later, Aey served as a camp counselor in northern Michigan. When she finished this assignment, she and her brother, Ace, who was then a student at the University of Colorado in Denver, visited us here in our home in Green Valley. What a delightful visit. Her parents were our houseguests some years earlier.

We were delighted when Ace, Dr. Suthep's son, invited us to his wedding in July 2005 and introduced us to his lovely bride, Bee. Leta and I made a special rip to Thailand for this occasion, arriving several days early because we were flying on standby status with Delta Airlines. Dr. Suthep and his wife, Dr. Ni, met us at the hotel where we were staying and brought us to the site of the ceremony, both in Bangkok as well as in the city of Phitsanuluk. While there were no vows exchanged between the bride and groom, the presider of the first ceremony was the former International Rotary President Bhichai Rattakul, which took place at the spectacular Shangri-la Hotel in Bangkok. The second event took place at the Amara Lagoon Hotel in Phitsnanuluk approximately two hundred miles north of Bangkok. The ceremonies were quite different but both festive. What a privilege to be considered as part of this wonderful Thai family. All of Dr. Suthep's grandchildren now refer to me as grandpa, including Ace and Bee's four children.

There have been a number of Friendship Exchanges to Thailand, all interesting and exciting. An focus of these Friendship tours is on service projects. While Rotary friendships are incredibly important, in the end, the projects prove the primary element that holds Rotary connections intact. These exchanges endeavor to enhance Rotary International's goals of promoting peace, fighting disease, providing clean water, saving mothers and children, supporting education, and growing local economies.

The events in these exchanges tend to run together in my memory. One event involved a current district governor, along with a dozen Rotarians and their spouses—an incident that could have proved serious but ended up being amusing. We were traveling in three nine-passenger vans and were attempting cross a river that didn't have bridge near one of the sites for our first water project. To cross this river, it was necessary (and intimidating for the uninitiated) to stay close to a twenty-five-foot drop-off next to a waterfall. One of the drivers was nervous about driving too close to these falls and managed to slip off a rock ledge on the other side of the falls. The van was at approximately a forty-five-degree angle and was filled with water that came up to the chests of passengers of the tipped side of the van. Each passenger, including District Governor Jim Aslin, valiantly carried their brides to safety. I kidded the governor, suggesting that he had just received a Buddhist baptism. The van was pulled out of the water and replaced with another van. Among the pleasant memories of the trip, this water experience will likely be among the most unusual.

Although as unique and varied as each exchange tends to be, they begin to run together in my memory. I was certain that what would be "never be forgotten" has not been, but placing of a certain event at a precise moment is more difficult. There are so many extraordinary people that have been involved over the years doing such incredible projects that they all tend to become one. This is not to say one is more important or more unusual, but that all of them have become a part of who I am. I have truly become a citizen of two countries: the United States and Thailand. I have extended family and friends in both. One exchange involved the then-current District Governor, Jim Aslin, along with a dozen Rotarians and their spouses.

Past District Governor Tom Tilton and his lovely wife, Maria, were on an informal Rotary exchange trip to visit a number of clubs. This proved to be Leta's last visit to Thailand. Among many places of interest, we visited the lovely gardens of the Queen Mother, who was a vital force changing the lives of local people. There is an opium museum that she had an influential role in creating. Everyone who visits the Golden Triangle must see it.

One of the valued memories of this trip was Tom contacting our daughter, Linda, in Salt Lake City, to describe her mother's smile as we sat in a restaurant overlooking the Mekong river. Across the river was Laos. Just to the left was Myanmar, formerly known as Burma.

Several exchange groups in Arizona will remember the outstanding water project completed in cooperation with the Rotary club of Song. Clean water was provided to seven or eight schools. Rotarian Samart Seemson was the engineer who was the guiding force behind the implementation

Our son Ed, his wife Micki, son Phillip, and daughter Rebecca chose to be part of an informal friendship exchange. A very special moment occurred while we were visiting the village of Song, the site of a newly completed Rotary-sponsored water project. An eleven-year-old girl, (the same age as our granddaughter, Rebecca) read a moving statement written in English, thanking me for bringing clean water to their village. (I'm not sure if she composed the letter that she read, but whoever composed it didn't realize that this was an international project with which many Rotarians had major involvement.) At any rate, I was so moved by her statement that I could barely restrain the tears. Here was Rotary in action in a powerful way.

Both Ed and Micki are now active Rotarians. Their experience in Thailand was a clearly a decisive element in their choosing to become Rotarians.

In April 2014, Dr. Bill Miller, a longtime Rotarian, and the love of his life, Ann, along with our daughter, Linda; grandson Michael Berrett and his wife, Rebecca; and Rosalyn Wright attended the graduation ceremonies at the Rotary-sponsored Peace and Conflict Resolution Studies at Chulalongkorn University in Bangkok. (Linda returned home for work after the ceremony.) They also attended the Rotary District Conference in the charming town of Utteradit. We visited our wonderful Rotary friends in Phitsonaloke, Phrae, Song, Lampong, Chiang Rai, and Chiang Mai. How can I possibly summarize all the wonderful vibes received at every place we visited? The Chiang Rai stop was with a very special friend, Anan. What a celebration of life we had in the Chiang Rai region. While we didn't cross the border into Myanmar, we experienced much of the charm of the border town of Mai Sai. We also took a longneck boat ride and rode elephants.

Ann was so taken with the elephants that she wanted to bring one home! She was certainly a standout on our team. I would be surprised to learn that she ever had an enemy. She loved life, loved being with people, and was devoted to the love of her life, Dr. Bill Miller. We were stunned to hear that she suffered a cerebral hemorrhage and died on January 29, 2015. I feel so honored that she touched our lives in very important ways. We are all richer because she walked among us.

—

At the 2012 Rotary International Convention held in Bangkok, Thailand, I had played a role in organizing the party that celebrates the accomplishments of the outgoing district governor, Michael Drake. While members of our district did come to this event, the Rotarians from northern Thailand were well represented. It was such a pleasure to see Dr. Suthep Nimpitakpong and his wife, Dr. Ni. Without the enthusiastic support of Dr. Suthep, none of the many projects jointly sponsored by our two Rotary districts would ever have taken place. Other members of the Nimpitakpong family were also present at this reception. Dr. Piyarat Nimpitakpong, known as Dr. Oh, has an earned a PhD from the University of Wisconsin in pharmacology. She is a dynamic Rotarian. Wansiri Nimpitkpong, known as Aey, has an MBA from a university in Japan. (She is currently the director of the lovely hospital that Dr. Suthep built.) Sathit Nimpitkpong, known as Ace, has a master's from the University of Denver in communications and is the director of technical services at the hospital.

A dozen or so Rotarians attended the International Rotary Convention in Bangkok and then participated in a Friendship Exchange. The coordinator of the Thai team that received us was Anan Loathamatas. (Anan and his family are pictured in the appendix.) Rotary District 5500 joined Rotary District in a grant that brought clean water to several schools in mountain villages. Our hosts took us to visit some of these schools, which were in remote settings with breathtaking views.

One of the outstanding memories of this exchange is related to Michael Finkelstein. He brought his trumpet and played the Thai and the US national anthems. It was very impressive. Michael reports that he listened to the Thai national anthem over the radio, where it played every morning, until he had memorialized it so that he could render the melody of this anthem accurately.

We spent a festive three days with the Rotary club in Phitsanoloke. We saw a number of water project sites that were a result of matching grants. The reception that we received in Phitsanoloke was typically Thai, joyful and spirited. Our group consisted of PDG Phil and Kathleen Silvers, DGN Nancy and Bill Cassel, Bill and Nancy McGibbon, Michael and Joyce Finkelstein, Bob and Virginia Juettner, and Meg Weesner. The next stop was at Phrae and Song. The Rotary Club of Song showed the new water system, which was the result of a matching grant between the two districts. Samart Seemson, a telecommunication engineer, took us to an ethnic mountain village known as Meaproa.

From there, we went to the city of Lampang. The incoming district governor, Anurak Napawan, owned an upscale porcelain factory. We received a first-class tour of the factory and designed our own coffee mugs. Once again, we received a Thai welcome. From there, it was on to the charming city of Chiang Mai, the second largest city in Thailand. We were introduced to the mayor and had a chance to see the sights and sounds of that beautiful area. Our final night was truly festive with singing and dancing and celebrating the coming together of two cultures.

The final stop was in Chiang Rai. Here, we experienced hour-long rides on elephants and visited an outstanding high school of thirteen hundred students who entertained us with Thai dances and live Thai music. Michael Finkelstein was a huge hit at the final social gathering when he played the Thai national anthem as well as the American national anthem on his trumpet. (Michael's wife, Joyce noted that she was the one who packed and carried the trumpet on the trip to Thailand.)

Dr. Suthep, who played a decisive role in forming the long-term relationship between our Rotary Districts, passed away in 2013. He and his family have in many significant ways become my family. I had the high honor of visiting his gravesite, located on the grounds of a beautiful resort that the family owns. There is impressive artistic memorial stonework that commemorates his life along with an accompanying guardian angel memorial statue. Small of stature, Dr. Suthep was a giant among his fellow being in the way that he served mankind.

In 2015, Tom Tilton, our daughter Linda, her husband Paul, and I attended the dazzling wedding of Naratta (Dew) Nanking. Deeply immersed in Buddhist traditions, it featured costumes and customs from ancient rituals that lasted nearly two hours. I was deeply moved as the bride and groom walked on their knees to each mother at opposite ends of the platform (both fathers were deceased) to ask both mothers for the blessing of their marriage. What an honor to be asked to give them my personal blessing. Incidentally, the bride has called me grandpa for several years. This festive event lasted until the wee hours and was attended by several hundred Rotarians. Thanks, Ti and Dew, for this wonderful invitation to attend this deeply moving ceremony and thanks for including me as part of your extended family. It was the most elaborate wedding I have ever attended.

A group of nine Rotarians from District 5500 were hosted in

a royal way by Rotarian Ratanaporn (Tim) Seenamngern and her daughter Namking (Dew) Naratta in the spring of 2017. Both were dynamic Rotarians in the spring of 2017; both outstanding Rotarians. Our group consisted of Kenneth and Sheila Frahm (Sheila is a former US senator from Kansas), Dr. Marvin Clark, Michael and Thelma Lundy (both past assistant Rotary district governors), Roni D'Eustachio, Candyce Pardee, her daughter Cassandra Pardee, and me.

They escorted us to the club of Khanuworalugsaburi, a recently chartered club in the city of Kampangpetch. This club is truly excited about Rotary and how Rotary changes lives.

Then we visited the Rotary club of Buddhachinara, which became the largest club in the district during its first year of existence, along with the Rotary club of Phitsanulok. The continuous relationship of more than two decades between District 5500 in Southern Arizona and District 3360 in Northern Thailand began here in Phitsanulok. We were given the opportunity of visiting the very moving memorial monuments honoring my valued friend, Dr. Suthep. It is located at the resort that his family owned.

Pat and Kan Pitrapan, who are pictured in the appendix, are among our closest friends. On each occasion of our many visits to Thailand, they have gone far beyond the call of duty to welcome us. They took our group to a Buddhist temple that I hadn't previously visited. It was a stunningly beautiful temple known as Wat Phra Si Rattana Mahathat, a temple that houses the famous Phra Buddha Chinnarat.

Tim and Dew entertained and educated the team in magnificent ways. The five days we spent with the Phrae Rotarians were informative, inspiring, and festive. Among the activities was a fairly lengthy visit to elephant training camps. It is (almost) a requirement that every Rotarian who has not ridden an elephant will do so during their time in Thailand. In additional to visiting various historical sites, our hosts took us to see an exciting orphanage, where many of us had an opportunity to interact one-on-one with these children.

Our hosts then introduced us to the Rotary club of Nam. Roni

D'Eustachio and Ken Frahm celebrated their birthdays in grand style. There were birthday cakes and much festivity in three different Rotary clubs to celebrate the new mileposts on life's journey. I suspect is the only time that Roni and Ken have celebrated their birthdays so often in the space of a couple days and in such grand style.

The hotel of the Rotary club of Chiangkhong is on the banks of Mekong River. Cross the river, and you are in Laos. The newly formed Rotary received us with great enthusiasm.

Kenneth and Shelia Frahm, Bill Miller, and I attended the Rotary district conference at Maesai, located at the Myanmar border. While we didn't understand the Thai language, we understood the content and celebrated the spirit of the exciting events that were taking place. It was an exciting convention to attend. It was a special privilege to hear an excellent choir composed of Hill Tribe members, some of whom did not have citizenship status with either Thailand or Myanmar. As we were leaving Maesai to catch our plane in Chiang Rai, my good friend Anan and his lovely wife met us at an excellent restaurant for lunch and a fond farewell. (Anan's picture with his family can be seen in the photo section of this book.)

—

There have been three Friendship Exchange visits from our Thai friends. The first visit was in 2006, when eight Rotarians from the Rotary club of Phitsanulok visited us. The highlight of this trip was when our club president, Will Bennett, was instrumental in arranging an outstanding steak fry around a fireplace at the Bill McGibben ranch. It featured a singing Hispanic group from Father Michael Shay's congregation. A number of prominent Rotarians throughout the district attended this event. I am still in touch with the Thai leader of this team, Cherry Ice. Incidentally, Will Bennett, Bill McGibben, and their spouses have been on Rotary Friendship Exchanges in Thailand.

The second team was hosted and led by Anan Loathatamos. On this occasion, the Thai Rotarians represented a number of different clubs. A number of Rotary clubs in our district participated in celebrating the presence of the team. The Old Pueblo Rotary featured an event in the park. The Tucson Sunrise helped support the cost of a steak dinner at a place where people have their ties cut off. It was great fun to see the Thais have their ties cut. We also visited clubs in Sierra Visa and had an excellent meal on the Mexican side of the border. Mexican Rotarians attended. An exciting highlight was the visit to the famous Kurchner Caves.

Past District Governor Tom Tilton arranged for a former exchange student from Mexico, who had been in the Pittapan home, to have a surprise visit with Assistant District Governor Kan, who wept with joy when seeing her former Rotary son. Her husband, Pat, was in on the secret plan to arrange this meeting. Powerful relationships that last a lifetime are born through these kinds of exchanges. I am convinced that only an organization like Rotary International has the capacity of doing it. Where, other than through Rotary, can a youth from Mexico meet his Thai "host parents" while each is visiting in the southwestern part of the United States? Rotary has the power and moral authority to bring this about.

Our Thai guests cooked a great Thai dinner serving approximately fifty people in our home. What an evening of celebration. My late wife suffered with dementia during the final ten years of her life. In the middle of the festivities, she was speaking to the Thai leader, Anan. She pointed at me and asked him if he could see that bald headed man in the next room. She then instructed him to be certain that "he doesn't run off with one his Thai ladies." While we were all amused (including Leta) by her statement, it shows that people who carry the heavy burden of dementia are concerned that they will one day be abandoned.

The third Thai friendship team of seventeen Rotarians came from the club of Phrae. It was led by the dynamic mother and daughter duo of Tim and Dew from this club. A van, borrowed from the United Methodist Church in Green Valley, plus a rented van and a pickup with trailer to carry the luggage of our guests, met our Thai team in Las Vegas. The following day, our caravan stopped for a quick look at the Hoover Dam, the Grand Canyon, and Sedona before going to Yuma, where the Rotary clubs there received our Thai guests with zest and joy. While they showed them the places of interest in that area, more importantly the Yuma Rotarians opened their homes and their lives in an endearing way.

The journey continued to Tucson, where the Thais enjoyed the rituals of having their ties cut off before continuing to our Sierra Vista Rotary family. The finale took place in Green Valley with an outstanding dinner prepared and served by our Thai Rotarian friends. About a hundred people attended this event, and $2,000 was raised for a service project in Thailand. The *Green Valley News and Sun* featured the event on the front page. The group also visited the Tucson Missile Museum, which was one of many missile sites that played a major role in the nation's defense during the Cold War. The most important and long-lasting aspect of this—and every— Rotary Friendship Exchange has been the friendship created, the projects completed, and the pure joy of people working together to create a more harmonious world. I have been enriched and blessed by my participation and friendships in Rotary in general and more certainly by my many Thai friendships in particular.

—

While Thailand and Uganda are very different cultures, I would be amiss if I didn't share some affirming word of my new-found Rotary friends in Uganda. While I have visited a number of different countries in Africa, Uganda is a special place for me. I visited a seminar that focused on empowering women at the invitation of Dr. Phil Silvers, who has served at the top echelon of Rotary International. Held at the lovely Banana Village in Entebbe, Uganda, this seminar enrolled about forty women from different parts of Uganda. These women were given skills and supervision that will empower them to be change agents in their communities. The women will be invited to return to assess their progress and enhance the skills that they have developed.

Jemimah Semakadde, owner of the Banana Village resort, was the president of the Entebbe Rotary Club between 2016 and 2017 and was a major seminar speaker at the Rotary International convention held in Atlanta, Georgia, in 2017. Rotary is a dynamic force in this country. Past District Governor Phil Silvers has also played a vital role in the life of Rotary in Uganda. I predict that the Rotary membership will double in a short time.

Rotary International has played a key role in dealing with the elimination of polio as a goal. I have had the privilege of being part of an immunization day in both Ghana and India, where an attempt is made to immunize every child under five.

I will never forget the moment when I held a newborn child who was only three or four hours old. I gave it the two drops of polio prevention and saw the smile on the mother's face when she realized that her child would go through life polio-free.

I also had the opportunity of being part of a team immunizing children in the harsh slums of Delhi, India. My pride in what Rotary is doing on so many fronts, including immunization, grew as I gave children those two precious drops in their mouths. They would spend their lives facing severe living conditions. Rotary is also providing impressive vocational activities in these ghettos that will enable the people there to enhance their opportunities for upward mobility.

I also had the privilege of visiting a hospital ward, where victims of polio with severe mobility problems from arm or leg amputations were given prostheses so they can gain their mobility and live their lives with new and exciting possibilities. This and many more experiences of service have had an important role in expanding my vision that all the peoples of the world are one—brothers and sisters in the same family of our planet called Earth.

62

The Use of Hypnosis— Milton Erickson Style

Dr. Erickson was considered the most prominent physician and psychiatrist in the world to use hypnosis in medical practice, particularly in the area of pain management. No stranger to pain himself, he had contracted polio as a teenager on his Wisconsin farm. He reports that the only muscular control he had was the movement of his eyelids. He used this period of enforced immobility to great advantage. He learned to pay attention to stimuli that most of us would miss.

I had the distinct honor of spending, along with several other students, an afternoon workshop with him. By then, he had suffered a stroke, and his face was partially paralyzed, forcing him to speak out of the side of his mouth. About an hour into his workshop, he turned to me and asked, "Have you ever been hypnotized?"

I responded that I had only experienced light levels of trance.

Looking me squarely in the eyes, he asked, "Do you want to be hypnotized?"

I responded that I was willing to experience this phenomena, adding that my fear was that, because I held him in such esteem and wanted very much to please him, I was afraid that I would fake it. I remember his smile. He began to tell some story that made no sense to me at all about some character in the South Pacific. Before I knew it, I was in a deep state of trance.

There are a multitude of stories about his treatment strategies that show how original and effective his methods were. I want to share a couple of these stories. The first occurred while he was a psychiatrist in a California mental hospital. Given my own experience as a psychologist in a VA psychiatric hospital, I can identify with the following story.

There was a patient, with a diagnosis of schizophrenia, who spoke in a word salad, a language only known to the patient himself. Dr. Milton Erickson, who had a great difficulty with mobility as a result of polio, noticed this patient sitting on a bench on the grounds of the hospital. Milton hobbled up to this bench and sat down. He carefully listened to this patient speak his unintelligible language until he picked up a certain sequence in his use of syllables. After detecting this pattern, he began to respond to this patient by imitating this speech pattern. They would carry on speaking in this unknown tongue until it was time for Milton to leave. After some time had passed, he would again find the patient on this same bench and began to speak the unintelligible conversation. Dr. Erickson repeated this behavior over several months. One day as he was seated, the patient said to him, "Hey, Doc, don't you think it's time that we started talking sense?"

What impressed and inspired me was the dignity with which Dr. Erickson encountered this patient and others. He responded to them not as patients but as people.

I remember a patient on the ward that I directed in the VA hospital with a diagnosis of paranoid schizophrenia. He stated that his father had come to see him, and the authorities wouldn't allow his father in to see him. Remembering Dr. Erickson's experience, I responded with the question of how he knew that his father had come for a visit and was being denied access. He stated that he had seen his father's car in the parking lot. We went together to inspect the car. While it was the same make and model as the car that his father drove, I pointed to the license plate, which identified the part of Michigan in which the car was licensed, and stated that I didn't know that his father was from Battle Creek. The patient responded that his father lived in Lansing. I pointed to an emblem on the car and stated that I wasn't aware that his father belonged to the organization represented by the emblem. After pointing out several more issues about the car that didn't seem to fit, the patient stated that he must have been mistaken about his father being there to see him. If I had attempted to challenge his paranoid ideation directly, I feel certain that it would have backfired.

One of the first things Dr. Erickson did when you went to see him for either professional counseling or seminars was to pass out a sheet of paper on which he asked you to respond if you were born in the city or in the country. (He obviously had a great appreciation for farm life, given his life on a Wisconsin farm.)

A lady who indicated she had a rural background was experiencing intractable pain. Her interview with Dr. Erickson began with the question as to whether or not her father had cattle that included a bull. When she responded in the affirmative, he asked whether she had been attacked by a bull when walking through the pasture where the cattle were grazing. She stated that while she herself had never been attacked by a bull, she had heard of those who had such a harrowing experience. Dr. Erickson then asked how much pain she would be experiencing if she were being chased by a bull. Her surprised response was that she would be so focused on escaping that she probably wouldn't feel any pain at all. In that healing moment, she recognized that she had a choice on whether she chose to focus on pain.

I attended the international conference in Phoenix to honor Dr. Erickson for his lifetime achievements. As I remember, over a thousand delegates from all over the world were present for this event. Dr. Erickson died just weeks before the conference was to be held. Countless professionals were impacted by Dr. Erickson's strategies and his way of experiencing the world around him.

Several of us had some training using what was known as Ericksonian hypnosis and decided to take a week out of our practices and hire a nationally recognized expert in this method for a week of concentrated training. As the week progressed, we came to a part of the training where we would practice inducing trances. I was selected to be the first one to try to put another into a trance state. The person I was to hypnotize was the assistant dean of the University of Arizona Medical School. To say that I was traumatized is something of an understatement. Not only was he a graduate of a medical school, but also a graduate of the Naval Academy as well as a talented Shakespearian actor.

In this exercise, my client was to play the role of an angry patient who had invested a great deal of time and money in the therapy that I had purported to provide. The only response that I could make to his confrontational statements was the two-word statement, "That's right." Incidentally Dr. Erickson often used this phrase. I could use any tone of voice and any facial or other body movement in using those two words.

The session quickly went downhill for me. He responded with heated anger every time I responded with "That's right." I tried every tone of voice or facial expression I could think of, to no avail. When I was in obvious difficulty, the instructor whispered in my ear, out of range of my client, that I had forgotten to breathe. I quickly realized that this behavior would lead to carbon dioxide buildup in the brain. I began gasping for air. The situation only worsened. My client's anger only intensified. After what seemed forever, the instructor again whispered in my ear that I should see him as a five-year-old having a temper tantrum. Suddenly, everything changed for me. This handsome, six-foot man with impressive credentials became that five-year-old tantrum-throwing child. My responses were still limited to "That's right," but something within me changed. My colleague playing the role of my client asked afterward what our guide had told me. He stated that he was no longer able to maintain his level of anger. It was a lesson to recognize the power of a new state of awareness.

Neurolinguistic programming, in which I became certified, gives considerable attention to sensory data. This system holds that we use all five senses, but we use them in a hierarchical order. A primary sensory mode for some may be visual while for others, it will be auditory. Still others may give priority to the kinesthetic mode or the sense of taste and smell. People who have a different hierarchical order from another can easily have difficulties communicating with each other.

I remember one couple having a great deal of stress in their marriage. I began to sense that the wife had strong kinesthetic sensory orientation while her husband's first sensory priority was auditory. I intentionally had them reenact an intense moment of conflict. When both were experiencing significant conflict, I had him take her hand. The tension quickly dissipated for her. I suggested to the husband that he had a powerful tool at his disposal. I then reminded her that when she became stressed out, the pitch of her voice reflected her intensity. The tone of her voice was very distracting to him. I began to help them focus on how they could use their primary sensory modes in an effective way to improve their communication with each other.

On another occasion, when meeting with a couple with a troubled marriage, I instinctively focused on the primary olfactory mode. The wife immediately broke into tears. As we explored where those tears came from, she related that when she growing up in Brooklyn, her father, who worked as a handyman, would come home after work. She was often on the couch, reading. The father attempted to show his affection by coming up behind her and covering her eyes with his hands. All she could remember was the stench of his hands. While he was not an unclean man, he typically didn't shower until it was time to go to bed.

This wife noted that when she went on her first date to a movie, the young man was wearing Old Spice aftershave. To her, it was a glorious smell. When she married, she married a man who was also a handyman, who, like her father, didn't bathe until bedtime. She stated that she repeatedly bought Old Spice products for him to use, but he felt that these products were feminine and refused to use them. Obviously, he now had a powerful tool if he chose to use her primary olfactory sensory preference to improve the communication in their marriage.

63

A Year at Louisiana State University

An unexpected call from my doctoral advisor from Michigan State University, Dr. John Jordan, revealed that he had joined the faculty at Louisiana State University. He asked if I would be willing to interview for a faculty position. To say that I was taken by surprise is something of an understatement. Leta and I went to Baton Rouge for the interview, but I was reluctant to leave Arizona. We met the dean of the department and some of the members of the faculty at a reception held for us and were shown around the city. I was being offered the rank of associate professor. The invitation was intriguing. A week, possibly two, after we returned to Arizona, I was offered the rank of full professor. This was hard to refuse. I somewhat hesitantly accepted and then only with the reservation that I would stay at the university a relatively short time.

We rented our house in Tucson and loaded our belongings in a U-Haul that I drove while Leta drove our car. I remember the distance across Texas was nearly a thousand miles, and the total distance was something like fifteen hundred miles.

We initially thought we would be there for two or more years but definitely for a limited time. We debated about whether to purchase a house or rent. We chose the latter. It was a lovely three-bedroom in one of the neighborhoods that had named the streets after the fabled story of *King Arthur and the Knights of the Round Table*.

While at Michigan State University, Dr. Jordan had been able to get a special line item funding from Congress to develop rehabilitation resource centers around the world. One of the US senators from Michigan had been instrumental in getting this program funded. Dr. Jordan attempted to move this program to LSU, where the faculty appeared to be more open to this kind of grant than they had been at Michigan State University. His gamble was whether he would be able to pull the political strings to get the funding for this program transferred from MSU to LSU. While I did some teaching at the graduate level, my place in the rehabilitation program depended on this gamble paying off.

Dr. Jordan clearly planned on me playing a major role in this project, but my duties were undefined and at best nebulous. It became increasingly clear that the governmental transfer of funds didn't get the political support that it had earlier. In light of this difficulty I, as well as other professors that Dr. Jordan had recruited, were at a loss how to define our roles—other than through teaching courses. The expectations that the university had placed on Dr. Jordan, as well as those he had placed on himself, resulted in intense pressures that were to have devastating results.

Meanwhile, we found the Cajun cultural influences of southern Louisiana to be extremely interesting. We went to political rallies just to get a feel for what happened at these functions. Mountains of favored Cajun food would be served, and political speeches followed. I developed a real fondness for genuine Cajun food.

We made friends at the Broadmoor United Methodist Church, where Leta and I sang in the choir. The pastor of this large church signed up for the course that I taught at the university. We found the people there to be gracious and very much in love with their culture. So many people we talked to were so entrenched in their history that they couldn't imagine living anywhere else in the world.

While I enjoyed the university setting, I became increasingly uncomfortable as Dr. Jordan became more tense and unavailable to me and other staff members as he desperately tried to hold together the international rehabilitation program. There was little for me to do as far as the international aspects of this rehabilitation program were concerned.

I designed a graduate-level class on holistic health that I had to nurture through the academic review committee. As I remember, about twenty students signed up for this course. I announced on the first day of classes that the students could choose their own grade at the end of the course. After developing the criteria on which they were asked to base their grade, I suggested that I would meet with each student at the end of the course and ask them to defend their choice based on the criteria given. I assured them that they would receive the grade they requested unless I became convinced that they had been fraudulent in their work or inappropriate about the grade they chose.

One of the students had been a medical student but had to drop out of medical school when he developed a brain tumor. While the tumor had not been malignant, he had developed grand mal seizures following surgery.

I knew that he had invested a great deal of energy and excitement in pursuing this newly designed course. When I met with him at the end of the term, I asked him, in light of the criteria given the first day of class, to describe how he had met these criteria. After he described his work, I asked him to select an academic grade. He began to stutter and nervously asked that I decide on his grade. I reminded him that I had announced the first day of class that each person was to select their grade based on their concept of how well they had met the outlined goals of the class. He got very tense and took a set of instructions from his shirt pocket that informed by-standers on what to do in the event of a grand mal seizure. He then announced that he was going to have a seizure and asked that I take him to a place designated on the sheet of instructions.

I then asked him to look around the room to see if there were any impediments in the room that would be harmful to him during a seizure. After he looked around the room and saw none, I invited him to lie down on the floor and have his grand mal seizure, adding that he had had many grand mal seizures before, and his body knew exactly what to do and how to perform when grand mal seizures occurred. He gave me what can only be called a shocked look and then followed my instructions. I assured him that I would make sure he didn't get in trouble while thrashing around the room and added that I would be looking over his class documents during his seizure.

He did indeed have a grand mal, which lasted what seemed like ten minutes, although I didn't time it. I was relieved that no one came knocking on my door during this event. When the seizure was over, he remained on the floor for some time in what appeared to be a mild stupor. When it became clear that he was fully conscious, I leaned over to him and asked if he had yet decided on the grade for the course. He gave me a look that seemed to say, "I don't believe you're asking me this question."

He finally stated that he wanted a B. I assured him that he would receive that grade for the course. When he was fully recovered, I then took him to where he was staying.

I later learned from one of his friends that one of his medical school professors had also been the surgeon for his brain surgery. This friend told me that while he was in the recovery room following surgery, this surgeon, who apparently had been a father figure to him, had unintentionally given him some hypnotic statements that included: "You don't have anything to worry about, no actions to take, no decisions to make." This friend stated that from this time forward, it became almost immobilizing for him to make a decision.

He called me the following morning to say that he thought he really deserved an A. I promptly changed his grade to match his request. I suspect that he learned through this experience that he had more power over his "grand mals" than he had previously thought possible.

—

If I had examined the invitation to join the faculty at Louisiana State University in a fully rational manner, the likely choice would have been not to accept. I certainly had no way of knowing that the federal grant awarded to the specific rehabilitation project to

Michigan State pending transfer to Louisiana State would not be approved. Looking back, I suspect that this transfer was blocked primarily on political grounds.

Given the principle that my friend Bob Price and I had formulated during our college years that we base our decisions on whether a given prospect was dynamic and alive, I think the decision to accept this invitation was appropriate. I had already started to sense that the private practice that had been so exciting was beginning to change because of the coming health maintenance organizations and their priority of cutting cost rather than providing quality medical services. I'll say more about this in the next section.

Another important dimension was the respect that I had for Dr. Jordan. Before accepting this position, I had stated that it was important for me that our relationship be built on trust. My decision to come was based on this sense of trust and respect. I further stated that if we were going to be in a close working relationship, our working relationship had to be transparent. If there were any misunderstandings or differences of opinion, it was important to deal with these dynamics openly and without delay. He quickly agreed.

As it became apparent that his project funding to develop rehabilitation centers around the world (a kind of United Nations approach to rehabilitation) was in trouble, Dr. Jordan became (or seemed to become) increasingly less available. In a program that had a great deal of ambiguity built into it, my feelings of isolation and discomfort began to grow. Leta was very supportive during this troubling time. She must have been feeling anxious as well, but she invested her energy in affirming me and my decision to come to Louisiana.

One day, I cornered Dr. Jordan and told him that we needed to talk. I pressed him for an appointment. One Friday afternoon in the middle of the spring term, we went for coffee in a local restaurant in downtown Baton Rouge. I told him that I was feeling impotent in my job and had decided to return to Tucson. We had several hours of conversation that seemed to clear the air. As we were leaving, he stated that it was the best conversation that he had had with anyone for months. I hadn't realized how isolated he had felt.

I was beginning to develop a small psychology practice on the side and had made an office out of one of the spare bedrooms. I was seeing a client after I had returned home from the visit with Dr. Jordan when I received a call from Mrs. Jordan stating that John wasn't feeling well. I told her that I would come over as soon as the counseling session had ended. When I later telephoned her to announce that I was on the way, she stated that he had been taken to the hospital.

I went directly to the hospital to learn that Dr. Jordan had suffered a massive brain aneurysm. He died that evening. I was glad that we had the conversation earlier that afternoon to clear up much of the confusion that had developed in our relationship. His memorial services were held several days later, with primarily the staff and faculty of the college of human development attending. The dean and I conducted the services.

64

It's Great to be Home in Tucson

After returning to Tucson, I had vague feelings of emptiness and depression. I realized that, although the Friday afternoon coffee session with Dr. Jordan just hours prior to his death had been a godsend, there was still some unfinished business. Dr. Carroll Rinehart, one of my closest friends, suggested that I spend the first thirty minutes upon awakening writing down my feelings. It was an important time when I expressed my confused and sometimes incoherent feelings. It proved to be a time of real cleansing for my troubled feelings.

Before returning to Tucson, I contacted my colleague, Dr. Richard Riley, who had developed the drug and alcohol program known as West Center. Initially, he maintained his own private practice of medicine but eventually became the medical director of West Center. He was most encouraging about my return to Tucson but felt that I should return as quickly as possible. He was helpful in directing a number of clinical referrals to me.

In the meanwhile, a group of internal medicine doctors, known as the osteopathic internists, invited me to join their practice. This relationship was outstanding in every respect. All the doctors had excellent reputations. While the number of clients I was seeing on a professional basis never reached the level that it had reached during the late seventies, I did a number of inpatient and outpatient consultations and saw a number of clients and patients in this office. A major difference in the practice was that the office personnel would type up my clinical reports and schedule appointments. Leta had done a great job running the office and typing the reports, but the new arrangement had a number of advantages. One of the advantages was using a Dictaphone to do my reports.

Still, the atmosphere was changing. The health maintenance organizations (HMOs) were having a definite impact on the referrals that were sent to me. Prior to the advent of the HMO, the physician had a choice about where they would refer patients. In the changing medical environment, the referring physicians had to, for practical reasons, refer patients to the specific health care professionals in a given HMO network. Actually, the entire practice of medicine was to change in a rather profound way.

A decade and half earlier, I had spoken to the medical director of Tucson General Hospital in the doctor's dining room. I had suggested that the majority of the patients in the hospital didn't really require inpatient care but could go home at night and return the next day for treatment. His response was, "What would Blue Cross and Medicare say?"

While I sensed that changes were coming, I didn't anticipate the way in which health care delivery was to be radically altered. I hadn't foreseen that some clerk at a distant location would be making treatment decisions and that professional health workers would be told what kind of coverage would be provided for patients who enrolled in that particular HMO. I don't think the medical community foresaw that CEOs of health care systems (as well as other organizations) would get huge salaries while cutting staff positions in rather radical ways. The major impact for my practice was that the referring physician could not choose to whom they would refer a patient. Because Medicare was to become a primary player, my practice was hit hard because Medicare, in most cases, did not cover psychological care.

65

An Invitation to Join the Staff at Saint Francis

While I continued to be involved in my psychology practice, I was pleased when Dr. David Wilkinson, the pastor of the Church of St. Francis in the Foothills, began a dialogue about my accepting a position on a part-time basis at the church. St. Francis began in the sixties and reflected the antiestablishment mood of that era. The church appealed to those who had checked out of the established church. It was important for this growing congregation to look different from the typical organized church. At the time I joined the staff, approximately 20 percent of the congregation had Jewish cultural and spiritual backgrounds. While most didn't see themselves as Christians, they did see themselves as on a spiritual journey.

Some members had a strong New Age focus, and this group wanted the church to sponsor seminars on astrology. The church services often used songs that were secular. At a mortgage-burning ceremony held in 2004, one of the former pastors talked about how chagrined he was when the soloist sang a hard-ass woman song and how insulted the soloist was when he, the pastor, had suggested the song was inappropriate. Traditional hymns were typically avoided, and there was an emphasis on what I referred to as camp songs—songs that could be sung around a campfire.

This church shunned the word "sermon" and insisted on using the word "commentary" to describe the Sunday morning message. This commentary was to be delivered without manuscripts or notes. They saw themselves as being an inclusive church, although they tended to be more inclusive to theological positions that were left of center.

If my memory serves me well, it was the first church in Tucson who openly welcomed those who had a homosexual or a bisexual orientation without identifying itself as a church with an exclusive gay ministry. Church services often focused on drama, particularly during Advent and the Lenten season. They would develop sequential dramas of excellent quality lasting from five to ten minutes, based on some secular drama that also focused on Advent and Lenten themes. Some of the themes that I remember included such classics as *Pinocchio, Beauty and the Beast* and *Knights of the Round Table*. It was fascinating to see themes dealing with birth, life, death, and resurrection come out of these dramas.

We sent up a program of volunteers who would emulate the ideas in *Knights of the Round Table*. These volunteers would seek to be of service to the community by babysitting for a young mother who needed some downtime or elderly persons who needed assistance. This group also initiated a religious celebration for those who were in prison. These groups were very active for a year or more.

On several occasions, full-fledged musicals were performed, primarily by the members of St. Francis. *Man of La Mancha* was performed twice. Both times, the senior pastor had the lead role. I had the privilege of playing the singing role of the priest during the first performance. In both of these instances, the church became a Spanish prison, where prisoners, including persons who were to be brought before the religious court of the Spanish Inquisition, were held.

When communion was served, both wine and grape juice was available. Those who were struggling with alcohol abuse would typically choose grape. When the elements were being consecrated, I would identify which vessel contained grape juice and which contained the wine.

On one Sunday, I forgot to check which vessel contained which element. The senior pastor, the Reverend David Wilkinson, found it amusing that as I was lifting the first cup, I first smelled it before announcing which cup contained what liquid element. David never let me live that lapse of attention down.

The impressive education building was built when I was privileged to be there. During the construction, David and I would tour the building the first thing in the morning and the last thing at night. It was the original intention to have a new sanctuary before phase two of the building project. However, funds were not available, so that plan was put on hold. This hold was to last for a decade and a half or so.

Someone generously donated nearly half a million dollars to pay off the indebtedness of the education building. The two pastors that preceded David Wilkinson, Cecil Williams and Dick George, and the bishop were present for this mortgage-burning event. Rabbi Joe Wiezenbaum, who heads the current Jewish congregation that meets at St. Francis, as well as the pastor of the Islamic congregation, Imam Omar Shahin, were also present. They shared their dreams and passion in vivid and often humorous and certainly inspirational ways. They have announced plans that the long-delayed new sanctuary is now revived, and it will be a place of worship for the three world religions that claim the spiritual heritage of Abraham: Christianity, Judaism, and Islam. It will be a Tucson first and a rarity in most of the world.

66

A Compelling Dream

While my time at St. Francis was exciting, I wanted to be part of creating a new congregation that would provide innovative ways to be the church in the world. Dr. Carroll Rinehart, who was internationally known for his creative work with children and opera, was also intrigued with the idea of bringing together a community of faith that would be something more than "church as usual." We had dreamed of a place where people from a multigenerational and multicultural background would come together to create a spiritual journey that would be contagious.

David Wilkinson and the Church of St. Francis gave me permission to spend some of my time and energy to bring this dream into fruition. We started with no constituents other than Carroll, Leta, and me. Our first meeting took place in the home of a university professor and his wife. A half dozen couples were present from a number of religious traditions. None of this group from this first meeting chose to become part of the permanent congregation.

In the first weeks and months, this nucleus often numbered a dozen or less. Our times together on Sunday morning were often spent sharing ideas about how to live out our faith. Carroll often took these ideas and assisted us in creating songs. As I look at it now, I'm surprised that growth didn't take place at a faster pace than it did. Nevertheless, a number of significant events took place during the first few years of our existence.

I remember our first Christmas Eve service. That night, snow fell. It happened to be the only time during my thirty years in Tucson that it snowed on Christmas Eve. In fact, it snowed about six inches. While the evening was incredibly beautiful, I remember that I was anxious that the snow might give the people who might consider attending this event an excuse to stay away.

We created a tradition of forming a circle in our closing moments together and joining hands. We would sing "Bind Us Together." It was a short song with a lovely lilting melody and a great message. This tradition continued for several years.

It took several months before an average attendance reached twenty people. This number gradually increased. By the end of the first year, thirty-five or forty people were normally present. The business meetings were generally short and quite casual. I remember choosing the name for this congregation. It took place around the dining room table of Kevin and Susie Oxnam. A consensus was reached in an hour or so. We chose the name Fountain of Life United Methodist, Fuente de la Vida. It took a while to get approval. We initially chose the Spanish part of this name but had to accept the English version because there was a Hispanic church in the Phoenix area. Even denominational headquarters knew how to practice the art of bureaucracy.

Carroll played a number of exciting roles: pianist, choir director, and cheerleader. A young medical student named Wesley Lewis, son of a Methodist minister, and a young engineer named Clay Chandler regularly played the guitar at the services for several years.

We had our first retreat experience at a center in Pine Canyon, located in southern Arizona. Initially, it seemed to be an anchoring experience for this developing congregation. Another retreat experience known as the Walk to Emmaus also held promise for this gathering group.

Introduced to this seventy-two-hour reflective spiritual event by my good friend, Reverend Douglas Bobbitt, I suspect that I would have been skeptical if I had not trusted Doug as much as I did. This event, developed initially in Spain, when a priest sensed that the men of his parish were missing important aspects of their spiritual development, took them on a life-changing retreat. Eventually, Spanish servicemen introduced this event to the priests near the US military base where they were receiving special training. Initially a Roman Catholic experience, it began to spread rapidly in a number of mainline denominations here in the States.

A friend, Reverend Dr. Larry Hinshaw, was instrumental in bringing the experience here to Arizona. It proved to be an influential event in my life. Our marriage had reached a low point, and I began to realize that I didn't want to perpetuate a marriage that had little energy. At the same time, I still wanted to have a caring relationship with my spouse, even if we didn't stay in the marriage. In large part because of this event, we eventually experienced a significant healing.

A number of members of Fountain of Life went through this weekend experience. With one exception, everyone stated that this had been a powerful experience. In time, I discovered that while this had been a peak experience for many, it didn't prove ultimately to be the unifying force that I had hoped it would be.

Even though I had grown up in a very conservative religious environment, for a number of years dating back to my active duty military experiences, I found that this conservative bent really didn't fit me. However, one of my dreams had been to witness a congregation that could embrace a person regardless of where they were on the theological continuum or where they were on their faith journey. As the new congregation began to develop, I began to sense that it would take a miracle to achieve this kind of integration. Part of the early developmental struggle was that people who had a strong conservative theological leaning were tempted to impose their convictions on the rest of the growing church family. These folks were obviously taken by the early excitement and promise of a new congregation but had difficulty allowing each person to develop and determine his or her own spiritual direction. It created a crisis that I wasn't sure that this young congregation could survive.

At a crucial moment, those who wanted to challenge our Methodist traditions gradually left and found churches that fit their theological mold. I found it disappointing that these folks, whom I personally valued (at least for the most part), were unable to stay and be a vital part of our growing family. But we survived this initial crisis.

As our congregation slowly expanded, we moved from the classroom to a small auditorium at the high school. This meant that we had to set up everything each Sunday and take all these items with us each week. With little warning, we received notice from the school principal that the facilities at the high school would no longer be available to us. The following Sunday, I announced to our budding congregation that I had good news and bad news to share. The bad news was that we had to move; the good news was that we would have an opportunity to develop beyond the limitations of being in a school setting. I added that I didn't have the slightest idea where we would move.

I had noticed that there was a Disciples of Christ Church a mile or so from the high school. I met with the pastor, Reverend Terry Immel, about the possibility of our congregation using their facilities at a different hour than their congregation used it. He was enthusiastic but added that he would have to present this possibility to his church board. We soon received word that the board had given their approval, and we would be able to use their facilities.

Our final service at the high school was a memorable one. We had our worship service with our weekly communion. As the last person was served communion, we began to gather all of our materials that we set up each Sunday and as quickly as possible left for the Capilla del Sol Christian Church, where we would complete our worship service by singing a final hymn, followed by the benediction. Reverend Immel was there to greet us as we arrived to welcome us and to give the benediction. This would prove to be an exciting relationship.

While the Capilla church family met at nine and we met at eleven, we found a number of ways to share activities. The most exciting was the joint participation in chancel operas Dr. Carroll Rinehart wrote. The first opera was entitled *How Was I to Know?*

This theme grew out of an event that occurred the previous Advent season. But I'm getting ahead of the story.

Carroll and I often gave the morning sermon in dialogue. That is, one would person would make a comment, and the other would respond to it, unrehearsed. These responses could be questions that forced the presenter to expand their original statements. We were ready to try any innovation in our effort to make what went on in the worship experience relevant.

Very early on, Carroll used a model that he had so successfully used in creating an environment where children would write their own operas. Some of our early worship experiences were spent creating songs. As a choir began to take shape, we would often sing songs that had just been created the week before.

On one occasion, when Carroll was en route to my home, he passed the Tucson mall, where he encountered a person who was obviously an unemployed person holding a sign that read: "Wife pregnant. Will work for food." He was deeply shaken by the sign the expectant father carried. In our discussion, we concluded that this twenty-first-century scene in some ways paralleled the first-century biblical scene where Joseph and Mary sought shelter in Bethlehem when Mary was in her final hours of pregnancy. Apparently, their financial resources and options were marginal at best.

Our dialogue sermon the following Sunday dealt with the economic and social limitations many people faced in the first century and in this one. We also talked about the dynamics of the innkeeper, who was so focused on the business opportunities that he missed a major event of history. An opera was born that both congregations performed.

Carroll developed a role in the opera for an unemployed carpenter that fit the description of the man that he had seen carrying a sign asking for employment near the Tucson mall. This unshaven man with his sign requesting work in exchange for food came down the aisle. The song was entitled "Wife Pregnant. Will Work for Food." This person had a startling effect on the congregation. Many thought he was actually a homeless person who had invaded the service. After he came up the aisle, making his plea, he stood off to the side, watching the arrival of shepherds and the Magi.

As Carroll developed the dialogue, the innkeeper's wife intervened when the innkeeper was turning this young couple away from the inn. When she noticed that Mary was very close to delivering a child, her motherly instincts took over. She took charge and overruled her husband's decision not to find space for this young couple. She had her servants hastily prepare a place in the stable for this young couple.

The innkeeper kept musing on the preposterous implications of a full inn. When the illiterate shepherds unexpectedly showed up at the inn, they were flush with the excitement over all that occurred. They spoke of hearing an angelic choir announcing a birth. We also focused on the dynamics of the innkeeper who was so focused on the business opportunities that he nearly missed a major event of history. By the time the impressive Magi from the East showed up, he was impressed and began to take credit for providing the shelter that provided a place for the remarkable birth.

In one of the closing scenes, the shepherds, the Magi, the staff of the inn, and the unemployed carpenter are gathered around the parents and child. There are deeply moving songs of celebration as the newborn is being shown to those assembled around the manger. There was the mother's lullaby and the unemployed carpenter speaking of the hope of the world. The song entitled "No Cozy Cradle" was a phrase that had been used in a Christmas Eve sermon given by Dr. John Blackwell. It so captured Carroll's attention that he heard nothing more of the sermon. This phrase eventually became a lullaby that Mary would sing to her newborn infant.

The finale of this opera was a song entitled "Glory to God." It was sung with a light rock beat, with all the participants still gathered around the parents and child. The singing of "Silent Night" followed this song and a communion hymn entitled "Take this Bread." Communion was then served.

The How Was I to Know opera received excellent reviews by the music critic of the Tucson Daily Star and eventually was published.

414

It was truly a dramatic moment in the life of Fountain of Life UMC and the Capilla del Sol Disciples of Christ.

Carroll was to write a second opera focusing on the final week of Christ's life. Again, both choirs participated in this drama. One of the moving songs reflected the anguish of a mother as she watches the one to whom she had given birth go through the ordeal of the crucifixion. It was a story with which every mother could identify.

Every newly developing congregation is faced with the immense hurdle of purchasing land. Even though the congregation had few financial resources, I felt it was important to start looking for land. This search lasted for months. Finally, we settled on an eight-acre site, which was on the edge of an area that was rapidly expanding. A wash ran through the property, dividing the area. We had anticipated that the smaller section would be an ideal future site for a youth center while the larger portion would be ideal for a future sanctuary. Funds began to be available in the most creative way, and the property was eventually paid for in full.

Mobile structures had been moved onto the property, and it was time for us to leave the Capilla del Sol congregation. While we looked forward to being in our own space, it would be difficult to leave our wonderful family at Capilla del Sol. On the appointed Sunday of the move, both congregations decided to have a joint service. The first half of the service would be at Capilla del Sol. The midway point occurred when the people were given the opportunity of sharing their tithes and offerings. At that point, both congregations moved the three miles or so to our new site. The worship commenced where it left off, with the singing of the doxology and the presentation and dedication of the offering. At the conclusion of the worship service, we enjoyed a family potluck meal together.

Another memorable moment was the surprise celebration of Carroll's seventieth birthday. It was truly a celebration. Carroll's favorite minister, Reverend Dwanne Zimmerman, then retired and now deceased, was invited to speak. The entire celebration was playful. Carroll, who was the choir director, was preparing to lead the choir in a given song. Unknown to him, the choir sang a different song than the one he had selected. After several bars into the song, he gave up and took his seat while the choir continued singing.

So many people played such a vital role in this congregation. Leon and Pam Vicars, Dr. Mark and Barbara Wise, Dr. Wes and Pam Lewis, Elsie Blakesley, Dr. Walter Moran, Trevor and Maxine Beecham, Clay and Kathy Chandler, Mary Jane Hickey, Chris and Jean Niccum, Grant and Joyce Paterson, Don and Sue Pell, Bob and Jessie Hansen, Bob and Sharon Whitney, Mike and Diane Edwards, Tom Verville, and, of course, Dr. Carroll Rinehart, who had a vital part creating the original dream—plus so many more. It is so tempting to share many more stories about these wonderful people from this vital community of faith that will be forever etched in my memories. But to do justice to these memories would take a miniature forever.

I can't resist the temptation to briefly share a couple stories. I first met Elsie Blakesley when her husband passed away. We had never met before, and the funeral director, a personal friend, had asked if I would do the memorial service since the Blakesleys didn't have a church home. Obviously, our meeting was totally fortuitous. Elsie arranged for a lovely lunch at one of the nearby restaurants following the memorial service. Several days later, I dropped in for an informal visit with Elsie to see how she was coping with the loss of her husband of many years. Mr. Blakesley had been an invalid for the last several years of his life, and Elsie had managed his care. I was concerned with how she would organize her day and begin to experience a healing of her spirits following his passing. In our conversation, I was essentially playing the psychology role and was suggesting some options for her to consider. As I was leaving, I casually mentioned that a church often provided a meaningful social and support group. To my surprise, she attended the following Sunday and shortly thereafter asked to join the church. She added that she had not been active in a church for well over fifty years.

A delegate from every church was expected to participate in the annual conference, normally held in June in the Phoenix area. I found out on the Saturday evening before the conference started four days later that both the elected delegate and the alternate delegate were in the hospital. The next day, I asked several members who attended the church if they would be interested in pinch-hitting as a delegate. The typical response was that they would be glad to do that but their weeks were already planned. The last person to leave the church was Elsie. I casually asked if she would be interested in that role. Her response was that she had no idea of what transpired at the conference but would be happy to accept this role if she could be helpful. I didn't tell her the official rule was that a minimum of two years of church membership in the congregation was a requirement to be an official delegate.

Every delegate was assigned to a legislative session, and the color-coded name badges reflected the specific session that each delegate was assigned to. Elsie received a green name badge. On Saturday morning, there was a special meeting of the delegates from our district. The district superintendent asked each delegate to introduce and share something about themselves. When it was Elsie's turn, she mused about whether there was a relationship with the green code on her badge and the fact that she was a greenhorn. She then proceeded to tell the story that she had been a member of the church for only six weeks (at that time I was trying to duck out of sight) and then added that she hadn't been to church for fifty years and accepted the first invitation that she got. The latter part of this phrase really caught the attention of everyone present.

Elsie was well into her eighties when she participated in travel programs that I had sponsored to Turkey and also to Spain and Portugal. Elsie was 101 years old when she peacefully passed away. It was always a joy to be in her presence.

Other than Carroll Rinehart, she is the only one from the former Fountain of Life Family with whom Leta and I had regular contact.

Among our closest friends during our involvement at Fountain of Life Church were Leon and Pam Vicars, although we have had little contact with each other in recent years. We shared so many wonderful times together. Their daughter, Kathryn Vicars, was in high school during the years that I was with this congregation. She stated that when she married, she wanted me to perform the ceremony. Nearly ten years after leaving this community, Leta and I flew to Virginia in October 2004, and I had the high honor of performing her wedding ceremony.

Leon had come to Tucson from Virginia to attend the University of Arizona, where he attained a degree in civil engineering. Among his many projects, he oversaw the lengthening of the runways at Tucson International Airport. He retired to his Virginia home, where he hoped to serve as a mentor to young engineers. Unfortunately, he succumbed to cancer. I had the privilege of speaking at the celebration of his life, held at Capilla de Sol Christian Church in Tucson.

67

Sons of Orpheus Male Choir

In the summer of 1993, I heard an announcement over the public radio station that a male chorus had been formed under the direction of Grayson Hurst, a former major opera singer who is now a retired professor of voice at the University of Arizona. I had been a seasonal member of a community choir a year or two before hearing this announcement. In response to my telephone call, Grayson invited me to join. With the exception of the 1994–95 season when I was leading a study group to Thailand, I have been a member ever since. (When I was giving lectures on cruise ships, I missed some of the performances yet remained with the choir.)

I always appreciated our director's philosophy that every man who could carry a tune could be in the choir, provided they were willing to accept the rather rigorous discipline of rehearsals. He has been very forgiving of those who haven't been able to legitimately keep all the rehearsal schedules. He has always insisted on performing challenging musical numbers that ranged from operatic choruses, classical compositions for men's voices, folk and sacred music from many cultures (in their original languages), Broadway and Hollywood show tunes, and cowboy classics.

The Orpheus members include both trained and amateur singers (I am clearly in the latter group) and retired and active businessmen as well as students. The professions included businessmen, scientists, physicians, psychologists, engineers, clergy, teachers, former agents of the FBI and CIA, a bus driver, a PBS radio announcer and a person who owned a school of real estate. During regular rehearsal sessions, the singers focused in on singing and typically don't have an opportunity to get to know each other well. One of the rewards of being on tour is the opportunity to get to know each other much better.

In addition to our annual spring concert, we annually perform with the Tucson Boys Chorus at the historic San Xavier Mission. This church is a national monument and dates back to the Father Kino era of the late seventeenth century. The setting for this Christmas performance is truly spectacular with its renovated artwork. The lighted candles and wonderful acoustics all provide a very special atmosphere. The six performances were sold out, with all proceeds going to the mission.

There have been a number of highlights for the Sons of Orpheus. The choir members will remember the thrill of singing in the East Room of the White House in Washington, DC, during the 1998 Christmas season. Sons of Orpheus made its first European tour during the summer of 2000 by performing in Germany, Austria, and Hungary. In 2002, the Sons of Orpheus made a concert tour of Ireland, Scotland, England, and Wales. So many wonderful memories are associated with both tours. While it is always interesting to visit places, our host choirs really made our tours memorable.

In July 2004, we performed in various places in Italy. Thanks to Dr. Vaughn Huff and Ivan Berger's extensive planning, this was a magnificent tour. For me, three events stand out. The first was the music festival event at the Alta Pusteria International Choir Festival that took place in the Italian Alps just a few miles from the Austrian border. One hundred choirs from seventeen countries with thirty-seven hundred choir members participated. (We were the only choir from the United States.) Our rendtition of *Nessun dorma* (an Italian favorite) at one of the venues at the Alta Pusteria was performed unusually well. At the end of this opera performance, the audience applauded for about ten or fifteen minutes. There were rousing cheers and tears from the audience as well as from members of the Sons of Orpheus choir. It will be an unforgettable moment for all on that tour, a memory that will remain as long as we have memory.

The Sons of Orpheus were invited with a number of choirs to perform at the White House during Christmas 1998. Being from Arizona, we sang the cowboy songs of Christmas in the East Room. We were given a breathtaking tour to see the Christmas trees in many of the rooms.

In addition to other tours in Italy, we had the honor of singing at one of the main chapels in the Vatican as well as visiting the famous Sistine Chapel in 2013. In the summer of 2017, we sang at the Notre Dame Cathedral in Paris as well as at the beautiful cathedral at L'Eglise de la Madeleine. What an honor! It was also exciting to be invited to be guests of a well-known male choir known as Le choeur d. AHmeD. So Enjoy. It was located in a scenic area about a three-hour bus drive from Paris. Both their choir and ours performed in a joint choral performance. We were hosted in their homes and given the royal treatment during our overnight stay with new friends who are part of an excellent male choir.

It was exciting to be invited to be guest of a well-known male choir.

On the last afternoon of this event, the choirs marched through the town to the village. Under one baton, the choirs performed Verdi's opera, *Coro Di Schiavi Ebrei*. It speaks of the Babylonian captives. What a thrill to be a part of this mass choir for this one performance.

Our choir was standing next to a Russian choir as we waited to march to the village. It was a real treat to sing our Russian numbers (in the Russian language, of course) to them and watch their reaction. What fun! I heard one of our members comment that it doesn't get any better than this.

The second event that will forever be etched in my memory was when we attended a performance of the Italian opera *Aida*. The setting was in an open-air amphitheater built in the first century in Verna. This theater was filled to capacity, with twenty-five thousand people present. While I have little formal knowledge of opera, it was awesome to hear the top opera singers in the world perform. How can you forget a night like that?

The third event has more to do with the setting. It took place at the Church of Santa Susanna in Rome. It was built in AD 330 and has had an active congregation since that date. That's more than a thousand years before Columbus made his way to the New World. Two major renovations have taken place: the first in the late eighth century and another in the twelfth century. What history! The Mariachi group from Tucson was with us on this tour. They were a big hit, particularly when they played spontaneously to the crowds at slack moments. Their finest moment was when they played a Mariachi Mass at the Church of Santa Susanna.

What a thrill it was to again visit St. Peter's Basilica and the Sistine Chapel, with all of its marvelous paintings by Michelangelo. I enjoyed walking miles through the city, basking in the glow of history so evident everywhere.

In the summer of 2016, the Sons of Orpheus sang at the Notre Dame Cathedral in Paris as well as in the beautiful Cathedral at L'Eglise de la Madeleline. What an honor!

It was also exciting to be invited to be guests of a well known male choir known as "Le Choeur d' Hommes d' Anjou" located in a scenic area located about a three hour bus drive from Paris. Both their choir and our performed in a joint choral performance. We were hosted in their homes and given the royal treatment during our overnight stay with our new friends who are part of this excellent male choir.

68

An Unexpected Move

The year was 1995. By this time, I had retired from my psychology practice and was spending my final years in the clergy. I had expected to be at Fountain of Life United Methodist Church until I retired. I received a sudden call from the district superintendent stating that she wanted to have a meeting with me. I was surprised when she said that the bishop had asked me to consider moving to the Green Valley Community Church as an associate pastor. Moreover, she had said that Reverend James Stewart had asked me to be his associate. When I asked how long I had to decide, I was given seventy-two hours.

It was an agonizing decision. The choice was mine to make, although the district superintendent clearly hoped that I would choose the new assignment. I walked over the nearly eight acres of saguaro-studded cactus ground where I visualized a church would stand in a few years. I estimated that we were three or four years away from building our first unit. It truly was a difficult time in making this unexpected decision.

Ultimately, the decision swung in favor of Green Valley. The factor that tipped the scale was the notion that a younger pastor at the Fountain of Life church could be in the position of staying with the congregation after an addition had been made to the church. I further felt that while I had no need to leave, a younger pastor might provide new energy and excitement for the congregation. At the same time, I felt I was leaving a very real part of myself at Fountain of Life.

When the district superintendent asked at the end of the three days what my decision was, I stated that it was "a jump ball." It could easily have gone either way. As it turned out, the district superintendent, in my judgment, made a mistake when it came to selecting my successor. It was a mistake of the heart rather than a rational decision. She selected a husband-and-wife team that simply didn't fit. A dynamic pastor by the name of Reverend Paul Caseman, who ultimately became the senior minister of a strong and successful church, made it known that he really wanted to come. If he had been chosen, my guess is that Fountain of Life would have become a vibrant congregation.

Within a year, the heart of the church membership had been destroyed, and ultimately, the church with such promise was closed a few years after I left. Every time I hear the name "Fountain of Life," my heart sinks. A part of me suffered great pain over this loss. I haven't fully worked my way through the grieving process. The district superintendent—different from the one who played an instrumental part, of my judgment, of choosing the wrong successor—asked me to make a retirement statement at the annual conference of Green Valley Community Church in March 2000. I stated, among other things, that I never regretted coming to Green Valley, but I have regretted leaving Fountain of Life, particularly when I "saw it going down the drain after I left, and there wasn't anything that I could do about it."

We arrived in Green Valley right at the end of June 1995. The house that we were about to purchase had been the church parsonage for a number of years. The church decided to "get out of the real estate business." I remember arriving at our new home, where large palm trees lined the street. (Leta was to arrive several hours later from our Tucson home.) A surprise awaited me. A large palm tree lay across the sidewalk in front of the new house. The day before, a large garbage truck had careened down the street without its driver and struck the palm tree that now blocked the sidewalk.

The downed palm tree blocked this garbage truck from continuing down the street, which was on a downward slope and likely prevented much more serious damage.

In fact, the previous clergyperson, who was in the process of moving from this house, had purchased a new car when he retired and had decided to move it from the curb to the carport just an hour or so before the accident. His new car would have been demolished had he not moved it. The driver of the garbage truck insisted that he had set the emergency brake before he briefly left the vehicle. The typical response of the neighbors was "yeah, sure."

While I had passed through Green Valley over the years before our move, I knew very little about it. I expected a sleepy-eyed adult community where not much transpired. Much to my surprise and delight, I found it an active community (that is during daylight hours) comprised of people who had held major leadership positions as university professors and CEOs of large corporations as well as people who had served at high levels of the military and other organizations. Even more surprising was the large percentage of people who performed major volunteer activates.

Prior to accepting the assignment at the church, now known as the United Methodist Church of Green Valley, I promised a young medical student from Mexico City that I would attend his graduation. I had no idea that his graduation would occur during my second Sunday at Green Valley. Still, I had promises to keep. So I was off to Mexico City to keep that promise.

I had met Francisco Delgado when I was on Rotary-sponsored trip to Mexico in the city of Durango in the state of the same name. The Rotarians there had received a group of us into their homes. I was assigned to be in the Delgado home. Francisco was a preteenager, and he had two younger siblings. His sister, Olijandra, was probably eight or nine years old. What I remember is that she invited her girlfriends over to see this gringo who was staying in their home. She also invited me to play some table games with her friends. Olijandra later became an exchange student with a Rotary club in Tucson and is now a licensed architect.

The president of the American School in Durango, Kenneth

Darg, told me that Francisco had been the brightest student that had enrolled in their school during the ten years that he had been there. I casually invited Francisco to contact me should he be interested in enrolling at the University of Arizona. I told him that I had some contacts there. It was a casual statement that I didn't think would lead anywhere.

Several years later, Francisco called to say that he was interested in exploring enrollment at the university. I called Dr. Mario Saldate, who was the chairperson of the Mexican-American Research and Study Center, and told him about Francisco's interest in the University of Arizona. He suggested that I come over and that we would go to the admissions office to see if a scholarship was available. We were very pleased when the admissions personnel informed us that a four-year tuition scholarship was available.

I then arranged for him to stay in the home of Professor Dick Rice. Initially, this arrangement was to have lasted for three months. I intended to find another place for him to get gratis room and board. At the end of this period, they requested that he stay with them as long as he was going to the university. They formed a relationship that continues to this day.

Francisco decided in his junior year to attend medical school in Mexico City. He was a top student there as well. I received a call from him a year prior to his scheduled graduation in which he elicited a promise that I would attend his graduation ceremonies from medical school.

When the graduation date rolled around, Dr. and Mrs. Richard Rice, Leon Vicars (Francisco's sister, Alexandria, had stayed in the Vicars's home when she was an exchange student in Tucson), and I were present. Since this was a Catholic university, I wasn't surprised that a priest spoke to the graduation class. He used the Biblical parable of the Good Samaritan to challenge this new class of physicians to focus on service rather than on their income. He drove home his point when he described a physician friend of his who owned seven Mercedes. For what, he asked! As one might expect, he reminded them that there was so much more than just the accumulation of things.

What surprised me most was that the students gave an extended standing ovation. The physicians I knew tended to be inattentive and sometimes downright discourteous when they were listening to speeches. Eventually, I found what was behind their enthusiastic response to the priest. He was also a physician and had been their instructor. I can still visualize him waving to the class, acknowledging their greetings. With his white hair and striking good looks plus a captivating smile, he made an important statement about who he was and the values that he embraced. It's a scene I will never forget. It turns out that the priest was suffering from pancreatic cancer and was making his final address to this class as well as to the medical school. I heard that the priest died a few weeks later.

A few years later, Francisco told me that he had met a Canadian young lady named Claude and asked if I would perform their ceremony in the Montreal area. It was an offer that I couldn't resist. The wedding took place at a lovely golf course. English was the second language for those who attended the ceremony. Claude's family spoke French, and Francisco's family spoke Spanish. I was truly honored to be part of this event.

We later visited Dr. and Mrs. Delgado in Nashville, where Francisco was doing a residency in infectious diseases at Vanderbilt Medical School. He had earlier completed a residency in internal medicine in Florida. They now have three beautiful daughters and have moved from San Miguel, Mexico, to Dallas, where Francisco has joined a medical practice. (Francisco called me in December 2006 stating that he would be joining an international medicine group in Indianapolis.)

Several weeks after my return, the senior minister, James Stewart, had a stroke that left him incapacitated for a couple of months. During that time, I attempted to cover his duties. He returned to his position but wisely decided to retire at the end of the conference year.

While I immensely enjoyed my role at the church, I also was quite pleased with the people that live in this lovely retirement community. People shared their lives with us in a profound way. I had the privilege of performing the marriage ceremony of Murray and Jean Triplette as well as doing the memorial service for Jean's son by a previous marriage. He had been executed in a Cambodian prison during the Reign of Terror that took many thousands of lives there.

There was Herb and Linda Turck, who touched our lives in so many ways. They influenced me to retire a couple of months early, on April Fool's Day in 2000, to be precise. More importantly, they played a significant role in my being involved in giving lectures on cruises. (I felt a real loss at Herb's death in the fall of 2006.)

It was my privilege to share powerful moments with Lloyd and Bonnie Britton during his final days. I so vividly remember standing around Lloyd's bed, holding hands with the two hospice nurses, Bonnie, and their grandson and repeating Psalm 139. This was followed by the familiar benediction: May the Lord bless you and keep you and make His face to shine upon you and give you peace. Lloyd, still a relatively young man, took his final breath when the Amen was spoken. There were so many powerful moments as this congregation so deeply shared their lives with me.

Beyond the typical pastoral duties, I had the opportunity to lead tours to Greece, Turkey, Israel, Spain, and Portugal. There was also a side trip to Morocco. There were obviously many memorable moments. In Spain and Portugal, we visited cathedrals and museums as well as the land of Don Quixote.

We were steeped in ancient history as we visited the places where St. Paul had journeyed. Who can forget the magnificence, both past and present, of the ancient city of Ephesus? Visiting the sites on the rocks of Meteora in Greece, where twenty-one monasteries had once stood, was unforgettable. Six of those monasteries still exist. The entrance to one of the remaining monasteries, the Holy Monastery of Varlaam, once required that you be hauled up in a basket that swung perilously for nearly thirty minutes as it climbed more than a thousand feet.

While sites with such fascinating histories are indeed important, being with valued friends and experiencing customs of local culture add so much to the color and memory in a distant land. One night in Tangier, Morocco, Nawas International Travel set up a belly-dancing event for the group that I had recruited. The members of this group, who happened to be members of the church I was serving, were greatly amused when the belly dancer came to me, removed my shirt, placed a brassiere on me, and asked that I imitate her dancing. I suspect I was set up in advance to be selected by the dancer.

I first met Harold Cox in 1946 at the Owosso College. Actually this church school also had a high school academy. Harold, who was later to be called Walter, was in the academy when I was in the first year of college. We got to know each other well during our time at the Owosso *Argus-Press*. I had a motorized paper route that involved traveling nearly a hundred miles per day while he had other duties in the circulation department. We got to be great friends and participated in a number of social activities together. When it looked like I was breaking up with Leta, he agreed to take the corsage that I had ordered for her in the event that we hadn't got it together for the junior–senior banquet. It couldn't be called a prom because dancing was strictly forbidden. Actually it was one of the few events where males and females could officially be together.

I spent the evening before I was married in his home. His father, a real tease from Texas, took the occasion to warn me about the hazards of marriage. It was actually a good-natured jest. Harold was present at my wedding. After graduation, we went our different ways. After I had enrolled in the graduate program at Michigan State in the early sixties, we had the opportunity of renewing our friendship.

It was sometime in the nineties when we could spend quality time with each other in Spain. He and his wife, Carol, met us in Madrid. From there, we rented a car and went to the Malaga area to spend a week together in a time-share. We traveled along the coastal area and visited the Rock of Gibraltar. What a fascinating place. The tension that existed between England and Spain over this site, which stands guard over the narrow neck of water that separates Africa from Spain, still exists. Obviously, this piece of real estate has had an enormous strategic value. We took the cable car to the top and then walked down a path to a large cave area that had served as a site for a hospital during World War II.

We also stayed in VIP quarters at the air naval base just outside of Cadiz, Spain, that is shared with the Spanish military. We also traveled to Barcelona. I was driving at about eighty miles an hour (most cars were passing me) when a large bird flew into our windshield. It could have been catastrophic, but the bird apparently hit the upper part of the windshield and glanced off. I watched the bird through the rear mirror as it was hurled straight up in the air for twenty feet or so and then fell back down to the pavement. While it is only an estimate, I judged the length of the bird's wingspan to be about a yard. We were so fortunate that this creature didn't break through the windshield.

Walt and Carol traveled on to Spain, but we left them in Barcelona to fly back to the States. It was wonderful to spend this time renewing our acquaintance of so many years past. We saw them the last several years at Owasso College reunions in Florida. It is interesting that this reunion has grown over the years, even though the college has not existed for more than two decades. Friendships formed in formative years continue to be so important.

69

Can You Believe It's Been Fifty Years?

It would be less than honest to say that the road to fifty years of wedded bliss didn't have bumps in it. There was little overt hostility or direct confrontation. Rather, there was a time, particularly during the middle years of time together, when there was little energy or excitement. We both went through the spiritual retreat known as the Walk to Emmaus. It proved to be a healing experience for us.

As we approached the fiftieth anniversary, I initially intended it be a quiet family event. Our daughter-in-law, Micki McCorkle, had other ideas that proved instrumental in changing our ideas about how this event would be celebrated. She invested a great deal of energy in bringing this event to fruition.

Both Leta and I came from very conservative religious and social backgrounds and had very limited experiences in the world. No one from either of our families up until that time had attended a college or university. Neither of our families had traveled extensively, although Leta's family had ventured out of their home state on a few trips. Neither of us could have anticipated that we would move beyond the life boundaries that we both had known.

I'm not sure where the urge came from to explore areas that were totally unfamiliar to me. It must have come from some genes inherited from some distant ancestor. In many respects, this urge has defined the direction that our life together has taken. Certainly, nothing in my family background would have predicted this ad-venturous streak. While Leta didn't initiate such actions as

my entering the military, becoming a bush pilot in South Amer-ica, or entering into graduate school after a family of three children had arrived, she was supportive once the decision was made.

Shortly after moving to Arizona, I anxiously began question-ing the appropriateness of leaving a well-established, relatively secure position as a director of a mental health center to go into private practice and not have a dependable income. In fact, we were so close to the wire financially that we could have been in serious financial trouble. Through all of this, Leta was as steady. When I would panic after initiating other actions that were scary to me, she was the solid one who wanted to stick it out. She didn't sup-port, however, my decision to enter the military paratroopers but quickly came aboard after I made my third jump.

In many respects, we were quite different in temperament. We look at the world quite differently and now have different political affiliations. She has retained her conservative bent while I have be-come quite liberal in the way I see life. In spite of these differences (or perhaps because of them), we are, at the date of this writing, in our sixty-first year of marriage. I will be eternally grateful for the supportive and loving role she has played in my life and the life of our offspring. Again, thanks must be given to our daughter-in-law, Micki McCorkle, who wouldn't let us get away with a simple family dinner for our golden wedding ceremony. It was a grand occasion.

The actual anniversary occurred on the Sunday before Christ-mas. Instead of giving a sermon per se, I played the role of the inn-keeper in the Bethlehem story in costume and basically followed the storyline of the opera that Carroll had written. This role was played out in monologue. The innkeeper, some thirty-five years af-ter the event of the birth of the Christ child, was reflecting on how he was so absorbed in the business aspects of running an inn on that special evening that he really didn't want to be bothered by a pregnant young woman and her husband who showed up un-expectedly at his door. However, his wife overruled him, because her motherly instincts prompted her to find a place in their stable that would be carefully prepared for this teenager about to give birth. I then spoke of the innkeeper's surprise when illiterate shepherds breathlessly and somewhat incoherently tried to share their encounter with the angels. The arrival of the Magi and their entourage is then described.

Years later, as I developed the story, the innkeeper remembers hearing about the exploits of a young rabbi who attracts both interest and controversy and is ultimately executed. Some thirty-five years had passed since that memorable evening in the stable of his inn. He hears the rumors about the rabbi's return to life that have energized his followers. Could this have been the Son of God, he ponders, that was born in the stable of my inn?

Two singers with opera experience were present to sing some of the songs in the opera, *How Was I to Know*, described earlier. The church choir sang the finale, *Glory to God*, with a light rock beat. (See Appendix II, An Innkeeper Tells His Story). In the afternoon, several hundred friends gathered in the sanctuary to hear operatic love songs as well as love songs from the fifties. We then gathered in the social hall, where both of our sons sang and played the piano, and our daughter shared her memories of what it was like growing up in our home. Our grandchildren, Kristina and Michael Berrett, played an instrumental number. My brother, Dr. Merle Friesen, and his lovely wife, Delores, came from Montgomery, Alabama, and shared some humorous memories that went back a lifetime. It was a celebration that we will long remember. As mentioned earlier, our relationship almost ended before it got started. I am profoundly grateful that we have shared this incredible journey together. Without her love and support, this journey would not likely have taken place.

The evening was capped by my participating in the Christmas concert with the Sons of Orpheus and the Tucson Boys Chorus, actually two concerts, which were performed at the beautiful San Xavier Mission. Our sons and daughter and her spouse, along with my brother and his wife, attended. It was an interesting way to complete a very full day.

When we started our journey together, there was so much we didn't know. Our view of the world around us changed dramatically along the way—not always in the same way. If Leta could have gotten a glimpse of me as I would be fifty some years down the pike, she may have been more cautious in accepting my proposal that we make a lifelong commitment to each other. She demonstrated her loyalty in so many ways, even when I went down a path that she wouldn't have necessarily selected. I am grateful for her love and commitment.

70

A New Community of Faith Is Born

Many residents of Green Valley want our city to remain a village. It is a city of twenty-five thousand or more inhabitants and growing rapidly. Its citizens, however, have voted on three occasions not to incorporate. As a result, the Pima County board of commissioners made the major decisions that govern the life of the city. The much smaller next-door town of Sahuarita, on the other hand, has decided to incorporate and has been growing by leaps and bounds. These dynamics played a major role in creating a new United Methodist Church.

Before the board of supervisors decided to preserve the old Canoa Ranch area (just south of Green Valley) and plans for a developing a major residential and business section were halted, the Green Valley church had decided to sponsor a new congregation that would have been the first church in the area. While I remained on the staff at the Green Valley church, I was responsible for providing the Sunday worship services during the next fourteen months before I retired. The worship services were held in the Santa Rita Recreation Center.

The first worship service was held on the first Sunday of February in 1999. There was standing room only. The Green Valley Community Church choir was part of this first service. After they performed, I invited them to leave so the persons standing would have a seat.

Easter Sunday of that same year was memorable. We had arranged to have sunrise worship on the open upper deck. That Easter morning was below freezing, with a high wind blowing. We decided to stay in our regular space until it was time for communion. Then we assembled on a very windy cold deck. One of the parishioners made the comment that I reminded him of Moses as I elevated the communion bread and wine and shouted the words of consecration into a bitter howling wind.

When the board of supervisors decided to block the Canoa Ranch development, the population growth quickly moved to the incorporated village of Sahuarita, which gave a developer by the name of Sharp permission to go full-speed ahead. This occurred just as I was retiring.

Incidentally, the new congregation, now known as the United Methodist Church of Santa Cruz Valley, has experienced phenomenal growth, thanks to the rapid population expansion of Sahuarita as well as the leadership of a dynamic young pastor named Brian Osborne. They have just chartered their congregation with well over a hundred members. Over 250 congregants worshiped together on Easter Sunday.

During the years we lived in Tucson, I never dreamed that Green Valley would one day be our home, a home that I can't imagine leaving. Five years passed so quickly, and so did my seventieth birthday. I somehow thought it would take a lot longer to reach that milestone than it did. The United Methodist Church requires their pastors to retire at age seventy. The conference year begins on July 1. However, if a clergy's seventieth birthday occurs after that date, they are allowed to continue for another conference year. By this rule, I was allowed to continue on active status for another nine months plus.

Early in the New Year, I received an invitation from Herb and Linda Turck to join them on a cruise from Florida to Spain on an upscale ship from the Seabourn Cruise Line that would sail on the last day of March from Fort Lauderdale, Florida. I decided to move my retirement date up three months and go with them. Since no chaplain had been assigned for this voyage, I was given the opportunity to provide the worship services for the three Sundays of the cruise. It was a sign of things to come.

71

Cruising into Retirement

We have been blessed that our daughter, Linda Berrett Greener, worked for Delta Airlines. My line is that every parent has a responsibility to guide at least one of their offspring to work for the airlines. Shortly after returning from our retirement cruise, I got a notice from a travel service that exclusively serves airline personnel and their parents that a world cruise was being offered on Princess Cruises for deeply discounted rates. We applied and were accepted. Days before we were to embark, we were informed by the travel agency that the cruise line had overbooked, and it was unlikely that we would be able to sail. We were offered a full refund plus a free cruise on another Princess ship. We hesitated and reluctantly decided to accept. If we had accepted at once, we would have sailed from Bombay, India, to South Africa, and from there to the United States via Istanbul. By the time we agreed to accept this offer, the portion of the cruise from Bombay to Cape Town, South Africa, had been filled. We accepted the fifty-two-day trip, sailing up the west coast of Africa around the northern part of Africa to Istanbul, Turkey, and from there to New York.

Before this cruise, I had never given a great deal of thought of traveling to Africa. It turned out to be a fantastic trip. Our fifteen-hour flight from Atlanta, Georgia, took us to Cape Town. I soon realized why travelers have often referred to the lovely city of Cape

Town as one of the most beautiful cities in the world. Several memorable events took place. One of them was truly romantic. Leta and I took the cable car that goes up to Table Mountain at sunset and then back down to the city below under a full moon. The city nestled by the sea was truly spectacular.

A trip down the lanes of history took us to Robbin Island, just off the coast nearby Cape Town. On this island, Nelson Mandela, later to become the first black prime minister, was imprisoned for over two decades. We visited his cell and the places where he and his fellow conspirators against the apartheid government had been sentenced to a lifetime in prison. One of the many moving stories is how Nelson Mandela graciously received the judge who had sentenced him to life in prison after he had been released and elevated to the head of state of South Africa.

We stopped at so many interesting ports of call as we cruised up the west side of Africa. In some ports, native dancers in costume were there to welcome us and, of course, invite us to see and purchase their interesting works of art. When we were coming to our third port, I was on the top deck watching the captain skillfully bring the ship into the harbor. I was to receive the surprise of my life. The psychology professor on board and her husband were wonderful dancers. While I attended their lectures, their dancing especially fascinated me. They clearly stole the show. Dr. Jean Waaben found me on the top deck and asked me for my name. When I told her, she replied, "I thought so. You hired me thirty years ago when you were the director of the mental health center in Lansing, Michigan."

She then was a new PhD. I had not recognized her, but she had recognized me. What a coincidence to meet so many years later, worlds away from Lansing, Michigan, on a cruise ship sailing up the ten thousand miles of the west coast of Africa.

There were so many interesting sights to see. I'll share only three. We were in a port of Ghana, about an hour's drive from the capital city of Accra. We had engaged the services of a cab driver and had intended to go to Accra. En route, we stopped at a most interesting casket factory. The caskets were made to meet the wishes of the clients. One person had been a ship captain. He had ordered his casket to be made in the shape of a ship. Another person had been a farmer, and he had ordered his casket made in the form of a Holstein cow. Another person, obviously fond of his beer, had ordered his casket made in the form of a beer bottle.

The second occurred in the capital city of Dakar, Senegal. Over the past century and more, this city was deeply involved in the slave trade. An island only a couple of miles offshore, known as La Maison des Esclaves de Goree, was where hundreds of thousands of slaves were processed and shipped, under conditions that defy description, to the New World and beyond as slaves. There is a porthole in a fortress wall, where slaves got their final view of their homeland as they left for the New World. Because half were expected to perish en route, the ships were loaded to compensate for this loss. I stood peering out this porthole for a long time as I pondered man's inhumanity to man. When we returned to Dakar a second time, I urged a black friend to visit this island. He did, and when he returned to his stateroom on the ship, he was so traumatized by this experience that he didn't emerge from his stateroom for several days.

The third incident that deeply touched me occurred in Tunis, Tunisia. It was a most interesting city, as was the nearby ancient ruined city of Carthage. Near this ancient city was a beautifully maintained US military cemetery. I stood in awe as I looked over many thousands of cemetery markers of the US soldiers who had fallen. I had forgotten that North Africa was the arena for major military conflicts in World War II as well as throughout human history.

I had contacted several cruise lines in an attempt to get an assignment either as a psychologist or a clergyman and was typically referred to agents who secured the professional speakers for the cruise lines. The usual response was that there was a long list of people waiting for such assignments, but they would receive applications.

One day I called Diane Zammel, who secured speakers for Norwegian Cruise Lines, to inquire about being a lecturer. She asked a few questions about the topic I would be presenting. I ended up being assigned to be the speaker on several cruises with Norwegian Cruise Line. A few months later, I got a call from Anthony Ciena, who got the speakers for the Seabourn Cruise Line. He arranged an Easter cruise from Florida to Spain.

The first cruise was to the Greek isles. We flew to Athens several days ahead of time to make certain that we would connect on the space-available flights on Delta. The cruise initially went from Athens to Istanbul. We were to revisit several of the islands we had seen on other trips. The most beautiful island for me was Santorini. It is a volcanic island with unique shopping areas and picturesque houses—all whitewashed. On this leg of the trip, Istanbul was our destination. What an interesting city! St. Sophia, originally an ornate Christian cathedral where emperors were once crowned, is now a museum. I found the entire city fascinating. From the port where the ship is docked, it is possible to climb a number of steps, perhaps three hundred steps or more to the top. I chose that route into the downtown portion of the city several times. I enjoyed stopping at the small hotels located on one of the main streets and had a wonderful massage for well under ten dollars.

En route to Barcelona, we stopped in the lovely country of Croatia. The city of Dubrovnik was charming. While this part of the country was impacted by the war that tore Yugoslavia apart under the leadership of Tito, this city experienced minor damage, most of which had been repaired by the time we arrived.

We then visited various Italian ports such as Venice, Naples, and Rome, and the French ports that were near Cannes and Monaco. We arrived at the lovely city of Barcelona. I was so fortunate to be the escort on many of these tours. Each of these cities had their own charm. What a breathtaking place the Isle of Capri was! Sharp winding roads that hugged the cliffs were truly impressive. In one garden home, there was a thousand-foot drop just beyond the wall that enclosed the garden.

The tour ended in Barcelona. We hurried home to get ready to board the *Norwegian Sun* in Singapore. This cruise would take us to several ports in Malaysia, including the capital city of Kuala Lumpur. We took the elevator to the tallest manmade structure in the world located in this city. (A taller structure has since been built in Taiwan. Very soon, the tallest structure in the world is scheduled to be in Beijing.) We were scheduled to make a stop in Bali, but this port stop was canceled for security reasons. Incidentally, our scheduled visit occurred several years before the bombing of the nightclub there. We were keenly disappointed that this stop was eliminated. Many of our British friends spoke highly of this lovely island.

We crossed the Australian barrier reef, although there wasn't much to be seen from shipside. Our first port stop in Australia was Darwin. It was late December, the summer season—hot and humid. In fact, much of the eastern coastline seemed to be tropical. Either in Cairns or in Townsville, I was the escort of the ship's tour to a crocodile farm. These crocodiles were enormous, some weighing close to a ton. One old crocodile had lost all of its teeth. It still had the amazing ability to crush objects in its jaws. In the tourist center, there was a large snake, which the guide placed on my shoulders. I hadn't volunteered for this display, but I was determined to be casual with this snake wrapping itself around my neck and its tongue licking my ears. No one volunteered to repeat this experience.

We stopped in Brisbane for an afternoon of looking around the city and then continued our voyage to Sidney, which was our tour's destination. We disembarked near the lovely opera building. We were on the grounds, but the building was closed. The following morning, I attended a Rotary meeting on a ferry docked nearby in full view of the opera building.

We were on standby status on British Airways for a flight to Thailand, a six- or seven-hour flight away. Since we were still in the Christmas holiday season, the flights were full with British folks who had been on holiday in Sidney and were returning to Great Britain. After missing several flights, we managed to get on a flight to Singapore in the late evening. It took a half a day or more to arrange to get to Bangkok on a standby basis.

Shortly after arriving at the Indra Regent Hotel, where we had stayed on previous trips to Bangkok, we contacted Dr. Suthep Nimpitakpong and his wife, Dr. Ni, who live in Phitsanulok and own a one-hundred-fifty-bed, state-of-the-art hospital. An active Rotarian and a former district governor of Rotary, Dr. Suthep and I were jointly involved in organizing a campaign to raise money to bring clean water to three villages close to Phitsanulok. The money we raised was matched by Rotary headquarters and supported by our local district office of Rotary.

There were several highlights of this particular visit. One was that we had the honor to be guests of Dr. Suthep and his family in their home. The second was to visit the site where three water towers now stand with the name of both Rotary districts emblazed on the towers in English and Thai. The third event was to be guests of their local Rotary meeting. We were treated like a king and queen. Incidentally, Dr. Suthep, Dr. Ni, and two of their adult offspring have been our guests here in our Green Valley home.

I had taken the train from Phitsanulok to Chiang Mai several times before and I wanted Leta to also have this experience. The scenery during this seven-hour ride changes from rice fields to mountain terrain. It's a great way to see the countryside.

When we arrived in Chiangmai, Dr. Surapong Lerdthusnee, a professor at the University of Chiangmai, was there to greet us and take us to their home as their guests. His wife, Dr. Kumsuma, is a physician of internal medicine. It was a real treat to be in their home. Dr. Pong (Thai folks typically abbreviate their names) took us to the elephant training camp. Leta had the experience of riding an elephant for some distance up and down a mountainside and through a river, an experience she will likely not forget. We returned to Bangkok for several days before starting the twenty-hour plane ride back to the States.

As an aside, our daughter, Linda, her three children, and her sister-in-law accompanied us to Thailand in October of 2004. We did all the tourist things like visiting the Buddhist temples in several cities, riding elephants near Chiang Mai, and attending a Rotary meeting with the club that had worked with clubs of our Rotary district to bring clean water to three villages. When I asked our granddaughter, Kristina, who had her nineteenth birthday in Thailand, to identify her favorite experience, I expected her to say it was riding elephants. Instead she stated that it was the Rotary meeting in Phitsunulok. They had welcomed our family in grand style.

Leta and I attended Dr. Suthep's son's wedding in July 2005. Ace and Bee's ceremony took place at the Shangri-La Hotel, a hotel that lived up to its name. It was truly a festive occasion. We also went to the second reception in Phitsanulok, a city two hundred miles north of Bangkok. Dr. Suthep and his wife, Dr. Ni, and their son and daughters have become family to us.

While we did a number of cruises on the Caribbean Sea, the most notable cruise in our hemisphere was a forty-four-day cruise around the horn of South America. While my official duties didn't begin until we reached Valparaiso, Chile, we decided to be passengers from Miami to Valparaiso. It was thoroughly enjoyable. On several of the stops before reaching Valparaiso, we rented a cab with Ed and Monica Pineda, who were natives of Chile but now live in New Mexico. We were together in the charming city of Lima, where we visited, among other things, the National Cathedral. Monica visited a school with us in Iquique, Chile, where friends from Green Valley, Ed and Natalie Barber, had worked as teachers in a beautiful school located near a lovely beach.

It was awesome to see the abundant glaciers as we traveled to the southernmost tip of South America. We attended a most interesting lecture by Chuck Richardson on Darwin's exploits in this part of the world. I was surprised to learn that Darwin was considered a mediocre student whose father in desperation urged him to get any kind of a university degree. He eventually graduated with a degree in theology.

I was interested to learn that there have been many shipwrecks in the vicinity of Cape Horn. It is 1,300 miles further south than the Cape of Good Hope in Africa and 600 miles below the latitude of New Zealand's Stewart Island, but it is still 1,080 miles north of the Antarctic Circle and 3,168 miles north of the South Pole. As we circled Cape Horn, the captain and the second captain poured water on the heads of all willing passengers. The cold water had been gathered from the three oceans that merge at this point: the Atlantic, the Pacific and the Southern Oceans. It was a rite of passage that I wouldn't miss, even though I had a cold.

One of the fascinating cities was Ushuaia, Argentina, which is described as the southernmost city in the hemisphere. It boasts of a railway, about ten miles long, which goes to the end of the world. From this city, Argentina launched their war against the British in an effort to gain control of the Falkland Islands.

I was surprised to see how loyal Falkland Islanders are to the British Crown and to their windswept island that still has warning signs of unexploded arsenal dotting the countryside. I remember meeting a sexton in an Anglican church. He was a retired banker who had lived all over the world. I asked him why he chose this spot to retire. He said it was "the safest place in the world," where crime is not present.

We had the opportunity to see the Magellan penguins here at the Falklands as well as cities on the coast of Argentina. While their walk is awkward, they are capable of swimming at twenty miles per hour and travel great distances at sea from season to season.

The city that had real appeal for me was Montevideo, Uruguay. A short distance from Buenos Aires, it has lovely shorelines and lovely nearby farms. I found the people in this city to be very friendly. I went to one of the fine hotels to get a haircut. Even though I don't have a difficult head of hair to cut, the barber was so meticulous and so attentive. I would certainly look him up if I were to return to that part of the world.

We arrived in Buenos Aires on Sunday morning and departed that evening. I was surprised how little activity there was on a Sunday in the downtown section that, in many ways, reminded me of Barcelona. While I had visited this city in the mid-1960s for several days, I felt I had experienced too little of its charm. This time, as we sailed away a few short hours after our arrival, I found myself desiring to stay longer.

The return trip to Valparaiso followed an identical route, except we didn't circle the rock known as the cape this time around. On the first trip, I was standing in the front of the ship when it lurched sharply enough that the liquor bottles fell off the cart onto the floor.

The rumor was that we had just missed a large rock looming just below the surface of the water. This rumor was given some credence when the captain announced an hour or so later that the pilot was still "on board." While the captain is in charge of the ship, it is the pilot's job to safely guide the ship in difficult passages.

As we were passing through the Magellan Straits into the Pacific Ocean, we encountered heavy winds that reached a velocity of about a hundred miles per hour. The captain noted that the waves were sixty feet high. (Come to think of it, that's five or six stories high.) He also reported that this hurricane-type weather had not been predicted. We especially became aware of the pitching motion of the ship when the TV in our room fell off the wall to the floor at the foot of the bed where we were sleeping. For one whole day, the ship was facing into the wind. The captain reported that our speed was 1 knot per hour for an entire day, causing the captain to cancel one of our ports of call. Understandably, no one was allowed on the outer decks. The cruise director gave me the option of canceling my scheduled lecture. I chose to give the lecture on a ship that was really rocking and rolling.

When we arrived in Valparaiso, I had arranged for a local tour guide that I had met on our first trip to this port city to take a group of us to the capitol city of Santiago. We passed through beautiful vineyards as we moved up in elevation from the sea. After a tour of the city, we ended up at the airport. We were on standby status. Since the flights were full, we were to spend several more days in this fascinating city. Delta Airline employees told us that an upscale hotel in downtown Santiago would provide us a room at Delta employee rates. On the fourth day, we were finally able to get seats in the business section on a flight to Atlanta.

We were on standby, waiting for a flight to London from Atlanta. The flight was oversold. The flight to Paris was also heavily booked, but we found out that we could get seats. This flight left before the London flight. (We later learned that we would have gotten on the flight to London.) We took two different trains to England; the second train was the high-speed train through the tunnel, and we got off just after having crossed through the tunnel and took several transfers to get to our bed-and-breakfast in the city of Folk-stone. Because we are typically flying on a "space available" status, we tried to arrive several days prior to sailing to ensure that we would arrive at the port city in time. While we enjoyed seeing some sights in the area, the primary purpose of our early arrival was to get ready to board the *Norwegian Dream* in Dover.

We sailed past the white cliffs made famous by a World War II song and on to our first port in Tallinn, Estonia. A colleague, Reverend Dr. David Wilkinson, had visited the Methodist church here that managed to stay active when the Russian government had taken over the country and closed the churches. Since we were in this port city for only a few hours and I had accepted duty as an escort for on the ship's tours, I didn't have an opportunity to visit this historic church.

We arrived in the city of St. Petersburg, Russia (formerly Leningrad), the day before the three-hundredth anniversary celebration, an event that drew people of influence and power, including the heads of state. The president of the United States arrived the day we left. I was fortunate to be the escort of a tour to the eighteenth-century Imperial Peterhof. It reminded me of the famous King Ludwig castles of Bavaria. The opulence that characterized the palaces of that time was much in evidence here. It was fascinating to read of the political intrigue that took place when this was the official seat of the Russian government.

Leta and I went to a special performance of a string orchestra in one of the mansions that dated back several centuries. The orchestra performed in the garb that would have been present several centuries past.

I was surprised to see that many of the church buildings had not only survived but were well maintained, although most were not active churches during the communist era. There was the Peter and Paul Cathedral, the fortress island, St. Isaak's Cathedral, St. Peter's Lutheran Church, and many other places of interest.

The day of the three-hundredth anniversary, we went to the Hermitage Museum. Local people were given free admission because of the anniversary celebration. Again, I was an escort. Since the people from the ship didn't have visas, we were not permitted to wander off and visit the sites on our own. When we went through the Hermitage, we stood in line for hours. It was wall-to-wall people. Once inside, we were literally pushed along by the rush of human traffic from room to room. Although there were lovely works of art, I was so busy trying to keep a group of nearly forty people together that I didn't allow myself to see what was in the museum.

Grayson Hurst, the director of the Sons of Orpheus Choir, hopes that our choir can travel to this wonderful city and be in concert in this place that has known great music.

The port stops in Finland, Sweden, Denmark, and Norway all had their special attractions. During our short stops in each of these countries, I was an escort of tours that primarily went to the lush countryside with the result of seeing little of the capital cities. We saw the exterior of the building where the nominations are accepted and where decisions are made as to who will get the Nobel Peace Prize as well as the Nobel awards for scientific achievement. The most interesting country to me was Norway, where we visited the Norway Ship Museum as well as the sculpture park and museum in Oslo known as Vigeland. Gustav Vigeland created this park, which featured one 121 stone figures of men, women, and children depicting their struggle for life.

I had taken my digital camera with me during my escort duties in Norway. In this role, it was part of my duty to urge everyone on the bus to check to see if they left any of their belongings. In a hurry to take my wife, Leta, who was waiting for me aboard the ship, on a short tour of the area before the ship sailed, I violated my admonition to the other passengers and left my digital camera on the bus—never to be recovered.

In 2005, I was accepted by an agency known as Sixth Star Entertainment. This agency provides the lecturers for a number of cruise lines with which I hadn't been involved. My first assignment was to do ten lectures on the relationship between mind, body, and spirit during a twenty-eight-day cruise that began in Cape Town, South Africa, and sailed to Sidney, Australia, in September.

We sailed on September 10 and stopped at two ports in South

Africa: East London and Durban. Both cities are described as having wonderful beaches. Leta and I took a shuttle into the shopping section of east London. We didn't see anything there that interested us so we took the next shuttle back to the ship.

When we docked at the city of Durban, the weather was rainy. Leta and I started to walk into town but quickly turned back. After Leta was back on ship, I walked into the city. I was walking on a rather broad sideway. I should have been watching my feet rather than looking at the shops on both sides of the street. I stepped into an uncovered manhole opening and could have fallen twenty feet into this manhole had I not caught myself by elbows. Fortunately, I sustained only a skinned ankle. One of the security guards near the shops where our ship was in port told me that manhole covers are frequently stolen.

Their interesting displays of native arts and crafts captured me, and I ended up purchasing a beautifully carved walking stick. When we disembarked at Sidney, I forgot to take this stick with me. Someone fortuitously found a great souvenir.

The next stop was the island of Madagascar. I was on escort duty in the very third-world port named Nosy Be, a name that we were told meant "big island." The markets and the village brought memories of Paramaribo, Surinam, where we once lived. We then sailed to the French island of Reunion, where we bought tour tickets to see the volcanic countryside. The tour bus ride through the mountain country reminded me of a tour we had taken several years before in one of the Canary Islands. The following day, we were on the Island of Mauritius. The most memorable experience here was to see a statue, about a hundred feet high, which was considered a sacred place of the Hindus. The waters of the nearby river are seen as being as sacred as the Ganges River in India.

The next eight days, we would be on the Indian Ocean en route to Fremantle, Australia. We would celebrate Leta's eightieth birthday in the company of our dinner companions, three Aussie couples. In addition to the lectures, we enjoyed the Broadway-caliber productions. We attended worship services led by Dennis and Bobbi West, who were entertainers. I discovered that Dennis, in addition to his outstanding musical talent, was also an ordained Assembly of God minister. I also attended several computer lectures from an instructor who really knew how to connect with his students.

After Fremantle, we docked in Adelaide, Melbourne, and went on the island of Tasmania. I was again on escort duty and spent most of the time in the country. On the final morning, I got up early to see our docking in the beautiful port in Sidney.

Tiananmen Square in Beijing is described as the largest square in the world. Built before Columbus discovered the New World, it has been a site where important events have transpired over the centuries. Who can forget the very dark chapter written several decades ago involving the bloody massacre of scores of people who were demonstrating for human rights that occurred at this very site? Located nearby, the Imperial Palace, also known as the Forbidden City, was an awesome place to visit. In earlier centuries, this site was open only to the members of the imperial court and to the many concubines typically selected while in their early teens. Once selected, they could never leave—even to visit their families. At the entrance of the square was a huge picture of Mao.

Built more than a century before the time of Christ, the famous Wall of China stretches across mountainous areas for more than four thousand miles. This distance is significantly longer than miles that separate coasts of the United States. What an engineering feat! Steeped in history, China is rapidly becoming one of the major powers in the world of the future.

Leaving Beijing, we embarked on the *Princess Diamond* on Thanksgiving Day 2005. As on the previous cruise, I was scheduled to give a series of lectures on the relationship between mind, body, and spirit. There were more port stops on this voyage than on the *Princess Pacific*.

Our first port stop was Busan, South Korea. I had remembered the city as being called Pusan. We walked the streets of this peninsular city for several hours before returning to the ship. I remembered that at a critical moment in the early part of the war, the North Korean forces nearly drove the United Nations into the sea. Pusan was pivotal in this struggle.

The next port stop was Nagasaki, Japan, the site of the second atomic bomb during World War II. Leta and I took the trolley to the Peace Monument sponsored by the Lions Club of Nagasaki and Hiroshima. It was awesome to stand at dead center of the blast. A small Catholic church, which had just managed to complete the church towers, was at this center. A fragment of the wall remains. A few yards from the center of the blast stood two large trees that appeared to be totally shattered. Somehow, these trees grew again and are now beautiful. The Japanese guide told us that if we touched the tree, we would find energy. Who could resist? I was deeply impressed by the friendliness and helpfulness of the average citizen of this seaport city. We were told that seventy-five thousand people, mostly women, children, and elderly men, died at the moment of the blast.

The next port was Shanghai. We arrived several hours later than planned because of heavy seas. Chinese immigration agents took several more hours to clear the vessel for debarkation. Since our time was severely compromised, I chose not to go into this dynamic city of nearly twenty million inhabitants. I hope to visit this city in the future.

After a brief stop in Hong Kong, the ship docked at Nha Trang, Vietnam, a seaside resort city. I understand that this was an RandR site for US military forces during the Vietnam War. Our major stop was at a hotel, where I made several telephone calls. It appeared to be a lovely place. It would be worth a second look. The next stop was Ho Chi Min City (Saigon). Linda purchased a pair of slacks from a very friendly English-speaking lady. Leta seemed to enjoy this encounter. The drop-off and pick-up place was the Rex Hotel, which we had visited the year before.

The next stop was the Port of Laem Chabang, Thailand. We chose to go to the seaside city of Pattaya instead of taking the long bus ride to Bangkok. Strolling the beachfront streets was a pleasant way to spend a few hours.

The final stop was in Singapore, where we would check into Pan Pacific Hotel. While it was a lovely hotel, I would prefer a hotel closer to Chinatown. The most interesting thing that happened during our three-day stay here was our attendance at a church called The Rock. I had called the office of one of the Methodist churches and asked for the nearest Methodist church to our hotel. I should have picked up on the clue that she was referring us to the church she attended. This charismatic church met in the third story of a mall. We were told that there were ten thousand worshipers at their three worship services. While I regret not attending the Methodist church, which was about a mile away from the hotel, it was an interesting one-time experience to attend The Rock. However, I wouldn't choose to attend this church again.

The only cruise in 2006 was on Holland America Cruise Line. The place of embarkation and disembarkation was to be Copenhagen. We had business accommodations on our flight from Atlanta but were surprised by the Comfort Inn Hotel in Copenhagen. It wasn't air-conditioned. Moreover, the weather was unusually warm. When we opened the windows, we discovered that very busy train tracks were just outside our room. Trains came by every few minutes during all hours of the day and night.

We were happy to board the Holland America ship, the *Rotterdam*, several days later. Because a major political summit was being held in St. Petersburg, Russia, eight or nine cruise ships were being rerouted. While we made several port stops, two stand out: Helsinki and St. Petersburg (Leningrad). Leta seemed quite content to stay on the ship and relax while I walked several miles into Helsinki. At this time of year, they were enjoying nearly twenty hours of sunshine. I don't think I would enjoy their twenty hours of darkness during the winter. I chose to walk to the center of the city — probably four miles or so and chose a different route to return to the ship. It is a charming city. (Several years later, I invited all the members of our immediate family to celebrate our sixtieth wedding anniversary in the dynamic metropolis.)

Both Leta and I participated in a great tour in St. Petersburg, a city of awesome cathedrals. I was told that most are museums, although worship services are occasionally held. I was impressed with the outside of St. Isaac's Cathedral, although I didn't see its interior since this wasn't included on our tour. Another nearby cathedral was called The Savior on Spilled Blood, purportedly so named because one of the emperors who sponsored the building of this cathedral was assassinated on this site.

We did visit Peter and Paul Fortress, where Peter the Great and his family are buried. We heard a male choir (or part of their choir) perform for the visitors. I purchased a CD of this group and passed it on to Grayson Hurst, our director of the Sons of Orpheus.

We had an interesting challenge trying to get a space-available flight back to the States. When we didn't get on the first flight from Copenhagen, we took the train to Brussels. Our daughter, Linda, stated that she had always been able to get on a space-available flight from there. We took two different trains to Brussels. It took us four days to get out of Brussels—and we were very lucky to make the flight that we did.

Traveling for Leta was difficult, although she continued to handle these challenges like a trooper despite the confusion that enveloped her on occasion.

I have only participated in two cruises as a chaplain since Leta's death. The first was on the *Queen Mary 2*. The cruise was twenty-four days long. I embarked on this portion of the world cruise in Singapore on April 2, 2011. This cruise would sail to Phuket, Thailand; Cochin, India; Dubai; Muscat; Oman; Sokhna, Egypt; Athens; and Lisbon. It would disembark in Southampton, England.

For me, the highlight of the trip was the two days in Dubai, home to what is now the world's tallest building. It has 163 floors and is 2,722 feet high. Among its many functions, it purportedly accommodates thirty thousand residential homes as well as several hotels, including a seven-star hotel. Certainly one of the modern cities in the world, its numerous innovative architectural structures boggle the imagination. Here, I first experienced a train ride that was totally computer driven.

The last cruise was on the Azamara cruise line from Singapore to Myanmar (Burma) during Christmas and New Year holidays in 2013 to 2014. This country, which had been ruled in a heavy-handed manner by a military dictatorship for several decades, was just beginning to allow tourists. I had been fascinated since I was a teenager by the stories of Rangoon, now called Yangon, and was excited by the prospect of visiting this city and surrounding areas. I was surprised and delighted that a strong security presence was not obvious as we toured the various sites. The Buddhist palaces seemed to be equal to similar sites in Bangkok.

We made various port stops in Malaysia and Sumatra, returning to Singapore. It is always a treat to be in Singapore, which is sometimes referred to as the cleanest city in the world. The year 2006 was a time to share in the celebration of a fiftieth anniversary of a college friend and member of our college male quartet. Art and Fern Taylor, who live in Grand Rapids, chose to celebrate their wedding anniversary in Colorado Springs, a city that brought back wonderful memories of high school years. Art had asked me to lead the ceremony involving the renewal of their vows in an outdoor ceremony with Pikes Peak as a backdrop.

In addition to spending special days with the celebrating couple, it was wonderful to see Art's sister and her husband, June and Jack Mitchell, from Phoenix, Arizona. My brother Merle also attended this event. We had a great time reliving the year that we spent with our parents in this charming city in 1942 and trying to retrace our steps of that time. As the years fade into history, old friends and experiences during the formative years have special meaning.

My brother Merle, along with Leta and I, drove to have breakfast at the home of a cousin, Dean Kornelson, and his lovely wife. Another first cousin, Jan and Ray Kohen were part of this breakfast. These cousins from different sides of the family had never met.

Earlier, I mentioned that we had little contact with our relatives in our childhood and youth. This has been true of our adult years. It was good to see them again.

Speaking of reunions, six of us who had been part of the youth group mentioned previously, Bob Molle and his brother Don, Bonnie Jean (Wiseman) Friesen and her sister Dottie, my brother Merle, and I were to get together for the first time as a group in sixty years. While our lives had been lived very differently, the twenty-four or so hours that we spent together was much more enjoyable than we had the right to expect. It was wonderful to meet Don Molle's charming wife. This group had shared an important moment during our developmental years. I believe that we all felt that we were richer for it.

Our daughter, Linda, and her three children, Kristina, Michael, and Justin, accompanied Leta and I on a trip to Surinam, South America, that was filled with nostalgia in midsummer of 2006. Nearly a half-century ago, Bob Price and I had set out to pursue an impossible dream. Our families, of course, were deeply immersed in this dream. Perhaps it should have been expected that this sentimental journey would have its own kind of hurdles to go through. Both Leta and I sent our passports to the Surinam Consulate in Miami for the necessary visas that were required before one could gain entry into the country. I was told by the consulate a couple days prior to our leaving that the pages of my passport had been used up (thanks to the repeated stamping of my passport by the immigration folks in Brussels weeks earlier because of all the full standby flights for four consecutive days. Each time we attempted to make these flights and failed, immigration officials stamped our passports as if we were leaving the country and then reentering.)

We arranged a hurried trip to Miami to get the passport from the Surinam embassy and take it to the US passport office to get the additional passport pages. In order to get same-day service, we had to provide evidence that an imminent trip was in the works. After standing in line for hours, I was told by the passport representative that my passport had been compromised and that I would have to get a new passport. This meant getting a picture for the passport in a nearby drugstore and then standing in line for more hours before the new passport could be processed—for a healthy additional fee. I had contacted the Surinam consulate, which normally closed at three o'clock. To my surprise and delight, they stayed open for several hours to process my visa in less than thirty minutes.

I rushed back to the hotel where Leta was waiting. Even though we were past the checkout time at the hotel when I returned, the clerk at the desk stated that we wouldn't be billed if we didn't stay that night. Unfortunately, I didn't keep a copy of the statement and was in fact charged for the room, even though we didn't stay the night.

We then flew to Nashville to spend a couple nights with our son Ed and daughter-in-law, Micki, before catching a flight to San Juan, where we would connect with a flight the following day for Trinidad. This flight to Trinidad was several hours late, so we barely connected with the flight from Trinidad to Paramaribo. A very nervous daughter, who was waiting for us in Trinidad, breathed a heavy sigh of relief when we emerged to board the flight to Paramaribo minutes later.

We arrived at what we had known as Zanderij Airfield, since renamed, in the wee hours of the morning. Our hosts, Roy Lytle and his gracious wife, Margaret, were there to greet us and show us to our quarters. Teachers normally used this building as a residence, but we were able to use these facilities because of the vacation period.

The Lytles were outstanding hosts. Roy arranged our trip to the interior to visit an Indian village as well as accompany us and serve as an outstanding guide. Linda and the grandchildren had the kind of introduction to village life that few people would have.

Flying over the vast jungles brought back so many memories. While the areas near the city were now more populated, the deeper recesses of the jungles were in so many respects the same as they were fifty years ago. Obviously profound changes have taken place in village life. The Indians, for the most part, are literate. I heard of one Trio family who now live in Paramaribo, where their children attend Dutch-speaking schools. Fifty years ago, their ancestors had never seen anyone from the outside world.

Obviously, other profound changes have occurred. Some, particularly what I refer to as the fundamentalist anthropologists, would be aghast and would have preferred to have them remain as "happy and carefree children in their jungle home." I doubt that many of us would prefer to be back in the horse and buggy days, and I suspect that these Indians wouldn't want to go back in time either.

While missionaries have frequently been targets of criticism, some of which is probably deserved, it is to their credit that they have seen the Indians through these profound changes and have sought to be a force for good. These missionaries have often dedicated much of their productive years to carrying out their vision and passion to serve with a minimum of personal or financial gain. This can't be said of many groups who invaded the territory of the interior and the Indian culture for their own gain rather than for the welfare of the Indians.

Enough philosophizing. Back to our trip to the interior. As we were approaching the airstrip, our grandson Justin asked where the airstrip was located and nearly panicked when the pilot pointed to a small field of green. I laughingly told Justin that this strip was twice as long as the ones we had used nearly a half-century ago. In fact, we had typically landed on strips a thousand feet or less and landed between tall trees.

The family got an orientation to life in an Indian village that few expatriates have an opportunity to examine. While much in the lives of Indians has changed in the last half century, much remains as it has been for centuries.

Back in the city, Linda had an opportunity to show her children where she had gone to school. All of us visited the home where we had lived. The current resident graciously received us. We also had an opportunity to share several meals in delightful Javanese restaurants. Some family members didn't have the time to develop some of the tastes that are unique and distinct. They didn't escape, however, the magic of the sights and sounds of this delightful third-world city.

72

Family Rituals and Ceremonies

My paternal grandmother died just a few months short of her ninety-seventh birthday. Until the last few months of her life, she lived in her own apartment in an assisted living community. Ten years before her death, she asked me to do her funeral services. She insisted on sending money for an airline ticket shortly after she made the request. My tongue-in-cheek response was that I would be happy to oblige if she would agree to do my services should I predecease her.

She had fallen and broken her hip and had to leave her small apartment. After surgery, she had been placed in a nursing home. The family members discounted and attempted to negate her statements that she wanted to die. When I saw her a few weeks before her death, she repeated her wish about death. My comment to her was that I wanted what she wanted. If she wanted to live, I would celebrate that wish. If she wanted to die, I would respect that wish. She seemed to be grateful for this response. In a few weeks, she died.

A famous western Nebraska snow blizzard was raging when I received word of her death. My father suggested that I not attempt to fly because of the weather conditions. My response was that I had to try to attend, adding that if the airports were closed when I arrived, I could then in good conscience know that I attempted to fulfill my grandmother's request.

The plane was able to land at the airport in North Platte, Nebraska. My father was there to meet me. It occurred to me that I had never hugged him as an adult. When I attempted to hug him at the airport, he was clearly embarrassed. I remember him looking around the lobby to see if anyone saw me attempting to embrace him. In his world, men didn't hug men.

The service was held in Grant, Nebraska. The snow was so deep that a burial had to be delayed. Hence, the committal was given at the Bullock Funeral home. I remember my father mentioning how generous Mr. Bullock had been to our family during my growing-up years. It was an honor to conduct the memorial service and to sense with deep appreciation how this funeral director had been present for my parents.

I learned that my grandmother, when she sensed that death was near, told my father where she kept a special shawl. She said that she wanted to be buried in a shawl because she "didn't want to appear uncovered before God." My father hadn't been aware of her commitment to this Old World religious custom.

—

My sister Myrna was born after I left for the Owosso College. I may have seen her five or six times before she became an adult. In many respects, we hardly know each other. But we have been present for each other at significant moments in our lives as adults. She graduated from nursing college in Oklahoma City and was married to Dennis Enders the following day. I was pleased to be invited to officiate at this ceremony. Now she is a grandmother. I have typically seen my sister at those ceremonial moments that are pivotal to us all. She and her husband attended our son and daughter-in-law, Ed and Micki's, wedding. We were together for the memorial services for our parents. In 2003, Leta and I had the privilege of being in her home in Imperial, Missouri. What a joy it was to walk with her in the rain and share valued memories and special moments together.

Linda's first serious romance, as far as I know, was with a Colombian young man named Eduardo. This relationship lasted for several years. Linda had stayed with his family while she was a student at the University of the Andes in Bogota. After this relationship cooled, she had a relationship with another young man from Bogota. While they remained good friends for a number of years, this romance never matured.

In time, she met Kent, who was working for Delta Airlines at the time at the Los Angeles airport while she was working at the Spanish desk. This relationship quickly blossomed. Our family was soon to meet Kent in the Los Angeles area. This was the first time that our nuclear family had all been together since Leta and I left Michigan in early 1974. Shortly after this meeting, both Kent and Linda were transferred back to the Delta desks in San Francisco.

On November 5, 1981, Linda and Kent exchanged wedding vows at the San Mateo United Methodist Church. Kent, a committed Mormon, strongly felt that children born to this union should be raised in a Mormon tradition. He readily agreed, however, to Linda's request that her father perform the wedding ceremony. It was an honor that I deeply cherished.

We were not to meet Kent's family until a rehearsal luncheon on the day of the wedding in the charming city of San Francisco. Instead of a rehearsal, Linda wanted to focus on the celebration of two families coming together. We celebrated by riding the famed cable cars and getting to know Kent's family.

A close friend, the Reverend Douglas Bobbitt, accompanied us to the wedding event. Doug, an engaging person with a wonderful sense of humor, added much joy to this occasion.

The unrehearsed wedding ceremony was very much a family affair. Kent's father, Reed Berrett, was the organist. Kent's sister, Pam, who at the time was a performer in Las Vegas, sang. Our son Edward also sang.

As I already stated in the Preface, I was totally unprepared for the emotions that would flood my being as I walked our firstborn down the aisle. I had performed hundreds of marriage ceremonies before and had often experienced a profound sense of drama. But this was different. What happened is unexplainable, really. It was like I was sensing the mystical connection between the generations—between the past and the future. When we reached the altar, I left her standing at Kent's side while I turned around and faced the bride and groom. I could barely speak. I wanted to weep, not from sadness, but because I was caught up in a profound moment. (My friend, Doug Bobbitt, commented afterward that he thought he might have to complete the wedding ritual.)

As I addressed our daughter, I spoke of vividly remembering the night when she was born and shared what a powerful moment that had been. I then traced some of the happenings that she had experienced during her developmental years and the dynamic impact that she had made on our lives. I commended her on her adventurous spirit and then detailed some of the risk-taking experiences that she had undertaken that had left her mother and me with some apprehension but much pride. I remembered the day we said good-bye to her at the Detroit airport, when she and other high school students boarded a chartered airplane filled with students who were leaving for summer exchange programs. I specifically remembered the look in her eyes, a look that spoke eloquently both of the apprehension and anticipation that she was experiencing as she gave us one final glance when she and the other fellow students walked into another room just prior to leaving for their European destination. I also recalled the night that she, as a college graduate, was leaving for Colombia, South America, on her final "leaving the nest for good" kind of experience. I remembered that her mother and I had lumps in our throats as we saw her flight disappear into a glowing sunset.

I then turned to Kent and welcomed him into our family—not simply as an appendage to our daughter, but as a son. Linda and Kent chose to symbolize the coming together of two families by having all the family join them at the altar in a circle as they were pronounced husband and wife.

I don't remember our son Edward having any serious romantic relationships during his high school and college years. He had a number of friends, and some of them happened to be female. When he enrolled in Garrett-Evangelical Theological Seminary, located on the campus of Northwestern University, he met a bright young lady from Kansas named Michelle McCorkle. Micki had been a teacher in a Mennonite mission school in the African country of

Burkina Faso. It apparently wasn't a "love at first sight" kind of relationship but, after several years, they did end up exchanging the vows of marriage at Micki's home church, United Methodist in Winfield, Kansas, on September 5, 1992.

It shouldn't be surprising that as theological graduate students they would end up creating their own marriage ceremony. Four clergypersons participated in this ritual of marriage. Among this group was Micki's close friend, Reverend Frances "Fran" Broadhurst, who was a Presbyterian minister and who had been the dean of women at the college where Micki had attended. It was my pleasure to be a concelebrant with Fran during the communion ritual, which took place at the wedding.

A climactic moment occurred in the ceremony, when Ed accompanied himself at the piano and sang a love song to his bride that he had just finished composing the day of the wedding. I don't think that there were many dry eyes as he sang.

Kristina Berrett, a niece of the groom, was the lovely flower girl, and her brother, Michael, was the ring bearer. The ceremony was rather lengthy and Michael, age six, had fallen asleep. When it was time for him to stand at the altar, near the end of the ceremony, Michael was awakened by his father and was taken to his place at the altar. Shortly after he arrived, Michael lay down on the altar steps and promptly fell asleep again. His embarrassed father brought him to his feet again and urged him to wake up. (I thought that the picture of Michael sleeping at the altar was beautiful and secretly wished that his father had not disturbed his sleep.)

I have had the high honor to be present and participate in the baptism of two of our grandchildren: Philip Wesley McCorkle Friesen and his sister, Rebecca Leigh Ann McCorkle Friesen.

Philip was baptized in April 1996 at the Claflin United Methodist Church near Great Bend, Kansas. Micki was the pastor of this congregation. Reverend James Reed, a longtime friend and their district superintendent, participated in this ritual. Philip's great-grandparents were present at this ceremony. This may have been the last travel experience of Leona Friesen, the great-grandmother, before her death.

I also had the honor of baptizing Rebecca in April 2001 at the

Greenwich United Methodist Church in the Wichita area. Rebecca's godparent, Reverend Gayla Rapp, gave the sermon on the occasion of her baptism.

As noted earlier, I left home without my parents' blessings. I was only sixteen years old and essentially penniless. My parents' concern was deeper than whatever anxiety they may have had about my financial instability or my tender age. Their religious orientation was very conservative, and they were afraid that I would lose my religious grounding, which they had so carefully nurtured. While they were clearly pleased that my goal was to enter the clergy, they were concerned that the Bible college I was entering was too liberal.

They seemed to be pleased that I became the first military chaplain of the denomination in which I was ordained, even though their tradition had been a pacifist one. They became alarmed when I eventually transferred to the United Methodist Church and totally confused when I got a doctorate of ministry degree from the Jesuit School of Theology at Berkeley.

Their conservative religious and political orientation never wavered. I was surprised and pleased when they asked, several years before their deaths, if I would officiate at their memorial services.

As I mentioned earlier, my father's death occurred while I was in Mexico City attending the wedding of Veronica Cerda, whose parents were close friends. Mexican wedding celebrations often go on until the early hours of the morning. I returned to my hotel at 2:00 a.m. and had a call waiting from my brother Merle, announcing that my father had passed on, apparently from a heart attack.

I returned to keep the commitment of doing a memorial service in the very Mennonite congregation that my parents had left when I was a child. I had a chance to speak to former Mennonite neighbors that I hadn't seen since then. The bully in my one-room schoolhouse was present. I was sorry that the funeral director rushed us on to the cemetery before I had an opportunity to speak to him as well as other people who had attended the memorial service. (I was saddened to hear that this person, who had terrified me in my childhood, died a sudden accidental death sometime after my father's death. It would have been good to connect as adults and senior citizens.) It was wonderful to see the way my father was respected in this community, even though he had often stated that he had accomplished little in life and even though he had gone through much of his life with little social standing. Five weeks later, I did the memorial service for my mother. They were just a few weeks shy of their seventieth wedding anniversary. I was struck with the fact that we had come full circle by having the services in this Mennonite Church in Grant, Nebraska. While I had traveled a road in my life with which my parents and most of the people of the community had little familiarity, the memorial services were, for me, a homecoming and a genuine celebration of my parents' lives.

Our daughter, Linda, had remembered when our family had been living in Munich, Germany, where I had been a chaplain with the military. She had begun her kindergarten years there. She wanted to show her husband, Kent, and her children, Kristina, Michael, and Justin, where she had lived as a girl. I was pleased when she asked us to accompany them to Bavaria. We were to stay in Oberammergau at a bed-and-breakfast with a view of the famous Passion Play Theater.

We had a great week touring the castles of King Ludwig and visiting the military recreational facilities in Garmish as well as Kimsee, where one of the castles was located on an island in the second largest lake in Germany. Leta and I had visited this castle in 1955. We attended a string orchestra concert at one of the Wagner concerts in the Hall of Mirrors, where more than a thousand candles had been lit.

The weeks passed quickly, and we were on the same flight to Atlanta. We said good-bye to our family at the Atlanta airport, not realizing that Kent would soon have a fatal heart attack on the golf course in Salt Lake City. Every Monday afternoon, following work, Kent and his buddies, who were also Delta employees, would play nine holes of golf without carts. Kent played the first eight holes but complained of being tired when they reached the ninth hole. His concerned friends insisted that they get a cart while Kent stated that he was feeling fine. His friends insisted on getting the cart. When the cart arrived, Kent climbed on the cart without difficulty but had a fatal heart attack before they reached the clubhouse.

Leta and I took the flight to Salt Lake to be with Linda and her children. We winced when we witnessed her pain. At the viewing the night before the funeral, Linda received her friends, who were fellow Delta employees and friends from her Mormon Church for three full hours. She was a source of inspiration to so many as she dealt with the shock and pain of loss with both tears and hope. The death occurred on June 16, 2003. I witnessed her dealing authentically with her grief without losing her focus on the need to go on with her life and be as fully present to her children as possible.

Her lovely daughter, Kristina, spoke eloquently at her father's funeral services. Kristina, who was adopted at age three from Colombia, South America, had a very close bond with her father. When Linda and Kent had received word that Kristina was ready for adoption, Linda had just had gall bladder surgery and was restricted on the amount of weight she could lift. Kent went to pick Kristina up in one of the providences of Colombia. Kent was given custody of her on their first meeting. The adoption process took about three weeks. Kent obviously was unaccustomed to spending twenty-four hours a day with a small child. During this time, a deep bonding occurred that would never end. When Linda met Kent and Kristina in Bogota for the first time, Kristina wasn't at all sure she wanted to share her newfound father with this new person she was meeting. After Kristina's eloquent tribute to her father at the memorial ceremony, I told her that I would be honored if she spoke at my commemoration service when I pass on to bigger and better things.

Since Kent's death, Linda has taken her children on trips to Rome, Ireland, and New York. She also took Michael on a trip to Brazil to celebrate his graduation from high school. From her papa's perspective, she appears to be doing an excellent job as a new single parent. We couldn't be more proud.

—

My brother Claire, who was a bit less than a year younger than I, died on February 15, 2004. He had worked in western Nebraska

in agriculture-related jobs. He and his wife, Bonnie Jean, had retired in Bernie, Texas. His memorial service was held in Ogallala,
Nebraska, where he is buried in the Wiseman family plots.

His wife, Bonnie Jean Wiseman Friesen, who was a high school
classmate of my brother and me, died on December 4, 2013. Her
memorial service was held on December 11, 2013, in Ogallala. I was
invited to lead her service (see Appendices). She was buried next to
her husband.

—

In the summer of 2008, our children and grandchildren (with the
exception of one son and one granddaughter) joined us in Shanghai, China, to celebrate our sixtieth wedding anniversary. While the
sights and sounds of this old and yet modern city were marvelous,
the highlight of the event took place in the Westin Hotel, where we
held our celebration. Different cuisines were located on different
floors of the hotel. We chose the Thai cuisine on the fifth floor. The
setting was elegant, and the food and the service were outstanding.
While this was described as an anniversary celebration, I wanted
the focus to be on Leta.

To cap the evening, I had intended to remind our children and
grandchildren of the different ways that their grandmother had impacted their lives. As I began to speak, I suddenly and unexpectedly
choked up. I could barely speak and wanted to weep. A quarter of
a century earlier, I had a similar experience when I was performing
the marriage ceremony of our daughter. At both events, there was
an unexpected realization that once again we were standing on the
cusp of one generation passing and another rising to the fore. While
Leta's progressive debilitation undoubtedly played a role, the larger sense was one generation passing the baton to the next. It is an
evening that will live in my memory as long as there is memory.
This was the last major event that our family shared together.

73

Have I Told You about Our Grandkids Lately?

No autobiography would be complete without saying a few words about our grandchildren. I will introduce them from the youngest to the oldest.

Rebecca Leigh Anne McCorkle Friesen was born on December 30, 1999. She missed being a millennial baby by hours. She was born by Cesarean section so the parents had a choice on which day she would arrive. Since we didn't have the opportunity to be grandparents in residence, it took a while for her to feel comfortable around us when we would visit her and her family.

Leta went to Wichita as soon as we knew Rebecca was going to be born via C-section. Leta's flight landed just an hour or two after Rebecca was born, so Grandma and Rebecca met in the first few hours of her life. After Rebecca came home from the hospital, Grandma Leta would rock her for hours on the recliner. Though Rebecca didn't want to be with any adults except her parents from ages one to two, these hours with Grandma were a foreshadowing of a long relationship to come.

As Rebecca got more used to her grandparents, she would spend hours on Grandma's lap. Grandma would read stories to Rebecca, or they would just talk. (Rebecca often did most of the talking.) Grandma Leta paid rapt attention to Rebecca, even if she did not know what she was saying. One evening when Ed, Micki, Phillip, and Rebecca were all visiting Green Valley, Micki said to Rebecca, "You and Grandma both like to read and snuggle don't you?"

Rebecca grinned and nodded. Grandma hugged Rebecca and said, "We are just two peas in a pod, aren't we!"

Rebecca repeated, "Two peas in a pod!"

From that moment on, Rebecca would remind her parents, "Grandma and I like to spend time together; we are two peas in a pod." She repeated that phrase to Leta sometimes too, who got great joy out of the fact that Rebecca remembered it and felt that way about her grandmother.

Rebecca graduated from Derby High School in Derby, Kansas. She accomplished this feat in the space of three years and graduated with honors. She continues the ballet lessons that she began at age three and is enrolling in junior college to supplement her skills as a dancer with training in physical therapy.

A bright, highly socialized young lady, Rebecca had a command of the alphabet and had developed early reading and writing skills before entering kindergarten in 2005. She takes her ballet lessons very seriously. She sees her brother as a protector and friend (at least most of the time). Rebecca and her grandmother Friesen have formed a very special bond that goes beyond the typical grandchild and grandparent relationship. They seem to have developed a "soulmate" kind of relationship. During our last visit to Kansas for Thanksgiving 2010, when Leta was ill, Rebecca was nine. For many hours, Rebecca sat with Grandma on the couch. This time, Grandma didn't read books, and Rebecca didn't tell Grandma all about her activities. They sat in silence together—hip-to-hip and knee-to-knee—holding hands. From time to time, they would look at each other and smile. No words seemed to be necessary for these two peas in a pod.

Rebecca graduated from Derby High school in three years with honors in 20016. In addition to her ballet dancing activities, she is pursuing training as a physical therapist.

Her brother, Phillip Wesley McCorkle Friesen, was born January 29, 1996. At the time of this writing, he is a junior at Wichita State University, where he is majoring in aeronautical engineering. His bent toward engineering was evident when he was a small child. When he would receive a toy, his first inclination was to take the toy apart and then reassemble it. He, like his sister, inherits strong intellectual skills from his parents. He excels in schoolwork and has an inquisitive mind. He was an enthusiastic drummer in the Derby High School drum line and shares his father's love of music. Phillip also has a well-developed sense of humor—thanks to his dad. Phillip is very observant and is a thinker. He is always processing information and thinking of things that can be done with it. He is the one who fixes things around the house and troubleshoots computer issues for the family.

Justin Eugene Berrett was born April 10, 1992. Justin, like his father, is devoted to sports and can quote an amazing amount of statistics relating to various sports. For years, he had no doubt in his mind that he would one day be an NBA basketball player. As time has passed, he is certain that he wants to work in the sports field, perhaps in sports medicine. Justin is personable, competitive, and bright, and he is a great deal of fun to be around. Justin received his Eagle Scout award on July 5, 2009. His natural talents will take him far.

Michael Reed Berrett was born on April 25, 1987. Michael was the first family member to become an Eagle Scout. When this honor was bestowed on him, he, accompanied by the trainer, held a live eagle in the air. He was a member of his high school swimming team. While he is a reflective person, he surrounds himself with many friends. Michael's high school graduation gift from his mother was a trip to Chile and Argentina. Michael completed six years in the air force and has a service-connected disability. He is now at Hill Air Force Base in Utah and is working as an avionics technician. He was deployed in both Qatar and Kyrgyzstan while on active duty. Michael and Rebecca have joined us on Rotary trips in Thailand, and he is now an active Rotarian and has been awarded the Paul Harris Medallion. Michael and his wife Rebecca are the proud parents of Mary Lou, a charming young lass who is very bright and quick on her feet. At this writing, Mary Lou is fifteen months old and has a wonderful disposition.

Kristina Marie Berrett, as mentioned earlier, was born in Colombia, South America, and arrived in this country when she was two and half years old. She raised her right hand and officially swore allegiance to the United States of America when she was three years old. I will never forget her timid first words to me (prompted by her parents, of course) in a telephone conversation. They were, "Te amo," which forever bonded her to me. At that time, she spoke no English. Kristina has superb social skills, was the captain of her swimming team in her high school, and has an excellent presence on the platform. In addition to working full time, Kristina has taken courses in journalism at a junior college. I predict that she will do well in whatever vocation she chooses.

Our son, Edward Alan Friesen, and his wife, Micki, are ordained as clergy in the United Methodist Church. Ed is a graduate of the University of Arizona, where he majored in music theory. Both Ed and Micki are graduates of the Garrett-Evangelical Theological Seminary. Micki received a master's degree from a Jesuit university and now is the pastor of the Trinity United Methodist Church in Dorado, Kansas. She is a member of the Rotary club in Dorado. Ed, a survivor of multiple myeloma, is now assigned as pastor of the Derby United Methodist Church in Derby, a suburb of Wichita, Kansas. Like his father, he is active member of the Rotary club of Derby.

Robert Arthur Friesen and his partner of forty years, Michael Cohen, live in Hilliard, Ohio, a suburb of Columbus. Bob is a graduate of Western Michigan University and had major experience with John Hancock life insurance company and has been a stockbroker with Smith-Barney. He is currently a financial planner with Nationwide Financial Services. He is a certified financial planner with all kind of certifications and credentials that I can't began to describe. He is a cancer survivor and is active in his Lutheran church. In the past, Bob has sung with the outstanding Columbus Gay Men's Choir. He is a highly intelligent and deeply compassionate person who has a strong social conscience.

Linda Marie Friesen Berrett Greener received her twenty-five-year pin with Delta Airlines in 2004. The Delta family has become very important to her. Thanks to the Delta connection, she and her family have traveled widely in different parts of the world. A devoted mother, she and her children accompanied us to Thailand in October 2004. She officially retired on July 1, 2005. I suspect that she will find interesting activities that will reflect her caring personality. At this writing, she is employed at eBay.

She is a graduate of Alma College in Alma, Michigan. She spent a semester attending the University of the Andes in Bogota, Columbia, and then returned to work with the street children of Bogota. She currently lives in Murray, Utah, with her three children and is our favorite daughter. She continues to travel widely with her family and friends.

Her twenty-five-year marriage to Kent Berrett, also a Delta employee, ended with Kent's sudden death at a golf course where he was with his Delta buddies, who had a longstanding tradition of playing nine holes of golf every Monday after work.

Five years later, she married Dan Corrigan on August 8, 2008. After nearly seven years of marriage, the dreams with which they began their life together began to fade. They decided to dissolve this union amicably.

Linda is now married to Paul Greener, and they have retired in Green Valley. It is great to have our only and hence favorite daughter and her spouse living nearby. Linda, Paul, and her close friend of fifty years, Dee Gill, and husband, Allen, are planning to join me on a trip to Surinam in September 2017.

74

About Leta's Life and Death

Earlier, I briefly described our romance and marriage. We were to have sixty-two years of marriage minus exactly three weeks. Naïve and rather insecure, both of us came from insulated and very conservative religious backgrounds and viewed politics in what would now be described as right wing terms. In the beginning, our views were fairly well matched.

Surprising to both of us, we were to experience a host of changes in the ways we saw the world. Over the years, we came to experience these changes in rather different ways. While she had an intermittent work history, she spent the bulk of our time together as a stay-at-home mom, a role that she found very satisfying. While she tended to shy away from making decisions having a major impact on our lives, she fully supported me once a difficult decision had been made. During the first dozen years or so while we were living at the poverty level, she never once complained about our limited budget.

In the next several pages, I will essentially retell some of our history together but will attempt to do so from her perspective, even though I speak in the first person. After graduating from Owosso Bible College, I enrolled at Taylor University in Upland, Indiana. We moved our twenty-seven-foot trailer from Michigan to Indiana just as Leta was two weeks away from delivering our first child. We had only enough funds to pay the first semester's tuition and the hospital bill. The kind and patient doctor who took her as a patient at this advanced stage of pregnancy and delivered our daughter, Linda, did not press us for payment.

As 1950 ended, we calculated that we had lived on five dollars per week, half of which went for baby food. When someone placed a dollar in our mailbox unannounced, Leta and I discussed whether to spend that dollar for bread or milk. There was never a time during this "trial by fire" that Leta complained or suggested that I should quit school or get a job. The university village of Upland had a population of fewer than a thousand people, not counting the students. Jobs were essentially unavailable.

Leta was clearly in for the duration as far as our time at Taylor University was concerned.

Three years later, while serving my first assignment as a pastor in Columbia, South Carolina, the promised salary of forty dollars per week turned out to be more like five dollars per week, although there were a number of weeks when there was no salary at all. Leta was certainly a trooper and never once complained that our income was almost nonexistent.

As stated earlier, Leta was fully supportive of my decision to go into the army as a chaplain, even though there were a host of unknowns. In 1954, she and the children were to join me in Europe some four months after my deployment there. Although she must have had a high level of anxiety about taking two young children, ages one and four, across the country solo to board a ship for a journey across rough seas and then boarding a train to the final destination in Munich, she did so without hesitation. None of her siblings would ever live more than two hours away from where they were born, but she was destined to see the world and adapt to wherever we went. She did, however, have real reservations about my decision to become a paratrooper while serving as a chaplain to an airborne unit—until she watched my third jump. After that, she became a fan.

The next major change in our lives came with the decision to contact Indians in the unexplored regions of Surinam. It was an agonizing decision that bordered on being foolhardy. While she wouldn't weigh in on the decision process, she was fully supportive, even though it would mean that we would invest all the money we had managed to save during our time on active duty. More than that, our future income would be very limited and uncertain. Her family must have wondered what crazy thing their unpredictable son-in-law would try next. Leta was unshakable in her support.

Leta and our two children, Linda and Bob, would join me in Paramaribo, Surinam, where we would live as the locals lived. During our time in Surinam, we would never have a refrigerator. Leta would ride a bicycle daily to an open-air market and try to communicate in a language in which she was not conversant when trying to buy groceries. This, for her, was to become a daily chore.

She would provide superb care of our children while I would spend days—sometimes weeks—in the unexplored jungles with no way to communicate with her. She had to face a host of unknowns, including my whereabouts as I flew over uncharted jungles. Characteristically, she endured these times of uncertainty without a complaint. As previously described, for one month, Leta didn't know whether out expedition had survived our initial contacts with "Indians who had never seen anyone from the outside world." The Trio Indian tribe, for whom I came to have the greatest respect, was similar to the ones who had murdered the five missionaries who had attempted to contact them. The fears that she carried were far greater than those I carried on that very uncertain mission.

When we returned to the States, just months before the birth of our third child, Edward, Leta was once again a real champ as I enrolled full time in a doctoral program at Michigan State University. In addition, I committed to be the minister of three Methodist churches to keep bread on the table. She never complained that I was stretched so thin that we continued to have little time together.

This heavy schedule would continue after my doctoral studies were completed. Leta sometimes became exhausted with mothering while I was away, and she was engaged in a host of other activities. This was obviously true during the times that I was serving a full-time church congregation as well as being a full-time director of a mental health center that grew to a staff of seventy, including professional and clerical staff. She fully supported the decision to leave the mental health center, where we had a decent income for the first time in our married life, and move to Arizona with no promise of an income. It obviously meant leaving a network of friends that she deeply cherished.

After our move to Arizona, the prospects of financial survival were rather bleak in the beginning. Leta held steady even when I was in a panic about having left a financially secure position to pursue yet another dream—a private practice in clinical psychology at the other end of the country.

As the private practice began to grow, once again, my time was stretched beyond any reasonable limits. By then, reacting calmly to these growing pains was a well-rehearsed behavior for Leta. However, she made the adjustments without complaint. Perhaps her appropriate response might have been "Enough, already."

My habit of making changes once I got comfortable in a given position wasn't over yet. I accepted, with considerable reluctance, an invitation from my former doctoral advisor, Dr. John Jordan, to join him on the staff at Louisiana State University. I hesitantly took the job only when I was offered the title of full professor and only then with the provision that I would return to Arizona within a short time. It soon appeared certain that, because of a change in the political winds, my colleague would not be able to transfer his grant, and it became clear that this very creative project was in jeopardy. Therefore, I began to make plans to return to Arizona. Again, Leta maintained her poise. In the midst of that tension, my colleague, Dr. Jordan, suddenly suffered a brain aneurysm that resulted in his death. The magnificent dream he had for creating a worldwide network of rehabilitation service disappeared. We were now free to return to Arizona.

Though going to Louisiana was truly risky, it proved to have a lot of merit, and the time in this setting was, from my perspective, beneficial. We had the opportunity to make a number of new friends, and Leta and I had the opportunity to spend some quality time with each other.

I sensed even before we left Louisiana that the atmosphere for delivering health care was beginning to change. Health Maintenance Organizations (HMOs) began appearing on the scene and that was to have a rather profound influence on the future of health care delivery. Physicians began having increasingly limited ability to refer their patients to specialists. They were largely limited to using the HMO's network of staff, which did not allow reimbursement to psychologists. My medical colleagues were most cordial in welcoming my return but were limited in their ability to make referrals to me.

I began to seriously consider returning to my other career as an active clergyman. Once again, Leta was supportive of whatever decision I would make. As previously stated, Leta and I have had an incredible journey together. Admittedly, there were times that were less than blissful.

Leta's Descent into Dementia

Leta's journey into dementia began shortly after her heart bypass surgery. She had had a violent reaction to the anesthesia. While still in the recovery room, she thought she was in a Nazi prison camp. Always such a gentle person, Leta uncharacteristically took a swing at the nurse she thought was a prison guard stopping her attempt to escape the camp. When the nurses called me in the wee hours, I went to the hospital, where she explained to me that she was in a Nazi concentration camp. I got permission to take her in a wheelchair to the chapel and attempted to explain that this was a chapel and not a prison.

She noted a crucifix on the wall and asked, "Who put that guy up there?" She began to suspect that I had been "brainwashed" because I was trying to convince her she wasn't in a prison and wanted nothing to do with me. This delusion lasted for several weeks.

She wasn't delusional again, with one exception, for most of the next ten years. The exception was when we were returning to Tucson from a vacation in Peru. She suggested that we drop by for a visit with her sister. I tried to reason with her that since her sister lived in Michigan and we were arriving in Tucson, it was not feasible to visit her sister, although I promised that we would plan a visit in the near future. She responded that her sister was living alone and seldom had a visitor, so she thought it very important that we visit her right then. Every attempt I made to suggest that an immediate visit was impossible totally failed.

Her response was, "If you aren't able to get me to visit my sister, then I will find someone who can."

When we arrived home, she went to her favorite chair. I assumed she would sit there quietly for a while, so I went to check the computer for messages. When I returned to the living room about thirty minutes later, she was gone. I alerted the sheriff's office and began to search where I thought she might be. Fortunately, she was wearing an ID bracelet Linda had given her. A neighbor found her wandering on the golf course. This was the only time that she wandered off without notification. She explained that she was searching for someone who would help her get to Michigan to see her sister.

Leta's descent into dementia lasted about ten years. Dementia might be compared to the disease of leprosy. Instead of part of the body beginning to fall away, part of one's personality begins to disappear. I first noticed the increasing deterioration when she could no longer manage our finances. She would spend hours trying to find minor discrepancies in the checkbook. She then began to lose her sense of time. When writing a check, she would inquire about the date. If she had been told the date was, for example, July 4, 1776, she would have put that date on the check. This was followed by the loss of her organizational abilities. As someone who could make a meal out of almost anything, she forgot how to organize a simple meal. When we would go on a trip, she forgot how to pack her suitcase.

As her dementia progressed, Leta would have been content to spend her days at home. Fearing that she would be mired in an all-encompassing sense of isolation, I insisted that we not draw the curtains and withdraw from the world. While she enjoyed our travels, both Rotary-oriented travels and our time on the cruises, as her dementia increasingly dominated her life, she began to find the cruises to be somewhat disorientating and preferred to be in the safety of her home—actually the safety of her favorite sofa. After that, I decided that I should limit our commitment to giving lectures on cruises.

In 2010, during the final year of life, we traveled to visit our Rotary friends in Thailand. We also visited our Rotary exchange "daughter" and her family in Peru. I believe this kept her mind clear and her body active. We also visited all of her living siblings and were in the process of visiting the last of our three offspring.

Our last visit would be to the home of our son Ed and his wife, Micki, for Thanksgiving. We saw Leta's physician, Dr. William Imboden, on the morning of our flight to Wichita, Kansas. All of her vital signs were normal. He gave her a prescription, and we filled it at Davis Monthan Air Force Base.

We had missed breakfast because I had difficulty getting her up. With the loss of her time perspective, she wanted to delay getting up because, "I'm tired and need to rest."

For several years, she experienced fairly frequent abdominal distress, and I tried to find some food at the Base Exchange food court that wouldn't upset her stomach. The only thing that I found that I thought would fit the bill was banana bread. I made the wrong choice. On the way to the airport, she began to experience nausea. I suggested that we cancel the trip and go home, but she wanted to continue on to Wichita. All the way to Atlanta, the nausea became increasingly severe. The flight attendants made every effort to assist her. I considered getting a hotel in Atlanta, but the continuing flight to Wichita was at the gate when we arrived. I decided to continue the flight because we had reservations at the air base in Wichita.

Leta became a bit more comfortable after we got to our room. I was reluctant to order food the next morning as we began our journey to Protection, Kansas, a small city about three hours from Wichita, where Micki, our daughter-in-law, was the pastor of a local United Methodist church. It occurred to me that she might be able to tolerate a milkshake. A stop at McDonalds did the trick.

She continued to have bouts of nausea during our stay with our son Ed and his family. After several days, I called a local doctor to determine whether she might be experiencing dehydration. After asking several diagnostic questions, he suggested that she likely was not suffering from dehydration. Several days later, her condition had not improved, so I contacted the physician again, stating that I wanted assistance in controlling Leta's nausea so we could return to Tucson and the care of her regular physician.

As it turned out, Leta needed to be hospitalized in the local hospital so she could be properly medicated. The next day, the physician informed me that she needed to be transferred to a Wichita hospital because she needed more care than the local hospital could supply. He added that he would arrange for a transfer by ambulance. I flatly refused the ambulance, stating that I would transfer her personally. The physician told me that I was acting contrary to his medical advice, suggesting that there could be consequences if she were not transferred by ambulance. I quickly added that I would accept those consequences, noting that such a trip for such a confused woman, riding backward in an uncomfortable ambulance while strangers (medical attendants) hovered over her, would frighten her.

The physician finally released her very reluctantly to my care. Our two grandchildren, Phillip and Rebecca, came by to see their grandmother before going with their mother, Micki McCorkle, to conduct the Sunday church service. Instead, the grandchildren accompanied their grandmother and me to the Wesley Hospital in Wichita.

The trip to Wichita was mostly uneventful, except for one short episode of vomiting. This three-hour trip was much more comfortable for her than a ride in an ambulance would have been. Leta was able to walk into the hospital. She was admitted at midday and shortly thereafter began another medication routine. During the evening, she became hyperactive. She was so medicated that she couldn't stand by herself. I held one arm while a lovely young nursing aide, who appeared to be in her early twenties, had the other. For the next hour and a half, Leta insisted on "charging around" most of the area on the hospital floor where her room was. She wanted to explore every patient room. By the time this evening was over, I was totally exhausted. The young aide who held her other arm kept talking to Leta in endearing terms. I was deeply moved by her compassion as well as her energy as we guided Leta to a number of locations on the floor while investing considerable energy in preventing her entering the rooms of other patients.

It was probably 10:00 p.m. when the nursing staff indicated that they would be referring Leta to the intensive care unit (ICU) because the ICU had more personnel to care for her. I followed as the nurses wheeled her. The personnel in ICU instructed me to go and get some rest and assured me that things were under control. When I returned the following morning, I witnessed Leta being led around the area in much the same agitated state that she had been in the night before — this time on the arms of the ICU nurses.

Linda had given her mother an ID bracelet, which included her name, address and the fact that she suffered from dementia. Leta had never taken off the bracelet. But in the final day of her life, she managed to remove the bracelet after much struggle. She gave the bracelet to me with a slight grin on her face that reflected a sense of accomplishment. When I told Linda this, she felt sure that her mother was saying that she would no longer need this bracelet.

I should explain that throughout her life, Leta had never been violent in any sense of the word. Her agitation continued through much of the day. I was so moved by the way that our grandson, Michael Berrett, who was stationed at the Air Force Base in Wichita, related to his grandmother. When Leta needed help, such as going to the bathroom, Michael gently assisted her without any visible shyness. Before he left, he spoke to his grandmother in very loving terms, adding how special she was to him. Michael had no way of knowing this would be the last time he ever saw his dearly loved grandmother.

Between 6:00 and 7:00 p.m., the nursing staff told me that they would be giving her heavier medication to calm her agitated state and suggested that I take advantage of that and get some rest. I went to my quarters at the military base and collapsed on the bed in total fatigue. It was about midnight when I received a call from ICU stating that Leta had been placed on the critical list. They suggested that I come at once. When I arrived, I found that she was wearing an oxygen mask and was receiving life support. They asked for permission to make aggressive physical interventions. I emphatically stated that I only wanted them to provide comfort care at this point.

Months earlier, Leta had made it clear that she didn't want to receive long-term nursing home care, and I fully concurred that I didn't want that for her or me. They removed the mask and the other life support. Initially, she struggled to catch her breath, and I heard the rattling in her throat. I had heard of the death rattle and wondered whether this was what I was hearing. She was given some medication, and soon her breathing became normal.

I was in the room with her for nearly four hours. Even now, I feel a lump in my throat as I share that she appeared so serene and in a peaceful sleep. The nurses, most of them young enough to be my granddaughters, were so professional and so caring in the way they carried out their duties. One young nurse was in the room when Leta took her last breath. With the equipment that she had been attached to already shut down, the silence was deafening. I will never forget the nurse's concerned look as she announced, "She's gone."

Soon, all the nursing staff came by to give me a warm hug, as if they had known Leta for a long time. It was truly a sacred moment. It was so important to me that Leta be able to die with dignity and not waste away in some lonely nursing home. I got my wish. Leta did too! The date was November 30, 2010.

I called all the children that we had raised together to inform them of their mother's death. Linda, our eldest, said she knew that her mother was dying when, during their final telephone conversation, her mother had referred to her as "her favorite daughter." Linda had often used that term in a lighthearted manner because she was in fact our only daughter. Linda reported that her mother never used the term but had typically just smiled when Linda used that description.

Both Leta and I had arranged for our bodies to be given to Science Care, an organization that harvests all useable organs for donation and then sends the cremated remains to the next of kin. I was on the phone for nearly an hour making arrangements for this organization to pick up Leta's body, thus fulfilling Leta's wishes.

I will never forget the emotions I felt as I was leaving the hospital now that death had parted our union of more than six decades. I was surprised to feel like a great load had been lifted from me. I had not expected that, even as I had watched her condition deteriorating. While I would have made every effort to care for her as long as I could, I realized that the day was rapidly approaching when I would no longer be able to care for her appropriately. I can't begin to explain how much I dreaded the day when it would be necessary to transfer her to a care facility. Thankfully, that day never came. It was so important to me that she die with dignity. She was now safe in the presence of a loving Creator.

I deeply appreciate that our son Ed; his wife, Micki; and their children, Phillip and Rebecca, drove the three hours from the village of Protection to be with me. I also deeply appreciated that our grandson Michael was there with me as well. But I, surprisingly, wanted to be alone. The sense of wanting to be alone became overwhelming. I said good-bye to my family and headed for the airport and home—alone. I would have loved to walk alone for miles and miles in the woods, reflecting on the meaning of our days, reflecting on the blessing of the incredible yet unlikely journey that Leta and I had enjoyed together.

75

Celebrating Leta's Life and Honoring Her Memory

There were two celebrations of Leta's life. Several years prior to her death, I asked her where she wanted to be buried when the time came and whether she preferred to go through the traditional embalming procedure or if she wanted to be cremated. She asked me what my preference was for my body. When I responded that I intended to be cremated, she stated that she wanted to do the same. Her ashes were placed in her family plot that included her parents and her siblings. She is the first member of her family to be cremated.

Because of the threatening Michigan winter weather, the graveside service was held prior to the service celebrating her life, which was held in the church where Leta had attended in her childhood and teenage years. Our son Ed read the graveside words of committal while I knelt at the small grave opening holding the vase of ashes that were her earthly remains. Then I placed the vase into the ground after the words of committal were spoken.

We proceeded to the church. It was a family-oriented service. Leta's sister, Carol, was the pianist; her niece, Joy Coffey, and her husband, Barry, provided the music; Ed, an ordained Methodist minister himself, conducted the service, and Linda and Bob both spoke. At the conclusion, I quoted Psalm 139. Finally, and briefly, I described our years together.

The second service was held about ten days later at the Green Valley Community Church, the local Methodist church in Green Valley, Arizona. A close clergy friend, the Reverend Douglas Bobbitt, assisted by our son Ed, provided the leadership of the service. (Leta and I had shared a meal with Doug and Judy Bobbitt just ten days or so before her death. They were valued friends we had known for years.) The Sons of Orpheus Male Choir, of which I am a member for twenty years, sang two songs; a twelve-year-old, highly accomplished violist named Nicole Skaggs accompanied another number. (I insisted on singing with the choir as they sang in Leta's honor.) Our choral director, Professor Grayson Hurst, who has a long history of singing in operas on the great stages of the world and is now a retired professor of voice at the University of Arizona, sang *The Lord's Prayer* in a breathtaking, operatic style. Many of those present stated this rendition brought tears to their eyes. This moment will remain etched in my memory as long as there is memory.

Next, four very special friends, Bob Kurtz, Tom Tilton, Harmon Myers, and Caroll Rinehart, spoke briefly about their memories of Leta. Linda movingly spoke of the impacts her mother had on her life. Reverend Larry de Long, pastor of the Valley Presbyterian Church, delivered the benediction.

In the summer of 2011, I decided to take a five-thousand-mile solo drive across the country to visit the places and people who had been important to us—a sentimental journey. A description of that adventure can be found in the appendix.

76

After Leta's Death

Following Leta's death, I wanted to offer to each of our children and their families a two-week trip anywhere in the world. It was to be seen as a gift from their mother and me. It was also a statement that memories were an important part of inheritance. Memories will last longer than money. Our son Ed, his wife, and their children chose a trip to Thailand.

Our son Bob and his partner, Michael, chose to go to Europe as part of their inheritance gift. Meeting in Amsterdam, we rented a car and drove to Cologne, Germany, the site of a magnificent cathedral. Then we went through the Black Forest and into Switzerland, where we visited Michael's ancestral home.

After spending a week at a military resort in Garmish, Germany, we then toured part of the German landscape associated with Martin Luther and his journey.

Ed and his wife Micki and children chose Thailand.

Our daughter, Linda, and her husband Paul, our son Ed, his wife Micki, and his son Phillip and daughter Rebecca joined us in Paris to hear the Sons of Orpheus perform at the Notre Dame Cathedral and other venues in France.

After these performances, Linda arranged for a Airbnb for a week's stay on one of Normandy's beaches. It was deeply moving to visit the American Cemetery overlooking Omaha beach. Many interred here were still in their teenage years. We walked the beaches as well as visited various museums located at different sites. All were very impressive and were an important reminder for us to reflect on the history that forever changed the world

The Airborne Museum dedicated to the 82nd and 101st Airborne Division, located in the village of Sainte Mere Eglise, totally captivated me. I was totally entranced by the mockup of a combat jump vividly reminding me of my experiences as a paratrooper. Inspired by this event, I have dreamed and would be thrilled to make a commemorative parachute jump with an active military that takes place each year on D-Day at Normandy. While the odds of realizing this dream are heavily weighed against me, I continue to actively pursue this possibility

Prior to visiting Normandy, Linda, Paul, and I visited the sites where the 82nd Airborne jumped into the Netherlands, including the site of Nijmegen bridge and the museum. In a crucial battle, this bridge was captured and defended by the 82nd Airborne Division. We also visited the Margraten Cemetery, the only site in the Netherlands where US soldiers are buried. We also visited the impressive war museum at Bastogne.

As described elsewhere, Linda and Paul as well as our grandson Michael and wife Rebecca have visited Thailand on several occasions. Also described is the visit in 2017 to Surinam by Linda, Paul, and me. Her description of the Surinam trip is included in Linda's section of the Appendix.

A Concluding Word

As I reflect back on that summer night in 1946 when the moon was full and I was sitting against a shock of wheat in a nearby field, contemplating what might be, there was considerable apprehension. I had little confidence in my abilities, had performed badly in school, and developed few social skills. Still, I somehow sensed in that moment that beyond the apprehension I was experiencing, there was an exciting world out there about which I knew little and wanted to experience. I could have so easily stumbled but for the grace of God and the guidance and presence of so many teachers along the way. It has been an incredible journey. I am indebted in so many ways to my wife, who came into my life while I was still a teenager. She has been fully supportive of the many bends and turns of our journey together.

With the psalmist I can joyfully chant: "Surely goodness and mercy have followed me all the days of my life."

Well, grandchildren, that's my story and the story of how your grandmother impacted your grandfather's life. It's also part of your story. When you reach middle age and beyond and begin to look at whence you have come and where you are going, perhaps you will choose to read and reread these pages and recognize in a new way that we belong to each other.

Enjoy your journey!

Postscript

A number of people who have deeply touched our lives have been mentioned throughout this book in which we have tried to share some of the dimensions of our story. Of course, many more persons have blessed us along with the way. We are deeply grateful for the lives of our children and grandchildren, who bless us in so many ways.

Bob Price has remained as one of my closest friends for nearly seven decades. His very talented wife, Flo, is courageously facing the challenge of multiple sclerosis. Dr. Carroll and Marilyn Rinehart, as well as Dr. Harmon and Edith Myers, have been special friends with whom we have celebrated our lives in so many ways for over three decades. Harmon and Edith were involved in a serious automobile accident in 2008. After making significant progress during months of rehabilitation and recovery, Edith suffered a fatal aneurysm

On July 4, 2009, Harmon Myers and Betty Zimmerman were married. Betty's deceased husband, DeWayne, had been the renowned pastor of the First United Methodist Church. DeWayne and Betty had been close friends with Harmon and Edith as well as Carroll and Marilyn. Leta's and my association with the Zimmermans would come later. The special relationship between the Myers, Rineharts, and the Friesens continues with our thirty-five-year participation in the Arizona Theatre Company and the celebrations of each others' birthdays and anniversaries—and any other event we can think of to celebrate. I have spoken at length of Leta's passing, but she was the second member of our group to pass from mortality to immortality. Marilyn, an outstanding church organist at both the First United Methodist Church and the Catalina United Methodist Church, was to the next to pass.

Women tend to outlive men in our culture. In the case of the three couples described above, all the women passed first. Edith Myers passed away in 2008, Leta Friesen in 2010, and Marilyn Rinehart in 2011.

Harmon and Carroll were to have their final days in the same nursing home, although they were in different buildings. I had come to visit Harmon just as he was experiencing a medical crisis, a crisis from which he didn't survive.

My daughter, Linda, and her husband, Paul, along with Rev. Dr. Doug and Judy Bobbit were visiting Carroll together one week prior to his death. I am the last person in this close circle of friends still living. I miss them all. I am so grateful that we enjoyed such a rich relationship for all these years together.

Family

Our wedding picture, 1948

*Daughter Linda, Kent,
and their family*

Eugene, Leta, and family

Leta's high school photo, 1944

Eugene as a paratrooper, 1957

Bob and his partner, Michael

Eugene and Leta
Photo by Life Touch, Inc. Used with permission.

Family photo, 1956

Leta in Viet Nam

Eugene and Leta with Thai friends

Eugene with three-year-old daughter Linda.

Grandson, Michael and great-granddaughter Mary Lou.

Son Ed and his family at Mount Saint Michael's Cathedral in Normandy.

Eugene with his family in Paris.

Our Thai family with family members

Surinam

Trio Indian children gather with Eugene around airplane

Bob Price and Eugene Friesen in Surinam

No. A/1/1959

S U R I N A M

DEPARTMENT OF PUBLIC WORKS AND TRAFFIC

DIVISION OF CIVIL AVIATION

VALIDATION

of a Certificate of Competency and Licence in accordance with the
provisions of Article 14 of the enforcement-degree to the
Air Navigation Act.

THE MINISTER OF PUBLIC WORKS AND TRAFFIC

Seen the request of ___F R I E S E N___ ___E U G E N E___
___W E S L E Y___

dated ___OCTOBER 23___ 19 59

tending to render valid the Certificate of Competency and Licence

___PRIVATE PILOT___ No. 1431121

issued by the Competent Licensing Authority in

___UNITED STATES OF AMERICA___

on ___JANUARY 7___ 19 59

to ___EUGENE WESLEY FRIESEN___

for Surinam, as provided in Articles 22 and 24 of the abovement-
ioned degree.

In virtue of Article 14 of the Enforcement-degree;

Has approved of granting the validation applied for, subject
to renewal, suspension or withdrawal (Please turn over), until:

___D E C E M B E R 1 7, 1 9 5 9___

Paramaribo, OCTOBER 23 19 59

for Minister,
The Director of Civil Aviation,

Eugene's Surinam pilot's license

Sons of Orpheus

Eugene with the Sons of Orpheus Alta Pusteria in the Italian Alps.

Sons of Orpheus at San Xavier Del Bac in Tucson.

Rotary

Eugene receiving Service Above Self award from Rotary PDG Michael Drake.

Jemimah Semanahl and Rotary PDG Phil Silvers in Ghana.

Rotary Exchange group to Thailand in 2012.

Anan Loathamatos with his family in Thailand, Friendship Exchange, 2017.

Pat and Kan Pattanta.

*Rotary District
Governor Tom and
Marie Tilton*

Rotary Exchange group to Thailand in 2017.

Eugene gives the couple a blessing at Buddhist wedding in Thailand.

Buddhist wedding in Thailand.

*Caricature of Eugene Friesen by Bob Swaim, a retired architect
of Swaim Associates, Ltd. in Tucson, Arizona.*

Appendices

Appendix I
An Innkeeper Tells His Story

There is something so profound—so mysterious—about the birth of a child that Christians have the audacity to call Jesus the Son of God. The drama of Christmas and Easter is so captivating that people who may not regularly attend church services are drawn to this special time of year. To think that the Creator of trillions of galaxies would send an only son to this speck of dust that we call home is beyond comprehension. Yet we dare to embrace this drama as if our lives depended on this story—this story that for most of us is part of our earliest memories.

The Gospels do not record that Joseph and Mary arrived exhausted in Bethlehem late at night on the eve of her delivery of a newborn baby, pleading for shelter. I once read that there was a novelist in the third century who created this vivid story that caught the imagination of the folks, and it became deeply etched in the way that the Christmas drama has been celebrated for many centuries. I searched for the source of this story but obviously didn't search in the correct place.

The Gospels do record, however, the fact that Joseph and Mary arrived in Jerusalem in response to the decree of Caesar Augustus and that, while they were there, Mary gave birth to her child.

In the late 1980s, I was serving a new and developing congregation where we, in an attempt to be creative, did a lot of experimenting in creating new worship styles. A close friend, Carroll Rinehart, who was a music teacher par excellence, was a part of this experiment. During one Christmas season, we were working on what would be presented for the following Sunday's worship. As we were discussing the role of the innkeeper in the Christmas drama, I made the offhand comment that after his negative response to this couple's plea for a room in the overcrowded inn and after the dramatic visit of the shepherds and the Wise Men, he was to shrug his shoulders and say, "How was I to know?"

That response triggered an opera that the music teacher wrote and that premiered in the worship services, with members of the congregation participating in the opera. With that backdrop, I would like to give the central concepts of that opera by the telling of the Christmas story as if I were that innkeeper pictured in the opera.

Let me introduce myself. My parents gave me the name of David in honor of our greatest king. I am a retired innkeeper. I am a member of the synagogue—more active now than when I was absorbed in running an inn, which, as I am sure you will understand, was very demanding.

I want to share a story that occurred in my inn about thirty-five years ago. It was at a time when a census was being taken of the whole empire by that despicable Roman emperor, Caesar Augustus. The results of this census were sure to increase the heavy tax burden that we had.

The village of Bethlehem was full to overflowing. This census required that folks who lived elsewhere but had their origin here had to return for this census. This particular day had been hectic, and our inn was filled to capacity.

Just as the sun was setting, this man, who looked as if he was approaching his middle to late twenties, and his young spouse arrived, obviously exhausted. More than that, his wife was in the latest stages of pregnancy. The husband was obviously very anxious as he explained that they were desperate to find lodging because the baby would arrive soon. As much as I would like to have accommodated them, I explained that the inn had been fully occupied for several hours, and there simply wasn't any room. I apologized but added that there was nothing that I could do.

My wife overheard our conversation. When she realized the woman was going to deliver a child soon, her motherly instincts took over. She usually didn't overrule me, but that night, she did. She told this couple to rest while she began to order our servants to clear a place in our stable, which was attached to our inn. She improvised a makeshift bed for this woman, who was probably in her middle teens, to lie down on. Sure enough, the contractions began shortly thereafter, and my wife became the midwife and assisted with the birth of the child. Shortly after the child was cleaned up and placed in the arms of his mother, several unusual and unbelievable things began to happen.

It was a clear and very still night. The sky was full of stars that seemingly reached down to the horizon on every side. Most of the village residents and visitors were asleep when some very excited shepherds from a nearby hillside awkwardly rushed into the inn. While they were all illiterate, and their language was certainly unpolished, there was no question but that they had had a profound experience that prompted their excitement. Words that were often incoherent came tumbling out of their mouths, and they had a hard time explaining what they had seen and heard. It was a little hard to make out what they were saying. They said something about seeing a bright star and angels in the sky singing the most beautiful songs that they had ever heard. They said that this angelic choir sang something about "peace on earth and good will to men" and I'm almost sure that they said words like "glory to God in the highest." They kept repeating that these were the most beautiful songs that they had ever heard. They were so excited about what happened that they just had to share this exciting event.

What made this scene so unusual is that under normal

circumstances, the shepherds, who were the "nobodies" of this part of the world, wouldn't have dared to behave like this. Imagine these guys, considered trash in our community, crashing my inn like that. They were considered so unreliable that their word wasn't ever accepted in a court of law. Here they were, unbathed and smelly, and yet they were the first to announce the coming of the promised Messiah — the Savior of the World. Amazing, to say the least. They were the first to get this heavenly announcement.

To put it mildly, I was stunned. It was clear that something profound had happened. I almost missed this amazing drama that unfolded before my very eyes. And I was going to turn this couple away! I had no idea that this babe born in my stable was indeed a very special child. It was all beyond me. But how was I to know?

After getting a glimpse of the baby and showing their joy and enthusiasm, the shepherds eventually left and returned to the sheep they were watching — obviously for someone else. They didn't have two shekels to rub together.

Well, as stunning as the shepherd visit was, the night wasn't over. The next set of unexpected visitors really bowled me over. At first I couldn't really figure out who they were. They appeared to be members of the intellectual class who studied the stars. They looked like they were members of some royal family. They certainly were not of the Jewish faith. In fact, we would have considered them heathens. They said that they had been guided by a star and had been traveling through the desert for months. They said that they had come to see and worship the newborn 'King of the Jews.'

Their first stop had been in Jerusalem, where they assumed that a royal birth would take place. Their visit to the palace caused quite a stir. Isn't it strange how those who seem to have the power of life and death over people can be so insecure? Well, Herod referred them to the chief priests but with sinister motives — but that's another story. The chief priests identified Bethlehem as the site of this royal birth.

As these scholars started for Bethlehem, they told us how they saw the guiding star again leading them to the manger of my inn. They spoke about how excited they were after months of travel to finally arrive at the birthplace of a newborn king.

As stunned as I had been by the shepherds, I was totally unprepared when these royal scholars came by the inn in the late evening. In contrast to the uncouth shepherds, they came with princely demeanor, showing great respect in such an elegant way and giving gifts appropriate for a royal birth. All of us at the inn were clearly overwhelmed by this attention, but the young woman had had an earlier encounter with the angels, who had informed her that she was carrying in her body the long-expected one. She didn't seem surprised at all. In spite of her young age, she was the picture of serenity and peace. She obviously was in on this holy mystery from the beginning.

Well, I have never gotten over that evening. If it hadn't been for my wife, I would have missed the whole thing. I was pretty macho in those days and tended to take credit for the whole thing even though, if my wife hadn't overruled me, I would have turned this couple away. I am really embarrassed about a couple of things. First, that I was so insensitive to this couple's dilemma, and second, that I didn't give my wife credit that she deserved that night when she arranged for this couple to stay and ended up being the midwife on that night of nights.

Over the years, I kept hearing about this babe now grown up. He became quite a teacher and healer and, at least in the beginning of his public work, he drew great crowds but also opposition from the religious hierarchy. Then I heard that he was crucified during the Passover holidays. I couldn't figure that out. Why? It left me this queasy feeling in the stomach. The angels had announced his birth, after all. Then I heard that he had risen from the dead. I couldn't figure that out either. I had never heard of such a thing. But I also heard that his disciples were so totally convinced of this resurrection, and they had become a real force in our part of the world.

I still don't know what to make of it. I still go to the synagogue, and in many respects, life goes on. But that night some thirty years ago still haunts me. Without question, something mysterious and profound happened—and I almost missed it because I was so wrapped up in my world of survival at the time. But then, how was I to know?

One more memory. The Roman soldier who probably didn't have any kind of formal religious belief as far as I could tell was in charge of the events at the cross during Jesus's final brutal hours. This Roman soldier made a riveting comment just as death occurred. It went something like this: "Surely this man was the Son of God!" I think he was right. I still can't get over it. This tiny baby born in my inn was the Savior of the world. I can't explain it, but I know that my life was forever changed on that very special night. How was I to know?

Appendix II
Taking a Look in the Rearview Mirror

The summer of 2011, I decided to take what turned out to be a fifty-three-hundred-mile solo journey to the Midwest. While I could have taken to the skies as I typically do, I wanted to do some completion work related to my wife, Leta's, passing. I decided that this could best be done traveling by car. I would take in the landscape of our beautiful country and visit the homes of our children and other family members. I would relish seeing high school and college friends as well as former colleagues. Some of these friendships reached back as far as seven decades.

I was not interested in seeing new sites, but I wanted to immerse myself in the familiar—places where we had lived, worked, and enjoyed life together. This trip would lead to Kansas, Missouri, Ohio, Indiana, Michigan, Minnesota, Nebraska, Wyoming, and Utah before reaching my home at the end of a twenty-four-day journey.

Perhaps the climactic part of the journey for me was at a place called Little America, Wyoming. I vividly remembered what had occurred in early February 1965. My military unit was transferred as a unit, referred to as "gyroscoping," from Munich to Fort Ord, California. Leta and I and two young children, ages six and two, had picked up our car at the port of debarkation in New York. En route, we had visited Leta's family in Michigan and my family in Nebraska. We were traveling on Highway 30 through Wyoming. (It was before interstate highways or credit cards. We were traveling on a budget. A lieutenant's monthly pay was then about $4,000 a year.)

The fence posts on both sides of the road had been set back some distance—apparently in anticipation of the coming Interstate 80. My memory tells me that the fence posts from one side of the road to the other were at least a hundred yards apart. About mid-day, snow began to fall, and soon the road was invisible. To make matters worse, I didn't see any traffic on the road. I was making every effort to stay in the middle of those fence posts. There were a series of long rolling hills. I would drive down the hill as rapidly as I dared and barely make it to the top of the next hill, slowed by accumulating snow. Leta was examining the map, but there didn't appear to be any town near us. It was about 1600 hours, and the sky was already dark. To say that I was in full panic is a mild under-statement. The temperature was subzero. I was only too aware that my family was in grave danger.

Out of nowhere, we came across a gas station and a small ho-tel that was not on the map. Although we had planned to drive through the night, on that night, I would have gladly given my last dollar for the shelter that we received. On the wall of our room was the true legend of how that place came to be. Years earlier, a young man, attempting to get cattle to shelter before a predicted blizzard arrived, wasn't able to accomplish his mission. As he huddled be-tween the cattle that night to keep from freezing to death, he prom-ised himself that he would build a shelter for people "caught in a storm." We were the grateful recipients of his kept promise.

Fifty-five years later, I again stayed in Little America, now a thriving enterprise, and spent the night in a room similar to the one my family and I had occupied. I remembered and gave thanks that we had survived that evening—and I was thankful for all the events that would follow.

Appendix III

Linda Friesen—Memories of My First Ten Years

My grandpa Loew was fatally injured in a farming accident in western Michigan a few days before my third birthday. We were living in Columbia, South Carolina, where my father was serving as an Army chaplain. Since time was of the essence, my parents decided that we should fly back to Michigan for his funeral. We were in luck in that there were some open seats on my first flight, probably due to storm warnings in the area. Our pilot flew around the storms to the best of his ability. I remember the horrified faces of the passengers seated around us as I yelled, "Whee!" I enjoyed the sensations of turbulence. I remember being so puzzled when my mother kept asking me to be quiet and wondered why the other passengers didn't seem to enjoy my first flight as much as I did.

Our home in Columbia did not have a driveway or a garage, so we often parked in the neighbor's drive. One evening after Dad parked our car, I jumped out (booster seats had not yet been invented) and announced that I would run ahead and turn on the porch light to light the way for my parents. I remember running across my neighbor's yard in the pitch dark toward our house when their dog charged me, barking fiercely. I remember an overwhelming terror, and I instantly froze in my tracks. Within a matter of seconds, I felt the arms of my strong daddy picking me up. Even though it was still dark and the mean dog was still barking, I remember feeling safe in my father's arms. I am still very cautious around strange dogs, and my daddy continues to be my hero.

My mother kept homemade cookies in a jar on a very high shelf in the kitchen. I knew where they were, and I also was quite resourceful in finding them "in case of an emergency," of course. I remember Mom heading out to do some errands one afternoon when Dad came home from work. Dad was always a softer touch than Mom was when it came to asking for special favors. I remember asking my dad if I could have a cookie. He said I would have to wait until after dinner and promptly went back to reading his paper. I used a chair, climbed up on the cupboard to where I could finally reach the cookie jar, and brought it in to my father. With an innocent look, I asked my distracted Daddy if *he* would like a cookie. He almost fell for the bait, realizing that if *he* ate the cookie, he should be polite enough to offer *me* a cookie as well. He knew my plan!

I was four years old when Mom, Bobby, and I left my grandmother's home in Michigan to join my dad, who had deployed to Munich several months prior. I don't remember much about the train trip from Michigan to New York, except that my grandmother had advised Mom to keep me safe by securing me with a dog leash. How absolutely humiliating! I remember pleading my case with my poor mother, who was only doing her best to juggle two active children and luggage by herself.

Our military ship departed late December from New York, a time when the Atlantic typically has rough seas, and this passage lived up to the reputation. We shared a small cabin with another military wife and her small children. The cabin had only two sets of bunk beds. I remember many passengers, including my baby brother, being violently seasick much of the time. I also remember feeling the strong winds and hearing the powerful ocean on the nights we had to comply with the mandatory life jacket safety drills on deck. I remember how my mother warned me not to get too close to the edge, or I might slip off and drown. I also remember how amazed I was as I watched the dishes move back and forth across the dining room tables, which had wooden planks built on the sides. Mom and I were very happy to see my dad when we finally arrived in Germany. My baby brother, Bobby, had forgotten who Dad was in our months of separation and refused to go to him, much to my exhausted mother's chagrin and my delight.

Mom, Bob, and I lived in Media, Pennsylvania, with "Aunt" Flo, Gail, and Melody Price while preparations were made for us to join Dad and "Uncle" Bob in Paramaribo, Surinam. One Saturday after my weekly (yes, weekly!) bath, I felt a great deal of abdominal pain and lay down on the couch. Around midnight, Mom took me to the emergency room. At almost nine years old, I remember Mom picking me up and carrying me in since it hurt too much to walk. I remember the doctor asking me if it hurt as he pushed his fist into my inflamed stomach and me crying out with unbearable pain. I recall being rolled into the operating room and later observing the doctors remove my appendix from my view from the ceiling. I have heard some people call this an out-of-body experience. I just thought it was an interesting and comforting view. I didn't share that experience with anyone for many years because I didn't want anyone to think I was crazy.

When I woke up, I was in a bed with side rails in the hallway. Mom couldn't visit till visiting hours. I remember having to use the restroom and ringing the bell for the nurse. After waiting till I felt I would burst, I gingerly climbed over the rail and found the restroom by myself. The nurses found out about this little escapade and sternly scolded me. I explained I would not have to climb over a railing if they had me in a regular bed instead of a crib. After all, I was almost nine years old!

After having my stitches removed and recovering for a couple of weeks, we started our journey to join my Dad in Surinam, South America. We flew from Philadelphia to New York's LaGuardia Airport. I remember Mom leaving me to watch my six-year-old brother, Bob, while she frantically rushed around, trying to find our international flight. She was apparently unaware that we needed to take a bus from LaGuardia to Idlewild Airport (now known as JFK International Airport).

I loved the flight on KLM Royal Dutch Airlines. The flight attendants were so nice and pretty and that started my dreams of working for an airline one day. We flew from New York to Curacao, where the airline provided a nice hotel with all meals for a couple of days while we waited for our connecting flight. We loved the swimming pool at the hotel and seeing the famous swinging bridge open and close so the ships could enter the port of Willenstad.

Most people are surprised that neither Spanish nor Portuguese is spoken in the northern South American country of Surinam. The Dutch and British traded the island of Manhattan for the entire country of Surinam in 1667. The Dutch motivation for this trade was to cultivate sugar to sweeten their famous chocolate. The old flag of Surinam best depicted the colorful melting pot of the people who live in this tiny country. The white star represented the Europeans; the black star represented the Creoles, who descended from African slaves; the brown star was for the Asian Indians; and the yellow star was for the Chinese. Both of the latter races arrived as indentured servants to work on the sugar plantations. The red star represented the Native American Indians. You hear multiple languages in Paramaribo, but Dutch is the official language.

Dad picked us up at the airport, and we spent our first evening in the country with our new missionary friends, Walt and Marge Jackson, and their children. In preparation for school the next day, Beth Jackson taught us our first Dutch phrase, *"Hoe heet je?"* (It's pronounced *who hate yah*.) It translates to English as, "What is your name?" I remember children gathering Bob and me on the playground the next day, and a little boy asking Bobby, "Hoe heet je?" I have to admit, I burst out laughing when he responded, *"Nobody hates me ... I'm perfect."*

Bobby and I, along with the principal, were the only people who spoke English in my elementary school. That necessitated our need to learn Dutch, fast. Since our original plan had been to live in Surinam for two years, the educational action plan designed by my dad and the principal was for me to repeat the second and third grades my first year and then catch me up to my proper grade level in our second year. I attended the second and third grades two times and never attended the fourth grade. I graduated right on time with my classmates with whom I started kindergarten.

A Dutch boy by the name of Donald Deuck (pronounced *Duck*, really!) and I were the only Caucasian students in my class, with most of the children being of Indonesian descent. I was really jealous of the shiny black hair of the Indonesian girls and decided to emulate them by putting Vaseline in my hair to make it really shiny. Needless to say, my mother did not appreciate my decision and shampooed my hair multiple times until the shiny Vaseline was gone.

Our classroom did not have glass windows—only open windows with bars. Our wooden desks had holes in the front just large enough for an inkbottle, since we were learning to use fountain pens. We would practice drawing the ink into the pen while trying not to get the ink all over our fingers. One time, during a practice session, the very naughty boy who sat behind me dipped my braided hair into the inkbottle. I guess, for him, it was too much temptation to resist.

Dutch standards were very strict. My father recalled his appointment with the principal being a little delayed as he watched the principal teach a young boy not to fail another test by whipping him. As a Dutch colony, we learned about and celebrated important days in the life of the Royal Dutch family in our classroom.

In order to expedite my fluency in the Dutch language, my parents hired an older Indonesian lady as my private tutor. She told me interesting stories about surviving the horrors of World War II. I was shocked when she told me food was so scarce that her family once paid a dollar for one egg. During those tutoring days, I had to take a public bus by myself and walk a couple of blocks past some very mean, barking dogs before I could get to my lesson. It is astounding to me that at nine years old, my parents allowed me to take a public bus, by myself, in a third-world country.

One of the greatest gifts my parents gave me was the mindset that I had been given unique opportunities never to be misconstrued as being given insurmountable challenges. With that mindset, after living in Paramaribo for only one year and four days, I became more fluent in Dutch than in English. I dreamed in Dutch and communicated with everyone except my parents in Dutch, including my brother. My parents never hinted then nor admit to this day that this feat was an exceptional challenge. The expectations were that I would not only thrive, but also soar, and they were right.

My father and "Uncle Bob" were local celebrities of sorts. They assisted the Surinam government by flying missions for "Operation Grasshopper," a project to locate natural resources and construct runways within the rugged interior of the country. In addition, the project included contacting Indians who had never met anyone from the outside world. Several pilots crashed and perished the year we lived in Surinam. My dad actually crashed his little Piper Cub aircraft twice in the jungles of Surinam. As a child, it never occurred to me that my daddy might die when he flew out of town.

My mother, who often could not communicate with Dad for days or weeks, never showed my brother and me any sign of the stress she must have felt. It was not until I had children that I recognized that my mother was equally, or maybe more, amazing than my dad.

As a child, I loved our home in Paramaribo, especially the large front porch, where we had a hammock next to a giant rubber tree with its big, cool shiny leaves. We grew pineapples, bananas, and coconuts in our yard. Surinam is a little north of the equator, and we had no air-conditioning or even a fan to cool us down. We had to leave the windows open most of the time to keep it as comfortable as possible, but doing so also allowed the mosquitoes and bats to enter our home without invitation. Mom made me the most amazing mosquito net, which was (of course) designed to keep me safe from the mosquitoes carrying malaria. I felt like a princess in that bed, with the beautiful white netting falling around me.

Our toothbrushes had to be covered when not in use since we didn't want to give the tiny wall frogs the opportunity to cool off on their wet surfaces. We had no refrigerator, stove, oven, or washing machine. Sometimes Mom would buy ice from a truck that frequented our neighborhood. Mom had to ride her bicycle to the market every day to purchase food from people she did not understand. She tried to keep us all healthy with good nutrition, but I know I gave her a very hard time over drinking the lukewarm, reconstituted powdered milk. It simply tasted horrible! In the end, both Mom and I had to take medication for intestinal parasites.

We had no television, and come to think of it, there was probably no television station in the country. If we had had a television, there would have been nothing to see. I never recall being bored, however. I often played with my Betsy Wetsy doll that I had brought from the United States. Most of the time, we played outside either in flip-flops or barefoot.

On one occasion, I remember encouraging my younger brother to follow my example and experience the sensation of floating down the steps with an umbrella (like my dad did as a paratrooper). It was so much fun that I jumped multiple times. I wanted to share this experience with my brother, so I gave him a gentle push, since I was sure if he tried it once, he would want to do it again. He rewarded my encouragement by breaking his arm, just to get me in trouble. The sad part of this story is that this little mishap occurred during the late afternoon on a Friday, and the emergency room at the hospital was closed till Monday.

The Indians once gave my Dad a green parrot and a toucan. Polly, the parrot, was mean and a little stupid. She did not learn to talk until the day she got battered around in a tropical storm. She promptly died the next day.

I *loved* the toucan that I named Pinto. Pinto would proudly perch herself on the handlebars of my bike as we went riding around the block. With her large, beautiful beak, she commanded the respect of the ducks, chickens, and the parrot at mealtime. She would dine to her heart's content and then the "dinner table" was open to the other fowl. In addition to the feed, Pinto loved our fruit trees, especially the cherry tree. She would put a cherry in her beak and roll it back and forth until it had enough momentum to go down her throat whole. I was absolutely heartbroken the day I watched Pinto swallow a cherry that was a little too large and watched her suffocate to death. It was one of the few days my mother excused me from school since she understood how devastated I was.

Some of my best memories of Surinam are centered on the 1949 black French Citroen that my parents purchased from the widow of one of the pilots who had perished in the jungle. The windshield wipers had to be operated by hand (preferably by a front-seat passenger) and the turn signals were little flags that popped out on the left or right side of the vehicle. Sometimes, when you least expected it, the driver's side wheel would roll off as we were driving down the road. I can't understand how the car kept upright with one missing wheel, but somehow it did. This car provided a lot of comic relief for our family.

We returned to the United States at the end of September 1960, a few days after my tenth birthday. Within three months of our return, I was the only family member who was not hospitalized. Bob had pneumonia. Dad contracted pneumonia and malaria. My new baby brother, Eddie, was born on the twelfth of December. I was aware that we were going through some very tough financial times. Our only source of income was the GI bill that my dad activated to begin his master's degree at the Michigan State University.

Kudos for my parents. I knew we didn't have much (any) money, but I never did realize that we were actually poor.

The world, my world has changed so much in the 57 years since my family left Suriname. New members have joined our family and others have sadly left.

My dearest friends understand that I treasure my Suriname experience and the lessons my family learned in that short fragment of time. I am deeply honored that my husband Paul and my dear friend Dee and her husband Allan were willing to join Dad and me on a trip to Suriname in September 2017.

To us, Suriname is much more than a country; it is an intimate insight into our past.

Most people have never heard of the country of Suriname, a place where I lived between September 1959 and September 1960. This small country in Northern South America, with a current estimated population of a little over a half a million inhabitants is a significant part of my family history. I really wanted to return with my father and share in person as much of this history I could with my husband Paul and my very dear friend Dee as well her husband Allan.

I checked the US State Department web site (Step.gov) and saw no warnings for US travelers even though Suriname's President was a former coup leader, convicted of drug trafficking and accused of murder by the Netherlands government. I was a little concerned how we might be treated since his son is currently serving a 16-year sentence in United States for drug trafficking, firearms charges, and offering a home base to the Lebanese paramilitary group of Hezbollah. I am happy to report that I never felt any danger while visiting Suriname; in fact, I felt like a valued guest.

Even in 2017, it is a challenge to get to Suriname from the United States with limited air service from the western hemisphere. Caribbean Air and Suriname Air fly a couple days a week from Aruba, Curacao and Trinidad but do not offer airline discounts and were quite costly. KLM flies four times a week from Amsterdam to Paramaribo and offers active and retired airline employees a discount, however, the discount isn't offered to parents. Travel plans were coordinated so that Dad would fly Delta standby to Aruba and then continue on Suriname Air to Paramaribo. Dee and Allan would fly standby on United Airlines to Amsterdam and meet up with me and Paul who would fly standby on Delta to Amsterdam. The four of us would fly standby the next day on a KLM 747 jet to Paramaribo.

There were a few scheduling obstacles we had to overcome in the 3 weeks prior to our trip. Dee and Allan needed to help one daughter by assisting other grandchildren with the arrival of a new grandson, then helped another daughter relocate out of state, and "closed" on a new home in Nevada. We had to make sure our departure did not conflict with the promotion ceremony of Paul's son Jeffrey to "Chief" in the Navy. There were also a few major hurricanes terrorizing the Caribbean, which concerned me about Dad's trip via Aruba. Somehow or another, the obstacles dissipated and we were all on our way. Fortunately, everything just seemed to fall into place.

Our Delta flight from Detroit to Amsterdam arrived Sunday

morning approximately an hour and a half prior to the arrival of Dee and Allan on United. We met up in front of the train ticket counter and made our way to the Marriott located in The Hague (DenHaag) since the hotels were extra expensive that night in Amsterdam. Even a 2-star hotel was over $222 a night, while we could reserve the Marriott with an airline discount 30 minutes south by rail for just a little over $100. We were hoping for an early check in since we didn't get much sleep on our all-night flights, but that wasn't possible. So, we stored our bags with the bell captain and bought a day tram pass and took off to find something to eat in the adjacent beach resort of *Scheveningen and then on to Delft. When we finally made our way back to the hotel, dead beat, we settled down for an early night's rest in preparation of our KLM flight the next morning to Paramaribo.*

KLM rarely upgrades and graciously assigned us the best coach seats possible on the 747 in rows 63HJ and 64HJ, a rare 2-seat section. We had brought along crew treats and were treated very well by our flight attendants on this 9-hour, 4667-mile flight. On a side note, I was surprised that many of the passengers in our section of the aircraft were Chinese who didn't appear to speak Dutch or English. The Chinese are emigrating in large numbers to Suriname and are welcomed as very hard workers. Most of the road construction and most of the businesses and casinos are owned by Chinese immigrants.

After passing through multiple time zone changes, again, we arrived in Paramaribo around 3:30 pm, made our way to purchase our tourist cards, pass through immigration, pick up our luggage and find Mark, the owner of the Airbnb who was transporting us to the apartment. After changing out of our travel clothing, Mark had his trusty assistant Anthe ("Anthony") take us to Restaurant Jawa for some tasty Indonesian food. The food was very flavorful, but the servings were a little too large for us to finish.

Our Airbnb was an upstairs apartment close to downtown Paramaribo with air conditioning in each bedroom, WIFI, kitchen, small living room, bath and a half, front balcony, and a lovely back patio area to converse, eat and enjoy the rain. Our hosts provided many breakfasts, washed clothing, and provided transportation to restaurants and sightseeing within the city and out to French Guiana. The attention to our comfort and enjoyment more than made up for a few errors in the ad they had posted on the Airbnb web site.

My elementary school *J.H.N. Polanenschool* has not changed one single bit since 1960 (57 years!). The principal's office is still the only room in the school with glass window panes. We walked around the school, took pictures, and then headed to our former home, which has been through an extreme update. The lady of the home tied up the dogs and then walked us around to the backyard for pictures. The tennis courts (across the street from our former home) have been expanded into a very nice private club with the addition of a swimming pool, meeting rooms, restaurant, and bar. We headed to Zorg en Hoop Airport where Dad used to fly in and out of the interior with his Piper Cub.

I had mentioned to Mark that I remembered a delicious fruit with very thick skin we called *pamplemousse*. Mom used to giggle when she peeled the very thick peeling and we would finally get down to the edible fruit. Mark took us to the Central Market, found some *pamplemousse* in the market, and asked if the seller could trim off part of the very thick skin for us. The English word for the fruit is Pomelo and it was as delicious as I remembered it!

I had asked Mark if he could help us arrange a trip to French Guiana since there are now paved roads. Mark was raised in Paramaribo but left to get his degree and live in New York during the years of turbulent uprising. He and his wife (a pediatric ICU nurse) were vacationing for a couple of weeks in Suriname and decided a trip to French Guiana would be a great idea. After stopping by the bank for some Suriname dollars, we started our 95-mile drive from Paramaribo to the far eastern border town of Albina on the banks of the Marowijne (Maroni) River. A small boat (without lifejackets) was arranged for our crossing into the French Guiana town of Saint Laurent du Maroni. French Guiana is an overseas department of France in South America. The first thing I noticed was that prices were much higher in stores as they were quoted in euros. Saint Laurent du Maroni is known as a former penal colony. The 1858 Camp de la Transportation has cells and a museum. Henri

Charrière, author of "Papillon," was reputedly an inmate. The administrative center of the prison, known as Petit Paris, is notable for its colonial buildings. Nowadays, it is reputed that some Suriname citizens cross the river to give birth and register their child's birth to claim dual citizenship Suriname/French. As soon as we stepped off the boat on our return to Albina, it started to sprinkle and then rain hard. No worries, we were on vacation; just a few minutes walking and a late lunch/early dinner. On our way out of town we hit a dreaded *Drempel* (speed bump) a little too hard and lost part of the apparatus which secured the spare tire under the vehicle. The spare was put in the luggage hold, and off we went; unable to make it to the traditional Maroon (Bush Negro) villages but a fun and enjoyable day.

There were strict weight restrictions for the charter flight to the Wayana village of Apetina in south eastern Suriname, so, unfortunately, Allan and Paul stayed behind. Due to the hurricanes in the Caribbean and fuel priority for humanitarian efforts, we were told that we were the only non-critical flight on MAF (Mission Aviation Flights). We were weighed along with everything we were bringing on board. I was a little concerned when the pilot gave us a safety briefing, which included letting us know where the red bag was located with emergency survival supplies as well as an additional emergency locator beacon. After the safety briefing, the aircraft would not start without a battery and jumper cables. They mentioned that they were sure there was more fuel in Apetina for our return trip. The seating was quite tight and a more than a little uncomfortable, but the views were amazing and Dad was having the time of his life in the right-hand seat chatting with the pilot. After we landed on the grass air strip, Dee and I rolled out of the aircraft and headed down a very steep, muddy hill to the dugout with an engine that transported us to the village.

The missionaries opened their house so we could comfortably rest in the shade and have some lunch. Dee and I were especially grateful to be able to use the inside facilities, although I must admit I jumped and almost screamed when a very small frog jumped out of the toilet paper roll. We were shown around the village by the missionaries. I visited this village in 2005 with both my parents and my children and noted some major improvements: an elementary school, rain water collection barrels, a generator for electricity, and the natives are now raising chickens and building a vocational/high school. There is an outside group called the Amazon Conservation Team which lives within the village seeking information from the Indians about ancient herbal cures. Many people now have cell phones and were not at all offended that we were interested in taking pictures. I was especially interested in seeing the sweet cassava bread and beverage process from root to shredding to baking over the fire and then letting dry on the tin roofs. One absolutely beautiful macaw appeared to pose for us as we took its picture with cassava bread drying on the roof in the background. We went to one hut where the couple were probably in their 60s. The woman was interested in our ages and our children and grandchildren. She admired my ugly floppy camouflage hat and was quite happy when I presented it to her as my gift. Before leaving the village for our return flight, a Trio Indian man came into the house to sell a few of his spears and asked to say a prayer on our behalf. It was quite touching, being prayed for in the Trio language.

We returned to the airstrip. This time it was much more challenging to get out of the dugout without capsizing the boat and climbing up the steep but now dry hill. The pilot checked the extra fuel barrels which were stowed under a thatched roof structure and found there was no extra fuel. He also checked the amount of fuel in the aircraft. Then off we went skirting around thunderstorms back to Paramaribo, seemingly unconcerned. I was happy to land safely at Zorg en Hoof airport and roll off the plane with Dee, even though the MAF manager mentioned to Dee that our exit from the aircraft was not very ladylike.

In the *have to see it to believe it* category, we had the opportunity to experience something that only happens on Sunday mornings in Paramaribo. Men gather together with their very small black *twa twa* songbirds in cages. These birds are purchased at a very young age from the interior of the country and taught to mimic specific melodies by listening to a CD. Four times in the year, there is a competition to determine which bird is able to sing the loudest with the closest replication of the melody from theCD. The latest competition had taken place earlier in the month, but every Sunday morning, the men met as friends with their bird cages on poles a measured distance apart, either in front of the presidential palace or on a soccer field. It is seemingly a social event for the men to get out of the house and enjoy each other's company. You could close your eyes and imagine you were in a Walt Disney movie listening to the beautiful singing birds.

Built in 1640 by the French, taken over by the British, and later by the Dutch in 1651, Fort Zeelandia is a well restored star-shaped fortress. The fortress is situated on a high plot of land in a sharp bend in the river Suriname. Its pentagon therefore has three bastions facing the river. The two other bastions, between the entrance to the fort, face inland where in former times a wall and moats supplied extra protection. After the Surinamese independence in 1975, during the military government in the 1980s, Fort Zeelandia was the location of the "December murders" of 1982 and was used to hold and torture and murder political prisoners. Today, the fort is used as a museum with many historical structures surrounding the area, a peaceful place to pass a little time.

On our return to the Paramaribo Airport, Anthe suggested that we stop and pick up 2 kilos of *Pinda Sambel,* a Surinamese/Javanese peanut sauce mix at a local distributor. Dee and I thought that would be a fantastic idea. She would carry back the spears from the jungle and I would find a place in my luggage for the *Pinda Sambel.* After making our purchase, we continued to the airport when Anthe noticed some men putting a very large anaconda snake into a pickup bed. We stopped to check it out but were unable to get any good photos of this snake, who was making itself comfortable in a vacated house. We got to the airport 3 hours early and each checked one bag and made our way to the waiting area. The PA system in the waiting area was difficult to understand due to the echoing, but I thought I heard my name. I approached the desk and was advised that I must follow the police officer since there was something questionable in my checked bag. I surrendered my passport and was asked to open my suitcase for further inspection by the young police officer who was my daughter's age. The *Pinda Sambel* apparently looked like a block of drugs to them. I explained that I lived for a short time as a child in Paramaribo and returned for a walk down memory lane with my father, husband, and friends. I pulled out my phone and showed the police officer the picture of all of us in front of my elementary school. She looked closely at the photo and said... I went to the *J.H.N. Polanenschool* as well. What an amazing coincidence and helpful in redeeming my integrity.

After being assigned into two very full rows on our KLM return flight to Amsterdam, we had Allan ask the flight attendant (since he was on the aisle) if we could move back to the 2-seat section we had on the outbound in rows 63 and 64 if it remained unused. Our request was accepted and the 9 hours back to Amsterdam were much more comfortable. Dee shared with the flight crew that we had celebrated my birthday in Paramaribo. Later in the flight another flight attendant who was celebrating her birthday brought us all first class amenity kits and some chocolates for me.

Luckily the Best Western at the Amsterdam Airport location let us check in as soon as we arrived, which allowed us to get a few hours of sleep prior to our leisurely canal cruise through scenic Amsterdam. We were up early the next day for our excursion to Haarlem to visit the Corrie ten Boom museum (The Hiding Place). I have visited this museum multiple times and it touches me deeply every time how the ten Boom family chose risking their lives by assisting over 600 Jewish people with the Dutch underground movement during World War II. We also found time for a canal cruise in Haarlem, a very nice way to see this beautiful part of the world.

Next morning, back to the US again, this time in Business class to Portland with the opportunity to take a comfortable nap in the flat bed seat. Then home via Los Angeles. More than 24 hours in transit. Very fun and memorable trip but so good to sleep in our own bed!

Appendix IV

Bob's Memories

Linda mentioned the open windows and bats. While my parents and Linda have different memories, my recollection was that the bats would invariably want to "visit" when we had company in the evenings. I don't remember the mosquito nets keeping all the mosquitoes out, but I remember the sound of the bats hitting them. Many years later, even looking at a picture of a bat would nearly paralyze me. It would take every ounce of effort just to turn the page to another picture.

Linda's mention of cookies makes me recall an incident that happened either in Sunfield or Three Rivers. I must have been around ten years old, and I was in the kitchen playing mountain climber, crawling up the cabinets. It never occurred to me that the cabinets weren't securely bolted to the walls. I was standing on a chair and reached up to pull myself up when the cabinets tore loose from the wall. There was a mighty crash! Mom came running, and I could see her tears. Those shelves held her prized china from her grandmother, and I destroyed the souvenirs of her past. I regret that to this day—one of my most painful and guilt-filled memories.

My best companions growing up were the pets we had. When we stayed with the Prices before moving to Paramaribo, there was a cat in the house named Mrs. Gray. In Surinam, there was the parrot and the toucan Linda mentioned, and we also inherited a bunch of chickens and a few geese that chased me (I was sort of afraid of them and avoided them). For my seventh birthday, my parents gave me a dachshund that I dearly loved. When she arrived, she was mangy, but we restored her to health. Linda wanted to name her Ginger, but I favored the name Peanut Butter. We finally decided on Peanuts. We gave one of her offspring to Bob and Flo Price, who named the male Brahms, and one of his offspring was given back to us. Again, Dad overruled my suggested name, Archie. (There was a man in the congregation by that name, and Dad didn't want to offend him.) So Archie became Snoopy. Snoopy had a companion, a Siamese cat named Misty, who would occasionally jump on Snoopy's back, and they would wander around the back yard that way.

Linda and I are close in age, but Eddie is quite a bit younger. We loved him to pieces, but he often got in our hair. On one occasion (living in St. Johns), he wanted to play "Houdini," but I was required to weed the garden. Solution: tie him up with old rope as he requested, put him in the bedroom closet, and go do my work. There was a wrinkle, though—as soon as I went outside, he started moaning. When Mom, horrified, found him he said, "Tell Bob whatever I did to get him mad, I'm sorry." And I was punished.

Another time, it was past his bedtime, but he wanted to eavesdrop by listening through the floor to something that was happening downstairs. Linda and I warned him to go to bed. No response. Again, no response. He fell asleep on the floor, and we painted his hands, feet, and face with shoe polish.

On a third occasion, at Christmastime, he wouldn't go to bed, so I hid his presents and wrapped up sticks and stones for Christmas presents instead.

Appendix V
Bonnie Jean Wiseman Friesen

In my view, three things need to happen to make a memorial service complete.

First, I believe that it is important to focus on our Sacred Writings, which have given comfort and strength to people of faith for millennia; second, to give at least a brief focus on the meaning of our days and hope for what is to be; and third, to celebrate the life of Bonnie Jean.

For our scripture references, I want to share Psalms 139 and 23 from the Hebrew Scriptures, and chapter 13 from St Paul's first letter to the Corinthians.

O Lord, you have examined our hearts and know everything about us. You know when we sit or stand or lie down. You chart the path ahead of us and tell us where to stop and rest. You know what we are going to say before we say it. You both proceed and follow us and lay your hand of blessings on our head.

This is too glorious, too wonderful to believe. I can never be lost to your Spirit! I can never get away from my God. If I go up to the heavens, you are there. If I go down to the place of the dead, you are there. If I ride the morning winds to the farthest oceans, even there your hand will guide me; your strength will uphold me. If I try to hide in the darkness, the night becomes light around me. For even darkness cannot hide from God; to you the night shines as bright as the day. Darkness and light are both alike to you.

You have made all the delicate inner parts of my body and knit them together in my mother's womb. Thank you for making me so wonderfully complex! It is amazing to think about. Your workmanship is marvelous and is so impressive. You were there when I was being formed in utter seclusion! You saw me before I was born and scheduled every day of my life before I began to breathe. Every day was recorded in your book.

How precious it is, Lord, to realize that you are thinking about me constantly! I can't even count the number of times a day that your thoughts turn toward me. When I awaken in the morning, you are still thinking about me!

In Paul's letter, we find these words:

If I speak with the tongues of men and of angels, and have not love, I become like a sounding brass or a clanging symbol. If I have the gifts of prophecy and can predict the future with accuracy; if I understand all the mysteries of the Universe and have accumulated all the knowledge available to human kind; if I have faith enough to remove mountains but have not love, I've missed the point. If I give all I have to the poor and dispossessed and am martyred for my faith not love, I've lost my way.

Love is very gentle and kind, never jealous or envious, never boastful or proud, never arrogant, selfish or rude. Love does not demand its own way. It is rarely touchy or moody. It doesn't hold grudges and will put other people's fault in the best possible light.

Love is very concerned about truth and justice and is

deeply offended when the rich and powerful have taken advantage of the poor and voiceless but celebrates when truth and justice have won the day.

All the special gifts and powers from God will someday disappear but love goes on forever. Someday prophecy and speaking in unknown languages will simply dissipate because they will no longer be needed. Even with this special knowledge, we know so little and even the words of the most eloquent preacher are inadequate. But when we have been perfect and complete, then these special gifts will no longer be needed and simply disappear.

When I was a child, I thought, understood, and spoke as a child. When I became an adult, I was impacted by so much new knowledge that my childhood ways of understanding the world could no longer cope with the vastness of this new information. In the same way, we now understand so little about God. It's as if we were peering into a shattered mirror. Someday, we are going to see God face to face. Now all that I know is miniscule and blurred, but then I shall see clearly. There are three things that are eternal: faith, hope and love, but the greatest of these is love.

The final scripture is the psalm that is universally known and loved.

The Lord is my Shepherd. I have need of nothing. He makes me to lie down in green pastures and beside quiet streams and there restores my soul. He leads me in paths of righteousness, for his name's sake. Even though I walk through the valley death, I will fear no evil for Thou are with me; Thy staff and rod comfort me.

You prepare a table before me in the presence of my enemies. You anoint my head with oil. My cup runs over. Surely goodness and mercy has followed me all the days of my life and I will dwell in the house of the Lord forever.

Now a brief word about our short journey through life: we live in a sea of miracles.

There is the miracle of the heavens. When I was a child of seven or eight, I used to sit all alone at night on the steps leading to the porch at our farmhouse near Madrid, Nebraska, and gaze into the starlit heavens for long times. It seemed to me that the stars reached down to the earth. I was amazed and somewhat apprehensive at the vastness of it all. In comparison, I felt so inadequate. I wondered how the Creator God could be concerned about me. I had no idea that, according to astronomers and other scientists, there are more than a trillion galaxies, and our earth that seems so vast to us is hardly a speck of dust in comparison.

Then, I didn't know anything about atoms or the delicate but powerful components of atoms. Only in the very recent past, as I understand it, has there been a microscope developed that is powerful enough to capture this mysterious world of the atom.

The miracle of birth, described in Psalm 139, is truly mysterious and wonderful. That two microscopic cells from among millions come together in a most profound way is truly beyond description.

Then there's the miracle of maturation. How is it possible that this child of miracles, so helpless, so defenseless, develops in so many amazing ways? We truly can't begin to grasp the potential of this newborn, vulnerable child.

Love is the most powerful dynamic and, in many respects, is the glue that holds everything, including the universe, together. Bonds of love are so powerful. At this time of the year, we remember that all of us have been loved beyond comprehension long before time began.

The aging process is equally mysterious. In so many ways, it is hard to comprehend how every person, regardless of their talents or status, must one day leave all that they have ever known and return to dust from whence they have come. In a short time, all of us here will join Bonnie Jean into what lies beyond what we now know.

Perhaps the greatest mystery of all is the notion that there is life after life. No explanation can possibly do justice to the mystery that we are part of that which is eternal. I can't begin to describe how we will be a part of that heavenly experience. Will I see and recognize my wife of sixty-two years in that heavenly realm? Will you see your mother and grandmother again? The scriptures are silent on this question. All I can say with assurance is that we will be in God's presence forever. For me, that is enough! Far more than enough! We cannot begin to imagine what the Creator of all life has planned for us.

And now it's time to celebrate the life of Bonnie Jean Wiseman Friesen. Bonnie Jean was a valued high school friend and a member of the youth group here in Ogallala. Let me tell you some of the reasons why she and the small members of this group were so important to me.

Nobody would guess that during my high school days, I was extremely shy and felt uncomfortable among most of my classmates. I remember that I dreaded to go out in the city for fear that I would meet these classmates and wouldn't know what to say.

But this shyness would disappear with my closest friends, Bonnie Jean, Dottie, Bob, and Don Molle. My brothers, Claire and Merle, would also be in that group in spite of intense sibling rivalry. In many respects, they were my anchors, my lifeline to life. Without them, I would have been extremely isolated, and my future would likely have been dismal. With them, I felt fully included, and I could feel hope for the future.

While my contact with Bonnie Jean as an adult has been limited, she struck me as a person whose personality didn't change over the years. I remember her as a pleasant, warm, receiving, and loving person.

The Friesen brothers probably weren't the easiest people to live with, but each of their wives handled the changing circumstances in their married lives with real poise and dignity.

This was certainly true in Bonne Jean's case. She was a real champion when their resources were extremely limited, especially in the early days of their marriage. My bride and I made a quick visit from Michigan to Nebraska on our honeymoon for her to meet my parents and my relatives for the first time.

We spent several days with Bonnie Jean and Claire just before that horrendous blizzard of January 1949, which arrived with such fury. We later learned that their pantry shelves were nearly bare, and there was no way to get to the grocery store. Claire and Bonnie cooked wheat from the granary to survive. Cherri was still an infant.

Bonnie Jean was a survivor for sure. She was one of the most loyal, accepting, and loving persons I have ever known. Her dependability was never in question. The Corinthians letter, which was shared earlier, spoke of love as being very patient and kind, never being jealous or envious, never selfish or rude. She wasn't resentful and didn't hold grudges. Her word was her bond. As far as I am concerned, she fits St Paul's description of love to a *T*.

I am proud that I was included in her family. My life has been enriched because Bonnie Jean lived, walked among us, and was part of my life.

DE WEST

Dagblad uit en voor Suriname

ver D. G. A. FINDLAY, Waterkant 10 Telefoon Prive 3337, Administratie 3338, Redactie 3339 P. O. B. 176 Administr

Friesen terug van de Sipaliwini-savanah

Na een afwezigheid van zes weken keerde de Amerikaanse zendeling-vlieger E. Friesen gisternamiddag terug in Paramaribo. Gedurende deze zes weken bevond de heer Friesen zich in het gebied tussen de Sipaliwini-Savannah en het Kaysser Gebergte. Hedenmorgen vertrok de heer Friesen opnieuw naar het zuiden.

De voorbereiding

Enige tijd geleden landde de heer Friesen op de Sipaliwini-savannah in een Piper Super Cub. Een stuk terrein op deze savannah werd toen schoongemaakt, zodat volgende vluchten met minder risico konden geschieden.

Vervolgens vloog de heer Friesen naar Brits Guyana en haalde daar de zendeling Claude Leavitt, die reeds tien jaren werkzaam is onder de Wai Wai Indianen, wier taal hij bestudeerd heeft.

Met de heer Friesen kwamen ook mede drie Wai Wai Indianen, respectievelijk genaamd Jafoema, Ketifaka en Kafeana.

Op 4 februari jl. was de heer Friesen terug op de Sipaliwini Savannah en met zijn vier metgezellen trok hij onmiddellijk naar het noorden.

Reeds de volgende dag werd contact gemaakt met een aantal Trio's. Op deze tocht passeerden de twee Amerikanen en de drie Wai-Wais de Alkalapi rivier, welke de Trio's Arro noemen.

Het eerste Trio dorp was niet groot. Er waren hierin nauwelijks vijftien personen.

Ook waren de kampen in dit dorpje opvallend klein.

Bij de komst van de beide blanken waren de Trio's zeer gereserveerd. Het was hun namelijk niet duidelijk wat de twee Amerikanen en de drie vreemde Indianen eigenlijk wil den.

Waren zij gekomen om vrouwen en kinderen te roven en mede te nemen in hun „vliegende corjaal?"

gen bij de vriendelijke Trio's.

De heer Leavitt begon onmiddellijk aan de studie van hun taal.

Van dit dorp uit keerden de Wai-Wais en enige Trio's terug naar de Sipaliwini Savannah om daar bijlen, houwers en andere goederen te halen. Deze werden de Trio's ten geschenke aangeboden.

Naar het derde dorp

Van het tweede dorp maakte de heer Friesen met één Wai Wai en enige Trio's een voettocht naar de derde nederzetting.

Die ligt ongeveer in het midden van de afstand tussen de Sipaliwini-Savannah en het Kayser Gebergte.

Ook in het derde dorp waren de Trio's zeer gereserveerd. Het kostte wel wat moeite om hun vertrouwen te winnen.

In geen der drie door hem bezochte dorpen zag de heer Friesen stenen bijlen.

Door ruil — hetzij van stamgenoten, hetzij van Boslandcreolen — komen zij aan metalen voorwerpen.

Geen hunner had echter een geweer.

De drie Wai-Wais spraken met grote bewondering over de giftige pijlen van de Trio's. Wat zij daarmede presteren, grenst aan het wonderbaarlijke.

Meer dorpen

In het derde dorp vernam de heer Friesen, dat ten oosten hiervan er nog één is.

Verder noordwaarts moet er

Friesen terug naar de Trio's. Alvorens te vertrekken, liet hij in een kampje op de savannah een brief achter, welke later door de heer Zaal, directeur van de S.L.M. gevonden werd.

Een nieuwe airstrip

Op betrekkelijk korte afstand van het derde dorp werd door de heren Friesen en Leavitt een airstrip aangelegd, waarop een Piper Super Cub thans kan landen.

Zaterdag jl. was de heer Friesen met twee Indianen terug op de Sipaliwini Savannah.

Zij bleven twee dagen met hem en vertrokken toen. Van maandag jl. tot gisteren was de zendeling-vlieger alleen in het kamp op de Sipaliwini-Savannah, waar hij de mail, welke de heer Zaal voor hem gebracht had, vond.

Geen boten

Op deze tochten zag de heer Friesen nergens corjalen. Ook de bekende schorsboten kwam hij niet tegen. De door hem bezochte Trio's zijn echte Bos-Indianen.

De twee Amerikanen en de drie Wai-Wais kwamen enige malen grote slangen tegen. Ook hoorden zij vaak het gebrul van jaguars.

Hachelijke avonturen beleefden zij gelukkig niet.

Gistermorgen werd de heer Friesen door zijn collega-vlieger Kelly gehaald.

Hedenmorgen vertrok hij naar het zuiden om voor het transport van de heer Leavitt en de drie Wai-Wais te zorgen. Zij zullen binnenkort terugkeren naar Brits Guyana.

Een nieuw vliegtuig

Z.a. onze lezers weten, verloren de zendeling-vliegers Price en Friesen bij de landing op een zandplaat in de Lawa hun Piper Super Cub.

De volgende maand wordt de heer Price hier verwacht aan boord van een Piper Family

Appendix VI

Friesen returned from Sipaliwini-Savannah

The West newspaper from and for Surinam
Saturday, March 19, 1960
Translated by Sonja Van Burren and modified by Eugene Friesen

After an absence of six weeks the American pilot Eugene Friesen, who is with a faith based group known as Door to Life Ministries, returned to Parimaribo yesterday afternoon. During these six weeks Mr. Friesen stayed in the area between the Sipaliwini savannah and the Kayser mountain range. This morning Mr. Friesen once again traveled southward.

Some time ago Mr. Friesen landed on the Sipaliwini -Savannah in a Piper Super Cub. Part of the area on the savannah was cleared, so that the next flights could land with less risks. Subsequently Mr. Friesen flew to British Guyana and picked up the missionary Claude Leavitt, who had been employed for 10 years among the Wai-Wai Indians, whose language he studied and speaks. With Mr. Friesen, three Wai-Wai Indians, respectively called Jafuema, Ketifaka and Kafeana joined him. On February the 4th Mr. Friesen. returned to the Sipaliwini-Savannah and with his four fellow travelers he immediately went on his way north. The next day they contacted a number of Trio's on this trip. They, the two Americans

543

and the three Wai-Wai's passed the Akalapi river, which the Trio's called Arro.

The Trio Indians were still at the "hunting and gathering" stage of development with no written language. There were only 15 or 20 persons living in the first Trio village. At the arrival of the two white persons the Trio's were very frightened. They were not quite sure what the two Americans and the three foreign Indians actually wanted. Had they come to kidnap women and children to take in their "flying canoe" It took weeks before the Trios became reassured that the strangers were there to assist and not to harm them. It seemed that the community of Aloepi on the Tapanani recognized some of them. The two Americans the three Wai-Wais stayed with them in their huts for the night.

The following morning, this group took these strangers to a 2nd village that was located about 5 hours of walking to reach.

Mr. Friesen stayed for only one day at this Trio village before leaving for a 3rd village accompanied by one Wai Wai and a group of 5 or 6 Trios. Meanwhile Mr. Leavitt immediately started to study their language two Wai-Wais and some Trio's returned to Sipaliwini-savannah to get some supplies that included axes, shovels and other goods. Mr. Leavitt would reach the 3rd village in 10 days or so with the remaining Wai Wai's and some of the Trios from village one and two.

The third village located in the middle of the Sipaliwini savannah and Kayser mountain range, approximately 50 miles from the Sipaliwini landing site. While the people in the third village the Trio's were also quite apprehensive in that they had never seen anyone who looked and dressed differently than they did. Over the 6 weeks of time, this apprehension seemed to melt away Nowhere in the three villages Mr. Friesen saw stone axes. Through barter – either from fellow tribesmen of from forest creoles they acquire metal objects. No one had a firearm. The three Wai-Wais spoke with great admiration about the poisonous arrows of the Trio's. What they achieve with them borders to the miraculous.

On February 21st Mr. Friesen was back on the Sipaliwini-savannah where he was to keep a prearranged meeting with Mr. Zaal, the director of S. L. M., who was concerned for the safety of Mr. Friesen and Mr. Leavitt. He waited three days for the arrival of a plane. Due to bad weather conditions landing on the Sipaliwini-savannah was impossible. Before leaving Mr. Friesen left a letter at the small camp on the savannah giving the location of the site where we were building an airstrip. Mr. Zaal then flew overhead and was able to inform Mrs Friesen that the contact with this group of Indians had been successful.

The airstrip, which was to called the Alalapalu, was carved out of the rainforests, to accommodate the landing of the Pipe Super Club was built near the 3rd village.

Six weeks from the original contact with the Trios, Mr. Friesen had arranged for a plane to pick him up from the original landing site on the Siplaliwini savannah near the Brazilian. Past Saturday Mr. Friesen accompanied by a Wai Wai and several Indians returned to Sipaliwini-savannah. After arriving at this site, they left the following morning with Mr. Friesen's permission. Mr Friesen didn't know that Mr. Saal would be delayed for 5 days from the original rendezvous. Mr. Friesen stayed on the Sipaliwini-savannah by himself during this unexpected delay without knowing the reason of the delay. During this 5 days of wondering about this delay, he remembers being alone in the darkness from 6 p.m. to 6 a.m. He states that he should have been concerned about the jaguars. Instead he concerned about jaguars, he was concerned about the reasons for the delay and when he would next see another human being.

Nowhere on these adventures Mr. Friesen saw canoes. Neither did he encountered the familiar wooden boats. The Trio's he visited are genuine forest Indians. Mr. Friesen would walk a total of 200 miles through mountainous jungle before the end of this expedition. During the entire expedition, Mr. Friesen and Leavitt would eat with the Trios. Their meals consisted primarily of cassava and monkey meat although one occasion the Indians were able to shot a deer with bows and arrows. Mr Friesen, on the trip back to the original land site, did see a herd of javelins. Unfortunately Ketifaja, who accompanied him on this trek, had the gun and was searching for a wild turkey.

As our readers know Price and Friesen lost their Piper Super Cub while landing on a sandbank in the Lawa. Next month Mr. Price will be expected on board of a Piper Family Cruiser. This plane carries the pilot and three passengers. It will also be used for work in the hinterland. Mr. Price will be joined by a medical professional. Soon these gentlemen will be working south of Surinam.